D0533569

Edinburgh for Under Fives

13th Edition
2012-2014

By local parents and carers, including NCT members
Published by Edinburgh for Under Fives

1st edition   1987, reprinted 1987
2nd edition   1989
3rd edition   1991
4th edition   1993
5th edition   1995
6th edition   1997
7th edition   2000
8th edition   2002
9th edition   2004
10th edition   2006
11th edition   2008
12th edition   2010
13th edition   2012

Edinburgh for Under Fives Committee 2011-2012
Diahann Whitefield (Convenor)
Sophie Kelsall (Treasurer)
Anne Cameron
Allison Davis
Rachel F Freeman
Joy Hutchinson
Andrew Jamieson
Kathy McGlew
Mary Ross
Imogen Russon-Taylor
Hannah Sanguinetti
Lizzie Smith

Editor: Cathy Tingle (tinglecommunications@gmail.com)
Editorial Assistant: Gill Gray-North (gillg1967@yahoo.co.uk)
Design & Illustration: Maggie Tingle (maggie@tingledesign.co.uk)
Cover photo: Taken at St Margaret's Loch, Holyrood Park,
by Susan Heaton of Clear Photography (www.clearphotography.co.uk).
Q&As: Andrew Jamieson
EFUF logo: Ann Ross Paterson

Published by Edinburgh for Under Fives
© Edinburgh for Under Fives
ISBN 978-0-9555161-2-2

Welcome to Edinburgh for Under Fives.

We hope that this book is a source of inspiration and help as you explore Edinburgh and its surrounding areas with your young family.

This edition we've added more information to our reviews, with new icons so you can see at a glance whether a venue has the facilities you need. We've also included an introductory chapter which points you to different areas of the book if you're in a hurry, and includes articles from some of our researchers about caring for under 5s in Edinburgh. Right at the back of the book, there's a handy key to icons and a map.

In 2011, Edinburgh for Under Fives celebrated its 25th birthday. Since it began in 1987 it has grown and changed but it has always kept its basic quality of being written and produced by parents and carers, for parents and carers. Our fantastic team of 80 volunteer researchers are ordinary parents and carers of under 5s – they're mostly mums but also include dads and two grandmas. (We'll try and get a grandad for the next edition!) With their little ones they've visited, assessed and reported back on venues throughout Edinburgh, the Lothians and Fife, and sometimes further afield. Huge thanks to these wonderful people – we simply could not produce this book without them. Find out who they are on our researchers' page near the end of the book.

The proceeds of Edinburgh for Under Fives book sales and advertising revenue finance the printing of forthcoming editions and support the work of Edinburgh NCT. So a massive thank you to our advertisers, booksellers, supporters and readers. This year we've also appealed for help from Edinburgh-based businesses so that we can look at updating our website in the near future and investing in projects that keep us current and useful to parents and carers. We're delighted to say that we've attracted a number of donors – details on our donors' page at the back of the book.

Edinburgh's a big and busy city and before you blink, things have changed! So if you visit anywhere in this guide and feel you have more up-to-date information to share with our readers, please let us know by emailing ed@efuf.co.uk. We'll put the changes on our website and tweet them to our followers. Talking of which, are you following us yet? We're @EdforUnder5s on Twitter or you can be our friend on Facebook – look for Edinburgh Ed.

We look forward to seeing you out and about with your little ones soon!

The Edinburgh for Under Fives Committee

The Edinburgh for Under Fives Committee, 2012

Diahann Whitefield
(Convenor)

Sophie Kelsall
(Treasurer)

Cathy Tingle
(Editor)

Joy Hutchinson

Andrew Jamieson

Kathy McGlew

Mary Ross

Imogen Russon-Taylor

Hannah Sanguinetti

Lizzie Smith

Thanks also to Anne Cameron, Rachel F Freeman and Allison Davis who spent time on the committee for the 13th Edition and were a great help!

Contents

Introduction

Welcome to Edinburgh!

Even if you've lived here your whole life, you're about to experience a whole new city.

When you have a child it's a bit like moving to a new place. Suddenly you need to find a whole new set of hangouts, you have to navigate territory that's suddenly unfamiliar with a pushchair and a baby that is by turns hungry, bored or needing changed. Your daily routine alters. You move in different social circles.

It can even be a bit nerve-wracking. With a young child, you can't confidently walk out of the door on a whim with just your keys, phone and credit card. It all takes a bit more thought, planning – and baggage!

But there are so many brilliant things about your new life. You can make a whole set of new and firm friends and discover places you never even knew existed. You find new haunts. You suddenly see things through different eyes. It adds a completely fresh dimension to things.

And the best news is, Edinburgh is a fantastic place to be with an under 5. It's a bustling city, which means you're always near help and support, great leisure facilities, libraries, playgroups, activities and classes. It has inspirational cultural venues and festivals, family-friendly cafés, restaurants and shops, amazing museums and exciting historical buildings. The transport is great yet it's reasonably walkable. There's a brilliant cycle path network criss-crossing the city. At the same time it has a wealth of greenspace and sea air. There are friendly people everywhere who love to smile at babies. And there is lots you can do for free.

In this book we introduce you to your new city and its surrounding areas through the eyes of parents and carers that have been there before

you to check it out. There are reviews of places to go, places to eat, places to shop and things to do. There are listings of where to get help, and there's information about childcare.

To start you off, this chapter, also written by parents and carers, describes life in Edinburgh with a new baby (or babies), suggests some essential activities once the newborn stage is over, looks at caring for under 5s from the perspectives of a grandparent and a full-time dad, and includes some examples of grand trips out. At the end of this chapter, from pages 30 to 31, there's a bit about how to use this guide so you'll be all ready to dive in.

WHERE DO I START?

In this section we look at some things you might want to know about life in Edinburgh with a little one. What should I do when? How do I find new friends? Can NCT continue to support me after my baby's born? How do I get out and about with a newborn? What if I'm having twins?

Timeline

With so much to think about in pregnancy and the early days of parenthood you might find yourself wondering what you need to be aware of, and when. Hopefully this timeline will help put a few things into context. Later in the book you'll find details of places that will provide further information: more on toddler groups and playgroups, information about childcare options, and healthcare contact details.

During pregnancy	Find out from your midwife what antenatal classes you will be offered by the NHS and book into private antenatal classes, such as those run by the NCT, if you wish. If eligible (on benefits or you're pregnant and under 18) apply for Healthy Start vouchers which you swap for milk, fresh fruit, fresh vegetables and infant formula milk. Consider exercises for antenatal women, such as yoga and swimming. Try the free NCT bra-fitting service (see p 221) to find a comfortable and supportive bra.
After 29 weeks of pregnancy	After the 29th week of pregnancy (and before your child is 3 months old), apply for the Sure Start Maternity Grant if you have no other children under 16/are on a low income. This is a one-off payment of £500 to help towards buying things for a new baby. Consider purchasing a trial pack of real nappies from Edinburgh and Lothians Real Nappy Project (www.changeworks.org.uk). Find out about maternity/paternity pay from your employers. Look at nurseries for when returning to work (ask your employer about childcare vouchers).
After 36 weeks of pregnancy	You can buy a feeding bra after 36 weeks of pregnancy. Local NCT bra-fitters are there to help.
Birth	Non-routine immunisation against tuberculosis (TB) for babies more likely to come into contact with TB than the general population. Non-routine immunisation against Hepatitis B for babies where mothers are Hep B positive.
10 days	Usually discharged by the midwife around this time and your health visitor takes over.
By 21 days	Register the birth and name of your baby with a local Registrar of Births. As soon as possible register your baby with a GP. Apply for Child Benefit.

2 months	1st routine immunisations (2 injections) to protect against diphtheria, tetanus, pertussis, polio, Hib and pneumococcal infection.*
3 months	2nd routine immunisations (2 injections) to protect against diphtheria, tetanus, pertussis, polio, Hib and meningitis C.*
4 months	3rd routine immunisations (3 injections) to protect against diphtheria, tetanus, pertussis, polio, Hib, meningitis C and pneumococcal infection.* Bookbug bag supplied by health visitor.
Around 6 months	Register your baby with a dentist. Start weaning your baby onto solid foods.
Around 12 months	Routine immunisation to protect against Hib and meningococcal C.* Second set of Bookbug books given out by health visitor. Between 1 and 2 years put your child's name on playgroup waiting lists if wishing them to attend later (most take children from 27-30 months). If considering private education, start looking at the independent schools and putting your child's name on the waiting lists.
Around 13 months	Routine immunisations to protect against measles, mumps and rubella (MMR) and pneumococcal infection.*
2 years	For council nurseries, put child's name on waiting lists as soon as 2 (eligible for free part-time place the term after their 3rd birthday). Usually some time between 2 and 3 years start potty training your child.
3 years	Join Road Safety Scotland's "Go Safe with Ziggy" programme, which helps parents/carers teach children about road safety. Bookbug Treasure Chest received by children in nurseries and from child and family centres. Between 3 and 6 years be alert to any apparent language delay, hearing or sight problems – contact your health visitor if any concerns.
3 years, 4 months to 5 years	Routine immunisations to protect against diphtheria, tetanus, pertussis, polio and MMR (second jab).*
3 years, 9 months +	Around November time, enrol your child for entry to your local school the following August (look out for dates of enrolment days at the relevant school). Children who are 5 years on or before the last day of February usually start Primary School in the previous August. If applying to defer your child's school entry until the following year, an application for automatic deferral (if your child's birthday is in January or February) should be submitted by the end of February and for discretionary deferral (if your child's birthday is between the first day of the Autumn term and the end of December) by the end of March.

*The website for up-to-date information and descriptions of vaccines, plus details of when they are offered, is **www.healthscotland.com/topics/health/immunisation/index.aspx.**

This timeline held current information as we went to print but do let us know if you come across anything in it that needs updating **(info@efuf.co.uk).**

Finding your "tribe"

When you're caring for a little one, it's important to find a group of friends who understand exactly what you're going through. Researcher Tasca Shadix, who was new to Edinburgh when her first child arrived, gives us some ideas about how to go about forming those vital bonds.

When my husband and I moved to Edinburgh seven years ago, I was pregnant with my first child. Homesick and anxious, I worried I'd be friendless and alone, with a new baby in a new city. Luckily, I soon met a wonderful group of friends in my antenatal class.

At first, we met every Tuesday without fail. Mum's Group was sometimes my only reason to leave the house that day! We've since gone on holidays together, formed a babysitting cooperative, and supported each other through good times and bad. I firmly believe that every mother needs and deserves a support network like mine, but it can be daunting for a new mum to try to meet new friends. Here are some tips on how and where to start!

Antenatal classes
There you sit, surrounded by total strangers, contemplating a plastic model of a pelvis. Awkward? Yes! Nevertheless, send round a sheet to collect their contact information, and suggest a meet-up! Don't be shy! These are your parenting peers, the women you may soon be phoning to say, "Please tell me your baby eats non-stop, too, so I know mine's normal!"

Typical mum hangouts
As you know, mums love parks, museums, softplays, and cafés with good nappy changing facilities! Consider having inexpensive "mummy cards" printed from a business card company. That way, when chatting to a new acquaintance, you can quickly hand over your card as a way of staying in touch, rather than scrawling your number illegibly on a soon-to-be-lost napkin.

Mum-and-baby classes
Classes are a great excuse to get out of the house and make friends. The setting provides time to get to know people gradually, which is nice for those of us who are shy. Try not to reject potential friends simply because you don't seem to parent in exactly the same way. You can learn new things from mums who make different choices!

School
Make an effort to talk to the other mums at your child's playgroup, nursery, or school. When your child makes a friend in class, why not suggest a play date, inviting mum to tea at the same time? Your offer will very likely be accepted – and greatly appreciated!

It can be intimidating to reach out, but it's worth a try! Remember that we are all in the same boat, looking for the kindness, reassurance and support that only great friends can provide!

Life after birth – NCT can help here too!

Most parents become familiar with NCT through antenatal classes. For many, this is where NCT support starts rather than finishes.

Many groups continue to meet up and for many mums this support is invaluable. A group of close friends to debrief regularly with, who are going through similar changes at the same time. For those that don't make it to the classes there is a chance to do the same at Bumps and Babies groups at Blackhall and Marchmont St Giles. These run weekly and the one at Marchmont has NCT specialist practitioners facilitating the group. There will also be the opportunity to attend postnatal groups when Joanna, our first postnatal practitioner, has finished her training.

Joanna explains her role as: "To facilitate discussions in groups of new mums, with babies from 0-6 mths. The group lasts for 6 weeks, each week lasting 2 hrs. Discussion topics are usually around the area of relationships, sleep, getting ready to wean, going back to work, adjusting to the changes of motherhood. I am there to facilitate discussions amongst the mothers, not to give out information. The useful information will come out in the chats as they realise that most of what they are experiencing is totally normal and they are not alone. Ideas will be stimulated as they learn from each other's experiences."

We also have a network for parents of children from toddler to pre-school age. We set up the Work, Sleep & Play network for those parents who have returned to work but still want to connect with parents as new boundaries are reached. We have had speakers on topics like sleep, managing change and play. With the group growing in numbers there is still much more to debate about our approaches to modern-day parenting.

With more than 700 in the capital, you are never far from an NCT member. Members are the first to be informed of events including the regular NCT Nearly New Sales, of which there are half a dozen during the year and the same number outside the city in East Lothian, West Lothian and Midlothian. Look online to find your nearest sale for everything from buggies to clothes to cots.

Nothing totally prepares you for being a parent, even if you read all the books or take all the classes. However, it can be so much more fun to share it with people who understand. It's not a job to be done on your own so be part of your local NCT parents' network.

Would you be interested in training to provide support for parents? If so, contact your local NCT branch online.

**www.nct.org.uk
www.nctedinburgh.moonfruit.com**

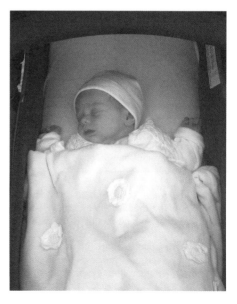

Getting out with a newborn

In those first few weeks with a baby, it can be difficult to get out of your pyjamas, let alone out of the house! Intrepid new mum Stephie Phipps shares what she learned after venturing into the city with her newborn.

Edinburgh is a city I thought I knew well – a few months ago I would have been confident in reeling off an extensive list of the best restaurants, shops and gorgeous coffee shops. Fast forward to 6 weeks after having my first baby, I've now realised that I have to think of Edinburgh as a new city to rediscover.

My daughter is beautiful and I have lost all sense of objectivity when it comes to her smile and chatter from her pram. For such a tiny bundle she has totally changed the way I look at things, for example, George Street – I used to think "brilliant shops or a cheeky cocktail after work", my first thought now is "how will I get my pram up those steps?", my second thought is "maybe we should try it anyway...". So, these are my new tactics with my lovely little girl and this great city:

– Try to plan ahead – think about keeping a bus timetable in your bag, charge your mobile, ask "what will the weather be like?".

– Be spontaneous (I promise I'm not contradicting myself!) – if you see an interesting place for a coffee, try it. What's the worst that could happen? If there aren't changing facilities, you'll soon find out.

– People in Edinburgh love babies! Be prepared for lots of "oohing" and "aahing" and even the odd silver coin put in the pram.

– You will be offered lots of help if you need it. I had planned my first trip into town with my baby to meet a friend for coffee. I'd managed the bus and was quite proud of myself for planning a stairless cup of coffee in Café Nero in Frasers in Princes Street. I pushed the pram through the doors and was met with the sight of steps leading up to the till. I

nearly turned around and got the bus home! Instead, I found a table, took my little one out of the pram and carried her to the till to order my lunch. As soon as the barista saw that I had a baby she offered to serve me straight away and brought over to my table a delicious panini and latte.

– If all else fails, head to John Lewis! It has amazing nappy changing and breastfeeding facilities. You will see so many other mums meeting in The Place to Eat at the top of the store that you will never feel uneasy about your crying baby who needs a cuddle and a feed. The views are lovely too, and the scones are delicious.

– Plan lots of stops for feeds and nappy changes and make yourself and your little one comfortable in case they feel like a longer feed or it begins to rain.

– Make a trip of it – rediscover some of Edinburgh's wonderful areas. Try über baby-friendly Bruntsfield, Stockbridge or

Morningside. It will feel like a day out. For the inevitable bad weather days, there's The Gyle or Ocean Terminal – brilliant parking and nappy changing. Also, check out The Gyle for Bookbug groups and Ocean Terminal for parent and baby cinema (yes, really, you don't have to miss out – the sound is lower, the lights are higher and baby chatter isn't discouraged).

– Use resources like Netmums. They provide information about local events, classes and groups. It can seem so daunting just turning up at a new group where you don't know anyone. I just kept trying until my daughter and I both found things we were happy and comfortable doing. We like Bookbug (check your local library) – it's great fun once you put aside that you are singing "The wheels on the bus". Next week we are starting baby massage and we are planning baby ballet! The possibilities are endless!

– Transport – parking is a bit of a pain in Edinburgh. Buses are great, but check out the rules about prams on buses and priorities with wheelchairs. We bought a baby sling for the days that the pram seems an effort. Apart from anything else it's another chance to have a nice long cuddle with my daughter!

Congratulations on your lovely new baby and I hope you enjoy Edinburgh with your little one.

5... great places in town for a quick nappy change

National Museum of Scotland, Chambers Street

National Galleries Weston Link

Fruitmarket Gallery, Market Street

Scottish National Portrait Gallery, Queen Street

John Lewis Parenting Suite (4th floor)

This symbol throughout the book means that you can find nappy-changing facilities on the premises – this means a pull-down changing table or a stand-alone unit. It does not mean a mat on the floor!

If, heaven forbid, you have mistakenly left your Edinburgh for Under Fives at home, NCT has released a new app which pinpoints and rates nappy-changing facilities all over the UK (including Edinburgh), so you can find your nearest facility, quickly! Download it free at http://www.nct.org.uk/about-nct/nct-babychange-app

Twins tips

Any parent will tell you that a little one is hard work, but what if you have more than one baby? Mother of twins Sarah Joss gives her top tips for two.

Just getting out the door with twins can be a challenge – twice as much packing, changing and dressing to do. Once you're out, where do you go and how can you get there?

Transport

Bus: Buses that can accommodate wheelchairs are also wide enough for double buggies (look for the symbols on the side). Be prepared to wait though, as if there is already a buggy on board your chosen bus, you'll have to board the next. You must also give up your space to a wheelchair user if required. Routes with a frequent service are best.

Cycle: For keen cyclists you can get double bike trailers. Pulling two children is not as hard as you might think and there are plenty of cycle paths. Plus it is free exercise for you.

Walk: You can get double slings for when the twins are small enough for you to manage both. The best of these can be configured in various ways on your front and back and separated into two slings, carry handles and emergency chair harnesses but they can be tricky to configure, expensive and the twins quickly become too heavy to carry together.

As twins get bigger, 3-wheeler buggies with large wheels makes getting about, especially over rough terrain, much easier and they are far lighter to steer even one handed. They can be a problem with narrow doors though.

When buying a double buggy check that it will not only fit into your boot but that you can also lift it in easily – some models are heavy. With some 3 wheelers the back wheels can easily be removed to help them fit in car boots.

Shopping

Best not to take the twins on the weekly shop. If you have to, find a shop with twin trolleys and try to keep them entertained with well-timed packets of raisins. Tesco car trolleys where one twin rides in the car and one in the trolley are popular with my twins. I use the timer on my mobile phone to keep turns fair.

Join the Edinburgh Twins Club (check out www.edinburghtwinsclub.co.uk) for a yearly fee of £12. There are discounts from major stores and Twin Club members get special out-of-hours access to some shops in the run up to Christmas.

Shoes: Some Clark's branches do a discount for Twin Club or Tamba members and the outlet in Livingston is also a good option when having to buy for 4 little feet at one time. Check ahead to see if you can make a fitting appointment.

Sales: Buying two of everything works out expensive so be prepared to consider second hand. NCT sales, the Twins Club sale, car boot sales at Omni or Asda at Chesser (weekends in summer), Polwarth parish church sale and also Gumtree can be an excellent source of good quality bargains.

Green spaces

Keeping an eye on one child is hard enough but two really is a challenge. Pick places that are quite enclosed and so if they do run off in opposite directions they can't get far. Reins can be a life saver, literally. You can now get little backpacks with a lead attachment for the back. Get them into a Road Safety Scotland programme as soon as you can so they can learn road safety. Saughton Winter Gardens provide a nice safe space with the option of the glasshouse for a warm refuge.

Play parks

Try to find a park that suits the age of your toddlers well. The more they can do safely by themselves the better as if you're on your own you won't be able to shadow both of them. This is for your stress levels as much as their safety! Very small playgrounds are often better until you are quite relaxed and confident about their abilities.

Swimming

Taking small twins swimming can be a real challenge and is really a job for two. There are a few things that can make it a bit easier. Take two bags to keep their clothes separate. Bring dressing gowns to keep one twin warm while you dry the other. Take car seats in for small babies. Xcite Livingston has really good-sized changing rooms to easily fit two adults and two children and most have pull-down changing tables.

Eating out

Make sure the venue has plenty of highchairs or you can get inflatable booster highchairs that you can bring with you. Take along some drawing things to keep them busy while they wait. Find somewhere you like and become a regular then they are likely to be delighted to see how your twins are progressing and forgiving when they have an off day and cause chaos.

Soft play

Same rules as for play parks – find somewhere with a level of challenge you are comfortable with. Scrambles at EICA is well supervised, making for a more relaxing experience.

Nursery and playgroups

Apply for nursery places early. Finding two places at once is more difficult. Look for nurseries that offer a second child discount. For playgroups find one where they won't make you take twice the number of turns helping out just because you have twins.

Groups

Make contact with other carers. The Edinburgh Twins Club has a network of meeting and educational sessions as well as numerous social events through the year. Don't just stick with other multiple parents where the subject of multiples can dominate, go to parent and toddlers groups and bask in the admiration of other parents who can't imagine how you manage it and who will usually be more than willing to help you out.

Activities and classes

Phone to speak to organisers of classes like baby massage and baby yoga as they may be delighted to help you out with one of the twins. They have a baby to demonstrate with and you get to spend quality bonding time with each twin in turn.

Help

Health visitors know having multiples is hard so ask them to find you some help if you feel you need it. If you can't get to see them, ask them to come to you. Home Start (www.home-start.org.uk) can offer you help from volunteers. TAMBA (www.tamba.org.uk) are a good source of help, advice and ideas.

You can get full contact details for Edinburgh Twins Club, Home Start and TAMBA in our Practical Information & Support chapter. Find out more about supermarkets and shoe shops in our Shopping chapter.

UNDER 5s ESSENTIALS

Once you get past those first few weeks, the challenge is often to work out what to do with your day. It helps to have a few tried and tested building blocks that you can construct your week around, and which offer enough variety and interest to keep both you and your under 5 happy.

In this section, we look at things that it helps to get into the habit of doing, so that you always have something to fall back on. Each of them links to a review or section later on in the book, so you can go straight there to read more if you feel inspired!

© Rachel Hein Photography

The great outdoors

Vicky Allan explains why the outdoors is great for young children – and for parents and carers too!

I grew up in the countryside, on a farm. So, perhaps, it should be no surprise that when it came to bringing up my own children, here, in a city, I wanted to give them a taste of that rural life: contact with the mud, the woods, the weather, and the big open spaces of nature. I hoped that they too would be tree climbers and berry pickers. Luckily, Edinburgh is a city with a lot of nature – with small lochs, trickling burns, a river, rolling hills, breath-taking views, wild sections of wood, ruins and beaches. And actually I believe this is the case for all cities and

towns – look for the wild woods and you will find them. I had, however, explored relatively few of the natural wonders of Edinburgh, until, last year, with Polly, an acquaintance who quickly became a friend, I decided to set up Let's Go Out, an informal outdoor playgroup.

Let's Go Out was inspired by a similar group Polly had been to in Glasgow, called Nurture in Nature run by Lusi Alderslowe. The idea is that we meet once a week in a pre-arranged outdoor location, bring snacks, do the odd activity, but mostly just hang out and play. When I look back over the last year, my most vivid memories are of these days in nature, and of the stunning range of places we visited. I recall, for instance, the stream in the Hermitage of Braid, and small teams of children paddling barefoot on a bright summer day. Or the same spot, later in the year, in the autumn, those same kids wading deep over the tops of their wellies. I think of faces smeared with blackberry juice, my son perched so high in a tree I had to climb up to get him down, of playing hide and seek in the high grass of Newhailes meadow. I also think of trying not to let my kids smear bus seats with muddy boots on the way home and wishing I had brought another set of spare clothes, or fighting with my son to make him wear his wellies. There's nothing special or complicated about this group and really anyone can do all the outings we have done on their own. One principle, though, is that we have done it whatever the weather – and there are virtues to this. The rain may look daunting as it trickles down your window, but if you persist in going out in it, rarely does the unpleasant weather last. Indeed, if you've got waterproofs and wellies, and a spare change of clothes, you can usually survive long enough to decide, yes, it has been a rather beautiful day.

For many of us the challenges of a bit of wind and rain are small compared with being cooped up with two small active children all day. Often when I go on these outings, I stand there looking at some tree or patch of sky, and think maybe I'm doing this as much for myself as the children. One of my inspirations for this group was Cathy Bache, who set up the Secret Garden outdoor nursery in Tayport, Fife (www.secretgardenoutdoor-nursery.co.uk), who told me that she believed "bad weather therapy" and time in nature were good for the mental health of people of all ages. I believe this is true. We could all do with a bit more of it. And children are a good excuse.

For those who are wondering what to do out there in the wet and wild, or even those searching for a good reason to go there, it's worth looking up www.childrenandnature.org, which includes among other things a Nature Club for Families Toolkit. And if anyone fancies joining us on Mondays, or even wants to set up their own group on another day, get in touch, at **letsgooot@gmail.com**.

5... ideal starter trips with small children

The Hermitage of Braid (also see p 74). Follow the stream from the main park entrance towards the Hermitage itself. One of the best paddling spots in Edinburgh is at a bend in the burn, next to a park bench. From there you can go on to the visitor centre at the house for shelter, warmth, games and information. And, for the more ambitious, there's the trek up Blackford Hills for stunning views.

Newhailes (also see p 65), a National Trust for Scotland property and one of the real wild gems of Edinburgh. Kids can hide in the woods round the side of the house, run across the lawns at the back, climb over walls, follow the path down past the shell grotto and throw sticks in the burn. Grounds are open all year round.

Cramond Island (also see p 89). Get the tides right and hit a beautiful sunny day, as we did, and this makes a magical walk. At toddler pace, you probably want to leave 45 minutes either way for the crossing.

Corstorphine Hill (also see p 50). One of the main landmarks on this hill is a tower – and so far we haven't made it there, despite that being a frequent ambition. This is partly because it's a long way from our meeting point, but also because there are so many distractions: rocks and fallen trees to clamber over, huge lawns to pelt down, and an enchanting walled garden to linger in.

Dalkeith Country Park (also see p 55). An easy trip out of town by bus. The main adventure is the playpark with its aerial wooden walkways, zip rides and slides. However, there are also beautiful grounds, a cave and, in July, we were raspberry picking.

See our Out & About chapter for more ideas about where to get some fresh air.

Playgrounds

Do you remember going on the swings as a bairn, falling off onto the hard tarmac and grazing your knee, dodging the dog mess to go crying to your mum? Scottish playgrounds are no longer so dismal, as Lizzie Smith discovers.

Brightly coloured, playgrounds now seem to have soft, all-weather surfaces and are usually gated to keep out dogs. The climbing frames are fun and often have quite imaginative little corners to turn them into boats or cars.

At our local playground in the centre of town you meet everyone: grandpas changing nappies, grannies with mum for the day, dads giving mum a break, and even nannies. The nannies are some of the keenest users, rain or shine, any month. They know about the secret of fresh air: it keeps kids happy and healthy. Even children in prams are known to benefit from a healthy dose of fresh, cold air every day.

Get the kit and invest in some waterproofs. All-in-ones are great for snow, as are wellies. I've even seen children playing in the bark chippings with a bucket and spade. Take a blanket to sit down for a snack – others will soon join you!

I find our playground is often crowded around four o'clock, just as school ends, or children are being taken back from going to the shops and stop off for a quick play before tea. Between 16.00 and 17.00 can be a difficult hour, with tempers starting to fray, so the playground is the best place to run off surplus energy. If you have ended up being indoors for a lot of the day, it's great to finally get out for some fresh air.

See our Out & About chapter for details of playgrounds in Edinburgh and beyond.

5... great playgrounds

Meadows Playpark (Meadows East)

Princes Street Gardens Playground

Barony Community Garden and Playground

Jack Kane Centre Play Area

Musselburgh Links Playground

Baby & Toddler Groups

Run by volunteers and offering an hour or two's entertainment for your child and a wee sit down with a cuppa for you, baby and toddler groups can be a lifeline.

Every weekday sleep-deprived mums and dads wander the streets of Edinburgh seeking refuge. Where might they meet fellow sufferers? Where can they entertain their little ones till lunchtime or teatime? And get a coffee – that's the number one priority. A bit of cake would be nice too.

Ah! A sign outside a church. A "Baby & Toddler Group". The smell of coffee drifts out. Heaven! At around £1.50 for entrance, coffee and as-many-biscuits-as-you-can-eat, it's cheaper than a café.

Staffed by lovely volunteers, many of these groups have been running for years. St Paul's and St George's Church on York Place (or "St P & G's" to those who go) is the biggest and now runs morning and afternoon on Thursdays. Sometimes over 80 pushchairs are parked in the hall under the watchful eye of the doorman. The snacks are well organised, there are lots of different play areas and a dedicated babies' area. The singing session is run by an American lady all miked up to lead the choruses. Stockbridge International Playgroup, two mornings a week, has a big space for running around and a songtime at the end. Inverleith Church Toddler Group on Ferry Road on Wednesdays has some of the best cakes in the city.

These groups are popular because they're a forum where carers get to meet other adults in a sometimes lonely job – and kids meet playmates too.

See the Pre-School Play & Education chapter for listings of baby and toddler groups (including parents' picks!) and playgroups.

Q&A

We asked Christine Craig of St. Mary's Episcopal Toddler Group …

Are you a parent? *Yes, I have a 2 year old daughter.*

Tell us about the toddler group: *It runs each Friday 10.00-11.30 in Walpole Hall, Chester Street, which is part of St Mary's Cathedral. Babies and children up to around 3 years are welcome. The group runs during all holidays and occasionally older siblings come along during school holidays. Format is active play followed by a 15 minute sing song. There is a range of toys including slide, trampoline, prams and buggies, duplo, drawing and playdoh. Having a big hall allows active toddlers plenty of space to run around. Tea, coffee and biscuits provided by parents and guardians on a rota basis.*

How long have you lived in Edinburgh? *Approx 25 years.*

How do you rate it as a child-friendly city? *I rate it highly as having a good variety of children's facilities and spaces to play and meet other parents.*

Recommendations: *Botanic Gardens, Inverleith Park, Edinburgh Zoo – family membership soon pays for itself and kids love the play areas as much as the animals, Pregnancy & Parenting Centre at Lower Gilmore Place for a wide variety of classes/groups, Ratho (EICA) and Molly's softplays.*

Find out more about St Mary's Baby & Todder Playgroup on pages 284 and 286.

Getting something for nothing

Free reigns

Why pay entrance fees to entertain your children when there are so many places to go for free? Here are a few ideas for things to do that don't need to cost you anything.

Get outside in the fresh air. Go up to the local Farmers' Market to soak in the atmosphere (and see if you can resist the smell of bacon rolls). Go to your local playpark, or one a bit further away – the playpark in the Meadows in Edinburgh is voted a top place to go.

Go to the seaside. You're never that far away in Scotland. In East Lothian there is beach after beach of sand: Yellowcraig, Tyninghame and Gullane are popular. Fife has lovely beaches – St Andrews has two big beaches; go up the coast to Tentsmuir near Leuchars and if you walk far enough along the beach you'll come across a large colony of seals. There are beaches further down the coast at Crail, Pittenweem, Anstruther and onto Aberdour and Dalgety Bay. Even in the city of Edinburgh you can get down to the shoreline at Cramond and Newhaven and a bit further down at Portobello. All round the coast of Scotland there are lots of secret beaches to be discovered.

Go to the library – a comfy, cheery place with soft cushions these days – and lie around reading a few storybooks.

Plus, there's Edinburgh's Botanic Garden and the National Museum of Scotland (reopened with fantastic new interactive displays); the city's galleries and museums, many of which have free entry, and Vogrie Park near Dalkeith. These are all firm favourites with our researchers – read all about them later in the book.

Free venues and activities are labelled FREE in our listings – you should be able to spot them easily!

Catching the book bug

It's free, it's fun, it's local and it's very popular! Bookbug fever is sweeping Scotland. New mum Stephie Phipps – a fan – explains why.

Before having my daughter I wouldn't have been able to name anything more than Mums and Babies Group as an activity to do with a young child. Oh, little did I know! My daughter is now 4 months old and I have discovered that there is so much to do in the "world of baby" that maternity leave doesn't seem enough time to experience it all. I feel like I have to choose quite carefully what will benefit my baby as the cost can add up. However, one of our favourites is actually free!

Bookbug is a regular free session created and run by the Scottish Book Trust and by Local Authorities throughout Scotland. Sessions are held in your local library or community centre and are very relaxed. They normally last about 30 minutes. Expect lots of songs and rhymes and some storytelling. The sessions are for babies and toddlers, and, of course, their parents, grandparents or carers.

Performing parents

Bookbug sounds innocent enough, but beware – you will leave all sense of adult etiquette at the door. If any of my work colleagues could witness our weekly trip there it would provide ammunition for a lot of jokes! Bea and I look forward to the half hour of singing "Old Macdonald", "The Wheels on the Bus" and "Little Peter Rabbit". I find myself "singing" (I can't sing at all so I am taking some artistic licence here when using that term) the songs to her throughout the week. There have been a few occasions that "The Wheels on the Bus" have saved us from a crying episode! Just don't let yourself sing it too loudly when actually on a bus – you get some very odd looks.

The adults find themselves singing whilst doing a baby version of the conga around the library holding our beautiful bundles up in the air, all the time trying not to make eye contact with the other mums who you have a sneaking feeling you may have once met in work. My advice: don't think about it too much, just try it! Your baby will probably absolutely love it. Bea giggles and carefully watches the other children – and afterwards, after getting her Bookbug sticker, that is, promptly falls asleep. This is exactly why Bookbug is such a nice experience – it is good quality time with my daughter which I know she enjoys. I know she is too young to learn to read, but I want her to appreciate words and books as early as she can and I think experiences like this will help with her social development.

Something for everyone

The best part of this half hour is how much the children actually love it. The babies get to kick about and join in with little stories and the toddlers do all the actions. Those who run Bookbug always have something up their sleeves (sometimes a puppet to add a bit of reality to "Old Macdonald") to liven up the session. Last week, my daughter's little eyebrows shot up when she heard the weekly story being read. It was a story in Scots. It was fantastic and really brought the language to life.

It's sometimes a little intimidating trying new things as a new parent or grandparent – however, I'd really encourage you to try it. As I discovered, we all love talking about our babies and it is very reassuring to meet people who are going through the same experiences as you.

Above all, don't feel guilty if you manage to coordinate activities like Bookbug with a cup of tea and a biscuit! That, I have discovered, is an important part of motherhood – making sure you remember to get the occasional warm cuppa!

Find out more about Bookbug in our Under Cover chapter.

Q&A

We asked Janet Smyth, Children's Director, Edinburgh International Book Festival ...

Are you a parent? *Parent of a 12 year old*

How long have you lived in Edinburgh? *I lived in Edinburgh for 12 years but now live in Bo'ness.*

How do you rate it as a child-friendly city? *In terms of spaces such as museums, parks, galleries, swimming pools and so on there's definitely lots to do. However, as a nation we still always want to segregate children so that some concerts, restaurants and bars prohibit under 14s. This isn't the case on the Continent where licensing doesn't restrict what you can take your child to.*

Any memorable experiences of Edinburgh as a parent? *I have really fond memories of long hours spent at the National Museum of Scotland before the refurb. There was always something new to see and as my daughter grew up the things she was interested in changed. The café and the changing facilities were always really good too.*

Recommendations: *I'm a bit out of touch with things for really little people but I would definitely recommend the National Museum of Scotland and The Art Cart weekend afternoons that the galleries run. These are a great way to introduce little people to art and get them to really focus on a picture and then do their own.*

You can find out about the Edinburgh International Book Festival on p 143.

Getting active

At your leisure

Edinburgh Leisure has a lot to interest parents and carers of under 5s – even the opportunity for "me time" while your children are kept entertained. With more than 20 locations across the city from Warrender to Kirkliston and Portobello to Ratho, you are never too far from an Edinburgh Leisure facility. Sarah Joss takes a look at what's on offer.

It is worth checking out the full range of Edinburgh Leisure's services. They include:
- 10 swimming pools
- gyms and fitness classes
- the Climbing Arena at Ratho, which also runs some outdoor courses
- Meadowbank Stadium
- 5-a-side pitches, sports pitches, tennis courts and sailing
- bowling
- golf
- soft play
- Portobello Turkish Baths, saunas and steam rooms
- children's parties
- school holiday activities
- aqua fit and aqua natal
- swimming lessons
- adult-and-child classes
- a range of children's activities from Learnabikes to Sticky Crafts.

Finding information

www.edinburghleisure.co.uk offers details of all venues, online booking for cardholders and a searchable timetable. There are also print timetables available from most venues offering full listings of coached activities for children as well as contact details and location maps. Pool timetables are available both online under each pool and as a booklet.

Leisure Access Cards and memberships

Facilities are open to non-members on a drop-in basis but if you wish to book activities in advance you must either have a Leisure Access Card or a membership. The Leisure Access Card is available for a one-off fee, currently £25/year for adults, with concession rates available. This card then allows you into classes, gyms and pools at a reduced rate as well as the loyalty points scheme. A free card is available for under 5s who attend classes to allow booking. Monthly memberships have several levels including swim only, gym-and-swim and climbing memberships. There are frequent deals to waive joining fees. Contact your nearest centre for details.

Where you can find soft play

Meadowbank Stadium, Ratho Climbing Arena and the Commonwealth Pool, as well as sessions at Portobello Bowling Club, Queensferry High Recreation Centre and Kirkliston. There is a soft play loyalty card on which you can save up stamps for free visits.

Time off for grown-ups

Sadly the crèches have now all closed, making it harder for parents and carers to exercise. The Healthy Active Mums scheme has also shut down. However, if you can get someone else to take the kids for a while, the Turkish Baths at Portobello are a great place to unwind.

If your children are old enough to attend a coached activity, usually 3+, adults can get a reduced price "Why Wait?" gym visit while your child is in a class. Most of the classes are very short though so it will have to be a flying visit.

As well as all the coaching opportunities for kids – tots tennis, gym nippers, mini kickers, mini athletics to name but a few – there is also a full range of adult classes. Yoga and pilates to unwind and stretch out; dance-based classes such as Zumba and Salsacise to put you through your moves; the full range of "Body classes" including Balance, Step, Pump and Combat; running classes; Tums and Bums, Swiss Ball and for those in need of a serious burn, RPM. With friendly, motivating instructors, a range of levels and introductory classes there is something for everyone if you are looking to get back into shape, burn off some stress or just keep fit enough to keep up with the kids.

Adults' highlights:
• Turkish Baths at Portobello Swim Centre
• Free weights room at Meadowbank – a bit spit and sawdust but great if you like that kind of thing
• Body Pump – much better than it sounds
• Body Step provides an excellent and (mostly) fun work out
• Aqua fit is low impact, suitable for pregnancy and very social
• Or there's RPM if you want to feel really virtuous.

Kids' highlights:
• Under 5s swim free
• Swimming lessons
• A range of birthday party options including a superb bouncy castle at Gracemount
• Soft play facilities
• Warrender has very good family sessions and good family change area
• The baby pool at Ainslie park – just a shame the Jacuzzi is so cold!

Practical points
A number of centres have been recently refurbished and they try to keep up with new equipment, such as ViPRs, power plates and the gravity gym. There are a few low points – the pools can sometimes be a bit cold, and during the week parking at Glenogle, Warrender and Dalry can be scarce and expensive. The children's activities can be a bit pricey especially if you have more than one child to pay for.

However, most venues are extremely accessible, with nappy changing readily available in both male and female or communal areas. In general they are well run, friendly and reasonably clean and well maintained considering the high level of use that they see.

You can find out about leisure centres and swimming pools in the Under Cover chapter, and about different Edinburgh Leisure activities in the Activities & Classes chapter.

Wee escapes

We all know how hard it is to leave the house without our children. Still, it can be helpful, and even fun, to do this on occasion! Grandparents, babysitting services and responsible teen neighbours can provide child care, but what if these are simply not an option for one reason or another? Tasca Shadix lets us into her babysitting secrets.

Consider forming a babysitting cooperative: There's a wealth of information online about how to do this. My friends and I ran one for years using a website. With a few willing participants, you can soon have free, reliable babysitting from people you know and trust.

Go on holiday with another family: One of our best holidays was with friends who, like us, had a 1 year old. We rented a cottage and took turns babysitting. We even took turns going out to dinner! If "It takes a village to raise a child," then don't forget to take your village on holiday!

Have a mummy sleepover: I've slept over at friends' homes so that they could go out, or even, on one occasion, to facilitate a surprise getaway for a friend's birthday! Don't be afraid to ask a mum friend to sleep over – she may be more than happy for you to return the favour!

Send your CHILD on a sleepover: At 6, my oldest happily spends the night at her best friend's house from time to time. She loves sleepovers, and we love the quiet time!

Go somewhere with a crèche: In a pinch, I've taken my daughter to the Parliament Crèche, just so I can have a cup of tea alone in the café. My husband and I have also been known to go on "dates" at IKEA. What can I say? Sometimes you're desperate.

Of course, your child must be old enough and comfortable enough with the proposed babysitters to make these options possible. Close friendships with other mums and encouraging your children to be comfortable with others will definitely make your life easier!

Enjoying a treat

My new and improved Saturday nights

Having children needn't mean an end to going out on a Saturday night. You just have to do it a bit earlier and take them along, that's all. Paula Skerry investigated what Hamilton's Bar and Kitchen in Stockbridge has to offer adults and children and found that the whole family could have a great Saturday night there – and then get home in time for the X Factor!

I LOVE Saturday night. I always have done. Saturday night is dressing up, dining out, hitting the town and, after a few vinos, the dance floor! That was all in the years BC (before children) when anything earlier than a 2am home-time was for wimps and Sunday morning was rarely seen! Now I have Strictly, followed by The X Factor, a Chinese takeaway (if I'm lucky) and then bed!

Comfort and cosmopolitans

This month I made a momentous decision: I decided to reclaim my Saturday nights and bring the whole family along with me. OK – so booking a table for two adults, one toddler and one baby for 5.30 on a Saturday night doesn't sound very rock 'n' roll but it's the closest I'm going to get for the next 10 years!

I am fussy, I work in the media, I like champagne – I am a cliché. Therefore I didn't want a restaurant for children where adults are welcome, but a restaurant for adults where children are welcome – and believe me there is a big difference. From the outside, Hamilton's in Stockbridge looked as though it would fit the bill perfectly. On entering, I liked the lively vibe with tables mixed in with comfy sofas and deco that isn't too fussy but still stylish. I also loved the extensive cocktail menu (anywhere that serves a cosmo gets a huge tick in my book).

Family fare

My husband liked browsing the good selection of beers and when it came to food the thick beef burger accompanied by a mini bucket of chips was a sure bet. As a mini-me, Lilian (10 months) likes to "network" with the other customers by smiling sweetly and getting their attention whilst sitting in one of the highchairs that are provided. The menu isn't vast but it's solid and safe with offerings like fish and chips, steak pie and vegetable lasagne. But be warned, leave room for the large selection of desserts. I had a honeycomb and pecan cheesecake – only my personal trainer would disapprove (I did say I was a cliché of a media type!). We didn't choose from the children's menu but Wilfred (2) loved the adults' fishcake starter accompanied by a glass of apple juice – but mostly enjoyed flirting with the friendly waitresses. This brings me to my husband's constructive one-line review: "The waitresses are very accommodating and very pretty."

The relaxed atmosphere was perfect for a Saturday night dinner but all good things come to an end as their licence laws mean no children after 8pm. That's fine by me – a Saturday night out followed by a Saturday night in front of the telly with Gary Barlow – bliss!

Get more ideas for your Saturday nights (or lunchtimes) in the Eat & Drink chapter, later in the book. You can read our review of Hamilton's on p 154.

Take your kids to the pub!

Doesn't sound very PC does it? But Scottish pubs are not the hard-drinking dens of old. Lizzie Smith tells us why she can be seen going into pubs at opening time, in the middle of the week, with a pushchair.

Pubs in Scotland these days are very different to the establishments I remember my dad frequenting in the 70s. Everywhere you look there are "bistros" and "gastro pubs" all vying for clientele. So much so, that they are actively seeking to appeal to non-drinkers – even the kids! If you are in and around Edinburgh, I can recommend two establishments to you: one off Leith Walk and one down towards the Royal Botanic Garden.

Swede success

Joseph Pearce's has filled a niche for a few years now. Run by Swedish couple and parents Anna and Mike Christopherson, they have made their venue more than just a pub. Between 11 and 5 they turn over a mezzanine area to children and parents, with big comfy sofas and a play area. As soon as you enter through the double doors, staff come out from behind the counter and offer to carry your buggy up the stairs.

Especially if you arrive for an early lunch, the staff are soon with you again to take your order from a fun, healthy menu including Swedish options. A children's menu is available too. The children's area is fitted out with a microwave, plates and even a bottle warmer. A stair gate is in discreet operation and highchairs are available for eating; but your little one will want to play with the toys on the carpet for most of the time – while you can relax and chat to your friends over a drink.

The pub also runs a weekly jogging club and hosts charity art exhibitions. Find "JP's" at 23 Elm Row, near Leith Walk.

Orchard near the Garden

If you're on a trip to the Royal Botanic Garden in Edinburgh and fancy lunch, given the queues in the cafés there it might be a better option to go out the East Gate and head for The Orchard Bar, 1-2 Howard Place. Children can actually stay in the pub for eating till 8.30pm if you are looking for an evening meal (romantic or not).

The Orchard has an excellent separate family room off their main bar, complete with ice cream counter. The pub rebranded itself a couple of years ago and has some great Scottish cooking. They often have game on the menu for pub prices and always have an Anstruther Catch of the Day – and goat's cheese soufflé. The children's menu includes a cheesy pasta or soup, and half portions from the main menu are also available. Another big plus is the provision of crayons to keep the little ones entertained.

Pub practicalities

Something pubs are not usually as swish about as restaurants is their nappy changing facilities. Typically it's in the Ladies – okay for the dads! – and the changing station is squished into a cubicle. This is still the case in Joseph Pearce's. However, The Orchard has changing facilities in the Gents too. Many cafés and hotels tend to have a bit more space for changing in the accessible loo.

Most mums are not so fussy about the décor of a pub – they just want to feel comfortable and welcomed as valued clientele. It's quite good for a pub – or even a café – to have a buzz about it by attracting a crowd. Pubs usually have a bit more space than cafés to park pushchairs and as mums come in the daytime they help to keep the place open all day round.

They say that pubs are a dying breed – but these two are opening their doors to the next generation and doing good business from it. So support your local – take the kids along and these fine establishments are all the more likely to be there when you need somewhere to take the grandkids. Use it or lose it!

There are lots of other family-friendly pubs reviewed in our Eat & Drink chapter.

CARERS AREN'T JUST MUM-SHAPED!

It's not just mums that look after young children of course. Grandparents and dads are just two other types of carer that enrich the lives of under 5s. We hear from a grandma and a stay-at-home dad.

The A-Z of grandparenting

Part of the original Edinburgh for Under Fives Committee in 1987, Kathy McGlew is an NCT Breastfeeding Counsellor and a grandma. Here are her tips for entertaining the youngest members of the family.

Art Baking Cleaning Dressing-up Errands Flowers Gluing Hospital-play Ice Joy Kitchen Love Music Nutrition Opera Pencils Quiet Rest Science Tidying Ukulele Vacuuming Water-play Xylophone Yarn Zoo

Going out and about on an adventure with my under-5 granddaughter and her baby sister is wonderful but she often asks "When are we going to Grandma's house?"

I have child proofed my house so most things are all right for grandchildren to touch. It just meant rearranging possessions a bit, packing away a few precious ornaments or placing them out of reach. I set a few rules so some rooms are just never played in and other rooms are fine for them to explore. Someone once wrote: "When you remove a temptation, you remove a rule and the fewer rules there are, the easier the child can live in dignity with the rules that are left."

We were thrilled with the arrival of our first grandchild, a beautiful little girl and then two and a half years later her gorgeous sister arrived. It was very simple at first because all that was needed at Grandma's house was a cot and a nappy changing station and I did acquire a baby bouncer.

I found there was no need to buy many toys for under 5s but a few chewing toys for a baby was a good idea. I tried being creative with what is

to hand like putting some teaspoons in a basket for the crawling baby to find. I also have a mystery basket into which I put small things of interest from around the house or small toys I pick up. This can appeal to both children. I add to it and remove things all the time. As the children have moved into age 2 and 3, I have bought crayons, pens, cookie cutters, farm and zoo animals, doctors kit, cars, puzzles and lots of books. Home-made play dough in different colours keeps a long time in a sealed container in the fridge.

I accept that there will be a (sometimes serious) mess after cooking, baking, watering the plants, (it helps to put a plant in the sink first). And thinking of the kitchen sink, it almost always pleases my under 5, even the youngest under 5, to play at the kitchen sink probably from the time they can reach it standing on a chair. Everything gets wet but the mess is not so bad as the child gets older. For this reason I keep a complete change of clothes for each child. Drawing, painting and gluing creates a mess but the children like to clean and tidy, wipe and sweep as well, especially if they get to maybe put on rubber gloves first. I found sometimes the clearing up was more fun than the messy activity.

I recently had a fun afternoon cleaning out my junk drawer with my granddaughter. I tipped the drawer out in a big mess on the kitchen table. There were definitely some risky things in that pile so I grabbed the pills and matches but everything else we sorted out and most was of interest. She figured out how to use the paper punch and it kept her busy for the rest of the afternoon: all those little circles – everywhere.

GRANDMA'S PLAYDOUGH RECIPE
1 CUP SALT
2 CUPS FLOUR
1 TABLESPOON CREAM OF TARTAR
Mix well and add
2 CUPS BOILING WATER
1 TEASPOON COOKING OIL
Knead well when it is cool enough to touch.
Add a few drops of food colour.

Adventures in daddy daycare

Around 6% of British fathers are full-time dads. One of them is Edinburgh for Under Fives committee member Andrew Jamieson, who gives us his insight into life in daddy daycare, with useful tips for parents and carers of all kinds.

It can be said that it is good to be challenged, constantly and often, to be shaken out of your comfort zone. Well, that is what I discovered when I became a dad. There was me, thinking, I'll pick it up along the way, why read any of these puerile lad-dad books, surely instinct will kick in?

It is hard now, looking back, to try and imagine what life was like before Princess M (as my toddler daughter shall be known throughout this article, as per her request ...) appeared on the scene. Self-preoccupied, without any real purpose, for sure, but generally not quite as tired ...

Now, so as not to bore the stitches out of your clothes, I'll not ramble too much about Princess M's birth, other than it was quite a time, involving an emergency C-section, and a fraught first 6 weeks at home, with my wife suffering from a double bout of mastitis (if you're familiar with such a symptom then you'll have some sympathy I'd imagine). And, well, I just wish I'd been a bit more prepared. Hindsight is delusional, I know, but a bit of friendly advice would not have gone amiss ... Mind you, would I have listened to any that was given to me? Probably not.

Anyway, read on for some insight into the life of an average full-time daddy, broken down into four easy parts ...

Part One: The Challenge

I look after Princess M full-time while my wife works. She is a full-time teacher. Due to cold and cruel financial sense, we decided that the logical decision would be for me to give up my poorly paid retail job to look after Princess M, when the time came for my wife to go back to work. That first week back was really tough on her. To see her so upset every morning when she had to leave made me feel like an absolute waste of space. Lots of soul-searching, lots of doubting. The only way to deal with that, I found, was to work hard, to make things easier for my wife. The way I see it, chores are my job. Whatever free time she has I try to make sure she is either spending time with our daughter, or relaxing. She is a wonder wife and a "yummy mummy", in the best way. She works harder than anyone I know.

As job changes go for me, it was quite dramatic. From selling books in a shop to looking after a baby and a home.

I look back now and can't help but think: how on earth did you cope?

Nothing can really prepare you for the responsibility of being, well, responsible. And responsible for another human being, at that. You just have to get on and do it, learn as you fumble. Sink or swim etc.

And us men are not quite as useless as:
a) most women would like to think we are, or
b) we believe ourselves to be.
Bar the exceptions, of course, who generally make the rest of us look bad.

Part Two: Playing Daddy

I am in a minority. Seems strange to write that, but it is true to an extent. I am more often than not the only dad at most playgroups I go to. I've spoken to some dads who find a room of chatting women quite intimidating. Not me. I have an ability to talk, to put it bluntly. Conversation is a difficult art, but an enjoyable one. And a very useful trait for playgroups.

Ah, playgroups.

My advice to the new dad is just go for it, get stuck in. Play with the toys, sing along to the songs, mingle with the mummies. And drink the coffee and eat the biscuits. It is a liberating experience, in some ways. It can be hard work at first, particularly if your child is young; you have to work harder to get them to play. The older they get the more independent they are, so you just leave them to it, for the most part. It can be a thrill to see them getting on with other kids and enjoying themselves.

Sometimes I do think that I get funny looks, the kind that I interpret as: what a loser, he's looking after the baby, he can't provide for his family so his other half has to. That kind of look. Or perhaps they're looking at the billboard behind me. Or maybe they're thinking (if they're a man): lucky swine, he's got it easy. Quite a lot to read into a look. Maybe I'm paranoid, maybe not.

I am certain, however, that looking after Princess M isn't easy. It is hard work, tiring, but the most rewarding job I've ever done. I'm my own boss (most of the time), working to a flexible clock, defined by playgroups and playdates. I am (mostly) in control of the household, making sure washing and cleaning are up to date, that bills have been paid, that food is being bought and made, etc. Oh, and I have become quite the baker. My wife and I sometimes engage in a mild bake-off. She is quite competitive.

I also feel very privileged. I know that, yes, I am in some respects a minority, but certainly a happy one. It isn't every dad that gets to spend so much quality time with their young child. I know there must be loads of fathers out there who wish they could spend more time at home with their families. I feel very fortunate indeed to be around so much for my daughter in the formative years of her life. Every day is a gift.

Part Three: Reality
When I left my old job to look after Princess M, I had another job lined up, a part-time position with more flexible hours that kind of fits in around our family lifestyle. Financially speaking, we couldn't cope just on my wife's wage. So my job helps to take care of our bills, like Council Tax (boo-hiss) and power. Sometimes there is a little bit of playtime money for daddy.

I work part-time for a homeless charity as a care worker, a few shifts a week, mostly weekends and some weekday evenings. It really brings into focus a lot of the important things in life. It can be very easy in our society to focus on the acquisition of more things, always thinking about what we don't have – as opposed to what we do actually have. A home, a family, food on the table, somewhere comfortable to sleep. These are luxuries that a certain section of the population don't have access to.

Can I recommend being a full-time dad? Yes. Our situation was forced on us through necessity. We couldn't afford to put our daughter into a nursery, but we feel we made the right decision at the time and, it so happens, we think that decision was the right one. You might think otherwise. That's fine. There are no hard and fast rules that are universal. What I've learned is that every parent finds their own way of doing things that works for them and, most importantly, for their child.

Part Four: Tried and Tested
I like to think that, along the way, I have picked up a few good habits and have learnt enough in this past year to be able to offer advice, of a kind, to the new dad, whether he be the main bread-winner of the family, or a full-time daddy like me. The key thing, obviously, is to be organised.

Below you will see a couple of lists, of some of my daughter's favourite things in life, and also some recommends from me.

Some of Princess M's favourite things:
• Going to wave at the trains from the bridge in Princes Street Gardens.
• Peppa Pig TV show.
• Grilled cheese on toast, yoghurt pouches, fruit!
• Shoes! (She is a girl after all!)
• Archie from the BBC's Balamory.
• Gromit (from Wallace & Gromit).
• Choc-choc.
• Her mummy and daddy, of course.

Andy recommends:

- The best playgroup in town, for my money, is at St Paul's & St George's Church (where York Place ends and Broughton Street begins). Loads of space, lots of toys, great staff and a fantastic sing-song at the end, all for a bargain £2 entry.
- Princes Street Gardens has a great playground/playpark, and from there it's a quick stroll to the aforementioned bridge to wave at the trains ...
- There is lots of space to play and wander in the children's section at the big Waterstone's at the West End of Princes Street – just don't make a mess! Or Caroline will find you ...
- Got housework to do? Princess M is happily distracted by: drawing, Peppa Pig and/or Balamory, her plastic tea set, her books ... You get the idea. If you need to get on with things, keep the little people entertained!
- Save Our Sleep by Tizzie Hall is a great book for learning how to cope with your wee one's changing sleep patterns. My wife swears by this book.
- Princess M has always had a great appetite so feeding her has never been a bother, really. But Annabel Karmel has loads of great ideas in her books if you're struggling for meal ideas.
- Some good books for the little one: Little Red by David & Lynne Roberts (a great spin on Little Red Riding Wolf); The Gruffalo, of course, by Julia Donaldson & Axel Scheffler (in fact anything written by Donaldson is a treat for the ears); A Bit Lost by Chris Haughton (mighty cute tale of a little owl); For Just One Day by Laura Leuck & Marc Boutavant (animal friendly fun); The Dangerous Alphabet by Neil Gaiman & Gris Grimly (possibly more fun for the adults...); Something Else by Kathryn Cave & Chris Riddell (beautiful book, important message).
- I touched on this before. Organisation. Always be prepared. This goes without saying to be honest, but us chaps need reminding, I think. Always try to plan the day ahead − I repeat: have plans, think ahead to meals and naps, make sure you have plenty of snacks to hand (for wee one and yourself) and be flexible. With the little people, nothing is ever set in stone, certainly not playdates or appointments.

Planning on leaving for somewhere at 9.30? Give yourself half an hour more than you think you'll need. Trust me.

About: Andy has written books, short stories and screenplays. He produces and edits a newsletter, the Edinburgh Geekzine, and its "big brother" website, **www.geekzine.co.uk.**

As Andy testifies, dads can get some great support from hanging out with mums. However, sometimes a dad just wants to be with other dads. Dads Rock, a new Edinburgh playgroup, allows them to do just that – and to give mum a couple of hours' peace on Saturday morning.

Part of Fathers Network Scotland, Dads Rock is not just Edinburgh's, but Scotland's, only father and child play/music group. It's FREE and suitable for dads and children from 0-5 years old, incorporating art and craft, reading and music into its Saturday morning sessions. The group aims to help fathers and their children increase their bond, while enjoying the company of other dads and their children.

There are regular visits from external agencies like art clubs and museums, and day trips planned to various venues across the Edinburgh and the Lothians.

At the moment there's no waiting list and dads are free to drop in any Saturday. They have to register and give a few details when they arrive in the building, which only takes 2 minutes. A free healthy snack is provided for every child at every session.

The group is held at Gate 55, 55 Sighthill Road, Edinburgh, EH11 4PB every Saturday from 10.00-11.30. Dads Rock is on Twitter (@DadsRockEdin) and Facebook (Dads Rock). For more information, contact David on 07511 533 432 or Thomas on 07813 461 571.

OUR GRAND TRIP OUT

We hope that you can plan some great excursions using the information and reviews later in the book. To inspire you and give you some handy tips, here are just a few trips out experienced by our researchers recently.

Baby boon

It can be hard to get out and about with a young baby, but make the effort and you'll be glad you did. To give you encouragement and a few ideas, Stephie Phipps re-traces the steps she took one Saturday with her little one.

What do you do on a slightly chilly Saturday with a 4-month-old baby? Picture the scene. It's one of those beautiful mornings that you only get in Scotland in the autumn. The kind when you imagine having a stroll in a park with the coppery trees as a backdrop and then stopping for a frothy latte in a cosy coffee shop. Then you remember the pram, changing bag, dilemma of coordinating nap times and heating feeds. Not such an attractive thought. But we have discovered that with a little adaptation, a Saturday adventure can be achieved for you and your little one. Just about!

Towpath treasures
Ratho Canal Centre was our starting point – either drive or get the 48 Lothian bus from town. Get out your pram (your baby might get jiggled about on the canal path a bit, but for Bea the motion sent her straight to sleep) or better yet, strap on your baby sling or carrier. Cross over the bridge – and start your stroll along the canal. The Union Canal has a lot of activity going on it from frequently passing canal boats to ducks that more than resemble Jemima Puddle-Duck, which your little ones will enjoy watching. If you are feeling more adventurous, get on your helmets and cycle along the canal path. The canal stretches further than you might think – about 30 miles from Fountainbridge in Edinburgh to Falkirk.

After a lovely hour of walking and chatting and stopping for a quick feed on one of the many (some of them beautifully designed) benches and picnic tables, we felt like we more than deserved lunch out, just to warm up more than anything else! We are great fans of The Bridge Inn in Ratho which has recently been refurbished. It does a lot to make children welcome – with an interesting children's menu and even a colouring-in competition. The food is hearty and fresh and is more gastropub than pub. There is a lovely beer garden overlooking the canal if the weather is nice.

Scrambling about
A big portion of beer battered fish and chips later, the baby is changed and fed and now looking for some entertainment after a long sleep in the fresh air in her pram. We are on a roll – where next? That's an easy one. We are near the Edinburgh International Climbing Arena (EICA) which houses a lot more than just the climbing centre. Scrambles soft play is suitable for children from babies to 9 year olds and even has a café area. The baby play area is great and has lots of seating near it so you can keep your changing bag near you. The older children's area and the play frame looks like a great adventure. My daughter is too young for this, but judging by my friend's children's faces and excitement – it is a lot of fun. Incidentally, this makes a good venue for meeting friends with children for coffee and a chat whilst the children play.

Whilst we were at the EICA we discovered the Honeypot Ceramics shop which would provide a creative afternoon's entertainment. Also, the coffee shop at EICA is spectacular with its views of the dramatic cliff face climbing wall and excellent coffee, scones and soup.

Phew! Exhausted and happy baby and parents are ready to head home for a spot of Saturday night TV!

Find out more about the Union Canal on p 181, about the Bridge Inn, Ratho, on p 93, and about Scrambles at EICA on p 122.

Flora, fauna, and a farm – for a fiver!

Researcher Susan Heaton decides that it is entirely possible to be a stay-at-home mum and not spend a fortune on coffee shops, soft play and overpriced baby and toddler classes (although one or two here and there is fine, right?). And the canny Scot in her intends to prove it, as she attempts an entire day out with a £5 budget ...

The day starts pretty late in our house as Poppy decided she would much rather stay up most of the night chatting with her friends round her cot. So a quick breakfast and off we go.

We catch the number 25 bus to Edinburgh's West End – £1.40 – with Poppy saying hello and goodbye to every passenger to pass our seats.

Animal magic (and a guinea pig that nearly disappears)
We get off the bus at Gorgie and head up the cobbled alleyway that leads to Gorgie City Farm – a world away from the hustle and bustle of Edinburgh City Centre. It's not long before we are transported into rural farm life.

There are lots of animals to see and interact with including sheep, pigs, cows, donkeys and rabbits. There are also pony rides – a fantastic day out for all the family! The indoor area houses birds, chinchillas and other small animals and Poppy even gets to pet some of them, including a very sweet guinea pig that could quite easily have slipped into my oversized change bag ... but doesn't, of course!

The staff here are helpful and informative, happily introducing the children to all the animals and, as we head back outside, a long queue can be seen forming at the petting area.

As the weather is unusually mild for this time of year, we have an impromptu picnic with some cream cheese sarnies, chopped fruit and pancakes. The picnic area has hand-washing stations to help keep the germs at bay, and swings for those who would rather play than eat!

We manage to spend most of the morning (well, what's left of it anyway!) chatting with the animals. Then the red rubbed eyes and threatening tantrum tells me it is time to get moving.

Hopping on another bus – £1.40 – we head towards the Royal Botanic Garden. This is a nice long journey that allows my now very snoozy toddler to have her afternoon nap. Which continues just long enough for me to grab a hot coffee and bun at the Botanics' Terrace Café – £2.20. I also get a stamp on my loyalty card which is technically a saving!

Crayon frying and cloud gazing
Poppy is soon wide awake though – there is nothing like a hot cuppa to wake a sleeping baby, every time without fail! Luckily, there is an ample play area in the café for her to get stuck into. She spends a good 20 minutes sorting out all the crayons and tasting them before cooking them with some bread and carrots in a pan.

All this cooking alerts her to the fact that it is almost time for a snack. Out come some delicious home-made banana biscuits and a carton of milk (thriftily, all brought from home) creating a few extra minutes for mum to sit and finish her cake.

This is a very child-and-adult-friendly café, with the children's play area sectioned off near the back. In fact, the whole Gardens are geared up for a family day out with ample attractions for people of all ages.

The rest of the afternoon is whiled away wandering through the flower beds and trees, saying hello to each and every duck on the pond and hiding in huge bushes! We take a short break to lie on the grass looking up through the trees and watching the birdies. We could be anywhere in the world, just my little girl and me. We laugh and point up into the darkening sky. Time to go home. There is so much to explore here that you could easily spend an entire day wandering along the winding paths in amongst the flora and fauna.

We walk home along the cycle path, stopping every so often to wave to the doggies or watch the hardy Water of Leith swans swimming alongside us.

One toddler, two buses, a £5 budget … total spend – £5!

Find out more about Gorgie City Farm on p 52 and about the Royal Botanic Garden on p 69.

5… great farm visits

Gorgie City Farm

East Links Family Park

Craigie's Farm and Deli

Muddy Boots, Balmalcolm, Fife

Almond Valley Heritage Centre

Edinburgh's other castle

Under siege at home with constant requests for juice, toast, things to do, missing toys and demands for more Octonauts, Sarah Joss decided it was time to muster the troops and storm a castle instead.

Despite living in the capital for over 20 years, like so many of the city's residents I'd never actually got round to visiting Craigmillar Castle. My twins Caitlin and Lucy enjoy a good castle, especially if it has a prison. Not yet 4, they already recognise a medieval bread oven when they see one. So, I decided it was time to check out Edinburgh's other castle.

Pleasant surprises

Expecting a small, mostly ruined building I was surprised to find a large castle in fantastic condition with numerous rooms, nooks, crannies and stairs ideal for tiring the legs of intrepid explorers. Craigmillar Castle, it turns out, is one of Scotland's best-preserved medieval castles.

Among other things, the castle is famous for hosting Mary Queen of Scots. The pact to kill her husband, Lord Darnley, known as the "Craigmillar Bond", was formed there in 1566.

A large wooden doorway leads from the outer to the inner courtyard. Inside the courtyard we were greeted by two very impressive, extremely climbable looking yew trees and a choice of doors into the castle itself.

The twins immediately ran off in opposite directions with shouts of "This way!". I'm convinced they contain opposing magnets, rendering them incapable of sticking together. After rounding them up, we began a more coordinated investigation of the building.

We soon became engrossed in a maze of spiral stairs, rooms and corridors. The castle was originally owned by the Preston family and then taken over by the Gilmours. Successive owners have added, altered and re-purposed, resulting in an intriguing higgledy-piggledy layout. Doors have been blocked off, windows widened, some kitchens converted to bedrooms and others to stables. There are stairways all over the place creating a labyrinth any Minotaur would be proud of.

Breezy heights

Eventually, after many twists and turns we arrived at the rooftop, Lucy's favourite part of the castle. From here you get fantastic views of East Lothian, Arthur's Seat, Edinburgh Castle, the Pentlands as well as the Park which would once have been the castle's hunting ground.

As well as the spectacular views outwards, there is also a dramatic view downwards through the machicolations (gaps for pouring boiling oil and projectiles down on attackers' heads). The girls were suitably impressed.

After the breezy heights of the roof, it's a relief to return to the Lord's Hall. Complete with wooden doors and leaded glass windows the hall and its adjoining rooms are a relatively cosy haven. Caitlin climbed into the fireplace to have a good peer up the chimney.

With so many rooms to explore and with most of the property still roofed, the castle is an all-weather attraction, although it is at its best on a day when the rooftop views can be enjoyed.

Lessons learned

The toilets are in a courtyard outside the castle. The number for the keycode is on the ticket. Despite being told to hang on to this, I'd misplaced it. Faced with desperation on the twins' faces, I eventually managed to dredge it up from memory. Mad panic ensued once we got back outside and couldn't spot Lucy anywhere. Thinking she was locked in we began frantically trying to recall the code. It turned out she was just around the corner. Relieved in more ways than one we continued our exploration of the grounds. Halfway around the kids declared they were tired and we retreated to the shop. According to the map of the castle park there is an adventure playground somewhere but we didn't made it that far.

The shop and visitor centre contains the usual mix of books, souvenirs, viking helmets and princess tiaras but no food. We should have brought a picnic but as we hadn't been expecting such an impressively extensive property we didn't think we'd need one.

Our review of Craigmillar Castle is on p 64.

Chapman's choice

What happens when you let your 4 year old decide what you're doing for an entire day? Diahann Whitefield (one brave lady!) decided to find out.

With the start of Primary One and his 5th birthday looming, I thought a "special day" to mark the occasion was in order. So, unsure of what I was getting myself into, and having visions of having to spend copious amounts of time in the candy shop filling up bags with pick and mix, I told our son, Chapman, that he could choose everything that we did for an entire day. The result did involve sugar, but mostly it was a day of breaking out of our normal routine, and sharing a fantastic adventure.

The big breakfast
We started at Wannaburger on Queensferry Street where in true 4-year-old style, only the highest seat at the highest table would do. This proved an excellent demonstration of the agility of youth versus the clumsiness of adulthood when I took my turn at being seated (there are lower tables available, however these are clearly not as desirable to the under-5 set!). However, the effort was well worth it for a filling and tasty breakfast, including a free refill on my coffee. With a varied menu from bacon rolls to pancakes, this was a great start to the day.

A rail adventure
Next stop – Haymarket station for a train trip across the Forth Rail Bridge. Children under 5 are normally free, but with Scotrail's "Kids Go Free" offer, up to two from 5 to 15 can ride free with each paying adult, making this a really affordable way to travel. You also get one free child admission at select attractions (such as Camera Obscura and Edinburgh Zoo) with your Kids Go Free ticket, so it's worth checking the Scotrail website for offers.

Chapman was absolutely delighted with the whole train ride, and hats off to Scotrail for encouraging children to ride the train. He got his own train ticket with a picture of a teddy bear on it, which made him feel important and grown-up, and he couldn't wait to hand it to the ticket collector for inspection. While riding the train may be a necessary mode of transportation for us adults, this was a real adventure for him – especially when it was time for our train to "race" the cars on the Forth Road Bridge (we won!).

Mummy the yes-machine
We got off the train in Aberdour, and walked to Silver Sands beach. Neither of us had been there before, and while I was delighted with the location and clean toilets, Chapman loved the bouncy castle, crazy golf, play area and snack shop selling candy floss (among other treats!). This being Chapman's day, we did all these things, with him looking at me with astonishment every time I said "Yes!" ("No" is a more frequent response in our home), and ultimately declaring, "Oh Mummy! You are the Yes-machine today!" We played on the beach, looked back at Edinburgh across the water, ate our picnic (though there is a café which sells good lunches), and then, with dark clouds moving in, decided we should head home.

On our way back to the station, Chapman spied Aberdour Castle (or, as it is now known, Aberdour Tower simply because it rhymes!), so we made a detour and visited the lovely walled gardens and terraced grounds. With my Historic Scotland Membership card, and kids under 5 going free at Historic Scotland sites, this turned out to be an affordable addition to our day.

When we arrived back in Edinburgh, I asked Chapman if there was anything else he wanted to do. Sensing the opportunity for one more "Yes", we headed to Princes Street Gardens for a ride on the carousel (there during Festival time), and a quick run about the playpark just as the rain started falling. As we headed home, we both had big smiles on our faces, and were looking forward to recounting our day to the rest of our family (and sharing our candy floss with them!). I'm not sure who had more fun on Chapman's special day – him or me!

You can read more about Wannaburger on p 161, Aberdour beach on p 91, Aberdour Castle on p 67 and Princes Street Gardens on p 68.

ABOUT THIS GUIDE

Edinburgh's zones

Many of the chapters in this book are divided by zone – Central, North, South, East and West Edinburgh, East Lothian, Midlothian, West Lothian and Fife. You can see the boundaries on the map inside the back cover. As in previous editions we've used postcodes to determine the areas in Edinburgh city.

Wherever possible we've listed postcodes in reviews so you can find venues using a map on the internet, your mobile phone or a sat nav.

Icons

Throughout, we've used a series of icons so you can check facilities at a glance. There's a quick key to icons at the end of the book, opposite the map, but here's an explanation of each icon in more detail.

Parking
The venue has lots of free on-street parking nearby, or a dedicated car park. Where parking is limited on-street, metered etc, we don't use the icon but usually put a note under the review so you know what to expect!

Accessibility
Our researchers have classed a venue as easily accessible to people with mobility issues, or a service as of special use to people with disabilities. Often we'll include notes explaining the situation in more detail. Do contact us with any issues or comments about our information on accessibility, on **ed@efuf.co.uk**.

Pushchair friendly
Pushchair access has to be easy in order to earn this icon. Certain venues will have areas where pushchairs must be parked in order to proceed further (at swimming pools for example). Where this is the case we've included an icon but explained these details in the notes.

Toilets
Used when we've been told by our researchers there's a toilet on the premises that the public can use. Occasionally we haven't been able to confirm this – in these cases we've left out the icon rather than guess!

Nappy changing
Facilities have to be more than a mat on the floor to earn a nappy-changing icon! There has to be a pull-down or freestanding table. Sometimes we mention where you can find nappy-changing facilities, but if we don't, you can usually find them in the accessible toilet.

Eating and drinking
Used for venues that aren't cafés and restaurants but where you can buy food/drinks. We haven't classed vending machines as eating/drinking facilities, although where there's a café area with a hot drinks machine (as in some of Edinburgh's libraries), we have.

Play area
Venues that aren't dedicated play areas (i.e. not soft play venues or playgrounds) but have play areas – like wildlife parks, cafés, museums or libraries. Play areas are anything from toys and books in a dedicated space to an outside multiplay. There will usually be something in the review to describe what's on offer.

Birthdays/celebrations

Used for venues and suppliers outside our "Party" section, pages 239-244, that are happy to host or help with parties, given notice.

Highchairs

At least one highchair – a separate chair rather than a booster seat. Often a venue will have at least 3 – we'll usually tell you if there is just one!

Children's menu

A specific children's menu exists rather than small portions on request from the main menu.

Vegetarian options

A number of vegetarian options are offered here.

Gluten free

Gluten-free options are offered here.

Licensed

Licensed to serve alcohol. This often means children are not allowed to stay after a certain time in the evening. We've included information about this where possible.

Food heating/bottle warming

We would expect any family-friendly restaurant or café to heat food or bottles when requested. We've only included an icon where researchers have told us that equipment is provided for you to do this yourself.

Breastfeeding

It's illegal to forbid breastfeeding in public in Scotland, so we've assumed that you'll be welcome to breastfeed anywhere in the book. We haven't included a breastfeeding icon unless the venue has provided a special dedicated area for nursing mothers.

If you are skimming reviews to check facilities, read from the bottom – look at the icons, then the notes underneath the review, then the review. Important details are recorded in all of these separate parts but the further down a review you go, the more likely it is that facilities will be mentioned.

Finally, bear in mind ...

What we've included in this guide are the views of individuals, sometimes based on one visit. Think of them as a personal opinion. Where we've received a negative review of a venue, service or activity we've left it out.

We rely on a team of volunteers, all of whom are busy parents and carers. Where they haven't managed to get to a venue we've verified that last edition's review still stands. However, if you feel that we've included out-of-date or incorrect information on somewhere you've been recently, please contact us at **ed@efuf.co.uk**. We'll put a correction on our website and ensure we have the details right for the next edition.

Some of our reviews are detailed but others are short and sweet, and occasionally there will be gaps where people haven't told us about facilities such as toilets, highchairs or a children's menu. Do contact the venue directly if you have any questions that we haven't covered.

Addresses are in Edinburgh, unless stated otherwise.

The odd fabulous place or activity does escape us sometimes. If there's something you think we should have included, please do tell us about it!

Q&A

We asked Caroline Watson, Buyer for Waterstone's Children's Department, West End ...

Are you a parent? *Yes.*

What do you like/dislike about your job? *I love my job! Coming from a heavy retail background anyway, it is extremely rewarding to be promoting and selling something so worthwhile. It is an absolute pleasure to see children (and sometimes more so, teens! Let's face it, they are the real tough customers!) roaming around the department, getting excited about books! My mother and mother-in-law are both librarians, so I do hope that my knowledge and obvious enthusiasm rubs off. A lot of my job is about chatting to the lil' uns and their parents and to hopefully recommend a book that they'll love, my only gripe being that sometimes I don't have the time to do this with every family. However, through the events and activity days that we hold (we aim to do this around twice a month at least) I hope to get to know and spend time with all my readers!*

How long have you lived in Edinburgh? *Since I was knee high to a grasshopper, but independently for the last 8 years.*

How do you rate it as a child-friendly city? *As a parent I have found it to be full of hidden gems, but for the most part, hidden they remain! It's astounding how much brilliant, friendly, innovative places there are for children and parents, yet most of it is only discovered by accident or on the say so of another parent. It can be frustrating that most establishments do not adorn themselves with their "child-friendly" badge, but instead wait for friends of friends to pass on the juicy titbits. This is, to me, what*

makes Edinburgh for Under Fives such a must-have, especially for first time mums or perhaps people who are the first to become parents within their social circle.

Any memorable experiences of Edinburgh as a parent? *I love that we live in a city with so much green put to such good use. My favourite memories are being red nosed and rosy cheeked, whether that be at Edinburgh Zoo, Gorgie Farm or in Princes St Gardens. It's a city kids can run in, and my most memorable experiences are of being able to escape from the city, within the city!*

Recommendations:
The Yard on Bonnington Road – Restaurant/ bar aiming for a European feel! Patio garden area with play equipment, as well as toys inside. Shows all main sporting events on TV and has activity days for children at weekends!

Our Dynamic Earth softplay – brilliant for 0-18mths. It is an underwater theme (soft, darkened lighting, wave sounds and fish projections) for a lovely sensory feel. Only £2 for entire day access – which is great if you want to go up to the café for a coffee and come back later!

Feeding the ducks at St Margaret's Loch in Holyrood Park – a brilliant activity for warmer days, located at the base of Arthur's Seat, take some time out from the hubbub of the city! Plenty of lovely child-friendly tea rooms nearby (including the Queen's, if you're feeling posh!).

Find out more about bookshops for under 5s on pages 214 to 217.

Getting Around

Getting Around

In this section we aim to prepare you for getting out and about in Edinburgh. We'll try to offer you the latest information on all the various forms of travel in our city in order of popularity with parents (in our experience). We'll pay particular attention to information relevant to travelling with under 5s – e.g. with pushchairs. To kick things off, you can find some useful sources of information below.

Edinburgh Council

www.edinburgh.gov.uk/transport
A useful site for finding out about general options for public transport in Edinburgh, walking and cycling options and roadworks etc affecting bus routes. Current information on the trams too.

Tourist Information Centre

Visit Scotland
Princes Mall, 3 Princes Street, EH2 2QP
0131 473 3820
0845 859 1006
info@visitscotland.com
www.edinburgh.org
Free literature, a booking system, discounts and transport information on Edinburgh and the Lothians. There is also a branch at Edinburgh Airport. Visit Scotland provides a booking and information service for the whole of Scotland too. See **www.visitscotland.com** for more.

Traffic Scotland

0800 028 1414
(24 hr Freephone Customer Care Line)
www.trafficscotland.org
Up-to-date information on motorways and trunk road networks in Scotland, including road accidents, traffic congestion, park-and-ride facilities, major events and even weather warnings. Smartphone app also available.

Traveline Scotland

0871 200 2233 (24 hr hotline)
www.travelinescotland.com
Information about public transport, such as timetables, details of available concessions, bus times to your mobile or details of transport for people with disabilities. The site can help with journey planning on public transport in Scotland and to major centres in other parts of the UK. It can also direct you to other sites e.g. Transport Direct, and help you plan a journey in Wales, Northern Ireland or England.

WALKING

Built on seven hills, Edinburgh is pretty steep in places with a lot of steps! It's not always the easiest city to negotiate with pushchairs, wheelchairs or with young children. However, the city centre is fairly compact so you can see a lot, quickly, and there are some brilliant greenspaces like Inverleith Park, the Royal Botanic Garden and the Meadows, which are free, have great views and are accessible for pushchairs and wheelchairs.

The council published a walking strategy in 2006 as part of its aim to promote more sustainable modes of travel. Here are a few useful resources for walking and road safety:

Walkit.com

www.walkit.com
A useful site when planning a walking route – however, it doesn't currently include information on accessible or pushchair-friendly routes.

Visit Scotland

www.visitscotland.com/walking
Includes routes throughout Scotland. A link on the right of the page takes you to information about disabled access for these walks.

Road Safety Scotland

www.road-safety.org.uk/education-and-families/preschool
www.gosafewithziggy.com
A new approach for early road safety in Scotland has been launched, and effectively replaces the Children's Traffic Club in Scotland. "Go Safe! Ziggy's Road Safety Mission" targets 3 key age groups (0-3, preschoolers, and transition to Primary 1). Age appropriate resources are provided to all children through the Bookstart programme, early education establishments and primary schools. Parents and children can also access the Go Safe With Ziggy website for additional resources and activity ideas.

Scottish Road Safety Campaign

www.srsc.org.uk

BY BUS

Two companies – Lothian Buses and First Bus – provide the majority of services in and around Edinburgh, although other operators provide localised transport. E&M Horsburgh and Edinburgh Coachlines are now taking over some routes in Edinburgh. Lothian bus tickets will not be valid on these services.

First Bus operates fewer routes in the city centre, but has more buses which service the outlying zones of the city.

Bus fares
Under 5s travel FREE on the understanding that they will surrender their seat for a fare-paying passenger. A maximum of two under 5s may accompany one adult, and a standard child fare must be paid for further children.

Fares are a flat rate for both adults and children, as well as for concessionary travel: currently, adults pay £1.40 for a single journey and £3.50 for a day ticket. The child's half-fare in Edinburgh is 70p (a child is 5-15). People who have concession passes for Edinburgh, East Lothian and Midlothian can travel FREE apart from on night buses and tour buses.

There are a raft of saver options available in addition to the great value day ticket – weekly, monthly and even yearly passes. There is also a RidaCard ticket available, paid by Direct Debit.

Bus times
Real-time bus information for in and around Edinburgh can be obtained from www.mybustracker.co.uk.

Pushchairs on buses
This issue is the subject of frequent media controversy in Edinburgh. The rule is, if there is already a pushchair on the bus you are boarding, you may need to be prepared to fold yours or wait until the next bus. Spaces may also need to be vacated for wheelchair users. Things seem to be getting easier with the introduction of a number of new buses with a dedicated space for an unfolded pushchair in addition to a wheelchair space.

These buses usually have a pushchair sign in the window. However, there may still be an issue with space on the bus if you have a certain type of side-by-side double pushchair. It's best to check with the bus company (numbers below) or chat to other parents.

BUS COMPANIES

First Bus

Carmuirs House, 300 Stirling Road, Larbert, FK5 3NJ
01324 602 200
08708 727271 (customer service)
www.firstgroup.com/ukbus/scotland/sescot

E&M Horsburgh

01506 432251
www.horsburghcoaches.com

Edinburgh Coachlines

0131 554 5413
www.edinburghcoachlines.com

Lothian Buses

Annandale Street, EH7 4AZ
0131 554 4494
0131 555 6363 (Bus times and information)
mail@lothianbuses.com
www.lothianbuses.com

All Lothian buses are low floor and easy access.

Lothian Buses Travelshops
– for enquiries, tickets and timetables:

27 Hanover St, EH2 2DL
Opening hours: Mon-Fri 9.00-18.00, Sat 10.00-18.00, Sun, local and bank holidays – closed.

7 Shandwick Pl, EH2 4RG
Opening hours: Mon-Fri 9.00-18.00, Sat 10.00-18.00, Sun, local and bank holidays – closed.

31 Waverley Bridge, EH1 1BQ
Opening hours: Mon-Fri 9.00-18.00, Sat 10.00-18.00, Sun 10.00-17.15, local and bank holidays 9.00-18.00.

Lothian Buses Lost Property
27 Hanover Street, EH2 2DL
0131 475 0652
lostproperty@lothianbuses.com
Opening hours: Mon-Fri 10.00-17.30 (closed 13.30-14.00), closed on local and bank holidays.

Megabus

0900 160 0900 (book by phone)
0871 266 3333 (general enquiries)
enquiries@megabus.com
www.megabus.com
Stagecoach also provides the Megabus intercity service. You can book tickets online. Under 3s go FREE, but are not guaranteed a seat – unless a specific seat has been purchased for them and the reference number provided.

National Express

08717 818181
www.nationalexpress.com/coach
Child fares apply to children aged 3 and above. One child under 3 can be carried FREE with each adult fare paying passenger.

Scottish Citylink Coaches

Buchanan Bus Station, Killermont Street
Glasgow, G2 3NP
0871 266 3333 (07.00-22.00)
www.citylink.com
Concessions for under 5s, check conditions of carriage.

Stagecoach Scotland

www.stagecoachbus.com
Website gives information about information on individual bus stations across Scotland, along with timetables, bus fares and online booking. Also see website for details of your local operating company.

BY CAR

Edinburgh is a fairly accessible city by car, if you can avoid travelling during rush hour. However, beware of tramworks which can slow your journey down along the tram routes, including Princes St and South Gyle.

Car parking
The main headache in Edinburgh is not driving but parking. This isn't the case with any of the outlying shopping complexes (the Gyle, Fort Kinnaird, Ocean Terminal, Straiton, Hermiston Gait, etc), where parking is usually ample and FREE. However, sometimes parking in or near the city centre cannot be avoided. In the last few years parking restrictions have become tighter and charges have become steeper.

There are now various parking zones around the city. The central zones 1-4 run from Haymarket to the West of the city centre to Calton Rd to the East, and from Heriot Row to the North to Melville Dr to the South. Restrictions usually apply Mon-Sat 08.30-18.30 and are generally charged at £2/hr. Central zones 5-8 generally apply Mon-Fri 08.30-17.30 and include areas such as Dean Village and Bruntsfield. There are also peripheral and controlled parking zones which charge at least 70p/hr.

There is now a facility called RingGo which you can register for using your mobile phone and credit/debit card. This is particularly handy if you don't have any change for the meter.

Car parking facilities

0131 469 5400
parking@edinburgh.gov.uk
www.edinburgh.gov.uk
There are also several different parking facilities available throughout Edinburgh:

Greenside Row Car Park
The largest car park available in Edinburgh is Greenside Row at the top of Leith Walk. This has an elevated walkway through to St. James Centre and is pushchair friendly.

Park Green Scheme
This scheme aims to make savings on residents' parking permits for those owners of cars with more fuel efficient vehicles paying less. Details on council website, above.

Park & Ride
There are 7 Park & Ride facilities in Edinburgh. These are generally FREE and secure and are currently based at: Ingliston, Hermiston, Straiton, Sheriffhall, Newcraighall, Wallyford and Ferrytoll Fife.

If you or your child have mobility problems you may be eligible for a Blue Badge parking permit which allows you to park FREE in on-street bays such as pay and display and designated disabled parking bays. You can find out more on the "Blue Badge" section of the council website.

Car safety

For up-to-date information on travelling safely and within the law with under 5s, please see www.childcarseats.org.uk

CAR SCHEMES

City Car Club

0845 330 1234
enquiries@citycarclub.co.uk
www.citycarclub.co.uk
An alternative to owning a car in Edinburgh is to join the City Car Club. You pay for the time you use a car for, plus a mileage charge.

You can join and book your car either online or by phone. Individual membership is currently £50/annum. For a hatchback, charges range from £5/hr to £104/72 hrs. You get 50 miles free fuel included in the first 24 hrs, and 24p/mile afterwards. Insurance is included within the membership fee, with a £500 excess. Cars are accessed by membership card and PIN. Keys are located inside the vehicle and cars are located throughout the city. You would have to provide your own child car seat(s).

Motability

0845 456 4566
www.motability.co.uk
Parents of children who qualify for the higher rate mobility component of the Disability Living Allowance can use it to pay a non-returnable deposit for the hire of a new vehicle. Sometimes there is no deposit, depending on the vehicle picked. There are a wide variety of cars to choose from, including MPVs. Repair and insurance costs are met over the period of rent.

To find out more about getting a disabled parking bay outside your house, call Clarence on 0800 232323.

Are you following us yet? We're @EdforUnder5s on Twitter or you can be our friend on Facebook – look for Edinburgh Ed.

By Bicycle

Cycling in Edinburgh, with its excellent network of cycleways, is fast, afford-able and healthy. Keen cyclists and parents Orla and James Hobson bring last edition's cycling section up to date, and add some useful tips of their own.

Edinburgh is the only UK city to have signed up to the Charter of Brussels, a commitment to city cycling that would see bikes account for 15% of all journeys in Edinburgh by 2020 – so there's never been a better time to get on a bike and join other families who are switching to pedal power.

Given the number of hills in and around Edinburgh, cycling may not be the first thing you think of doing with your baby or toddler, but with a wealth of benefits associated with it, maybe you will be inspired! Your child will certainly be thrilled by feeling the breeze and watching people and objects go by.

TOP TIPS

Before taking off, a few guidelines that will help you and your baby or toddler enjoy that first trip, cementing a great foundation for many more fabulous family adventures.

Your bike

Fundamentally, you need a bike. Maybe you're buying a new one, in which case all reputable bike shops will have set it up for you to be roadworthy.

If, however, you are digging out an old bike that has been sitting in a shed or have obtained a second-hand bike, it's advisable to give it a good check over before heading out. A good number of bike shops offer various forms of bike health checks. Depending on what's required, basic services cost around £20-£30 whilst a full service could cost around £80.

As an alternative you may consider learning some basic maintenance skills under the supervision of experienced bike mechanics. A number of cycle shops now offer this service either as a class or via an hourly hire of a workstand, tools, and guidance. Learning some

Your first trip

start small... and don't be too ambitious. Use a Spokes, Innertube or Council map to plan a route (see p 41).

You may find that wider handlebars give **better control** over the steering, but if you are using a mountain bike, change the knobbly tyres for smooth ones to reduce resistance on off-road paths and tarmac surfaces.

stay warm and take an extra top. Long sleeves can help if your baby likes to suck fingers.

check the weather forecast!

If using the more common rear-mounted child seat, it is advisable to carry any necessary **luggage** in front panniers to balance the weight front and back.

Compared with cycling along, you will find that the bike feels **heavier** with a child on or attached to your bike. But hopefully you will now make full use of those low gears.

basic skills in bike workings helps you keep your bike well maintained and makes journeys easier if you get a puncture! Pay special attention to the brakes and the wheels, as if you are carrying kids they will be under greater strain than normal.

Check out pages 224-228 for essential cycling gear and where you can buy it.

What to wear

Wear a helmet and ensure that your baby, toddler or child wears a helmet at all times both on road and off road.

Whether you cycle alone or with your child, dress brightly and make use of fluorescent strips to maximise visibility, and if it may get dark while you're out, remember to have working front and back lights. The use of a flashing red rear light in addition to the legally required steady red light is recommended.

It is key to remember that although you are cycling and generating warmth, your baby/toddler is not. Therefore it's important to consider the weather conditions for your little passenger. All in one baby/toddler suits and waterproof suits are great, and don't forget a warm hat for under the helmet and some snug gloves.

On the road

Beware of the effect other road users' actions, such as car doors opening unexpectedly, may have on you, and of the effect your actions, such as overtaking a stationary queue of traffic at a junction, may have on other road users. A simple rule to follow is to assume no one has seen you. And finally, no matter how tempting, never jump the red lights at pedestrian crossings.

stock up

on emergency favourite snacks! Don't forget to fuel the engine too – that's you!

CARRYING CHILDREN

Although some keen cyclists have been known to tow babies as young as a few weeks old in child trailers, it is not advisable to take them cycling until a baby can support its head and sit up unassisted, usually around 6 months. Babies and toddlers can be taken cycling in a child trailer towed behind the bike or in a rear-mounted child seat, which clips into a bicycle's rear rack. There are pros and cons to both and what is suitable for you will depend on the type of cycling you intend to do and your budget. You can read all about the options available in the Shopping section, pages 224-226.

Once the trailer or child seat has been outgrown (3-4 yrs depending on size), the choice is a trailer cycle, which attaches to your bike or a tandem bicycle. Again there are pros and cons to both.

The Spokes leaflets "How to be: a cycling family" and "Cycle-commuting with kids" (both available from the Spokes website, www. spokes.org.uk) provide a wealth of detailed information about different methods of conveying children by bicycle, as well as real-life stories and experiences.

For fully comprehensive information you should try a book such as *Bicycling with Children* by Trudy E. Bell.

BICYCLES ON TRAINS

Cycles travel free of charge on Scotrail trains, though reservations may be required. It's best to make your enquiry when you are booking your ticket.

CYCLING IN PREGNANCY

If you are reasonably fit and used to cycling, there is probably no reason not to keep cycling during pregnancy, but do follow your doctor's advice. www.nhs.uk does advise that you shouldn't cycle after 26 weeks due to the risk of falls. Consider lower gears and inverting dropped handlebars to enable a more upright sitting position for greater comfort. Be aware that your balance may change as your bump grows.

The Sustrans booklet "The Bike Belles Guide" (available from www.sustrans.org/ resources/Bike-Belles) offers useful information about cycling in pregnancy, as well as lots of tips for women in general who are interested in cycling.

BIKE STORAGE

One of the main obstacles to regular cycling in Edinburgh, especially for those who live in flats or tenements, is the issue of bike storage.

While some tenement-dwelling cyclists may have a suitable area in the stairwell to store their bikes securely and without causing an obstruction or nuisance to neighbours, many others do not have this luxury and are faced with the unappealing prospect of lugging their bikes up winding staircases and then taking up precious storage space within their flat with a grimy bike.

Spokes and Edinburgh City Council are working hard to come up with innovative solutions for bike storage in tenements to encourage more flat dwellers to cycle regularly. The Spokes leaflet "How to be: a cycling flat dweller" (available from www.spokes.org. uk) gives some good ideas for bike storage, and information about the Council's proposed strategies.

YOU'LL NEED A MAP …

A map is vital until you know your way around Edinburgh's routes, since you are often out of sight of the usual street names and landmarks that help you navigate when you're on the road. Although some of the cycleways are well signposted, other areas are not, and access and egress points can be easily missed without a map. These are a few of the maps available:

Spokes Maps
The Lothian cycle campaign produces excellent maps of where to cycle in Edinburgh (and East, West and Midlothian). Roads and paths are marked according to cycle-friendliness and objects of interest are pointed out. The maps currently retail for between £4.95 and £5.95. For your copy, visit: www.spokes.org.uk/wordpress/ spokes-maps.

Innertube Map
Created by The Bike Station with lottery funding, every line on the Innertube Map is an uninterrupted, car-free cycleway and footway. You can access it FREE online and download it as a pdf from www.thebikestation.org.uk/ innertube-map. Find out more about the Innertube project on www.innertubemap.com.

Other resources
"Explore Edinburgh by Bike" maps are available FREE from Edinburgh City Council. You can download them from the website (www. edinburgh.gov.uk) or order them from Clarence: 0800 232323/clarence@edinburgh.gov.uk.

Sustrans produces maps and guides – available from bike shops, bookshops or direct. You can also download FREE leaflets, containing routes and maps, from their website. Visit www. sustrans.co.uk.

ROUTES TO GET YOU STARTED

Water of Leith Walkway: much of the Water of Leith walkway is also designated as a cycleway and provides a traffic-free, well-surfaced, fairly level route which takes you away from the hustle and bustle of the city and into the scenic, tranquil riverscape. The whole route from Leith to Balerno is about 15 miles, possibly too long to do in one go unless you have spectacularly patient children, but it is easily broken up into segments of a few miles each, which can provide an easy enjoyable ride, e.g.:

• The Shore to Botanics/Inverleith Park
• Botanics/Inverleith Park to Scottish National Gallery of Modern Art
• Scottish National Gallery of Modern Art to Water of Leith Centre in Slateford, via Murrayfield and Roseburn Park.

Holyrood Park and Innocent Railway Path: A fabulously scenic cycle around Arthur's Seat (5km), or, if you don't quite fancy the slog up the main uphill section, the Innocent Railway Path (via the Innocent Tunnel) can take you all the way out to the coast by linking to paths to Bruntstane, Portobello, Joppa and Musselburgh.

Union Canal Towpath: You can cycle the whole way from Edinburgh to Glasgow along the flat canal towpath via the impressive Falkirk Wheel (again, patient children a requirement). However, you could also just do smaller sections such as Fountainbridge to the dramatic Slateford Aquaduct.

Silverknowes Esplanade: Cycling along the esplanade from Granton to Cramond is a pure pleasure on a nice day. In the future this section of cycleway will link up with sections along the rest of Edinburgh's waterfront at Granton, Newhaven, Leith and Seafield all the way to Portobello and Musselburgh.

If you're inspired to get on your bike, don't forget to check out our cycling section in the **Shopping chapter – pages 224 to 228.**

CYCLING ORGANISATIONS

You can get more information on cycling from the following organisations.

CTC

0870 736 8450
cycling@ctc.org.uk
www.ctc.org.uk
Britain's largest national cycling organisation. It campaigns for all cyclists regardless of age, ability or type of bike. Members receive a range of services, and there is a local group, the CTC Lothians District Association. Local contact: Bill Coppoch (Secretary), email secretary@ ctclothians.org.uk. www.ctclothians.org.uk.

Cycling Scotland

24 Blythswood Square
Glasgow G2 4BG
0141 229 5350
This organisation aims to establish cycling as an acceptable, attractive and practical lifestyle choice.

Spokes

St Martin's Church
Dalry Road EH11 2JG
0131 313 2114 (answering machine)
www.spokes.org.uk
A Lothian cycle group which campaigns for better conditions for cyclists, Spokes is an entirely voluntary organisation. It produces cycle maps of Edinburgh and surrounding area, including offroad routes.

Sustrans Scotland

Glenorchy House
20 Union Street EH1 3LR
0131 539 8122
scotland@sustrans.org.uk
www.sustrans.co.uk
A charity working on sustainable transport projects, the flagship project being the National Cycle Network. Sustrans also offers advice on Safe Routes to School projects.

BY TAXI

There are two types of taxi in Edinburgh – black taxis and some private hire cars. Black taxis are able to be flagged down and take up to five passengers plus a wheelchair, and most vehicles are accessible. Private hire cars must be booked in advance and can take up to eight passengers. All taxis should display licences and have ID badges shown, and they should all be registered with the council and have standard rates operating under a meter system.

Travelling with under 5s by taxi can be tricky but you should be able to fit your car seat in the taxi should you wish, or secure your pushchair in black taxis using wheelchair straps.

There are possibilities for taxi fare reductions for over 2s with mobility issues. Phone Clarence to find out more – 0800 232323 (freephone).

Handicabs

0131 447 9949
www.handicabs.org.uk
Handicabs provide two services to people with limited mobility – Dial-a-Ride and Dial-a-Bus – which operate door-to-door. Dial-a-Ride runs 7 days a week and all buses carry wheelchair users. Book in advance. Fares are reasonable.

BY TRAIN

National Rail Enquiry Service

08457 48 49 50 (24 hrs)
www.nationalrail.co.uk
For all train times and fare enquiries. You can also use the website to check parking facilities, accessibility, toilets and nappy changing at each station.

If you are planning a journey, you could also check out Traveline (p 34).

There are currently four main passenger service operators in and around Edinburgh:

Arriva Cross Country

(England via East Coast)
www.crosscountrytrains.co.uk
0844 811 0124

East Coast

(East Coast to London/Inverness/Aberdeen)
www.eastcoast.co.uk
08457 225333 (Customer Relations)
08457 225225 (Assisted Travel)

First Scotland

(trains throughout Scotland)
www.scotrail.co.uk
0845 601 5929 (Customer Relations)

Virgin Trains

(West Coast to London)
www.virgintrains.co.uk
08450 008000 (General enquiries)
08719 774222 (Telephone booking)
0844 556 5650 (After-sales)
08457 443366 (Travel Assistance)

TRAIN STATIONS

The four main Edinburgh stations are:

Edinburgh Waverley, EH1 1BB
Waverley Bridge entrances step free. Lifts to all platforms. Nappy changing. Parking limited. Buses stop near station.

Edinburgh Haymarket, EH12 5EY
No step-free access to platforms 2, 3 or 4. Nappy changing. Parking reduced due to engineering works.

Edinburgh Park, EH11 4DF
Step-free access to all parts of the station. No toilets or nappy changing. Parking at shopping complex.

South Gyle, EH12 9EU
Step-free access to all parts of the station. No toilets or nappy changing. Parking.

More information on the accessibility of stations and trains can be found on www.nationalrail.co.uk. Stations Made Easy, a new interactive tool on the website, gives you the ability to plan your route through a station avoiding features (such as stairs) that might be difficult to use.

TRAIN FARES

As a general rule, under 5s travel free, on the understanding that they will give their seats up to fare-paying passengers. An adult can be accompanied by up to two FREE under 5s. A variety of special fares are available for families, including saver, cheap day returns and family railcard. Always ask to check the cheapest way to travel before buying your ticket. There is usually an abundance of leaflets with special deals available.

BY AIR

Edinburgh Airport

EH12 9DN
0844 481 8989
www.edinburghairport.com
The airport is 8 miles west of Edinburgh, just off the A8 dual carriageway and close to the M8 and M9 motorways. The website provides live flight information, how to get to and from the airport, flight destinations from Edinburgh, how to book flights, plus information on parking, hotels nearby and airport security.

Bus links

0131 555 6363
Buses pick up and drop off outside the terminal building, just by the main entrance. Lothian Buses operate the 3 main services into Edinburgh. Details about other longer distance buses can be found on the airport website.

Get the most up-to-date information on
www.efuf.co.uk

Airlink 100

www.flybybus.com
This runs to and from Waverley Bridge to the airport. The journey time is approx 25 mins with buses leaving Waverley Bridge every 10 mins during the day. Most Airlink buses are of the low floor, easy access type. Fares: adult £3.50 single, £6 open return; child £2/3; under 5s free.

Night Bus N22

www.nightbuses.com
This runs from the airport to the city centre (via South Gyle) and onto Ocean Terminal, Leith, 7 nights/wk. It runs every 30 mins and takes 28 mins from the airport to Waverley. Fare: £3.

Service 35

www.lothianbuses.com
This also runs to the city centre and Ocean Terminal. Drop offs include the RBS Headquarters, Scottish Parliament and Holyrood House. The service runs every 15 mins at peak times, and takes about an hour from the airport to Holyrood. Fares: £1.40/adult, £3.50 for a day ticket.

AIRPORT PARKING

Short stay
There is a new Fast Track service which offers 150 dedicated spaces 1 minute's walk from the terminal building. These are currently charged at £26/day. Preferential rates available if you book in advance.

General Short Stay Parking is available for a few hours or for short trips, and prices currently range from £2.10 for 15 mins to £21.50 for 12-24 hrs. Short stay parking can be booked in advance for convenience.

Blue badge holders, or drivers carrying blue badge holders, are given 15 mins free access to the Short Stay car park Drivers carrying blue badges should show their tickets to the ticket desk on the ground floor of the car park for validation.

Long stay

Long Stay Edinburgh

Located within the airport boundary, linked to the terminal by a courtesy coach service, which runs every 10 mins and is a 5 min journey. The cost per day is now £9.10 for 24 hrs or part thereof.

NCP Scotpark Edinburgh

Located outwith the airport boundary (follow signs to "Eastfield Long Stay"), the complimentary coach runs every 7-10 mins and takes 5 mins. Pre-book to secure a charge of £3.95/day - bookings must be made at least 24 hrs in advance.

AIRPORT TAXIS

There are three options for taxis and cabs at Edinburgh Airport, and separate ranks for each.

Private hire airport taxis are managed by Onward Travel and are located outside the Terminal building beside UK Arrivals. Tel: 0131 333 2255, www.onwardtravel.com.

Pre-booked private hire taxis can be arranged via Edinburgh City Private Hire. The collection point/rank is located on the ground floor of the multi-storey car park, directly opposite the Terminal. Tel: 0131 477 4000.

City "Black Cabs" can be found outside the Terminal building beside UK Arrivals.

A journey to the city centre typically takes 25 mins. Many taxis are pushchair and wheelchair accessible.

EDINBURGH AIRPORT FOR UNDER 5s

Essentials: Boots after security has nappies, formula, wipes and baby food. Most eating facilities in the airport offer a children's menu.

Security: The rules around liquids, medicines and baby food and drink are constantly being updated, so check the airport website (Security Control section) before setting out.

Nappy changing: There are 4 changing rooms in the terminal building: in UK Arrivals near Costa, on the 1st floor near WHSmith, and after security near Gate 11. There are also facilities in the international baggage reclaim hall.

Play areas: There are some interactive play screens dotted about the airport, and a play area near Gate 3 (after security) with toys and puzzles.

FLYING WITH UNDER 5s

Let the airline know in advance that you'll be travelling with a baby or toddler and check out the facilities on board and at your destination airport when booking, along with any relevant airline policies, e.g. baggage and pushchairs.

If you have a lively toddler, it may be worth finding out if you can use a car seat on board. You may have to pay for the seat, depending on the airline and how busy the aircraft is. Other options include booking a separate seat for your child, though this is usually charged at adult price, or some airlines allow you to select your seats when booking your tickets, so you can select a block of seats together.

Car seats and pushchairs can also travel in the hold – but check your baggage allowance.

Take tried and tested snacks and toys for in-flight entertainment.

During take-off or landing, swallowing food or drinks, or bottle-feeding, will help prevent earache arising from changes in cabin pressure. Nappy-changing facilities vary with each aircraft.

FLYING WHILE PREGNANT

It's always best to check with individual airlines as to their policy, as well as checking your insurance policy. General advice is that the safest and most comfortable time to fly is after week 14 and before week 28. Most airlines will require a medical certificate after 28 weeks to allow you to travel.

BY TRAM

The tram works in Edinburgh are ongoing, and you should check the changing situation on the website. Currently, the aim is to complete the route to St Andrews Square by summer 2014. For up-to-date information, contact:

0800 328 3944
info@edinburghtrams.com
www.edinburghtrams.com

Toilet stops

There are 32 public toilets in Edinburgh for which the Council's Environmental and Consumer Services are responsible.

You can access information on any of them and see them pinpointed on a map at **www.edinburgh.gov.uk/directory/61/public_conveniences.**

To talk to the Council about them, contact:
**City of Edinburgh Council
Environmental and Consumer Services
0131 529 3030
publicconveniencesandnightcleansing@edinburgh.gov.uk.**

Please note that the Council reserves the right to alter opening times, and may need to close toilets when cleaning takes place.

There are other automated loos (e.g. St Andrew's Sq and Portobello Promenade) but you'll need to spend more than a penny (more like 20p) to operate them!

Key:

 Facilities for people with disabilities. These toilets are part of the national key scheme.

Facilities that allow 24hr access for disabled users.

Facilities for changing nappies, usually a pull-down shelf and separate bin.

Ardmillan 10.00-20.00
Bath Street 10.00-20.00
Bruntsfield 10.00-20.00

Canaan Lane 10.00-18.00
Canonmills 10.00-20.00
Castle Terrace Car Park 10.00-20.00
Castlehill 10.00-18.00 (summer 20.00)
Cathedral Lane 10.00-20.00
Colinton 10.00-18.00
Cramond 10.00-18.00
Currie 10.00-18.00
Granton Square 10.00-18.00
Hamilton Place 10.00-18.00
Hawes Pier 10.00-18.00 (summer 20.00)
Haymarket 10.00-20.00
High Street, South Queensferry 10.00-18.00 (summer 20.00)
Hope Park 10.00-18.00
Hunter Square 10.00-20.00
Joppa 10.00-18.00
Juniper Green 10.00-18.00
London Road 10.00-20.00
Middle Meadow Walk 10.00-18.00
Mound (Gents only) 10.00-22.00
Mound (Paraplegic) 10.00-22.00
Nicolson Square 10.00-22.00
Pipe Lane 10.00-20.00 (summer only)
Ross Band Stand 10.00-20.00 (summer only)
St James 10.00-18.00
St John's Road 10.00-18.00
Taylor Gardens 10.00-18.00
Tollcross 10.00-20.00
West End 10.00-22.00

Out & About

Out & About

There is a huge variety of places to have a really great time out and about with under 5s in Edinburgh, the Lothians and Fife. We have concentrated on those most children should enjoy and which could be visited comfortably by parents with young babies too.

Because every child is different, not every venue might be ideal: the content of some may offer little stimulation to a toddler, but could catch the attention of a 4 year old or be great for visiting with a baby. Others, due to the physical structure of buildings (dark rooms and corridors, narrow turnpike stairs, etc) may concern rather than excite your particular child.

Wherever you choose, there are considerations which concern every parent: will my child be able to access most or all of the venue; are there suitable toilets and nappy-changing areas; and if we want to eat, is the venue geared up to cater for children? We've tried to answer these points too!

When you're out and about with young children, if you go with the old adage, "if something can go wrong, it will", you'll have most bases covered. So, lightweight waterproofs are always worthwhile; put anything spillable or burstable in a sealable pocket or in a plastic bag; and take a change of clothes. In nice weather always remember sunscreen and a sunhat.

Here we've listed our venues by type, then by geographical area within Edinburgh, the Lothians and Fife. If you feel like exploring further, more far-flung venues are covered in the chapter "Further Afield", later in the book.

 Visit our website for updates:
www.efuf.co.uk

COUNTRYSIDE AND ANIMALS

NORTH EDINBURGH

Cammo Estate   •FREE

Cammo Road, EH4 8HW
A fantastic introduction to countryside walking and nature – 85 acres of woodlands, meadows, marshes, a ruined estate house, stables and a folly (which looks like a mini castle). You can take any bus that goes down Queensferry Rd, get off at the Barnton junction, turn left into Cammo Rd and follow the path to the estate. No entrance fee, no shops, no cafés, no ice cream vans – take a picnic and enjoy the countryside. Many routes for beginners, some for the more advanced, and some suitable for pushchairs and wheelchairs. Under 5s will love playing hide and seek behind the giant trees, watching nature change with the seasons, seeing frogspawn in the giant pond at springtime, and exploring the ruins. There is a visitor centre at the main entrance, open Tues and Sun 14.00-16.00 and Thurs 10.00-16.00. Here you will find lots of information on the estate, leaflets on walks (useful if you visit regularly) and toilets.

Craigie's Farm

West Craigie Farm, South Queensferry, EH30 9TR
0131 319 1048
john@craigies.co.uk
www.craigies.co.uk

A great outing for children and adults alike. A family-run working farm with wonderful views and FREE entry. Meet Mango and Chutney (the resident rare breed pigs), or collect your own eggs from the chicken coop (get an empty egg box from inside the shop). Well worth a visit during fruit picking season as there is a huge variety on offer throughout the summer. Children find out where fruit really comes from and will have loads of fun in doing so. There are a number of paths and trails for walking and cycling. The nature detective trail is probably the best for young children. Download an "Around the Farm" map from the very informative website, or ask the friendly staff for details. Runs many events throughout the year e.g. farm weekend, nature weekend and farm tours. Once you have visited you will return again and again!

Craigie's Farm Deli and Café
Family-run, family-friendly, extremely popular, and with very friendly staff, this excellent café also has fantastic panoramic views. It offers delicious seasonal food at reasonable prices, produce direct from the farm, from small suppliers and farmers a little further afield. Daily hot specials, homemade cakes and slices, and fantastic breakfasts. No specific children's menu, but you can get a child's portion of anything off the menu. There is a basket of books and toys for the little ones. A wonderful deli accompanies the café. With great scotch eggs, a butcher's counter, fresh produce and ice creams it is very difficult to leave without buying something. Dogs are very welcome too and have their own menu! Free Wi-Fi. Seats around 100.

Opening hours: 09.00-17.00 (last PYO entry and food order 16.00). **Play area:** *An outside area that includes a great children's tractor.*

SOUTH EDINBURGH

The Pentland Hills · FREE

Regional Park HQ
0131 445 3383
pentlands.enquiry@edinburgh.gov.uk
www.pentlandhills.org
A beautiful range of hills spreading along Edinburgh's southern edge. Supported by City of Edinburgh, Midlothian and West Lothian Councils and Scottish Natural Heritage. Consists of two country parks, reservoirs (no swimming permitted), nature reserves and other private areas. Within the Regional Park there are several areas of interest to parents with young children. These include Glencourse (p 55), Hillend (p 56), and also Bonaly (p 50), Harlaw and Red Moss (p 53).

Swanston Village

**Accessed from Swanston Road,
off Oxgangs Road, EH10 7DS**
On the outskirts of Edinburgh, this village provides a pleasant stroll for all the family. We like to park and wander past the village and the golf club to The Steading pub for lunch. This is about a half a mile, good for toddlers, but not ideal for pushchairs. Alternatively there are walks to the Hill End ski run. Highland cattle are visible. The paths up the hill afford splendid views – just go as high as your little legs will take you.

WEST EDINBURGH

Bavelaw Bird Reserve

Balerno
Parking at Threipmuir – see reviews on Harlaw and Threipmuir Reservoirs (p 53). There is a picnic table here and information board with maps. A short footpath, unsuitable for pushchairs, leads down to Threipmuir Reservoir and along to Harlaw. With a pushchair the best route is to turn left out of the car park and follow the road along towards a bridge. On your right is the Red Moss Wildlife Reserve. This area is boggy so keep to the boardwalk. Continue over the bridge and up a steep tree-lined hill. Bavelaw Bird Reserve is on your right and there is a bird hide on the shore, over a stile and along to a narrow boggy path. Note: the key is held at Balerno Post Office.

A signpost at the top of the hill gives walking options. Only the left continues to be suitable for pushchairs until you reach the stile opening onto the Pentland Hills. This walk is exposed and can be cold but worth it on a clear day for the views. Sheep and cattle in the fields, waterfowl and fishermen on the reservoir below.

Bonaly

EH13 0PB
Where Bonaly Rd crosses the city bypass there is a fork in the road. The right turn, Torduff Rd (public vehicle access for only a few hundred yards and limited parking), leads up to Torduff Reservoir and is surfaced, but is a long push for pushchairs and small cyclists. At the reservoir you can turn left for a walk across to Bonaly Country Park – steps and a grassy path, but good views over the city. For pushchairs, a better walk is to follow the west side of the reservoir to the end where there is a short push up to Clubbidean Reservoir, ¾ mile. Here there is more space for picnics and there are sometimes anglers in boats to watch. The path alongside Clubbidean is rougher for pushchairs but energetic parents with backpacks may like to continue on to Currie, 1.5 miles.

Following Bonaly Rd from the city bypass as far as it will go brings you to a car park. This area is known as Bonaly Country Park and from here you can walk up to the hills. There is an information board with maps and a picnic area. Of the 3 paths up from here, the left is too steep for youngsters, the right takes you over Torduff Reservoir and up into the heather. The middle path, possible with pushchairs and for reasonable walkers, leads up through a plantation of trees to Bonaly Reservoir.

Corstorphine Hill Local Nature Reserve

Panoramic views of the city and beyond are offered from the 531ft summit. Terrain is varied with large areas of woodland and also a steep, rocky section (including a flooded quarry). At the summit is Clermiston Tower, built in 1851 to commemorate the centenary of Sir Walter Scott's birth. Access to the tower by arrangement with Ranger Service, or on Sundays in summer courtesy of Friends of Corstorphine. Between the tower and Clermiston Rd is the Walled Garden which has been restored by Friends of Corstorphine into a woodland walk for the

community. There are several routes to the summit: Clermiston Rd (3 paths; the one near the hotel is rough and steep), Queensferry Rd (steep and rugged), Craigcrook Rd (between new houses up a fairly steep but smooth path, some steps); Ravelston Dykes Rd (200 yds north of Murrayfield Golf Clubhouse) and from Cairnmuir Rd at junction with Kaimes Rd. The latter is easiest for pushchairs though muddy after rain. Path follows the edge of the zoo.

Parking: Limited parking at Cairnmuir Rd/ Kaimes Rd, or in other streets adjacent to Hill. *Accessibility:* Some paths are steep and rocky. *Pushchair friendliness:* Only on some paths.

Craiglockhart Dell

Beautiful wooded glens with the Water of Leith and its walkway running through the centre. Plenty of paths to explore, although those with pushchairs will have to search for flat routes. Bridges for "Pooh Sticks" and open grassed areas next to the river are ideal for picnics and games. Access includes Dell Rd, Colinton, Katesmill Rd, pathway from Lanark Rd, near Dovecot Pk and behind the Tickled Trout pub on Lanark Rd at Slateford.

Craiglockhart Hill

Street parking at Craiglockhart Terr, Lockharton Cres and at Craiglockhart Sports Centre. Level paths from the sports centre and from Craiglockhart Terr are suitable for pushchairs and take you to the pond which is home to ducks, moorhens and coots, the nests of some of which can be seen in early summer. There is a map of the area at Craiglockhart Terr and at the pond. Many interesting and attractive plants. Off the level path you'll find steep sections, some with steps, that go up through seminatural woodlands to the top of the hill. The highest part is open and gives impressive views of the city and countryside beyond.

Edinburgh Zoo

134 Corstorphine Road, EH12 6TS
0131 334 9171
info@rzss.org.uk
www.edinburghzoo.org.uk
Just 10 mins from the city centre, Edinburgh Zoo is home to over 1000 rare and endangered animals and is one of Europe's leading zoos. Just recently it has famously welcomed giant pandas Tian Tian and Yang Guang. With an inspiring array of daily events and much to see and do, you will be kept busy here! At the ticket office you will receive a map and daily events list, and there is a notice board detailing any new arrivals/babies. There are plenty of animals to particularly amuse the under 5s – our favourites are the penguins (of course!), sea lions, sun bears, gibbons, chimpanzees in the impressive Budongo Trail, and capuchin and squirrel monkeys in the Living Links enclosure, to name but a few. Don't miss the famous penguin parade daily at 14.15 – get there early to get a good space. The underwater penguin viewing area is great fun too. There are plenty of indoor animal houses and undercover

viewing areas for a rainy day. The Hilltop Safari bus runs regularly up the hill to the very topmost attractions.

There are several safe play areas for under 5s, close to some of the main attractions. The Ark is close to the lemur enclosure, and has slides, hidey-holes and a rope bridge beside a small picnic area. Next to the penguins is another boat-shaped climbing frame with slides. A large play area with climbing frames is just above the Budongo Trail, and right at the top of the hill is a small all-age play area. Plus cafés, kiosks, picnic areas and a super gift shop – everything you need for a great day out!

The zoo now has a wider selection of eateries on offer. The new **Grasslands Restaurant** serves a wide range of hot and cold food including a daily carvery option, pizzas, home-made soup and sandwiches as well as a separate deli counter for coffees, baking (including gluten-free) and pre-packed sandwiches. Children's options include a lunch box for £4.25 which includes a ham or cheese sandwich, juice, jelly and fruit. Soup is around £3.50, carvery £5.95 and sandwiches £3-4. There are also sweet selection packs for treats. The environment is light and airy with lots of soft seating for little ones to play on. Definitely the highlight in terms of catering options and a very pleasant place to lunch on your zoo outing.

The **Jungle Café** has a pizzeria, burger bar, chip shop and ice-cream coffee bar. It also has a soft play so good for colder days. Only open at weekends in the winter, however. The **Penguin Coffee Bar** serves machine-made coffee, pre-packed sandwiches and baking. There are also kiosks selling drinks, snacks and ice cream throughout the zoo, weather permitting.

*Opening hours: 09.00-18.00 (Apr-Sep), 09.00-17.00 (Oct/Mar), 09.00-16.30 (Nov-Feb). **Cost:** Zoo – adult £15.50, child (3-15) £11, conc £13, under 3s FREE. Family tickets available, plus annual membership (pays for itself by 4th visit and you get a 10% discount on food!). Softplay at Jungle Café – £2 for 30 mins. **Parking:** Plenty, although a fee applies and it can get busy at peak times. Reduced fee for members. **Accessibility:** The Zoo is on a hill with some steep areas. Ask at reception for recommended route guide. FREE manual wheelchair loan*

*available. All attractions are accessible and a courtesy vehicle runs regularly to the top of the hill – this can be busy at peak times. Carers get in FREE. **Pushchairs:** Most cafés have space for pushchairs. The Mansion House has a "no pushchairs" policy. Pushchairs welcome on the Hilltop Safari bus, space permitting. **Nappy changing:** Available in toilets in cafés and other points throughout the zoo. **Birthdays/celebrations:** Parties available including a tour of the zoo. The Mansion House can be hired for private functions.*

Gorgie City Farm

51 Gorgie Road, EH11 2LA
0131 337 4202
info@gorgiecityfarm.org.uk
www.gorgiecityfarm.org.uk

A great place for children to experience farm animals. There are lots of lambs and piglets born during the year. There are two entrances from Gorgie Road, the first (coming from town) is for cars and the second for pedestrians. It is just before Tynecastle High School.

The pet lodge houses small birds, gerbils, guinea pigs and a snake amongst others. There is a sensory herb garden which is also home to the ducks, a wildlife garden which has an owl and a small pond where there are lots of frogs to spot in the summer. The main farm has goats, sheep, a pony, a cow, pigs, lots of chickens and turkeys and rabbits. There are chickens wandering freely round the farm which the children seem to enjoy and a big red static tractor. There is also an area where children can see vegetables being grown.

There is a café, selling coffee, tea, sandwiches, homemade soup and basic meals, which is trying to promote healthy eating and uses produce from its own gardens. There are also tables and chairs outside for when the weather is fine. The education centre can be hired for parties and classes.

Opening hours: Apr-Oct 09.30-16.30, Nov-Mar 09.30-16.00. Cost: FREE (Donation suggested). Parking: A £2 donation is required for parking. Birthdays/Celebrations: Parties arranged for £8.50/child. Contact the party co-ordinator through the "Contact us" section on website.

Harlaw Reservoir

EH14
0131 445 3383
pentlandhills@edinburgh.gov.uk
www.pentlandhills.org

For a child-friendly visit to the Pentlands, park at Harlaw or Threipmuir car park and follow a variety of well-marked paths, many of which are accessible by pushchair. Near Harlaw car park, stop at Harlaw House where there are several picnic benches and in the wildlife garden, a pond (where frogs can sometimes be spotted) and a number of child-friendly explanatory panels. Inside the house is further information on the Pentlands Regional Park and a handy toilet. Although there are no changing or feeding facilities, there is plenty of room in the house in case of emergency!

Accessibility/Pushchairs: A flat walk can be chosen for those with mobility difficulties or for pushchairs.

Red Moss Wildlife Reserve, Balerno

Pentland Hills Regional Park Car Park Threipmuir, EH14

Parking is about 300m from the entrance to Red Moss and the way is through woods with a narrow path and lots of tree roots. Part of the route has been widened to allow pushchairs but some is still too narrow and forbids their use, meaning the route is not circular for pushchairs. In the nature reserve the path is very clearly marked, mainly because you are restricted to a board walk covered in a fine metal mesh. Our daughter walked along it and was happy enough not to jump off into the peat bog alongside. However the peat is very wet and clingy, so the consequences could be quite serious if a child did fall off the edge (not least in washing bills!). The pushchair-friendly section of the path takes you to a small pond with a sheep field nearby where you can sit on wooden steps down to the pond and have a picnic – picturesque and remote. The views of the hills and countryside as you walk along are very pleasant and the peat and unusual plants growing in it are quite other-worldly, so offer some potential for imaginative play. However, younger children are unlikely to be entertained for long. Worth a visit as part of a general trip to nearby Threipmuir Reservoir but unlikely to satisfy day trippers as the whole thing can be done in less than an hour.

Threipmuir Reservoir

pentlandhills@edinburgh.gov.uk
www.pentlandhills.org

An easy walk for pushchairs but you can't link up with the car park at Red Moss if you have a pushchair as there are kissing gates at the other end. It is not possible to walk around Threipmuir Reservoir. A variety of birds can be seen on this walk, keep your eyes peeled for herons and cormorants.

Parking: At Threipmuir and at Red Moss Nature Reserve. Take first left in Balerno Village after High School. Follow road for approx 2 miles out of the village past the animal sanctuary to the car park.

EAST LOTHIAN

East Links Family Park

Dunbar, EH42 1XF
01368 863607
grant@eastlinks.co.uk
www.eastlinks.co.uk

This definitely deserves a star! One of the best venues around Edinburgh for entertaining children of all ages for a good, full day out. For under 5s, highlights are the opportunities for watching, handling and feeding small animals, the train ride, the 9-metre high fortress with a 4-lane covered slide and tunnels (for older under 5s), and the ball blast room. On top of that the attractions include go-carts, the jelly belly, numerous low level trampolines, milk churn skittles and a pirate ship multi-play centre and the indoor haybarn. Pony rides for a few hours each day on weekends and holidays from Apr-Oct, depending on the weather. There is an indoor picnic barn, a welcome sight on a wet and windy day. Special events at Christmas (e.g. Santa sleigh train, grotto, nativity scene with live animals and a snowman treasure hunt) and a great Easter Egg Hunt at Easter. The website's newsletter keeps visitors posted on new arrivals at the farm and you can follow them on Facebook for up-to-date information and discounts. There is a gift shop with a range of reasonably priced small toys.

Tea in the Park Café

Offers a range of hot and cold snacks, such as baked potatoes, paninis, filled baguettes and toasties as well as a soup and main meal of the day. It was very busy when we visited (school holidays) so was noisy and a bit chaotic but the staff were friendly and helpful if a little stressed! There were plenty available if needed. We were served efficiently and found a table with hot food arriving 5 mins later. Reasonable prices. Children's menu is standard – burgers/chicken nuggets/beans on toast, all £2, plus kids' trays for £3.50. The café also caters for people not visiting the park.

Opening hours: 10.00-17.00 (normal hours) 10.00-18.00 (summer holidays), 10.00-dusk (winter). Last orders for hot food in café 16.00. *Cost:* Adult £11, child/OAP £10, under 2s FREE. Annual Membership £45/adult, £40/child, admission to the park £1 each per visit thereafter. *Accessibility:* Pathways are gravel chipped and there are ramps into all the buildings. Ramp for access onto the train. FREE electric wheelchair and scooters available for customer use (phone to book). *Birthdays/celebrations:* Birthday parties cost £9/head (includes free animal feed and a reserved area for lunch), the top of the Fortress tower can be booked for an additional £25 and party food boxes can be arranged for £5 per head. *Bottlewarming/Foodheating:* There is a microwave available.

John Muir Country Park   •FREE

A1087, Dunbar
www.eastlothian.gov.uk

The park encompasses a large section of the East Lothian coast, with a variety of places to visit. There is Belhaven Bay, a beautiful stretch of sandy beach, a clifftop walk from the beach to Dunbar harbour, and a large area of woodland between the beach and the idyllic River Tyne estuary. Suitable for walking, cycling or watersports, the park has a large car park, with picnic tables, BBQ facilities and public toilets. Any children (or parents) who enjoy the unspoilt outdoors, space to explore and run about and beautiful picnic spots will enjoy a day out here. Parts of the park are accessible to off-road style pushchairs. Be sure to check tide times if you want to use the bridge at the Dunbar end of Belhaven Bay, as this is cut off at high tide. Belhaven Bay does get a lot of surf, so don't always expect to be able to use the water.

Scottish Seabird Centre and Café

The Harbour, North Berwick, EH39 4SS
01620 890202
www.seabird.org
Award-winning visitor attraction perched on the sea. A great family day out. Children's workshops during holidays and at weekends, and boat trips out to the Bass Rock. Centre has a wildlife cinema, events and exhibitions. Depending on the time of year, interactive live cameras allow visitors to watch gannets, puffins and other nesting birds on the Bass Rock and Fidra, and grey seals on the Isle of May. Cute seal pups live on camera are a great attraction! Seals and dolphins can sometimes be seen from the observation deck. In the main area downstairs there is a small soft play area for toddlers. Lovely café with a good menu, including a children's menu. Members of the centre get a discount in the café.

MIDLOTHIAN

Dalkeith Country Park

Dalkeith Country Estate, Dalkeith, EH22 2NJ
www.dalkeithcountryestate.com
Large country estate with marked trails for woodland and riverside walks. Grounds also include a large wooden adventure playground with raised walkways, huge slides and zip wires. Small version for toddlers. Ice cream kiosk in adventure playground, open weekends. Cycles welcome and picnic tables provided at various locations. Private BBQs allowed. Ranger-led walks and other events held throughout season.

Stables Tearoom is an informal, reasonably priced café serving drinks, ice creams and light snacks. All can be taken away to be consumed at outside picnic tables or elsewhere in the grounds.

Opening hours: Park – Apr-Oct 10.00-17.00. Café – 11.00-16.00, 10.00-17.00 during Midlothian school holidays. **Cost:** *Adult/child £4, family of 4 £10. Under 5s/seniors – FREE.* **Accessibility:** *Some trails not suitable for wheelchair users.* **Pushchairs:** *Nearly all paths OK, some off-road, some steps.* **Birthdays/celebrations:** *Park – BBQs welcome. Café – on request.*

Glencourse Reservoir   ►FREE

Off the A702. Start and end at the
Flotterstone Information Centre.
Pentland Hills Ranger Service
Boghall Farm, EH10 7DX
pentlands.enquiry@edinburgh.gov.uk
www.pentlandhills.org
We missed the ranger visitor centre beside the reservoir as we visited after 18.00. There were lots of maps and information available and some fantastic leaflets. The Great Glen Mystery is one which has an activity trail for families starting at the Flotterstone Information Centre. The walk is 4km long and should take 1-2 hrs. Some of the paths are unsurfaced and include short uphill sections. We did not stray from the tarmac road with our double pushchair and two sleeping children but the tarmac road took us right to the reservoir and past two picnic areas and one BBQ area. Watch for local traffic on the road as 4 cars passed us on our stroll. Depending on your pushchair you could follow the older filter road. It would be fun to try the unsurfaced paths with a back pack. Two other leaflets: Enjoy the Pentland Hills Regional Park and Discover the Pentland Hills Regional Park are fantastic for advice and other walking ideas. Please see the website too.

Accessibility/Pushchair friendliness: In parts.

Hillend Country Park

Follow the Biggar Rd out just beyond Lothianburn Golf Course on the right and turn up to Hillend. The No 4 bus stops on the main road and there is a long path up to the ski centre. There are picnic tables to the foot of the slope. Notice board with maps and general information about the Pentland Regional Park. At the top of the road there is the Hillend Ski Centre and a large car park. A chairlift at the artificial ski slope may be used by non-skiers. It is open daily, but check (0131 445 4433) as it closes in poor weather. No pushchairs. There are several bench-type seats so you can tuck tots in between adults and there is a stop halfway up if a child becomes frightened. Very active toddlers should not use the chairlift. At the top there is a viewfinder and paths through the heather, which energetic tots or parents with backpacks could cope with. The weather can change quickly though so don't stray too far from the chairlift. In the ski centre reception there are toilets and refreshments.

Roslin Glen Country Park

Roslin, EH25 9PU
01875 821990
midlothianrangerservice@midlothian.gov.uk
www.midlothian.gov.uk/info/200144/roslin_ glen_country_park
We had a thoroughly enjoyable time discovering the stunning countryside in Roslin Glen – the walks are especially varied and interesting which is good for keeping your little one entertained. Some of the stores and mill buildings from a former gunpowder factory still stand there. My daughter particularly enjoyed

looking for the wildlife – ducks and birds. The walkways are mostly accessible for pushchairs although there were steps up to bridges which were more difficult. It is such a peaceful location and excellent for getting away from the noise of the city! There were lovely spots where you could have a paddle in shallow waters and beautiful locations for having a super family picnic. I will definitely visit again – we had a very enjoyable time and would definitely recommend this as a fantastic place to go for an interesting scenic country walk for the family!

Opening hours: 08.00-20.00 (May-Sep), 08.00-17.00 (Oct-Apr). Accessibility and Pushchairs: Mostly accessible, but steps at some points.

Almond Valley Heritage Centre

Millfield, Livingston, EH54 7AR
01506 414957
info@almondvalley.co.uk
www.almondvalley.co.uk
We are regulars and hold a very worthwhile membership. Our children really enjoy the tractor trailer ride and the train trip (50p and £1 additional to entrance costs). There is a newly modernised soft play for under 2s. The apple tree decoration, gorgeous lighting and secret windows have made this the most delightful sensory and clean soft play we have found. A fantastic new addition has been made to the play park area in the form of a play mill and truck – beautiful and such fun to play on. The museum and various and seasonal activities within in it are fabulous. There is a new bouncing pillow and trampolines dedicated to toddlers. The archaeology dig sand area makes the farm a truly all-weather option. The animals themselves just seem so well cared for and happy. The extremely helpful staff make Almond Valley so special – everyone has time to help.

Morag's Tearoom is kept very clean and there are art activities for children. The staff are very helpful and kind. The food is good quality and portion sizes are good. Lunch for 2 adults and 2 children was around £12. It is a busy place!

*Opening hours: Daily 10.00-17.00 except 25/26 Dec and 1/2 Jan. Tearoom closes at 16.30. **Costs:** Adults £5.50, children and conc £4.00. Under 3s FREE. Soft play £1/30 mins. **Accessibility:** All buildings, except one small area of the mill, are accessible. Rough ground in parts but ramps have been provided where possible. On the narrow gauge railway trip there is no ramp access to the carriage and a child may need to transfer from a wheelchair to the carriage seats. Staff are more than willing to assist with this, and with storage of chairs and equipment. **Breastfeeding:** Café has a breastfeeding award. **Birthdays/celebrations:** Party assistant available. Two rooms, each can accommodate 30 children.*

Almondell & Calderwood Country Park and Oakbank

01506 882254
almondell&calderwood@westlothian.gov.uk
Country park offering woodland and riverside walks with many bridges for children to discover and explore. Paths vary from well paved to more rough muddy paths in the Calderwood section of the estate. South entrance is in East Calder and the north entrance is at Broxburn. These provide access to the most accessible paths with the north car park being nearest to the visitor centre. There is also parking at Mid Calder and

the Oakbank entrance near Livingston. Visitor centre hosts the ranger service which organises various events and talks and also a small gift shop, café and aquarium. Small play area next to visitor centre. BBQ area, which should be booked to avoid disappointment.

The Oakbank area is a reclaimed shale bing. The forest here is starting to mature and provides a surprisingly nice walk with excellent views across West Lothian. Some paths have steps and can be quite rough so better suited to toddlers, slings or all-terrain pushchairs. The Almondell section is particularly spectacular in autumn.

Opening hours: Some car parks close at 17.00. Parking: Parking for Oakbank off A71 just before Livingston, at East Calder entrance and Broxburn entrance. Accessibility: Disabled parking at visitor centre. Paved surfaces but quite steep hills. Toilets: In the visitor centre. No toilets at Oakbank end. Eating: Café in the visitor centre.

Beecraigs Country Park **FREE**

Nr Linlithgow, EH49 6PL
01506 844516
mail@beecraigs.com
www.beecraigs.com
Two miles south of Linlithgow, set in stunning countryside with pushchair-friendly woodland walks, trout farm, deer farm and reservoir as well as a variety of activities for all ages including water sports and other outdoor pursuits. Access to the park is free, activities extra. There are several car parks, one next to an information centre just opposite a caravan and camping site with plenty of facilities. For refreshments there is an on-site restaurant with extensive children's menu and highchairs as well as plenty of picnic tables and BBQs (for hire). Small gift shop in the information centre. The brand new attraction is an adventure play park which has equipment/ play structures for all ages and is lots of fun!

Opening hours: Summer: 09.00-17.00 (Fri 09.00-16.30). Winter (from 31 Oct): every day 10.00-16.00. Closed 25/26 Dec 1/2 Jan. Accessibility: Plenty of paths on level ground. Parking spaces for disabled badge holders by information centre and restaurant. Birthdays and celebrations: Environmental birthday parties with tailor-made activities and use of a room. Provide own food.

Five Sisters Zoo Park

Gavieside, West Calder, EH55 8PT
01506 872924
enquiries@fivesisterszoo.co.uk
www.fivesisterszoo.co.uk
A great day out and good value for money. 140 species of animals including meerkats, giant rabbits, monkeys, a crocodile and reptile house, deer, goats and miniature donkeys. The park is small and easily explored on foot with an under 5. There is a play area which features a new outdoor castle and pirate ship complete with ladders, rope bridges and slides, all contained within a "sea" of blue rubber chips – so very safe. Although there is a baby area in the play area, overall probably best suited to the over 3s. The zoo park is currently being extended to include a snack kiosk, picnic

area, rope swings and rides for under 5s plus a large grassy area to run around in. Highlights included the friendly resident cockerel who followed us round the park and even jumped on the carousel with the children! The pirate ship is also fantastic and nice to have an outdoor option for some fresh air and exercise. The tearoom/café and toilets could do with a bit of attention, however the food in the café was fresh and tasty.

Opening hours: 10.00-17.00 (Oct-Apr), 10.00-18.00 (May-Sep). **Cost:** *Adults £7, Child (3+) £5, family £20, season passes £35, conc £5. Play area additional charge of £5 for 2 hrs discounted to £3 with zoo ticket.* **Accessibility:** *Narrow double door to tearoom/café.* **Pushchairs:** *Need to fold pushchairs inside tearoom/café as limited space.* **Birthdays/Celebrations:** *Party room in play area. Book by contacting Leaping Lemurs (details on website).*

Polkemmet Country Park

Whitburn, EH47 0AD
01501 743905
polkemmet@westlothian.gov.uk
www.beecraigs.com/Country_Parks/polkemmet.htm
Take the M8, J4, through Whitburn, onto the B7066 towards Harthill. Park is on the right. It boasts an all-age adventure playpark – a pleasant surprise. Visitors can take "coloured" route walks through the woodlands (visit the famous "horn" sculpture, part of the M8 art project), though only certain routes are pushchair friendly. Situated within a former private estate along the valley of the River Almond, the park has beautiful grounds with plenty of wildlife to spot and is soon to be home to the Scottish Owl Centre. Designated picnic and BBQ site. Café refurbished and under new management, serving freshly made hot and cold food and drink. 9-hole golf course and driving range. A good afternoon out for all the family. "It's very nice and beautiful. There's lots of things to do here" said my 3 yr old. "Dogs!" said my youngest.

Opening hours: Every day except 25/26 Dec, 1/2 Jan. Visitor centre – Apr-Sep 06.45-21.30, Oct-Mar 08.45-16.15. **Accessibility:** *At least one coloured route walk would be suitable for wheelchairs – surfaced routes and ramps. Accessible parking spaces close to visitor centre.* **Pushchairs:** *At least one coloured walk would be pushchair friendly.* **Birthdays/celebrations:** *Countryside Ranger Service offers a range of environmental activities suited to school groups and small parties.*

Fife Animal Park

Auchtermuchty, KY15 7UT
01337 831830
www.fifeanimalpark.co.uk
On the B937 half a mile south of A91 Milnathort to St Andrews Rd. A fun day out with a good variety of domestic and exotic animals. We visited with our 10-mth-old boy who loved the outdoor trail around the animal enclosures, and they were as fascinated by him as he was by them. Most of the attractions are outside so wouldn't be so much fun on a rainy day.

Fife Animal Park Restaurant is more of a café, but a handy place to stop for reasonably priced refreshments. Good range of hot meals, snacks and cakes, and children's portions available including steak pie, scampi, mince and potatoes, and fish fingers. Could be overrun with groups of schoolchildren if you are visiting midweek. 50-60 seats indoors and a few tables outside.

Opening hours: 10.00-16.00 winter, 10.00-18.00 summer. **Cost:** *Adult £8, under 16 £6, under 3 £2, family (2 adults, 2 children) £26.* **Play area:** *Indoor and outdoor areas – fee applies.* **Breastfeeding:** *Separate parent and child room for breastfeeding, beside restaurant.*

Lochore Meadows Country Park

Crosshill, Lochgelly, KY5 8BA
01592 583343
Travel north on M90. Take Kirkcaldy, A92 turn off. Follow Lochgelly exit from this road, then B920 to Crosshill. Park is signposted on the left.

Offers a multitude of activities including a playground, woodland trail, orienteering routes, picnic and BBQ areas, café, birdwatching, canoeing, hillwalking, sailing, horse riding and golf/putting. Maps showing waymarked walking routes are available to buy at the Park Centre.

Accessibility: Accessible bird watching hide at the west end of the loch. Building all on one level.

Opening hours: Summer – Mon-Sat 09.00-17.00, Sun 10.00-17.00. Winter– Mon-Sat 10.00-17.00, Sun 10.00-16.30. Last kitchen order 30 mins before closing. *Cost:* Varies throughout the year. Ultimate Play pass £8. Ride, Slide & Bounce pass £5 (not including quad train). *Toilets:* Include a special child-sized toilet with sink and mini Dyson hand-dryer. *Birthdays/ celebrations:* Options from £6/head, including soft play, pottery painting and craft project parties. Party food options from £2.95/head.

Muddy Boots, Balmalcolm Farm

Balmalcolm, Fife, KY15 7TJ
01337 831 222
We loved Muddy Boots (we've actually been loads over the past year!). We've been in all weathers too as there is a great indoor play barn, a giant soft play castle that is not completely enclosed. If you go on a colder day (we went in November) take slipper socks for the play barn then you can play for as long as you like! There are also animals in a small field beside the under 7s play area and a pottery studio. There are lots of mini-tractors to play on and, as there are separate areas for the over 7s, it means the little ones have a great time.

Muddy Munchkins is the under 7s outdoor play area and includes gyro cars, a jumping pillow, tractor track, sandpit, playhouse and tyre swings. There's also a great café with gluten-free options. Our best bit has to be that it is an actual working farm as well, so we saw lots of proper tractors! Great excitement, especially as there were sometimes doggies on them too!

I would give this 10/10! I really can't praise this place enough. It has a great café, fab play area, and a wonderful farm shop! We had a 0, 1, 2 and 3 year with us and everyone had a great time! "I love Muddy Boots!" – Charlotte, 2 ½.

The Scottish Deer Centre

Cupar, KY15
01337 810391
info@tsdc.co.uk
www.tsdc.co.uk
Located on A91 4 miles before Cupar, Stagecoach bus Edinburgh to Cupar passes the Deer Centre. There's a deer farm walk to meet the deer, nature trail, picnic area, aerial walkway, etc. Wolves are a recent addition! There are also falconry displays 3 times a day, and trailer rides in summer. Covered all-weather adventure barn. Superb outdoor adventure playground. Restaurant, coffee shop and shops.

HISTORIC BUILDINGS

We've a wealth of historic buildings on our doorstep: from castles and palaces straight out of fairy tales to stark, eerie hulks that are the stuff of nightmares, and everything in between!

Despite changes in legislation, historic buildings, some areas of castles, palaces and even houses and museums may be hard to access due to the nature of the architecture. Slings are recommended for very young children but backpacks may be forbidden. If you're a member of Historic Scotland or the National Trust for Scotland, you gain free entry to many monuments, and if you have National Trust or English Heritage membership you may also get free entry.

While a visit to a country house may not be high on the list of things to do with young children, many stately homes now have family-friendly facilities including decent tearooms and nappy changing. Many estates now have nature trails and play areas.

CENTRAL EDINBURGH

Edinburgh Castle

Castlehill, EH1 2NG
0131 225 9846
hs.ticketing@scotland.gsi.gov.uk
www.edinburghcastle.gov.uk
My son didn't want to leave Edinburgh Castle! We took him for the first time aged 4. For a first visit, it's worth concentrating on just a few areas; if coming back again, allow more time to revisit previous areas and explore new ones.

Our top tips:
- Kids like climbing on cannons. The national war memorial has sentry boxes outside – popular to stand in.
- The one o'clock gun can be fun, though loud! Queue early for a good view, or stand higher up the hill. Bear in mind that it doesn't fire on a Sunday.

- Some children like viewing the "mini church", St Margaret's Chapel.
- The Crown Jewels section is impressive. This section can be busy, but you can always nip back for a second look.

Guided tours, subject to staff availability and the weather, are included in the price. Hire audio guides online or from the Audio Guide Pick Up point, just after the portcullis gate in the castle. Audio guides are available for children for £1.

The site is relatively steep, and some sections of it would be difficult to access by wheelchair or pushchair. However, we saw staff offering help with wheelchairs. Various sections of the castle are easily accessible, including cafés and the forecourt area where the one o'clock gun is fired. Other key areas are also easy to get to via low ramps, including St Margaret's Chapel, the Great Hall, and the Crown Jewels exhibition. Some sections of the castle would not be accessible except by steps, including the small exhibition on the one o'clock gun, and the Prisons of War exhibition. There is a courtesy vehicle from the esplanade to Crown Square. Contact the castle for more.

There are toilets in a number of locations. There is a brightly lit toilet block close to the castle entrance, with a separate room for breastfeeding and nappy changing containing a chair with proper back support, plus a small toy area. There is a locking door for privacy but no flush toilet or sink. There are also toilets in both cafés. Those at the Queen Anne Café were the nicest of the facilities on site.

There is a gift shop just before the area where tickets are checked, with a wide range of children's items, with some at pocket money prices, including toy swords, dressing up items, etc. There are two more gift shops on-site – one halfway up the castle complex with whisky and books, and the other in Crown Square with jewellery, china, tapestry-inspired items and a princes and princesses range for kids.

Castle entry also allows you to access the National War Museum which is within the castle complex.

to respond and open to requests about where to sit. Possibly the best Earl Grey tea I have had in a café. Generous-sized scones, with very creamy butter and jam. My son worked his way steadily through a large blueberry muffin, and smiled throughout. Cakes were generously sized too. There was a children's menu with healthy main course options and ice cream for pudding. I hadn't initially ordered a drink for my son, but the waiter spotted this when bringing our food, and offered tap water at no additional cost. Staff were child friendly and made an effort to respond in an age-appropriate way.

Opening hours: Summer (1 Apr-30 Sep) 09.30-18.00, Winter (1 Oct-31 Mar) 09.30-17.00. Last entry 45 minutes before closing time. Closed 25/26 December; reduced opening hours on 1 Jan. Hot food in cafés 11.30-15.00. **Cost:** *Jun-Sep adults £15, conc (over 60s) £12, child 5-15 £8.50. Otherwise, adults £14, conc £11.20, child 5-15 £8.20. Entry FREE for under 5s and Historic Scotland members. You can book your tickets through the fast track link on the website (top right hand corner).* **Parking:** *No parking on the Esplanade. However, there are limited spaces for disabled visitors. If you want to access one of these, phone 0131 310 5114. The nearest paid parking is at Castle Terrace and Johnston Terrace.* **Eating:** *Apart from the Redcoat and Queen Anne Cafés (above) there are benches in other areas of the castle complex, if you bring a picnic. Perhaps the best area is the Crown Square courtyard at the top of the complex, which has 10 good-sized benches.*

The Redcoat Café
Styled as a mix between a carvery and an old-fashioned café. It feels clean and informal, and is self-service. A good range of meals, both hot and deli type, plus sandwiches, drinks and appealing-looking cakes. Prices low to mid-range. There is a child's meal deal, where you can get 5 items for just under £5 (sandwiches, fruit, yoghurt, cake and drink). Cakes are a good size, and you could probably share them, if doing more of a coffee and cake visit. Alternatively, there were a good number of healthy options in the deli section, and you might want to share some salads.

There are 3 separate areas: picnic tables outside, a mid-section with a mix of tables/booths, and a back section with tables that has low windows, and great views over Princes St Gardens. A good area for children to see out, but is understandably popular.

Queen Anne Café
A quiet and very pleasant mid-priced café, at the top of the castle complex. Waiter service at tables. A wait to be seated, but staff are quick

Greyfriars Bobby

Corner of Candlemaker Row and King George IV Bridge, EH1
www.edinburghmuseums.org.uk
www.greyfriarsbobby.co.uk
A small statue dedicated to the faithful Skye Terrier who came to be known as Greyfriars Bobby. Situated opposite the Greyfriars Kirk

gates at the junction between Candlemaker Row and King George IV Bridge. Although this can be a very busy place to stop, my 16-mth-old daughter was really taken by the little statue. For older children, it is worthwhile retelling the story beforehand and taking a pleasant stroll around the churchyard opposite to visit his grave. There are lots of cafés and restaurants nearby.

Greyfriars Tolbooth and Highland Kirk ●FREE

Greyfriars Place, EH1 2QQ
administrator@greyfriarskirk.com
www.greyfriarskirk.com

A fascinating and quaint little church and kirkyard made famous by Greyfriars Bobby. The kirkyard is on very uneven ground so difficult with a pushchair and is littered with ancient tombstones, which offer a fascinating glimpse into the history of Edinburgh, but is perhaps not a safe environment for young children who would need to be kept close. The visitor centre is within the kirk and contains a museum full of interesting artefacts telling the kirk's story, starting after the Reformation with the signing of the deed of covenant in 1638. There are arts events such as concerts and exhibitions on throughout the year. The kirk is still used as an active place of worship for a Church of Scotland congregation and welcomes all visitors.

Opening hours: Kirk open all year round. Visitor centre Apr-Oct, Mon-Fri 10.30-16.30 and Sat 11.00-14.00. Accessibility: Unassisted access into the visitor centre. Accessible toilet.

St Giles Cathedral ●FREE

Royal Mile, EH1 1RE
0131 225 9442
info@stgilescathedral.org.uk

www.stgilescathedral.org.uk
A magnificent building steeped in history. As well as being a living church with an active congregation, it is host to some 400,000 visitors every year. Inside there is a great deal of space to explore and for a toddler this is quite exciting. There is no particular focus for children, but mine enjoyed the stained glass and running through the chairs. Children are welcome and the space is big enough for you not to worry about disturbing someone in prayer. Be aware that some parts are roped off and may be a challenge for the more adventurous child. The Thistle Chapel is worth a visit – it's full of detail and we enjoyed spotting the beautifully carved animals. Look for the angels playing bagpipes.

Volunteer guides are on duty each day to answer questions and conduct guided tours on request. There are information desks situated at the main west entrance and at the Thistle Chapel. Permits for photography, including camcorders, are available from the information desk for £2.

Opening hours: Vary according to season – check website. Cost: FREE – though donations gratefully received. Toilets: At the back of cathedral beside café. Eating: Café (see p 159).

NORTH EDINBURGH

Hopetoun House

South Queensferry, EH30 9SL
0131 331 2451
enquiries@hopetoun.co.uk
www.hopetoun.co.uk
Described as "Scotland's finest stately home", approaching it via the sweeping drive certainly creates quite an impact. There is a magnificent art collection throughout the impressive rooms – and pleasant guides who will explain interesting features such as serving bells to under 5s. The gardens are extensive with lots to explore for more adventurous children. Watch out for ha-has though (ditches to keep animals in fields – there's one to the left of the main drive), and the large pond to the rear of the house. Also

a picnic area, nature trails and deer. In the old stable block there is a flora and fauna exhibition for older children. Various events throughout the year.

Stables Tearoom
While the tearoom looks quite formal, everyone was very friendly when we visited, and there are food options which would suit children, plus snacks such as scones. Drinks include milk and still fruit drinks. Anything from the adult menu, including a very delicious afternoon tea, can also be made up in a children's portion. Recommended as a treat for after a visit to Hopetoun House rather than for a specific visit.

Opening hours: 10.30-17.00 (22 Apr-25 Sep), last admission 16.00. Closed 30/31 Jul and 6 Aug. Cost: House and grounds/grounds only: Adult £9.50/£4.25, children 5-16 £4.90/£2.50, conc £8.00/£3.70, family £25.00/£11.50, registered disabled £4.90/£2.50. Accessibility: Steep steps up to the house. Lift for wheelchair access. It's possible to borrow wheelchairs. Assistance dogs welcome. Wheelchairs cannot access the bedrooms at the top of the spiral staircase but there is digital access to the upper floor via a computer. Pushchairs: The terrain in the grounds makes access tricky. You need to leave your pushchair in the entrance to the house and carry your children/let them walk around the house. The house is accessed up a fairly steep flight of stairs, staff happy to help.

EAST EDINBURGH

Craigmillar Castle

Craigmillar Castle Road, EH16 4SY
0131 661 4445
www.historic-scotland.gov.uk
The castle is best known for its association with Mary, Queen of Scots. It has a tower house, courtyard, giftshop and gardens which include the remains of a fishpond in the shape of a P,

after the Preston family who once lived there. Initial impressions were frustrating as the entry door was difficult to negotiate with a pushchair.

Recommended for children who are walking, but keep an adult close by as there are steep turnpike stairs without handrails, different levels and long drops from low windows and balconies. See page 28 for our feature on Craigmillar Castle.

Cost: Adult £5, child 5-15 £3. FREE for under 5s and Historic Scotland members.

Palace of Holyroodhouse and Holyrood Abbey

Foot of the Royal Mile, Canongate
0131 524 1120
This is the Queen's official residence in Scotland and all state and historic apartments are open to the public. Audio tour equipment is provided, including a special "family" edition. You can also visit the ruins of Holyrood Abbey, dating back to the 11th century. There is a limited amount of interest for under 5s. Pushchair access limited to the ground and first floor. There is a family room with interactive activities just off the Great Gallery. The Palace is closed when the Queen or Her Commissioner is in residence.

Queen's Gallery
Situated in the Mews area of the Palace. Contains exhibitions from the Royal Collection. There are 22 steps up to the main exhibition area, with a lift for pushchairs and wheelchairs. Toilets are available in the Royal Mews, where changing and feeding facilities for babies are also available. There is also a café and gift shop with helpful staff.

Café at the Palace
0131 524 1032
Large selections of cakes and coffees/teas available as well as sandwiches and baked potatoes. Spacious dining area so plenty of room for pushchairs if you choose a table at the side. Easy access as café and toilets (with nappy changing) are all on the ground floor.

WEST EDINBURGH

Corstorphine Dovecot ·FREE

Dovecot Road, Corstorphine, EH12 7LE
www.historic-scotland.gov.uk
Maintained by Historic Scotland, this is a large circular beehive-shaped dovecot. It's possible to walk round the outside, but there are some steps. An interesting educational visit to tie in with doing something else in the area – St Margaret's Park or Corstorphine Library are very close by.

Parking: On Dovecot Rd.

EAST LOTHIAN

Dirleton Castle

Dirleton Road, Dirleton, EH39 5ER
01620 850330
www.historic-scotland.gov.uk
A great place to explore with children of any age, with everything young children must expect from a castle. Lots of the rooms are largely intact and children can really get a feel for what life in the castle was like, exploring the kitchens, great halls and bedrooms. The moat and large wooden bridge make an impressive entrance and the surrounding gardens are great for a good run around or a picnic. I would definitely recommend visiting on a sunny day to make the most of it. Best age range – toddlers and up.

Opening hours: Apr-Sep 09.30-17.30, Oct-Mar 09.30-16.30. Cost: Adult £5, child £3, conc £4. FREE to Historic Scotland members. Accessibility: Grounds accessible, but there are two steps into the castle and it would not be possible to enter all rooms. Pushchairs: Most of the castle and grounds is pushchair friendly and there are plenty of places to leave them.

Newhailes

Newhailes Road, Musselburgh, EH21 6RY
0844 493 2125 (reservations line)
newhailes@nts.org.uk
www.nts.org.uk/Property/Newhailes
A 17th-18th century house with a "lived-in" feel, reflecting the interesting history that has taken place within it. Dr Johnson described its library as "the most learned room in Europe". Access only by tour at set times – reservations recommended at busy times – so probably not the most suitable historical property for under 5s. However, Newhailes is set in an estate (designed in the 18th century) which is open all the year round and includes marked footpaths (that visitors are encouraged to keep to). In terms of accessibility and pushchairs, there are cobbles and uneven surfaces although there is one all-ability path. Best for older under 5s who will enjoy the grounds with its varied open spaces and wooded areas. Regular "Nature Nippers" events for under 5s, see website.

Opening hours: House, Visitor Centre, Shop and Café – Easter weekend (Fri-Mon) and 1 May-30 Sep, Thur-Mon 11.00-17.00. Oct Sat/Sun 11.00-16.00. Tour of house lasts approx 1¼ hours, starting every 30 mins from Visitor Centre. First tour departs 12.00; last tour departs 15.30. Allow 15 mins prior to tour departure to collect tickets and view film. Estate – Open all year, daily, car park closing at dusk. Cost: House – adult £11.50, family £28, 1 parent £21.50, conc £8.50. Parking: Pay and Display £2. Toilets: In Visitor Centre area (so only open part of the year). Eating: Café at Visitor Centre (open when House is). Picnic tables.

Preston Mill

East Linton, EH40 3DS
01620 860426
www.nts.org.uk
The oldest working water mill in Scotland, beautifully maintained and presented by the National Trust for Scotland. Although probably

not worth going inside with pre-school children, a lovely place to go for a picnic. Drinks and ice cream are available, and the friendly staff are happy for you to bring along your own food and use their large picnic tables. After lunch, there is a lovely walk past the water wheel, over the river (a few steps to negotiate) and through the fields to Phantassie Doocot which is also still fully intact. This is a sunny day destination for inquisitive toddlers – our 3 yr olds had a great time throwing sticks in the river, picking flowers and having races.

Opening hours: May-Sep only Thurs-Mon 12.30-17.00 (check website for exact dates). Cost: Adult £6, conc £5, family £15.50. NTS members FREE. Eating: Hot/cold drinks and ice cream only.

MIDLOTHIAN

Crichton Castle

near Pathhead, EH37 5QH
01875 320017
www.historic-scotland.gov.uk
Nestling in the Midlothian countryside, 2½ miles SW of Pathhead overlooking the River Tyne is this 14th century tower house. It was a noble residence for 200 years, first for the Crichtons and later for the Bothwells. A 600m dirt track, steep in parts, leads up to the castle where you can explore the courtyard with an unusual diamond-faceted facade, kitchen, dining room, pit prison and Grand Hall. It is particularly good for older under 5s. Visitors with mobility problems can telephone in advance to arrange to be dropped off at the castle. However, the castle has uneven surfaces throughout – cobbles, steps, different levels. There is a field by the car park which is good for picnics and playing, but note – there are no toilets!

Opening hours: Apr-Sep 09.30-17.30. Cost: Adult £4, conc £3.20, child £2.40, Under 5s and Historic Scotland members FREE. Parking: Small car park.

WEST LOTHIAN

Linlithgow Palace

Linlithgow, EH49 7AL
01506 842896
hs.rangers@scotland.gsi.gov.uk
www.historic-scotland.gov.uk
We had a great time exploring the ruins of Linlithgow Palace. I would definitely say that this attraction is aimed at the older child. A short quiz is available when you buy your tickets which would be fun for older children. Unfortunately the weather was rather wet and windy which made our visit more difficult as you are out in the open a lot and we did get cold by the time we had explored the Palace. However, it was really good fun exploring the ruins and there are so many interesting alcoves and corners. My daughter particularly enjoyed playing peekaboo around corners and hiding from her Daddy! The setting of Linlithgow Palace is simply stunning and you can get fantastic views of the water, boats and swans – my daughter enjoyed looking at the view from the Palace windows. There is also a good play area just down from the Palace and close to the water front. There is a gift shop too. It was definitely a very interesting and varied place to visit but perhaps better for older children!

Opening hours: 9.30-17.30 (Apr-Sep), 9.30-16.30 (Oct-Mar). Cost: Adult £5.50, children (5+) £3.30, concessions £4.40. Get details about membership of Historic Scotland on the website. Parking: Available at the cobbled entrance. Toilets: Accessible toilets.

FIFE

Abbot House Heritage Centre

13-15 Maygate, Dunfermline, KY12 7NE
01383 733266
www.abbothouse.co.uk

The oldest house in Dunfermline: "The People's Tardis". Permanent displays of Dunfermline/ Scottish life from the Picts to the 1960s and of famous people, such as Andrew Carnegie. Also hosts exhibitions and craft fairs. A virtual tour of the house offers access to upper floors which are unsuitable for pushchairs. Café and shop on the ground floor are accessible. Café has a "sitooterie" with a view of the Abbey. Under 5s can play in the gardens and in the adjoining Abbey grounds, but be aware of attractive hazards such as the fountain. Eating your own food in the grounds is not allowed.

Opening hours: *09.30-16.30.* **Cost:** *Adult £4, conc £3, accompanying child FREE.* **Accessibility:** *On-site accessible parking.*

Aberdour Castle

Aberdour
01383 860519
www.historic-scotland.gov.uk
Visited on a very cold and windy Good Friday! Great experience for two high energy toddlers who loved exploring the ruins and pretending to be knights. We had taken a picnic along which was fortunate as the tearoom is very small with no real access/space for pushchairs and not conducive to accommodating our sleeping 3-mth-old baby. However, it had a good selection of home-cooked soups, sandwiches, cakes and coffee, and a children's menu for £4.65 (sandwich, drink and fruit). Three picnic tables provided overlooking the beautiful walled garden, although these would most likely be restricted to café customers in better weather. Gift shop at entrance with reasonably priced toys for children, guide books etc. Overall good value and definitely worth a visit. Would recommend combining with a trip to Aberdour beach (p 91) to make a day of it. Likely to appeal most to toddlers and children 3+ yrs.

Opening hours: *1 Apr-30 Sep 09.30-17.30, Oct 09.30-16.30, 1 Nov-31 Mar Mon-Wed, Sat/Sun 09.30-16.30. Tearoom open daily in* summer and Sat/Sun only in winter. **Cost:** *Adult £5, children over 5 £3, conc £4. Children 0-5 FREE.* **Parking:** *Free parking adjacent to castle or park at Aberdour railway station, a short walk away. Disabled badge holder spaces at both.* **Nappy changing:** *In accessible toilet at main entrance (access via the shop upon request).*

Falkland Palace and Garden

High Street, Falkland, Cupar, KY15 7BU
0844 493 2186
falklandpalace&garden@nts.org.uk
www.nts.org.uk/Property/Falkland-Palace-Garden/
Set in a pretty medieval village, Falkland Palace dates from the 16th century and has beautiful gardens. It was the country residence and hunting lodge of 8 Stewart monarchs, including Mary, Queen of Scots. Much of the palace is ruined, but visitors can see furnished rooms, the chapel, and a Real Tennis court which was built in 1539 and is still in use. The palace tour is of limited interest to under 5s, but I-Spy sheets are available. The guides, dressed in elaborate historical costumes, were engaging and drew our attention to a monkey in the tapestry, a primitive privy and an intriguing punishment chair designed for a squirming royal child. The gardens and grounds are suitable for picnics, and children's events are held regularly. Grounds are accessible for pushchairs, but not the Palace. No café, but plenty in Falkland.

Opening hours: *Mar-Oct – Mon-Sat 11.00-17.00, Sun 13.00-17.00.* **Cost:** *Adult £11, family £27, one parent £21, conc £8. NTS members FREE.*

Get the most up-to-date information on
www.efuf.co.uk

Hill of Tarvit Mansionhouse & Garden

Cupar, KY15 5PB
0844 493 2185
robrown@nts.org.uk
www.nts.org.uk/Property/Hill-of-Tarvit-Man-sionhouse-Garden/
A beautiful house set in lovely grounds – you could take a picnic and walk around the paths using a baby sling or back carrier. We did not visit the house as felt it was unsuitable for our 9 mth old but they do have family trails for older children. Staff very helpful and welcoming.

Small tearoom with a good selection of drinks, sandwiches and home-made cakes. Ice creams available. Reasonable prices. 10 tables.

Opening hours: Garden and grounds – closes at dusk. House, shop and tearooom – 1 Apr-31 Oct, Thurs-Mon 13.00-17.00 (last entry 16.15). *Cost: Adult £9, family £22, one parent family £16.50, concession £6.50. Babies "usually" let in free.* *Parking: Suggested donation of £3 – reimbursed if you visit house.* *Accessibility/ Pushchairs: Route to house accessible but stairs and grass areas not accessible. You can enter through the house to get to the tearoom, which is an easier route for pushchairs and wheelchairs.*

GARDENS, PARKS AND GREENSPACE

CENTRAL EDINBURGH

Calton Hill

Great spot for strolling with a pushchair. Fabulous views over the city. Good open space to run around and a brass cannon to climb on.

Home to "Edinburgh's shame", a monument based on the Parthenon that was started in 1822 but never completed. This provides climbing opportunities for older children. Also home to the Observatory and Nelson's Monument, but neither are particularly suitable for young children.

Pedestrian entrance off Regent Road unsuitable for pushchairs due to steps. Gate next to Parliament House provides step-free route. Pushchair access also possible from quieter Royal Terrace, but this is steeper.

Princes Street Gardens

Princes Street
Edinburgh's most famous park runs alongside Princes St under the lee of the castle. A useful rest point for weary parents, mid-shopping, as there are plenty of seats and trees for shade on a sunny day. It also provides an open space for toddlers to let off steam. There is a playground in the West Gardens, see below.

There are lawns, trees, flowerbeds, statues and sculptures. Look out for a tree with a hole through it (near the gardener's lodge in the West Gardens). The park's patrol officers will be pleased to point this out, or help you out with any other questions or problems. Please note that dogs must be kept on a lead.

The presence of the railway line in the gardens is a bonus, especially the bridge behind the Ross Bandstand from which children can safely and easily see trains coming and going. Drivers usually oblige with a wave and a toot!

Home to many events such as concerts in the Ross Bandstand (West Gardens), the Winter Wonderland over Christmas (East Gardens) which includes a fairground and ice rink, the Hogmanay Concert on 31 December and the end-of-Festival fireworks in September.

East Gardens
The park is divided in two by the Mound. The East Gardens may be accessed from the Mound, Waverley Bridge and Princes St. Access to the lower level of the gardens is via steps at the Mound end and via a steep sloping path at the Waverley end. The Scott Monument, a Victorian, high-gothic memorial to the author

Sir Walter Scott, and a convenient landmark, can be climbed for an admission fee. The spiral stairs are very steep and narrow near the top and would probably not be enjoyed by small children or mothers-to-be!

Next to the Scott Monument is a kiosk selling sweets, ices, and hot and cold drinks to take away. There are plenty of birds and squirrels to feed and some of the kiosks sell nuts and bird food. The station platforms and trains can be viewed from the path at the side of the National Gallery.

West Gardens

Accessed from the Mound, Princes St, Johnstone Terr and King's Stables Rd. The famous Floral Clock, next to the steps down to the park at the junction of Princes St and the Mound, is a source of delight for both children and adults alike. It is composed of up to 35,000 small plants and functions all year round except when being replanted. A cuckoo emerges briefly from a wooden house every quarter of an hour. It was the original idea of an Edinburgh clockmaker in 1903 and there are now copies all over the world. There are several rain shelters at the Mound end of the gardens, close to the foot of the Floral Clock steps.

Be ready for the Castle's one o'clock gun – it is loud and might give you a fright if you're not prepared for it. There is some vehicle traffic in the gardens, especially when the Ross Bandstand is being used, but many under 5s will enjoy admiring forklift trucks and the gardeners' tractors.

The Ross Bandstand is situated in the middle of the West Gardens. This is used for various events throughout the year and during the Edinburgh Festival Fringe there are usually daily events and entertainment there.

Over the railway, the south side of the gardens is less formal, with a steep grassy slope (covered with daffodils in the spring) leading up to the Castle. There is a gate into the Castle Esplanade via a steep zigzag path with steps, but the gate can be locked at times (especially during the Edinburgh Military Tattoo). There is a level entrance to the Gardens from King's Stables Rd opposite the multi-storey car park and a sloped entrance from Johnstone Terr round the side of the Castle. These paths join

up and cross a railway footbridge (no view of trains) into the gardens near the playground. A path also leads from the bridge, alongside the railway to another bridge (excellent view of trains) at the Ross Bandstand.

Princes Street Gardens Playground

A really clean and well-kept play area with a variety of fun and imaginative large structures and equipment. Most suitable from 1 yr upwards although there are often many older children playing there too – due to its central location and popularity it can be quite noisy and boisterous! Loosely based on a castle theme, the multiplay has ramps, tunnels, slides and walkways suitable for toddlers and a climbing wall, upper level and covered slide for older children. There are no swings. Although the playground is unfenced, dogs are required to be kept on a lead in the gardens. Located in Princes St Gdns West, the furthermost entrance at the west end of Princes St is nearest to the playground via a long flight of steps. There are also a series of ramps along Princes St, which give access to the gardens. Level access also from King's Stable Rd and through St Cuthbert's Churchyard.

Opening hours: Locked at 22.00 (23.00 during the Festival). Toilets: At Ross Bandstand and near playground in West Gardens (where there are nappy changing facilities). You may have to get key from attendant. Eating: Lots of kiosks serving café style food and ice cream.

Royal Botanic Garden, Edinburgh   •FREE

Inverleith Row and John Hope Gateway at Arboretum Place, EH3 5LR
www.rbge.org.uk/the-gardens/home
The "Botanics" is a firm favourite among adults with young children, and for many Edinburgh folk is part of the fabric of their childhood – many families will have a picture of a toddler among the daffodils or rhododendrons in their albums. The staff are tolerant, friendly and

helpful to small people and their carers. My grand-daughter and I love this place. We have a well-worn route, starting with the film loop with its amazing animal and plant pictures in the John Hope Gateway, followed by fascination at the twirling wind vane on top of the building, then a walk east through the Chinese garden and pavilion and down towards the ducks on the pond, taking in squirrels on the way, followed by the fish in the aquarium, and back for a snack at the Terrace Café. The Gardens are where she perfected her walking (and now running) technique on the grassed areas, splashed in puddles in her wellies on rainy days, and learned to observe the details of plants and their names, shapes and colours. Recently she was in a blue phase. One afternoon we rounded a corner and to her delight, came upon a sea of blue flowers. The picture says it all!

The Glasshouse Experience
It is such a surprise to enter the luscious wonderworld of the glasshouses. I had no idea they were there although I've been a regular at the Botanics for years! After paying entry, go past the desk in the tallest glass palace, leading to a network of 10 or so others. There are tropical flowers, hanging vines, gurgling waterfalls and the sort of lilypads you could float your baby on! The hot humid temperatures are super on a winter's day. Cacti, orchids and large goldfish will have you watching out round every leaf. A refreshing change and fascinating fun! Take special care with toddlers as path and pond are on the same level with no guard.

East Gate Café
A fairly recent addition to the Gardens, this is a friendly first port of call for parents/carers when they make their way through the East Gate, often having had a little walk or a bus ride (buses stop right beside the East Gate). There's a toilet with nappy changing and space for a pushchair. Having grabbed your takeaway coffee and perhaps a sandwich, you can either sit at one of the outside tables, find a nearby bench or go and stand by the duck pond to enjoy your refreshments while your little one looks at the wildlife. As well as coffees, teas, hot chocolates etc there is a range of sandwiches, cold drinks, biscuits, cakes and crisps that's fairly limited and not terribly cheap, but we always find this a well-pitched and welcome stopping point.

Gateway Restaurant
Located upstairs in the John Hope Gateway building (with level access from the Gardens), this restaurant attracts families by the dozen and it's easy to see why. The sense of space and the waiter service feels luxurious compared to the Terrace Café but it's still friendly and welcoming. The food's good whatever the time of day, from breakfast to afternoon tea with a great lunch menu (risotto, posh burgers, cullen skink) in between. Prices are what you'd expect to pay in a bistro or restaurant – £6.50-£10.50 for a main course. The 3-course children's menu is fine – sausages and mash, fish and chips, a healthier vegetable dipper starter. Popular carvery for Sunday lunch at £15/adult and £7.95/child. The outside tables are popular in the summer and provide a nice area for families whose little ones need to burn off some energy – the decking is a good place for a run-around.

Terrace Café
A busy self-service café ideal for those needing to rest and refuel! A good place to bring children; plenty of seating both indoors and out, highchairs, nappy-changing facilities, a small children's play area with tables and chairs and space for pushchairs. The food is a tad overpriced but nice enough – a range of sandwiches, soup, hot meals and snacks as well as coffee and cake. A choice of lunchboxes and half portions for children. Bottle-warming facilities and staff will warm up baby food. Gets

very busy at weekends, especially on sunny days, so prepare to queue as there is no table service. On busy days the café can get a little messy and neglected towards the end of the day, including the changing facilities and the play area. Packed lunches are not allowed in the café's outside seating area, but the beauty of the Botanics is that you can always bring your own packed lunch, sit out on the grass nearby and enjoy the gardens and the view that way!

Opening hours: Feb-Oct 10.00-18.00, Nov-Jan 10.00-16.00. Cost: Gardens – FREE (donations welcomed). Glasshouse: Adult £4.50, conc £3.50, child £1, family £9.00, Members FREE. Parking: Metered throughout the week, FREE at weekends. Accessibility: Unassisted access in gardens. Cafés accessible. The Glasshouse Experience is on one main level, except the aquarium on the lower level. Every door has assisted access with buttons to open. Toilets: In John Hope Centre, restaurants and cafés. One by glasshouses. Nappy changing: At John Hope Centre, also in restaurant and cafés. Birthdays/celebrations: You can hire outdoor areas for parties and BBQs – 0131 552 1974, sales@prestigescotland.co.uk.

NORTH EDINBURGH

Dalmeny Estate

South Queensferry, EH30 9TQ
0131 331 1888
www.dalmeny.co.uk
While we wouldn't recommend Dalmeny House as a place to visit with young children, the estate is pleasant to walk around. There is a beach, shore and woodland with sheep, pheasants and a statue of a horse. There is a sheltered woodland walk through rhododendrons and azaleas called the Garden Valley. The house can also be reached by the 4.5 mile Shore Walk from Long Craig Gate in South Queensferry but

as the ferry is closed you can no longer access Cramond this way. The path is negotiable with a pushchair or with children in backpacks, and passes through several sites of special scientific interest – including nesting and feeding grounds for several rare species of birds – as well as giving wonderful views of the Forth.

Inverleith Park and Playing Fields • FREE

EH3 5NZ
www.inverleithpark.co.uk
A fantastic large open green space offering a wide range of activities – recently won a Green Flag Award, which rated the park excellent on criteria of cleanliness, accessibility, safety and environment. Includes playing fields (cricket in summer and rugby and football all year round), a network of paved footpaths, a large pond with ducks and swans (and remote controlled boats on a Sunday), rose garden, free tennis courts, free basketball courts, an area for playing petanque and an enclosed playground. The park hosts annual events such as Taste of Edinburgh and the MoonWalk and during the summer holidays there are various activities for school-age children. There is also a fantastic view of the Edinburgh skyline. The playground is located on the east side of the park, accessed from Arboretum Place, and is fenced off. Dogs are not permitted there. Seating for adults, and for children a good mix of equipment – a large ship with various attachments for climbing up/ sliding down, a smaller multiplay with slide, two swing sets including bucket swings, a seesaw and a sit-in wobbly whale. There is also a higher climbing structure for older children. All equipment sits on a rubberised surface and the area is clean and tidy. The park is open at all times and has level access from all sides.

Parking: Mostly within the zone so £1/hr during the week (or more outside the Botanics), however you can park for free a little further up East Fettes Ave beyond Inverleith Pl where the zone ends.

Lauriston Castle Grounds

2a Cramond Road South, Davidson's Mains, EH4 5QD
0131 336 2060
lauristoncastle@edinburgh.gov.uk
www.edinburghmuseums.org.uk/Venues/Lauriston-Castle.aspx
This beautiful public park is one of Edinburgh's undiscovered treasures. It overlooks the Firth of Forth, Cramond Island, the Fife coast and the mountains of Perthshire beyond. The wind from the water can be chilly, so wrap up warmly, even on milder days. The gardens include a large lawn, woodland, a tranquil Japanese friendship garden, croquet lawns, a meadow and several ponds. No dogs allowed. Picnic tables by the car park. A huge space for running around, and plenty to fascinate children. We like the snowy-white decorative pebbles, pinecones and statues. We spotted a pheasant hen, ducklings and a heron in May, and lots of brambles in autumn.

Ravelston Park and Playground

Craigcrook Road, EH4 3PG
0131 447 7145
countrysiderangers@edinburgh.gov.uk
Lovely open green space for running around at the foot of Ravelston Woods Local Nature Reserve (LNR). Countryside Rangers Service, guided walks, interpretation panels and woodland walks that run through the nature reserve with plenty of wildlife spotting, but paths are probably unsuitable for pushchairs and you need to take care with steep drops. There are plenty of suitable paths within the park for pushchairs, all safely enclosed from the busy road. The playground within the park has basic equipment such as seesaws, swings and climbing frames. One of the slides was quite difficult for my 3 yr old to access, but a smaller one nearby was fine. Serves locals very well or would make a good escape stop at rush hour, although no nearby toilets. "Lots of room to run around" said Grace.

There is also a ball court and dogs are allowed. Parking on Craigcrook Road. Great for a picnic as benches and colourful picnic areas are available.

EAST EDINBURGH

Figgate Park

Baileyfield Road, EH8 7SE
http://www.edinburgh.gov.uk/directory_record/10836/figgate_park
A boarded walkway extends across one end of the lake that provides easy access for pushchairs. Picture boards help with identifying wildlife. The east side of the park continues along the Braid Burn. This area of the park is enjoyed by dog walkers and provides a popular area for learning to ride a bike on a sunny day. The playpark is on the west side. It caters for all ages with climbing frames and slides including a twisty slide. It also has a view of the train line.

Holyrood Park

Holyrood Park Road, EH16 5BT
0131 668 8600 (general enquiry line)
hs.communications@scotland.gsi.gov.uk
www.historic-scotland.co.uk
Arguably the stunning heart of Edinburgh, Holyrood Park is spectacular, overlooked by the extinct volcano, Arthur's Seat. The park is a Scottish national treasure, and within its borders are contained history and archaeology dating back 1000s of years. For the little ones there is lots of space to run free! The park is so vast you could easily spend at least a day exploring its delights. There is also an excellent Education Centre, just behind the Palace, plus an equally visit-worthy exhibition, celebrating the park, at the Holyrood Lodge Information Centre next to the new Parliament.

Opening hours: 09.00-18.00 (check website

for seasonal variations, weather affects, etc). **Toilets and nappy changing:** *At the Education Centre by Holyrood Palace.* **Birthdays and celebrations:** *Contact the Education Centre (0131 652 8150).*

Rosefield Park

Rosefield Place, Portobello, EH15 1BD
0131 529 3111
Pretty park accessed at Rosefield Pl, West Brighton Pl and Baileyfield Cres. Large grass areas for ball games and picnics, benches for sitting and the Figgate Burn with footbridge for Pooh Sticks. Enclosed within a lovely brick wall and arched gate, the play park has swings and a climbing frame with two slides – one large and one small. Park popular with dog walkers although dogs not allowed in play park.

SOUTH EDINBURGH

Braidburn Valley Park

168 Cormiston Road, EH10 5TE
www.braidburnvalleypark.org.uk
Really picturesque park on the south side of the city just up the road from Morningside. Highlights are the bridges for playing pooh sticks from, daffodils and blossom trees in spring and the slopes for sledging on when snow permits (but beware of the shallow burn which runs through the middle of the park, it's cold) and for rolling eggs down at Easter. The Friends of Braidburn Valley Park also stage a number of events throughout the year, the busiest of which is the Fun Day, usually held in September, which includes a Duck Race. There is a smooth path along the length of the park which is great for trainee cycling, skating and scooting and children who are old enough to recognise numbers and letters might be kept busy for a while with the permanent orienteering course which is spread out around the park. A map for this can be downloaded from the park's website. As ever in parks, watch out for dogs.

The Braids

Grassy slopes and hills, good for kites, walking and sledging. Access and parking at the entrance to the Braid Hills Public Golf Course on Braid Hill Approach and along Braid Hill Drive. There are usually horses to be seen in fields nearby at Liberton Tower Farm.

Bruntsfield Links

An area of open parkland, great for letting your kids run around and burn off energy. There is a fenced playground, which is often quieter than the larger one on the Meadows, and wide, well maintained cycle paths. The Links is home to a nine hole golf course, so you need to keep an eye out for stray shots, but the golfers tend to be friendly and don't mind the constant stream of toddlers, dogs and picnickers wandering around the course. My 2-yr-old son loves it.

Toilet: At Bruntsfield Pl. A RADAR key is required for the accessible toilet.

Hermitage of Braid and Blackford Hill

69 Braid Road, EH10 6JF
0131 447 7145
countrysiderangers@edinburgh.gov.uk
www.snh.org.uk
A great open parkland in the city where you can spend a good few hours and the views from the top of the hill are well worth the climb. Most routes are suitable for a pushchair, but some include steps and streams and are less appropriate. Route maps can be picked up from the Visitor Centre (near the Braid Rd entrance) which also offers a range of activities and information for younger visitors. It's worth taking a picnic as there are no catering facilities at the site. The area is popular with dog walkers so do watch out for dog mess.

WEST EDINBURGH

Saughton Park

Balgreen Road, EH11 3BQ
0131 529 7921
parks@edinburgh.gov.uk
www.edinburgh.gov.uk/directory_
record/10910/saughton_park
Saughton Park was developed in the 1900s on the then western outskirts of Edinburgh. The park is split into three main sections: the walled garden, the playpark/skatepark and the sports complex. The walled garden is exactly that, a large gated garden with lots of flowerbeds, plenty of

benches to sit at, grassy areas to run about, rose gardens, sensory and Italian gardens, plus the winter garden in the glasshouse which contains a wee fish pond, the toilets, plus some seating with tables. There are pedestrian entrances from Balgreen Rd, Gorgie Rd and opposite the playpark. The park is lovely to walk around with a pushchair as it is very open and quiet, small children will love running though the little gardens and trying to find the fish before going to the playpark. A visit to the nearby Balgreen Library is easy too. Between the walled garden and open playing fields is the children's playpark and new skatepark. The playpark is large with lots of space to run about. There are 6 baby and 6 children's swings, a roundabout, large sandpit, 2 large climbing frames, rope climbing frame and caterpillar rope swing. Beside the skatepark is The Food Box selling very reasonably priced takeaway hot and cold food and drink. Saughton Sports Complex is accessed via Stevenson Rd and contains 5 grass football pitches, seven or 11-a-side third generation synthetic pitches, an athletics track and changing facilities.

Opening times: (Walled garden) Mon-Tues 10.00-16.00, Wed-Fri 10.00-15.30, Sat-Sun 12.00-16.00. Parking: FREE parking at Balgreen Rd/Fords Rd entrances to park.

Spylaw Park

Spylaw Street/Gillespie Road, EH13 0JX
One of Edinburgh's most beautiful parks, a hidden gem which can prove tricky to find on a first visit. Both entrances through woodland are sloping and can be quite muddy so a little taxing for pushchairs, but worth the effort. Fenced playground at the far end of the park is well shaded by trees. A path runs alongside the Water of Leith, so close supervision of children is required. Best bits include meeting lots of friendly dog-owners (and dogs!) and watching kids play pooh sticks from the bridge.

Union Park

Carrick Knowe Drive
A nice big space for kids to run around and kick a ball in.

Accessibility/Pushchairs: Gravel path.

EAST LOTHIAN

Inveresk Lodge Gardens

24 Inveresk Village, EH21 7TE
0844 493 2126
inveresk@nts.org.uk
www.nts.org.uk/Property/Inveresk-Lodge-Garden
A pleasant and tranquil garden with ample space for toddlers to run free. It is very hilly with several steps, so would suit babies in slings, walking toddlers and older children. Lots of pretty and fragrant floral displays to investigate, but my daughter was most enthralled by the bunny rabbits hopping about! Picnic tables/benches dotted around for soaking up the view.

Opening hours: 10.00-18.00 (or dusk if earlier). Cost: Adult £3.50, family £8.50, one parent family £6.50, conc £2.50. FREE to NTS members. Parking: Limited spaces directly outside and unrestricted parking on the road. Toilets: Single accessible toilet within the glasshouse.

Lauderdale Park

Bayswell Road, Dunbar
Excellent park for all ages and abilities. The Garden Path Café within the park serves a fine range of light meals and snacks. Combined with a visit to the swimming pool (see p 109) this is definitely a great day out. The park is accessible and laid out so that it can be enjoyed by more able-bodied children as well as those who are less mobile. There is suitable seating in the picnic area and tables with spaces for wheelchairs.

Toilets: Public toilets are very good, particularly the accessible ones (get a key for the accessible toilet from the attendant).

Lewisvale Park

Newbigging, Musselburgh, EH21 7JA
0131 653 5200
info@enjoyleisure.com
www.enjoyleisure.com
This is a great park with lots to do. Come through the gates opposite the leisure centre and on your left you'll find an aviary with lots of small birds to watch. There is a good formal garden area with lots of paths in front of the aviary for running or cycling round. Further along the path is a small play area with a Noah's Ark-themed play frame, some kids' swings and rocking animals. Walk further along and there is a big grassy area with a bandstand, so plenty of space to run around or sit and enjoy a picnic. At the far end of the park is a large wooden slide and climbing frame and a roundabout. The climbing frame is more suited to older children but everyone can enjoy the roundabout. Nearest toilets are in the leisure centre just across the road.

Parking: Unlimited on-street parking on Newbigging, or park in the leisure centre car park just across the road

Lodge Gardens

North Berwick
Wonderful sheltered gardens, new playpark and aviary. The gardens consist of herbaceous borders, a dry bed and lots of mature trees in a large green area. The gardens receive lottery funding and have won the Green Flag award 2010/2011. Local children and their parents suggested what they would like to see in the playpark. There are 2 baby swings,

BBQ areas that can be hired. Ride-on miniature railway on Sundays during the summer which my 2½ yr old was very excited about. Regular events throughout the year, some perfect for young children. Remember to buy a parking token (£1) at the white box before the gates!

Cedar Tree Café
Serves reasonably priced sandwiches, jacket potatoes, home baking, breakfast rolls etc. My roll and coffee were both lovely. Children's plate with sandwich, crisps and cake plus some fruit and veg. There are steps up to the café and it seemed clean, but you may have to wipe down your highchair before use! As well as welcoming children the café is also dog friendly – dog chew provided! Softplay area. Around 40 seats.

Opening hours: Park – 07.30-dusk. Café – 10.00-16.00 every day except Tues. Open 7 days during school holidays. **Cost:** *Park – FREE. Softplay in café for under 5s £2.* **Parking:** *Buy a £1 token before entering the car park. Disabled spaces.* **Toilets:** *Accessible toilets near car park and other toilets near adventure play area. Accessible toilet in the café downstairs (by lift).* **Eating:** *As well as the café there are picnic areas and BBQ areas to hire for groups.* **Birthdays/celebrations:** *Soft play can be hired inc. sandwich platters for children. Tea/Coffee, cakes can be organised in addition for adults.*

swings for children with additional needs and a roundabout. The aviary has budgerigars, lovebirds, zebra finches and cockatiels. There is a census of breeding songbirds carried out each spring as part of the management of the grounds.

Accessibility: Accessible but manual gates at main entrance.

MIDLOTHIAN

Vogrie Country Park

Gorebridge, EH23 4NU
01875 821716
MidlothianRangerService@midlothian.gov.uk
www.midlothian.gov.uk/info/200142/vogrie_country_park
Lots of walks, including short ones suitable for the kids, a great play area for children of all ages and a smaller one by the car park perfect for little ones. Plenty of picnic areas including large

WEST LOTHIAN

House of the Binns (grounds only)

Linlithgow, EH49 7NA
0844 493 2124
houseofthebinns@nts.org.uk
www.nts.org.uk/Property/House-Of-The-Binns
Opportunity for picnic and walks in a beautiful location with super views over the Forth. Lots of animals for children to spot on the drive up

and around the estate – we saw sheep, cows, rabbits and some very friendly peacocks! Ample parking on the grass beside the house and plenty of picnic tables. Follow signs for the 20 min circular woodland walk, which will take you up the hill to the tower, and will be quite an adventure for older children. The path is easy to follow and well marked but involves steps so is not suitable for pushchairs. If you want to visit the house, be aware that it is open from Jun-Sep and only by guided tour at specific times.

Opening hours: Estate open all year daily until dusk. House open from 1 Jun-30 Sep. Cost: Grounds FREE. House – Adult £9, family £22, 1 parent £16.50, conc £6.50, FREE for NTS members.

FIFE

Craigtoun Country Park

By St Andrews, KY16 8NX
01334 473666
Located 2 miles SW of St Andrews off A915. Plenty to do for all the family including: miniature railway (seasonal, buy tickets), trampolines, bouncy castle, putting, crazy golf, adventure play park, toddler play area, aviary, formal gardens and glasshouses. Countryside Centre and lots of parkland to roam and picnic in. Calendar of events throughout the year.

Opening hours: Apr-Sep 10.30-18.30, last admission 17.30. Eating: Café (open end of Jun to end of Aug).

Pittencrieff Park

Dunfermline, KY12 8QH
01383 722935
Lovely park close to Dunfermline Abbey, with wooded glen, wide open areas and great play park. Animal houses, glasshouses and

pavilion selling coffee ice cream etc. Free entry to park. Pittencrieff House Museum in the centre of the Park is worth a visit, free entry.

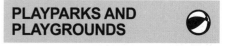

PLAYPARKS AND PLAYGROUNDS

If it's play equipment you're after there is plenty in and around Edinburgh. Each playground should have a notice displaying its name and a number to call to report any damage. Nearly all playgrounds have benches and litter bins. Newer playgrounds in particular will have taken into account the needs of wheelchair users and children with other additional needs.

CENTRAL EDINBURGH

Barony Community Garden and Playground

Barony Place, EH3
www.elgt.org.uk/index.php?page=barony-community-garden
Extensively refurbished in 2009, this delightfully tranquil garden and playground with ramped access has been described as an urban oasis. There is a large and colourful multiplay including slide, climbing wall, trapeze-style monkey bars, wobbly bridge, fireman's pole and cargo net. At ground level, for smaller children, there is a steering wheel with gears, a ship's wheel, a mini cooker and a spinning picture-maker. There are wide steps up to the slide which is separated from the rest of the multiplay so you don't have to worry about your toddler stepping off any high bits! There is also a seesaw, a giant basket swing and a bicycle roundabout. The play area is set on colourful safety surfacing. There is ample seating around the play area, lovely drystone raised flowerbeds and a handy shelter for any emergency al fresco nappy changing.

King George V Park

Eyre Place, EH3 5EN
0131 529 5050
sfc.northneighbourhood@edinburgh.gov.uk
www.edinburgh.gov.uk/directory_
record/10864/king_george_v_park
Fenced and gated area for young children keeps them safe and dogs out. It has a good variety of equipment including baby and children's swings, rope climbing net, climbing frame with walkway, slide and fireman's pole, low-level roundabout and bouncy seesaw. Equipment is surrounded by wood chippings for soft landings and there are good grassy areas and benches for snacks and picnics. Park area outside the enclosure has a play area for more adventurous older children, and grass and paths for walking practice and expeditions for toddlers and younger children. It's a popular place for dogs, whose owners are generally responsible about cleaning up after them. Handy pedestrian/bike tunnel to Tesco at Canonmills a few mins away for shopping and snacks, away from roads and traffic.

The Yard

22 Eyre Place Lane, EH3 5EH
0131 476 4506
www.theyardscotland.org.uk
The Yard has a wealth of play opportunities for children with additional support needs. There are a large range of adapted bikes, a bedswing and ball-cone, sandpit and soft play, a sensory garden, music trail, stream, musical instruments, an art room and a calming sensory room. Open sessions for families and siblings on Fri 13.00-16.00 (during term time) and Sat 10.00-16.00 (all year round). At quiet times local families are welcome to use The Yard on Sat from 13.30 at the discretion of the Play Team Manager. Every Mon from 15.00-17.00 The Yard runs a pre-school club for children aged 3-8 years. Please phone prior to your first visit and someone will meet you on arrival – The Yard is popular and used by lots of older children

and young people which might prove daunting to a younger child using it for the first time.

Broughton Road Play Area

EH7
Lovely modern park with soft matting under all equipment and benches, plus a small grassy area with pergola. Low and high slides both off climbing frame with rope bridge and climbing net, toddler swings and a large bowl swing, a rope roundabout, bouncy seesaw and bouncy horse. Metered parking on Broughton Rd.

Clermiston Park

Clermiston Gardens
Playground with 2 bucket swings, separated from the rest of the playground by a metal fence, 4 other swings, a multiplay with rope climbs and slides, roundabout, seesaw, and 2 springy animals, all set on rubber matting. Benches and litter bins. The surrounding park is grassy with lots of young trees. There is a hard surface next to the playground with basketball/netball nets.

Cramond Walled Garden

Off Cramond Glebe Road, behind Cramond Kirk, EH4 6QU
This Garden does indeed have walls but it is not particularly magical due to a few parts of the pirate ship falling victim to vandals' spray paint. The pirate ship features look-out posts, two levels, steps and slides. Benches allow weary parents places to sit while children run rampant, but at time of writing the swings had been removed. The adjacent larger grassy area features a basketball court and a space big enough to kick a ball or throw a frisbee – so this is a good spot for a family with children of varying ages. Biggest downside is that the garden is under a direct flight path to the

Edinburgh airport and can be noisy! If you walk to the Walled Garden behind Cramond Kirk, then be sure to look at the Roman fort ruins. Parking is not visible from the garden – behind Cramond Kirk and then a walk to the garden. Public toilets and cafés at Cramond Esplanade nearby.

Dalmeny Street Park

36 Dalmeny Street, EH6 8RG
0131 529 7061
citycentreteam@edinburgh.gov.uk
The park has a play/climbing area, a basketball court and a general grassed and benched area. The play equipment is more suited to school aged children. However kicking a ball around in the open space and riding around on a trike proved a hit in itself. On-street parking.

Davidson's Mains Park

East Barnton Avenue, EH4 6AQ
Playground within large grassy park.

Granton Crescent Park

Granton Crescent, EH5 1NY
0131 529 5050
sfc.northneighbourhood@edinburgh.gov.uk
www.edinburgh.gov.uk/directory_
record/10844/granton_crescent_park
Small playpark on grassy slope with views to the Firth of Forth (just visible behind the towerblocks!). Bucket swings, seesaw, slide and climbing frame and 2 benches for parents. Good for under 5s but wouldn't keep older chlidren entertained. Surrounding grassland provides opportunity for ball games. Accessible toilets in Granton Square, 0.8 miles – no nappy changing facilities.

Granton Mains Development

Granton Mill Crescent, EH4 4UT
Playground with 2 multiplay units, plus a roundabout. Grassy area within and around the playpark.

Haugh Park

Brae Park Road, Barnton, EH4
This is a really delightful park, pretty well hidden from the beaten track. You access it by driving along a fairly muddy track and can park right by the park. The park is easy access with bark covering on the ground. There are two entrances. Much to the delight of the toddlers I was with, it was right next to a field of Shetland ponies ("mummy, mummy clip clop clip clop", with much gesticulating and handwaving!). There are 2 swings for toddlers and a climbing frame for bigger children (pre-school), with 2 slides, a car, a climbing rope and some steps. There is also a bucket swing. It is very clean and very colourful. We had a terrific time there.

Parking: No specific designated spaces but there is lots of space. Terrain is slightly rough underfoot (muddy/potholes etc). Accessibility: The terrain is a bit uneven, other than that there are no obstacles to accessibility. Pushchairs: Easy to take pushchair from car to park and lots of space in park to leave it standing. It is slightly rough terrain to push over.

Hopetoun Street Development

McDonald Road
A very small, but colourful playground tucked away amongst the residential development on McDonald Rd. Access is by way of steps from McDonald Rd and there is pay parking right outside the park or by turning off McDonald Rd and into the block of flats where access is

direct (i.e. no steps). There is only one climbing structure consisting of a slide, climbing frame, ladders and a hump bridge. It is definitely for children in the upper age bracket (3-5). Very clean with a soft cover on the ground. Railings all around it.

Accessibility: *Only accessible if entered through flats. Access from McDonald Rd is via steps.* **Pushchairs:** *Accessible if entered through flats.*

Keddie Gardens Playground

Largo Place, Off Ferry Road
Playground with toddler multiplay and other equipment, includes swings and helter-skelter slide. Adjacent grass area close to steps down to Water of Leith walkway.

Leith Links

EH6 7EZ
0131 529 5050
www.edinburgh.gov.uk/directory_record/186515/leith_links
Popular, but not too busy play area in the middle of Leith Links park. Lots of play equipment ranging from baby swings to small and medium-sized climbing structures with slides, rigging etc., and from a large basket swing to an exciting flying fox. Large rope climbing structure for older kids in another enclosed area adjacent to play area. Large enclosed grassed area attached to play area, suitable for picnics, group games, etc. Well maintained, but litter can be a problem. No toilets/nappy changing but Duke St Tesco (with customer toilets) is just a 5 min walk away.

Lochend Park

Lochend Road South, EH7 6DQ
0131 529 3111
sfc.eastneighbourhood@edinburgh.gov.uk
A pleasant park with a large pond and a small fenced play area, which has a large climbing structure for older children, 2 toddler swings and a small roundabout. The park and play area are both well kept and were a pleasant spot for a short stroll on a sunny afternoon. The footpath runs around a large pond, and offers some nice views over to Arthur's Seat. Although the pond is entirely fenced it did appear to be home to a range of birdlife and a good spot for feeding the ducks with no risk of falling in!

Montgomery Street Playground

Montgomery Street, EH7
Centrally located, this large park is not the most modern but has a great variety of attractions for all ages; smaller climbing frames, slide and swings for toddlers and also more advanced and exciting things for older children including a tractor climbing frame with slide and another with a bridge tunnel, swings, and a high helter-skelter slide. Railings separate the playpark from the road and a large concrete basketball/football area – there is also an adjoining grass park with benches. Handy for Leith Walk and London Rd. The area is well served with cafés and restaurants.

Get the most up-to-date information on
www.efuf.co.uk

Muirhouse Linear Park and Playground

Near Muirhouse Drive
Playground with adjacent grass area, basketball court, BMX area and skateboard park.

Muirhouse View

At east end of Pennywell Gardens
Playground with toddler play area off Pennywell Gardens.

Northview Court

Pennywell Grove/Pennywell Gardens
Playground – play area off Pilton Crescent.

Pilrig Park

Bonnington Road/Pilrig Street
A good range of play equipment, suitable for babies/toddlers and older children. There are toddler swings and standard swings, so a good park if you have children in different age ranges. Opportunities for sliding, bouncing and climbing. All the equipment is well spaced and there is good space for running about, and benches for a well-earned rest. Easy area to get to and reasonably clean and litter-free.

Redbraes Park

Broughton Road, EH7
Fenced-off modern playpark set in large grassed park on Broughton Rd towards Pilrig St, which has free and open parking. Toddler and regular swings, climbing frame with chute. Good for all ages, soft matting surrounds all equipment.

Sandport Play Area

Sandport Street, Leith, EH6 6EP
0131 529 5050
www.edinburgh.gov.uk/directory_record/18667/sandport_street
Small but pleasant play area. Enclosed, leafy and safe, but near main road, so quite noisy. Older kids playing football within play area when we were there with our two 2½ yr olds and a 9 mth old – a bit annoying, but no one got hit. Nice, well-maintained play structure. Wood chip ground cover for safety. Swings, but no baby swings for the little one. Certainly not a "destination" playground, but the girls enjoyed the change from our usual haunt and it would be fine for a quick play if it was your nearest play area.

St Mark's Park

Warriston Road, EH7 4HN
0131 529 5050
sfc.northneighbourhood@edinburgh.gov.uk
www.edinburgh.gov.uk/directory_record/10919/st_marks_park

Beaverbank end
Tucked away in the new Beaverbank housing area at the entrance to St Mark's Park, this enclosed, under-2s gated play area is great for toddlers. Equipment includes sturdy and easily negotiable slide with platform and space for

hiding underneath, baby swings and bouncy seesaw. Rubberised surfaces to cushion falls and grass to sit on. Wooden bridge to park and riverside path is a good place to encounter very friendly ducks on the Water of Leith, who will waddle out to greet you. Given other users, animals and water, reins are advisable for toddlers on the riverside path.

Powderhall end
Sloping grassy area between the Water of Leith at Powderhall and the cycle path. Ideal for viewing one of Anthony Gormley's "6 Times" life-sized human sculptures standing in the water. The playground, just off the cycle path, has 2 multiplays with slides, tightrope, cargo net and steering wheel, all on safety surfacing. Watch out for the high drop from the larger multiplay. There is also a roundabout, benches, and some picnic tables on a grassy area. Plenty to entertain all ages but could do with a lick of paint.

Victoria Park and Playgrounds

Newhaven Road, EH6 5PY
0131 529 5050
sfc.northneighbourhood@edinburgh.gov.uk
www.edinburgh.gov.uk/directory_
record/10928/victoria_park
Lovely, open grassy space with pedestrian and cycle paths running throughout and two playgrounds. At the Newhaven Rd end, the toddler playground has two swings, a roundabout, a dome-shaped climbing frame and a small multiplay with slide. The playground at the Craighall Rd end is set on wood chipping and is suitable for around 3+ yrs although even my 5 yr old couldn't reach some of the assault course inspired equipment. There is a multiplay with a climbing wall and slide surrounded by various swinging activities. Plenty of picnic tables and benches around the park but can be busy at lunchtimes with schoolchildren. The playground for older children is soon to be refurbished and plans to amalgamate the two playgrounds is under consultation.

Parking: Plenty of free parking on Craighall Rd and Newhaven Rd.

EAST EDINBURGH

Craigmillar Park   `•FREE`

Niddrie House Square
Multiplay plus other equipment.

Gracemount Playground   `•FREE`

Gracemount Drive, EH16 6RN
The playground is not easy to locate until you realise that it is adjacent to Gracemount Leisure Centre – park in their car park. Ideal for younger children and toddlers, older children may find it a bit limiting. There are 2 bucket seat swings, a slide, 2 spring bouncers and a roundabout, all with soft surfaces underneath. The playground is clean and quiet and there is easy pushchair access. Toilets and nappy changing in leisure centre.

Inch Park   `•FREE`

225 Gilmerton Road, EH16 5UF
Playground set in expansive green parkland. There are 2 play areas – one for younger children and one for over 5s, both are gated. The equipment is well maintained and fenced for safety and for restricting dog access. Some of the play equipment will be challenging for toddlers. Best for pre-school and upwards. The surrounding green park land has extensive sports facilities for teenagers and adults – for football, cricket and basketball. The park is best accessed from Glenallen Dr, but you can also enter at Cameron Toll shopping centre car park.

Parking: Lots of street parking, also parking in Community Centre car park and at Cameron Toll.

Jack Kane Centre Play Area

Jack Kane Sports Centre, 208 Niddrie Mains Road, EH16 4NE
0131 669 0404
info.jksc@edinburghleisure.co.uk
www.edinburghleisure.co.uk
A large enclosed play area with a soft bark floor. For under 3s there are some baby swings, a small climbing frame with a slide and a small roundabout. For older children there is a larger slide and climbing frame, a large roundabout, some beams for balancing and a flying fox. Immediately outside the park there is a huge grassy field for running around and a BMX track – probably beyond the cycling abilities of most under 5s but my kids love running around it pretending to be on a bike.

I like this park because it is clean and secure and there is lots of space inside to run around. There is also a good mix of play equipment so it's a good place for families with mixed ages or abilities. You can park at Jack Kane Sports Centre beside the park but there is a £1 parking charge. Toilets and nappy changing at the sports centre.

Opening hours: 07.30 till dusk.

Joppa Quarry Playpark

South Morton Street, Portobello
Large play structure in a big grassy park. Good hill for rolling children or easter eggs down. The main play area is more suited for over 3s but there are swings, a roundabout and some small rocking animals for the younger ones.

The railway line is right next to the park so you might see some trains rushing by. You can park on Morton Street or Coillesdene Crescent, then walk across the bridge over the railway.

Accessibility: You can access without crossing the railway from S Morton St, but this is a narrower street with less parking.

Magdalene Community Centre Playpark

Magdalene Estate, Off Milton Road
Small playpark in between the primary school and the community centre. It has 3 pieces of play apparatus which each stand on a soft surface. The park would suit children from walking age. There are 3 chutes to use. Lots for climbing on but no swings. Surrounding the playpark there is a fence with 2 gates. The playpark is open even when the school and community centre are closed. Access through school gates.

Northfield Broadway

• FREE

Next to Northfield Community Centre
Toddler playground.

Prestonfield Park

• FREE

EH16 5EU
A nice local park. The play area (upgraded in 2009) is fenced off. There is one large piece of equipment incorporating multi-level play for all age groups. This includes a walkway, helter-skelter, fireman's pole and small slide. Additional equipment includes 2 traditional swings, roundabout, seesaw, multi-person swing and springy animal. Benches and picnic table are a welcome addition for parents. Access from Prestonfield Av or Prestonfield Rd.

Seven Acre Park

Stanedykehead, Liberton
Set in farmland with a breathtaking view over to Arthur's Seat and beyond, the park has an enclosed play area with 2 bucket seats, a "castle" multiplay and roundabout, with a separate area with basketball hoops. There is also a grassy area around the play area with picnic tables. As it's in quite an exposed location, it is fairly windy, but this does mean it's great for flying kites! My son liked the castle best as he could be "king of the castle".

Not the easiest place to find or to know where to park, and there is a bit of a walk for little legs. The park itself is pushchair friendly, but the access road is not good so could be a bumpy ride in a pushchair. When we were there, the farmland immediately beyond the park looked like it was being dug up to lay some sort of access road, so it is unclear if the peaceful location would be soon interrupted.

Straiton Place Playground

Straiton Place, Portobello
Small play park on Portobello Promenade. The play structure is shaped like a boat with a small climbing ladder, a slide and a small table and chairs. It is easy to use and most suitable for younger under 5s. Large grassy area around for running or ball games, and there are no dogs in the park so the grass is always clean. There is an area of sand for digging. Parking on Straiton Place right beside the playground. Large "superloo" outside the gate.

Accessibility: All flat but "cattle grid" at gate.

Tower Bank Playground

Just off the Promenade, Portobello
A small playground right on Portobello prom, with a multiplay unit, swings, balance beam and

seesaw. Probably best for children aged 2+. There has recently been some refurbishment work done to the sheltered area. Gets very busy after school with children from the nearby primary. Public toilets nearby on Bath St and Pipe Lane. Numerous small cafés along the prom and Portobello High St.

Buckstone Park

Buckstone Circle, EH10
A decent well-kept pre-school playground with a flat grassy park and wooded area nearby, ideal for hide and seek. The park can be hard to find unless you know the area. Basically keep going uphill through the Buckstone houses and the park is at the highest point, near the school. There is a footpath which gives access from Mounthooly Loan. Nearby links to wooded walks around Mortonhall.

Fairmilehead Park

Camus Avenue, EH10 6QU
Also known as Camus Park, the play area was updated in 2011 with brand new play equipment including a large climbing frame and slide, a smaller climbing wall and cargo net, a zip wire, swings and a witches hat roundabout. There are goal posts nearby. The park is great for older under 5s and school aged children although baby swings and a low level seesaw are available. This park is a bit out of the way – it can be accessed from Camus Ave, Pentland View and Pentland Dr. On-street parking. Café nearby at the Buckstone shops.

Falcon's Gardens Playpark

Pleasant, small playpark tucked away from the road and a little off the beaten track, except for the pupils of St Peter's Primary School next door who visit straight after school (so best avoided then if possible). Two toddler swings and 2 traditional swings, multiplay with small helter skelter, 2 other slides, rope climbing frame and small climbing wall. Small, steep grass area.

Entrances on corner of Falcon Rd/Falcon Gdns beside St Peter's Primary School, and on Canaan La opposite Woodburn Terr.

Meadows Playpark (Meadows East)

An excellent playpark, full of fun and innovative play areas that keep both older and younger children happy for hours on end. There is a large sandpit and water play area, along with several large multiplays of varying difficulty, and swings for babies, toddlers and children with disabilities. This is such a popular playpark that people will travel across the city to visit it, many of them spending the whole day with a picnic when weather allows, so it can get busy during weekends and holidays. There are toilets nearby, although they don't have nappy changing facilities. An ice cream and burger stand is usually in operation during the summer, and there are a handful of coffee shops within walking distance. Some on-street, metered parking in nearby Newington and Marchmont.

Eating: Summer only (kiosk).

Morningside Park

A lovely, well-used playpark which has been repainted and spruced up generally with new plants and a picnic table thanks to its "Friends" group. Four toddler swings, 4 traditional swings, toddler multiplay, climbing frame/slide, helter-skelter and sit-in roundabout. There are also grassy areas, hopscotch, a tennis court and a large hard-surfaced area for football, bike riding etc. The park can get very busy, especially in late afternoon, when it is sometimes used by the local after-school club.

WEST EDINBURGH

Bloomiehall Public Park

Juniper Green
At the end of Juniper Park Rd, accessed from Baberton Ave, where you can park too. This is a pleasant playpark in a lovely setting within a large grassy area for ball games, picnics, etc. There is a path around the circumference for pushchair access. The under 5s area is based on a railway theme with carriages, a station and a ticket office. There are 2 bucket swings on rubber surfacing. Large section for older children which is not fenced off completely from the toddler area, with slides, rope climbing, bridges, balancing beams, rope pyramid and a zipwire. Access to the playpark is via gates and has benches. The only complaint was that at time of visiting there was graffiti on some of the toddler equipment.

Accessibility: Gravel path.

Colinton Mains Park

Oxgangs Road North, EH13 9EB
0131 527 3800
sfc.southwestneighbourhood@edinburgh.
gov.uk
www.edinburgh.gov.uk/directory_
record/10814/colinton_mains_park
Spacious park with football pitches and basketball hoops. Modern play area with swings, climbing frames, seesaw and slide. Benches. There is a path all the way round the park. Some rubbish and graffiti but generally quite clean. Definitely worth a visit if you live close by!

Corstorphine Hill Playpark

Craigcrook Road, Just N of Hillpark Green
Playground with 4 rocking animals, toddler multiplay with slide and rope climbing frame. Close to path leading up to Corstorphine Hill Local Nature Reserve (see p 50).

Curriemuir End Park

Off Wester Hailes Road
This playground has to be approached on foot, using either the path that leaves Wester Hailes Rd close to the junction with Viewfield Rd, or the underpass beneath Wester Hailes Rd that links Clovenstone estate to the park.

Mainly wooden equipment. Surrounding park is grassy and hilly, and there are several picnic tables nearby. As part of the Pentlands Open Space Strategy Plan, plans are in place to raise the Park Quality Assessment grade of this park from fair to good between 2010 and 2020.

Dean Park, Balerno

31 Marchbank Gardens, Balerno, EH14 7ET
In terms of under 5s, Dean Park's best bit is the playpark, which has a range of equipment (but no bucket swing) for kids to enjoy, even at a very young age. The playpark is split into items for older children (such as a big "satellite dish" swing which seems to attract young teenagers by the handful) and items for younger children including rocking animals and a climbing frame with bridges and a slide. The whole thing is fenced off and has a gate which is easily opened (perhaps too easily, if you have an adventurous toddler like us). It is located right next to Dean Park Primary School, which has an adjacent car park, so is convenient for people dropping older children off at the school. Although it offers a range of activities for toddlers, there is little incentive to visit unless you happen to live near Balerno or are travelling through as it is a fairly standard playpark surrounded by lots of houses. It has provided many opportunities

for our daughter to test her developing climbing and adventuring skills.

Fauldburn Park, East Craigs

Lovely space to take kids to burn off energy, and the play area was nice and clean when we visited! Great for football, and loads of wooded areas to explore nearby.

Accessibility/Pushchairs: On grass, footpath to park.

Gyle Park

Wester Broom Place
A large expanse of grass including a playpark, football pitches, skate area and basketball court. Accessible via the Wester Broom/Gyle estates or via the road leading to the David Lloyd Leisure Club.

The playpark is securely fenced and consists of 2 frames, one suitable for toddlers and one aimed at 2+ yrs. There is also a flying fox, swings (baby and older) and on the ground a hopscotch area and paintings of ducks and frogs which you have to find throughout the park. I would highly rate this park as my son loved it and could manage all the equipment.

The general green area is also in very good condition, with raised areas with trees. Perfect for a wee picnic and some playing in the park.

Harrison Park

West Bryson Road/Watson Crescent
Fenced park with tree-lined walkway along the banks of the Union Canal. Set near tennis courts, playing fields and a bowling green. There are 4 bucket swings, a seesaw, a slide and a small climbing frame.

Murieston Park

Murieston Crescent, EH11 2LQ
sfs.southwestneighbourhood@edinburgh.
gov.uk
A small fenced off open green space in the middle of a residential crescent. Within it there is a small playground with a slide, climbing frame and a couple of other bits for younger children. Great for locals.

Pentland View Park

Lanark Road West, Currie
Standard playpark set within playing fields. Two toddler multiplays, one for slightly older toddlers as it's higher, both with slides. Two bucket swings, 4 other swings, 2 benches. Situated on busy road, but fenced off within the fields.

Parking: Car park for shopping centre right next to park.

Roseburn Playpark

Roseburn Crescent, EH12 5PH
0131 529 7440
sfc.westneighbourhood@edinburgh.gov.uk
www.edinburgh.gov.uk/directory_
record/10908/roseburn_park
Small enclosed playpark behind Roseburn Primary containing one large multiplay unit, but no swings. Open playing fields to side. Not suitable for babies.

Sighthill Park

Broomhouse Road
Playpark with two areas: toddler area equipment includes a sit-down roundabout, a multiplay and 2 bucket swings on a special low frame to help eliminate the disappointment of swing wrap round. The junior area includes a multiplay and more adventure style equipment, including a "Space Climbing" net. Next to the playground on the surrounding grass there are two small goal posts and a skateboarding ramp area.

Stewart Terrace Park

off Gorgie Road
Enclosed toddler park which is bright, clean and inviting. There are 2 bucket swings, two springy animals, plus a multiplay which has tunnels, a slide and climbing structures. There are also grassy areas and benches.

St Margaret's Park

Corstorphine High Street, EH12
Popular park with children's play area which was renovated in 2011. The play area is enclosed so children are kept in and dogs are kept out. Play equipment now includes a 4-seat crazy daisy springer, a dish roundabout, swings and slide. Also at the park are playing fields, bowling, tennis courts, putting, and the heritage centre and café which is open on Wed and Sat mornings for tea and coffee. Parking on nearby streets (Dovecot Rd, Orchardfield Ave) is a short walk to the park.

Opening hours: Mon-Fri 12.00-21.00, Sat-Sun 11.00-17.00. Eating: Wed/Sat mornings only.

Wester Hailes

This area has very few large playgrounds, but it has benefited from a programme to create small play centres within individual estates.

White Park

Gorgie Road, EH11 1TZ

A decent-sized playpark just along from the main road from Gorgie Farm (see p 52), sheltered on three sides by buildings and fully gated from dogs etc, with some area laid to grass on both sides of the play surface. Two picnic benches on one side, along with 4 other park benches for seating. The playpark itself consists of 2 swing sets, one double baby heavy-based swing set, and the other a set of 4 traditional swings, all in very good condition. There is also a stand-up style roundabout (suitable for 3+ yrs) and a main frame area with a climber made from rope, shaped with 2 bridges, 2 slides (one low and one very high). The children have to climb up the rope net to get to the high slide, which proved great fun for my 4 yr old. However, should your child go up to get on the high slide, and chicken out at the top, then the only way to retrieve them is to go up yourself! The slide is super slidey, so lots of fun. The lower slide can be accessed from the drawbridge so you can take a younger toddler up this and slide down with them. There is also a cargo net on the other side. The play surface is in good condition and all the equipment in very good working order with little or no graffiti. I would recommend this park to those with children 3+ yrs as the climbing frame would be too daunting for a younger child I think. My 10 mth old went on the swing and I slid down the lower slide with her. Great wee park though within 2 min walk from Gorgie Farm so worth a visit next time you are at the farm or passing through Gorgie. Entrances both from Gorgie Farm side and also from White Park.

Have you any information you would like to add? Email us at info@efuf.co.uk

EAST LOTHIAN

Musselburgh Links Playground

Fisherow Links off New St. Follow signs for Links and Bowling Green. Themed around pirates, this playpark is imaginatively designed and is packed with interesting and unusual play equipment. There's an outdoor gym for older children, a crow's nest slide complete with skull and crossbones hiding a seating area, large sandpit with diggers, huge swinging hammock, plus smaller swings for the younger children. There's also a multiplay unit with slide, climbing wall and balancing beam, a few springy animals and a balancing beam on its own (for walking the plank?). Challenging for my 17 mth old but it didn't stop him giving everything a go. Brilliant for slightly older under 5s. We'll be going back.

BEACHES

Swimming in the sea

Paddling and swimming in the sea can be great fun but remember sea water can be extremely cold even on sunny days so be ready to wrap up afterwards. Edinburgh's beaches are generally reasonably clean, but standards can change from season to season and after heavy rain, so always check before going into the water, and obey the notices posted – just because it looks clean doesn't mean it's safe. The Scottish Environment Protection Agency (SEPA) monitors and reports on water quality of other recreational waters as well as those which are EC recognised (see www.sepa.org.uk for results), but only Jun to mid-Sep.

Some beaches in urban areas can be affected by sewage debris and have higher bacterial concentrations during and immediately after heavy rain, caused by storm sewer overflows and run-off from streets. All the EC-recognised beaches in Edinburgh, Lothians and Fife meet EC water quality standards. Other beaches away from towns are generally safe to play on but do not have official EC recognition because they are too sparsely used.

NORTH EDINBURGH

Cramond Beach and Esplanade

Great place to let little ones run around and let off steam. In the summer, there is usually an ice-cream van at the Cramond Beach end, and there are some cafés to have a coffee and cake while out and about. The Fish sculpture by Ronald Rae is a firm favourite with us, and walking out to Cramond Island is a great day out with kids and dog, just keep an eye on the tide! Loads of kids ride around on bikes and skate along on blades. You'll need to watch out for dog mess too – sadly not all dog owners are responsible ones!

Cramond Roman Fort is nearby, which is interesting to look at, and there is a great playpark behind the Kirk, just up the hill from the Esplanade itself, in the Walled Garden (see p 78). See p 92 for more walks from Cramond.

Parking: Plenty, both at Lauriston Farm and at Cramond Village (beside the Roman Fort).
Toilets: At Cramond Village end, but never particularly clean or accessible/child-friendly.
Eating: Two nice cafés.

EAST EDINBURGH

Portobello Beach and Promenade

Rain or shine, Edinburgh's seaside has something to offer: sandcastles and ice creams in the summer, and puddles and bracing walks in the winter. Stretching from Seafield Rd (near the Edinburgh Dog and Cat Home) to Esplanade Terr in Joppa (just near the solar-powered public toilets!), the promenade is a wide paved space ideal for pushchairs, bikes, scooters and for exploring on foot (no traffic to worry about). There are a couple of playparks along its length. The pool at one end (p 108) and the bowling club at the other (p 121) make ideal places for snacks and toilet stops. The Seafield end is the more commercial area with amusement arcades and fast food bars, while the promenade and beach nearer Joppa are much quieter. The beach is very clean (early morning visitors can enjoy watching the tractors skim the sand) but is used by a lot of dog walkers so best to watch out! There's plenty of free parking along Portobello's streets, on the Musselburgh Rd and in a public car park in Bridge St.

EAST LOTHIAN

Aberlady Beach

EH32
www.undiscoveredscotland.co.uk/aberlady/ aberladybay/index.html
We had an excellent visit – a beautiful scenic area and perfect for a family outing, picnic and a good play on the beach! The Aberlady nature reserve is very pretty – my daughter had an excellent time trying to jump along the pedestrian walkway bridge. We drove along to the Longniddry beach and had a super time collecting shells and paddling in the water. It is an extremely picturesque place and very worthwhile visiting!

Pushchair friendly: Generally, though the sand may pose a problem with pushing. Eating: There were some lovely wee cafés and places to eat in Aberlady.

Gullane Beach

This is undoubtedly one of the most beautiful and family friendly beaches in East Lothian. It is easily accessible and located within the lovely town of Gullane (follow signs for Gullane Bents). It holds a Blue Flag Award as a clean beach. There is a long stretch of soft, golden sand, with rocks at one end and dunes behind, if you have slightly older children who want to explore. The beach slopes very gradually giving plenty of paddling space at high tide, and as the beach is within the Forth estuary, the water is usually very calm. There are some nice cafés in Gullane.

North Berwick Beach

Nice clean beach, with an easy walk to the town centre. Lots of parking nearby. A walk along the beach is a great way to get fresh air, exercise and a napping baby!

Parking: Bay/on-street parking. Accessibility: Ramps onto sand. Eating: Cafés in North Berwick.

Seacliff Beach

East of North Berwick on A198
We really enjoyed our trip to this beautiful quiet beach. It was deserted the day we visited it and we were the only car parked in the car park. The

views of the Bass Rock were stunning and the beach seemed sheltered. My 3 yr old enjoyed exploring the rock pools. The toilet block for male and female was open, relatively clean but remember your own toilet roll! Paying £2 at the entrance barrier seemed a bit steep but after finding the beautiful beach and the setting it seemed justified.

Cost: £2 at entrance barrier. Parking: Two small car parks. Accessibility: Steps from first carpark but if you drive on you can park near the toilets and pull a wheelchair to the beach. Pushchairs: Access from second car park.

Tyninghame Beach

Take the A199 out of Haddington and turn on to the A198 towards North Berwick. After passing Tyninghame village there is an unmarked turn off to the right, through an avenue of trees, leading to a small car park. From there a track leads down to the beach, and also off through the trees for various woodland walks. Not ideal for pushchairs, so take a sling or backpack. The beach has lots of rock pools and can be quite exposed. No toilets. There is a café with gift shop and toilet in Tyninghame village.

Yellowcraig Beach

Dirleton
Fabulous beach 30 mins drive from Edinburgh. Great playpark beside the car park with lots of ropes and climbing frames. Under 3s will find some smaller things to play on but much of the park is aimed at older kids. The park is in a forest area with lots of space to run around in, and some great trees for climbing. Follow a rough path to the lovely, clean beach with views out to the island of Fidra and the lighthouse. You can book a barbeque area on 01620 893957.

Pushchairs: Easy access to the play area, path to beach is rougher. Would be OK for all-terrain pushchairs but consider using a sling or carrier. *Toilets:* Along a grassy path signposted from the main track. Clean but basic.

FIFE

Aberdour Beach and Playpark

Aberdour, KY3
0845 155 0000 (Fife Council)
www.fife.gov.uk
Despite the very cold and windy weather on the day of our visit we enjoyed our trip to this sandy beach which boasts a Blue Flag and Resort Seaside Award. Clean and well maintained with good facilities including: toilets, first aid, lifeguards, dog restricted and dog exercise areas and a nice new café. The bouncy castle (£1.50 for 10 mins) was well received by the toddlers in our party. Small yet well-maintained playpark area built around a climbing frame (no swings!) suitable for toddlers. We will be back in the summer to spend more time here. There are some stairs from the main car park so I'd recommend a baby sling on this trip.

The playground on Shore Rd is well worth a visit. Lots to do for all ages of under 5s, plus plenty to interest older children. The tightrope walk was our favourite. Parking available at the shore or if that's full try the large car park by the railway station (also near the castle).

Parking: Ample car parking on Hawkcraig Point (£1.20) with a short walk (200 yds) to the beach. At the beach is a small car park, reserved for disabled drivers during the busiest times.

Elie Harbour Beach

Large, sandy, blue-flag beach (also winner of a Seaside Award in 2010) with a café at the harbour. The nearby Ship Inn is a good family-friendly place to eat, with activities and cricket to watch during the summer. Elie Watersports (01333 330 962) at the harbour hire out pedal boats, inflatable rides, canoes, dinghies, windsurfers, etc.

Kinghorn (Pettycur Bay)

Safe, sandy, award-winning bay (it has recently won a Seaside Award) with two ice-cream shops/cafés on the front. Fife Council Environmental Health Department gave it a good/excellent rating for its water quality.

St Andrew's Beach

East and West Sands Beaches: Two lovely large sandy beaches. Clean – and the water status is checked regularly. West Sands continues to hold a Blue Flag award.

Tentsmuir (near Leuchars): 2 miles from B945. Follow signs to Tentsmuir Forest and Beach. A huge sandy beach and forest with extensive walks and cycleways. There is a car park, picnic and barbeque area with toilets, a play area, and an information board. The car park kiosk sells a small selection of snacks. Swimming not recommended here.

FUN ON FOOT

Edinburgh is a wonderful city for walks and you'll find ideas for places to stretch your legs earlier in this chapter.

Below we've listed a few tried and tested walking routes, including the wonderful Water of Leith Walkway. Be aware that not all of the paths in these routes are pushchair friendly or accessible. Many are near water so watch little ones, and many of the routes are favourites with dog walkers, so look out for mess. As ever when walking, particularly on off-street routes, take care, consider inviting friends to walk with you and please don't use these routes after dark.

Cammo and the River Almond   `•FREE`

The path along the River Almond can be joined from Cammo. Routes not pushchair-friendly.

Start on Cammo Rd. A signpost leads you through a gate on the right and down a rough wide path to the river where the riverbank is steep. The path continues to follow the river upstream towards the airport. There are stepping stones about halfway along or turn up the path to the left near the bridge and you will eventually rejoin Cammo Rd. Along the path you pass Craighall Temple, a locked tower, or turn right over Grotto Bridge. The river here looks spectacular after rain, as the water thunders underneath. Watch the cattle grid just over the bridge. The path follows the river downstream and can be rough with steep steps down to the water. It ends near the Cramond Brig Hotel.

Walks from Cramond

Cramond Village is situated at the mouth of the River Almond. There are swans and seagulls to feed and lots of small boats to look at. Walks radiate in all directions from the yachting centre. There is a large car park on Cramond Glebe Rd, below Cramond Kirk and above the Cramond Inn. A ramp leads down to the esplanade. Below the Inn are public toilets. There are also two cafés serving teas and ice creams.

Cramond was home to an established Roman settlement. There is a partially excavated site in the upper car park, beside the 17th Century Cramond Kirk.

North – to Cramond Island

There is a causeway across the tidal mudflats out to Cramond Island, which is negotiable at low tide. Tide charts are pinned up at the start of the causeway monthly but often get torn down. Check the tide times with Forth Ports or the Ranger Service before setting out. Take a picnic to your own small uninhabited island. Good views of the Forth Bridges but keep an eye on the time for returning before the tide comes in again.

South – the River Almond

About 1.5 miles. The walkway starts on the esplanade, near the yachting centre, and follows the river upstream on a wooded path. The path is wide and on one level, and is suitable for pushchairs and bikes, but can be muddy. The river is tidal up to Cockle Mill Cottages, where the path opens out into a grassy area – watch for dog fouling. There is also a small car park, access from Whitehouse Rd via School Brae. The path continues up to Fair-a-Far Mill where there is a waterfall and a fish ladder. The mill is a ruin and children can enjoy running through the arches and up a few steps. The river is railed at this point but toddlers can get underneath quite easily. People throw pennies into the top of the fall and children collect them later! The path continues to the Cramond Brig Hotel and Haugh Park, but there is a steep flight of steps and pushchairs would have to be carried.

East – the Esplanade

A broad paved footpath runs for 2 miles from Cramond through Silverknowes to Granton Point, West Shore Rd. An attractive area for promenading with the pram, roller-skating or for learning to ride a bike. Superb views across to Fife on clear days. Suitable for picnics on the Grassy Banks at Silverknowes where there is parking along Marine Drive – but look out for dog mess. You can also walk up to Lauriston Castle from Silverknowes.

Tide charts are available in summer. Ice cream vans, pipe bands and entertainment over some summer weekends. The beach itself is sandy at Cramond and stony elsewhere. It can be oily and there are often pollution warnings about collecting shellfish. The beach is gently sloped but the tide can come in fast and maroon you on a sandbank – be prepared to paddle!

Union Canal

www.scottishcanals.co.uk
The canal runs out from Fountainbridge in the city centre to join with the Forth and Clyde Canal at the Falkirk Wheel. There are various access points along the length of the canal, Harrison Park is a good start point. The towpath is on the North Bank and is suitable for pushchairs, obviously children need close supervision. Walking from the city centre you pass industrial and commercial buildings before coming to suburban gardens and parks. Ducks and swans can often be seen as well as members of the rowing club swooshing along the water. At Slateford the Water of Leith Visitor Centre is accessible down a long flight of steps or continue on carefully over the magnificent 12-arch Slateford Aquaduct.

THE WATER OF LEITH WALKWAY

The Water of Leith rises in the Pentland Hills and runs through the villages of Balerno, Currie, Juniper Green and Colinton and into the heart of Edinburgh before flowing into the Firth of Forth at Leith. In its 24 miles it flows through wooded dells, past abandoned mills, elegant Georgian terraces and new housing developments, before opening up into a broad river surrounded by the buildings of Leith docks. It is designated an Urban Wildlife Site by the City of Edinburgh Council. Look for herons, especially near weirs.

It's worth taking a map as the signposting is sometimes unclear, and there are alternative routes which might make you muddled. There is a comprehensive guide to the walkway with a map and historical notes by the Water of Leith Conservation Trust. This is available at the Visitors' Centre or can be sent to you. However, it's an idea to also take a street map to ensure you have a full grasp of your location!

The guide highlights parts of the route best suited for wheelchairs and cycles. The walkway runs along most of the river in the City and most parts are negotiable with a pushchair, fewer with a wheelchair. Access is not always so easy and below we have tried to list alternatives to steps. Some sections are well used by dogs too. Keep an eye on young cyclists as the banks can be steep and there are not always railings.

The brown water is due to peat. Giant hogweed, a tall plant (up to 3m) with tiny white flowers, has established itself on several stretches. Touching this plant or blowing through sections of its hollow stem may cause an allergic reaction and photosensitivity of the skin. These plants are routinely cleared but return each year. Along stretches of the river are raspberries and brambles which should be safe to eat, but remember that dogs may have been there before you – pick high!

Interested in becoming a researcher for Edinburgh for Under Fives?
Drop us an email at ed@efuf.co.uk.
All you need is a bit of time, some commitment and an under 5!

Water of Leith Visitor Centre

 FREE

24 Lanark Road, EH14 1TQ
0131 455 7367
admin@wateofleith.org.uk
www.wateofleith.org.uk/centre

Located at Slateford, this centre in a renovated schoolhouse provides a bit of context to your walk with an interactive exhibition all about the Water of Leith, its history and its wildlife.

There are lots of hands-on things to do for under 5s and this is a pleasant place to while away perhaps an hour. Based on water and nature, the activities include building flood defences out of Lego and then turning on the flood to see what happens and altering the river flow to turn water wheels. Toddlers will enjoy playing at the "Flood Plain" and "Mill Lades and Water Wheels" and budding ecologists will have fun at the nature-based audio wall, complete with peepholes. Our 2 yr old took particular pleasure in having a good old splash and floating Lego bricks down the river at the "Flood Plain". A great place to visit in its own right and also a relaxing stop off for a walk. Shop selling maps and books also on site.

Opening hours: 10.00-16.00. Closed 24 Dec-3 Jan. Cost: FREE (£1 donation per person suggested). Eating: Snacks and juice available. Birthdays/celebrations: For 5-10 yr olds, environmental-themed parties.

"Borrow a Buggy" scheme

 FREE

Provides buggies for children with limited mobility to access countryside, beaches and hills – places that may have previously been inaccessible to them. Although registration of the carer is required (take along photo ID plus home address ID), it's a free service. Buggies are kept at the Water of Leith Visitor Centre and at Craiglockhart Tennis Club. After registration and a 15 minute familiarisation session, you will

be able to borrow a buggy. If available, they can be hired for half days, full days or weekends. Once registered just call in advance to reserve.

The Water of Leith Walkway route

Balerno to Juniper Green

The walkway begins to the north side of Balerno High School, Bridge Rd, and follows the track of an old railway, making it ideal for pushchairs and cyclists. There are a number of access points along the route to Currie – Waulkmill Loan is easiest for pushchairs. At Currie Kirkgate there are steps up to the walkway, next to the bridge. Here it is better for pushchairs if you continue under the bridge and up the road to Currie Baptist Church, where there is access to the walkway via an old goods yard; you can park here. The walkway continues for approx 1.5 miles to Juniper Green. There are steps up from the walkway to Blinkbonny Rd bridge. There is a section here where a 20ft wall drops sharply down to the river below, so hold on to tots. The path then crosses to the north side of the river again. Access in Juniper Green is from Baberton Loan, next to the Post Office where you can park.

Juniper Green to Slateford

Along this attractive and peaceful section of the river the walkway continues on the old railway, passing under the city bypass and into a wooded dell, crossing the river several times. Good access next to the Post Office in Juniper Green, West Mill Rd, Gillespie Rd by the bridge, or through Spylaw Park, Colinton where there is a good play area. Continuing on, the walkway enters an old railway tunnel, dimly lit but not as long as it looks and a superb place for echoes. Look out for a silhouette on the wall of a Balerno pug, the small engine specially designed for the steep sided Colinton Dell. The path emerges way above the river with other paths below. From Dell Rd, Colinton, down past the church, the walkway runs through the wooded Colinton and Craiglockhart Dells. This section is difficult for pushchairs as there are steps every so often. Access points include Katesmill Rd, Redhall Mill and behind the Tickled Trout, Lanark Rd, at Slateford.

Colinton Dell

The Dell extends along the Water of Leith Walkway from Colinton Parish Church towards Slateford and contains a mixture of mature and ancient woodland along a well established path. It is a natural habitat for wildlife, including numerous bird species, and occasionally roe deer (although I have never seen any!). The walkway and cycle path also pass by some of the original mill buildings, not forgetting the old tunnel (locally known as Henry's Tunnel, in reference to the character from popular children's TV series Thomas the Tank Engine) that dates back to when the path was part of the local railway line. Great for cycling and prams if the weather hasn't been too wet! There are some large patches of grass along the path which are suitable for picnics. Play areas at Spylaw Park/Harrison Gdns are on the route.

Parking: At Spylaw Park, Slateford or various points along the path. Accessibility: Can be accessed without coming down steps at Colinton and Slateford. Pushchairs: In dry conditions. Toilets/Nappy changing: In Colinton Village.

Slateford to Roseburn

This section of the walkway gets off to a pleasant start by the Visitor Centre, around the allotments and on to arrive at Saughton Park where the formal garden and Winter Gardens are worth a visit. Easy going for pushchairs and bikes. The next section along from Saughton to Murrayfield is not so pretty but picks up again once you cross the A8 at Roseburn.

Roseburn to Dean Path

Access the path from Roseburn Cliff where shallow steps lead to a concrete path right next to the riverside. It is easy to follow to Belford Bridge where you can leave the walkway and visit the Scottish Gallery of Modern Art – there are steps at the bridge so easier to leave by the back of the Belford Hotel. From Belford Bridge the Dean Bank footpath is surfaced and runs on the riverbank, a precarious few feet above the

water. Some sections have a handrail about 3ft high – useful for adults but small children can slip underneath quite easily. Easiest access is at the centre of Dean Village via Damside from the north or Hawthornbank Lane to the south (a few steps). There is an awkward, steep cobbled corner to negotiate – slippery if wet and liable to flooding after heavy rain.

Dean Path to Stockbridge

On a sunny day this is an attractive, scenic stroll. Accessible via Dean Path in Dean Village (follow the signs), this is a quick way to get to Stockbridge whilst taking in the beauty of the Water of Leith. Dean Bridge, for example, doesn't look more stunning than from the view you have when approaching it on Dean Path. The path itself is wide for pedestrian use so is ideal for pushchairs and prams. A lovely walk.

Dean Path takes you into Stockbridge, where there is good eating and shopping, among other more cultural attractions, i.e.: Stockbridge Library, Inverleith Park, the Botanic Garden. Public toilets on Hamilton Pl.

Stockbridge to Warriston

Steps down to the Deanhaugh Footpath from Deanhaugh St in Stockbridge. Easier access from Haugh St or Falshaw Bridge at the other end of the pathway. At Falshaw Bridge turn left, and immediately right onto Arboretum Ave. At the end of Arboretum Ave you reach the Rocheid Path with views across the river of the Colonies. Easiest exit from this path is via Inverleith Terr Lane onto Inverleith Row. If you cross the river the path becomes rather overgrown and there are steps up to Canonmills. At the time of writing, parts of the path are diverted due to engineering works as part of the flood defence scheme, but diversions are signposted.

Warriston to Leith

To continue to follow the river, take Warriston Rd and follow the riverbank at the bridge. It is possible to take a pushchair along this path, but hard pushing is sometimes required. An easier but less scenic route is to access the Warriston Cycleway from the corner of Canonmills and Broughton Rd. The two routes join at Connaught Pl where you can continue along the old railway line and rejoin the river after 500 metres. Or take the flight of steps up to Newhaven Rd, cross the road, turn right and walk towards town, and after 50m the walkway will take you across the river to Anderson Pl. Upon exiting at the road, turn left then right along West Bowling Green St and then rejoin the walkway where the sign indicates on the left side.

The scenery changes yet again as the now broad river enters the docks of Leith and you can treat yourselves to a well-earned cup of coffee. There are plenty of buses to various destinations from the bottom of Leith Walk.

FUN ON WATER

Inchcolm Island and Isle of May

There are two choices for exploring the Firth of Forth by boat. Both offer exciting opportunities for wildlife viewing, island walks and picnics. Familes are welcomed but children must be carefully supervised at all times. Duration of sailing and island stop-offs vary, phone for details.

Maid of the Forth, Inchcolm Island
0131 331 5000
www.maidoftheforth.co.uk
Sailings depart from Hawes Pier, South Queensferry, easily reached by car, train and bus.

Anstruther Pleasure Cruises, Isle of May
01333 311808
www.isleofmayferry.com
Sailings depart from Anstruther Harbour, Fife.

FUN ON WHEELS

Edinburgh Bus Tours

0131 220 0770
info@edinburghtour.com
www.edinburghtour.com
Buses are all painted in distinctive colours. The tours are: City Sightseeing Tour, The Edinburgh Tour and The Majestic Tour. Some buses are fully open-top, some part-covered. So depending on the weather and the friskiness of your under 5 you can choose to be inside or outside.

The Forth Bridges Cruise Bus and Boat Tour provides a bus link from the city centre to South Queensferry for a boat tour out on the Firth of Forth aboard the Forth Belle. See www.forthtours.com or their leaflet for details.

The city tours, all approx 1 hr, depart regularly from Waverley Bridge. Tickets are valid for 24 hrs and you can "hop on-hop off" at designated stops. While all tours are run by the same company at present, they offer slightly different experiences and take slightly different routes round the city. You can buy tickets from the tour bus drivers, Waverley Bridge ticket sellers, or from the Lothian Buses Travelshops at Waverley Bridge, Hanover St and Shandwick Pl. You can also buy tickets online.

Some tours have recorded guided tours (in up to 9 languages) and provide your own personal headphone set for your journey. Others have real-life guides providing commentary over loudspeaker. Tickets offer discounts on various other Edinburgh attractions. Ask the ticket seller or see their leaflets for details.

Trainspotting

There is a footbridge that connects West Princes St Gdns to the lower ramparts of Edinburgh Castle behind the Ross Bandstand. Its mostly transparent sides provide a perfect viewing point for the small train enthusiast. The bridge crosses the 4 main railway lines into and out of Edinburgh Waverley Station. The trains are of various types and run to numerous destinations both near and far. Drivers tend to be friendly and will usually blow their whistles and wave back to any children that are on the bridge.

A return ticket to North Queensferry on a nice day means a trip across the Forth Bridge – a very pleasant way to spend train time with an enthusiastic youngster.

Under Cover

Museums & Attractions
Swimming
Libraries
Soft Play

Under Cover

Sometimes the weather in our part of the world isn't all we'd wish for. Often this isn't a problem, but sometimes you just don't feel up to braving the elements. This chapter concentrates on those activities you can enjoy with your under 5 that are under cover, or where shelter is very near!

MUSEUMS & ATTRACTIONS

CENTRAL EDINBURGH

Camera Obscura and World of Illusions

Castlehill, The Royal Mile, EH1 2ND
0131 226 3709
info@camera-obscura.co.uk
www.camera-obscura.co.uk
This is the oldest purpose-built visitor attraction in Edinburgh. It is probably more suitable for older under 5s – we visited with our 3 yr old and 5 yr old and they loved it! The venue supports the "Kids in Museums" programme (www.kidsinmuseums.org.uk), so children are encouraged to make noise, touch interactive exhibits (with notices where touching isn't appropriate!), and use their imaginations throughout. Stools are provided so smaller children can reach exhibits, electrical outlets are covered, and there are nappy-changing facilities. The exhibits extend over several floors, with attractions such as a mirror maze and vortel tunnel (may be scary for younger children), photos of Edinburgh past, interactive optical illusions, holograms, heat camera, shadow wall, and a computerised "face transformer" that our children found hilarious. Well-stocked gift shop on site. Of course, there is the Camera Obscura itself on the top level, so try and choose a bright day to visit to get the best view of the city!

Opening hours: Apr-Jun 09.30-18.00, Jul-Aug 09.30-19.30, Sep-Oct 09.30-18.00, Nov-Mar 10.00-17.00. *Cost:* Adults £9.95, students/ seniors £7.95, children (5 + yrs) £6.95, under 5s

FREE. Pushchairs: No lifts. Pushchairs can be left near the front desk. Baby slings available. *Birthdays/celebrations:* Party room for 16, £24. Includes cooking facilities, fridge, freezer, crockery. Surprises include finding out that one of the bendy men on the viewcams is holding a sign wishing the person a happy birthday.

Museum of Childhood `FREE`

42 High Street, EH1 1TG
0131 529 4142
www.edinburghmuseums.org.uk/Venues/ Museum-of-Childhood.aspx
A chance for your little ones to see the toys you played with, and for them to spot Paddington, Rupert, and Winnie the Pooh. My 3 yr old loved the ride-on cars, and was desperate to take one home. Some parts are a little old and tired, but it is free admission and a great way to spend an hour. Great shop with lots of pocket money toys. Vast collection of trains, boats, planes, dolls, teddy bears and many more playthings of the past. Gallery 1 has a few coin operated working models. Gallery 2 has a rocking horse, hands-on puppets and trains for children to use. Gallery 3 has dolls and teddy bears with feely boxes, games, a dolls' house and activity sheets. Gallery 4 has board games, reading corner and Lego. Gallery 5 has period room sets with sound effects and a dressing-up box. Some of the displays are low level for small children. The museum is partly suitable for both pushchairs and wheelchairs, but there are many steps. There is a place to leave pushchairs on the ground floor (just past the

shop). Lift between Galleries 1, 2 and 3, ramps to Gallery 3.

Opening hours: *Mon-Sat 10.00-17.00, Sun 12.00-17.00.* **Accessibility and pushchairs:** *Partly accessible.* **Toilets:** *In Gallery 4 and basement.* **Nappy changing:** *In accessible toilet, in basement (by lift).*

National Museum of Scotland

Chambers Street, EH1 1JF
0300 123 6789
www.nms.ac.uk/scotland
You will not get a better trip out with your under 5s (or any age) than the newly refurbished National Museum of Scotland.

Sixteen amazing new galleries, loads of space, things to touch, buttons to press, even costumes to try on! Experience the world under one roof – meet a life-sized Tyrannosaurus Rex, pedal against the fastest animals in the world, see rocks that have fallen from outer space, and create your own piece of music with sounds from different countries. It would take a book in itself to mention all the fantastic things you can do, so I will go for the main crowd pleasers. (As suggested by my very enthusiastic family.)

The **Imagine Gallery** (level 1) gives families with young children a very special experience; allowing them to spend time together imagining and creating stories, pictures and 3D structures, inspired by real objects from around the world. There is a story corner where parents and children can relax as they read and listen to stories, myths and legends from around the world. Story bags containing replica objects, book boxes and simple jigsaws allow you to connect objects in the museum to the enchanting stories they bring to life. You can experiment with musical instruments and dress up. Make your own geometric jigsaw, play tunes on a dance mat, create your own teapot, or build a fantasy landscape using ideas from a 16th century Italian mosaic table design – and that's just one room! After leaving the Gallery,

check out the chiming millennium clock.

Adventure Planet (level 5) is based on nature and our planet. You will find a tree in the corner with some very interesting pull-out drawers, a sand box where you can excavate dinosaurs, lots of puzzles and a fantastic game where you camouflage your own fish so it's not eaten by a shark. There is the best dressing-up box – be a diver complete with aqua lung and flippers, a bee keeper and much more. I really did not think I was ever going to get my children to leave this room.

Other favourites were the **Connect Gallery** with Formula 1 car, Dolly the sheep, Rocket and Space Man. A big hit with my 4 yr old was the giant money box where you could watch your coins spin round to the bottom, well worth saving up loads of small coins to take with you. My personal favourite was the very impressive **Animal Room**. From an adult's point of view the building is magnificent and **Grand Hall** breathtaking.

There is an ongoing series of family events and activities. See website for details.

Opening hours: *10.00-17.00.* **Accessibility:** *Plenty of lifts, ramps and accessible toilets. You can arrange special tours with handling sessions for the visually impaired, or book a BSL interpreter in advance.* **Eating:** *Balcony Café, level 3. Museum Brasserie, entrance hall. Tower Restaurant, level 7. Plenty of packed lunch areas, level 2. Seated areas in grand galleries, outside the learning centre.*

The People's Story Museum

163 Canongate, Royal Mile, EH8 8EN
0131 529 4057
www.edinburghmuseums.org.uk/Venues/
The-People-s-Story.aspx
An interesting museum tracing the life and work of ordinary people from late 1700s to the present. Includes reconstructions of a fishwife, prisoners, servants, tea rooms, and a wash house. Some under 5s may find the mannequins

a little frightening. The visit is enhanced by photographs, sounds, and displays of everyday objects. A 22 min video complements the story. The video room is up a spiral staircase on the 2nd floor. Accessibility and pushchair access is limited – lift access to the 1st floor and stairs thereafter. Pushchairs may be left by the front desk. Some under 5s will be fascinated by the everyday objects of yesteryear.

Opening hours: Mon-Sat 10.00-17.00. During the Festival – Sun 12.00-17.00 too.

EAST EDINBURGH

Our Dynamic Earth

Holyrood Road, EH8 8AS
0131 550 7800
www.dynamicearth.co.uk
An interactive tourist attraction which tells the story of our earth and its elements. Not primarily designed for under 5s and you are more likely to take a young child when visiting with older children. Some little ones may be scared when it is dark with the flashes of light or in the volcano experience, however, many under 5s will love it. Expect to spend over an hour travelling through time. You can exit earlier – just ask a member of staff. You can meet a life size pterodactyl, feel volcanic tremors, experience a tropical rainstorm, and touch an iceberg. Everywhere is wheelchair and pushchair accessible with lifts where necessary. There is a shop which sells earth themed gifts including pocket money toys. The Ocean Commotion soft play area is through the gift shop and for children 1-10 yrs but is particularly great for under 5s, with climbing wall, ball pit and yellow submarine. Entry is free with an admission ticket. Great café (see p 175). A variety of events during the year, some suitable for under 5s, see website. Upon admission you could buy an Annual Explorer Pass for a few pounds more. Our family did, and we have found it a useful stop off near the Royal Mile for a quick snack and a play at Ocean Commotion.

Opening hours: Nov-Mar Wed-Sun 10.00-17.30. Apr-Oct Daily 10.00-17.30, Jul/Aug 10.00-18.00. Last entry 1 hr 30 mins before closing. Cost: Adult £10.80, child 4+ £7.20, under 3 FREE. Concessions £9.50. Annual Explorer Pass – adult £14.50, child (4+) £10.00. Ocean Commotion soft play £2. Free with an admission ticket. Parking: Paid. Eating: Food Chain Café (see p 175). Birthdays/celebrations: From 4 yrs. Different packages available.

The Scottish Parliament

Holyrood Road, EH99 1SP
sp.bookings@scottishparliament.uk
creche@scottish.parliament.uk (to book a crèche place)
www.scottish.parliament.uk
The controversial Scottish Parliament building (controversial because of its eventual cost!) is well worth a visit but is perhaps not the most stimulating environment for under 5s. There are quizzes which are designed to keep older children entertained as they make their way around the building, but nothing specifically aimed at under 5s. You can book guided tours and tickets to see parliamentary debates or for the First Minister's question time or wander round and look at the various exhibitions on display. There is an excellent FREE crèche, available to visitors while they are in the building, staffed by a local nursery. It seems well run with lots of activities for all ages and friendly and helpful staff. Open 08.00-18.00, Mon-Fri for up to 4 hrs at a time. You can book a place or use it on a drop-in basis (subject to availability). There is a café open Mon-Sat serving drinks and snacks at reasonable prices and a shop selling traditional Scottish gifts (whisky, shortbread, tartan etc).

Opening hours: Depends on the time of year. Mon-Sat 10.00-16.00 is the shortest opening.

EAST LOTHIAN

Museum of Flight

East Lothian, EH39 5LF
0300 123 6789
info@nms.ac.uk
www.nms.ac.uk/flight
The airfield is big, so limit your visit to a few buildings. Do try the interactive building (Fantastic Flight) exploring how flight works, and what skills pilots need. For a "whole family" experience you can all join in on the steering for the simulation of piloting an airship to land.

Concorde, the big attraction, is narrow inside. Keep moving through, but don't miss a look in the cockpit before exiting. The BOAC plane (in the same hangar) is wider to walk in, has things to touch, and allows you to "try out" seats on a plane. The Concorde hangar also included a flight-related board game, pens and crayons, plus instructions on how to make paper planes and quizzes. There is a play area close to the ticket office/Concorde. Lots of space for kids to run around in, a relaxed atmosphere, and friendly staff. My son liked "everything!".

Aviator Café
0131 247 4464
Light, airy and decorated with a flight theme. Open to non-museum visitors. Food and drinks straightforward but tasty. Tea came in a comfortingly large tea pot and decent-sized mug. Cakes, traybakes, soup, sandwiches, baked potatoes, toasties, and hot meals including home-made chilli and stovies. Fruit available, juices, and water. Reasonable prices. Seats around 70. My son loved the doughnuts!

Opening hours: Apr-Oct 10.00-17.00 7 days/ week, Nov-Mar 10.00-16.00 open weekends only. Cost: Adult £9.50, conc £7.50, child £4. Under 5s FREE. Entry FREE for Museum of Scotland members. Parking: Car park 1 closest to ticket office and café; car park 2 in opposite direction but still not far. Parking spaces for disabled visitors next to main hangar. Accessibility: Wheelchair accessible, free wheelchair loan. Shuttle service to take visitors around the site. Some of the display aircraft are not wheelchair accessible, including Concorde. However, there are plenty at ground level. *Eating: Café, large picnic area with 16 tables. Birthdays/celebrations: Packages from £10/ head (or £12.50 with Concorde). Celebrations last up to 2½ hrs and are adapted to suit child's age. Food in the Aviator Café is included.*

Myreton Motor Museum

Aberlady, EH32 0PZ
07585 356931
www.myretonmotormuseum.co.uk
Take the A1 to Haddington then the A6137 towards Aberlady. An interesting collection of bicycles, cars, motorcycles and World War II military vehicles, among others. Also has displays of posters and toy cars and related memorabilia.

Opening hours: Apr-Oct 10.30-16.30 7 days/ week, Nov-Feb 11.00-15.00 open weekends only. Cost: Adult £7, conc £6, child £3.

Prestongrange Industrial Museum

Morrison's Haven, Prestonpans, EH32 9RY
0131 653 2904
www.prestongrange.org
Not much of this old industrial site is actually "under cover" but the visitors' centre offers shelter, refreshment and an indoor play area. A great venue for under 5s with an interest in trains or machines. There are lots of old train carriages and engines to climb over and the remains of old industrial buildings to explore. You can follow the old railway tracks into the forest and we were lucky enough to see two deer up close when we visited. If trains and machines are not your thing there is a lot of outdoor space to run around in, or you can enjoy the great children's play area in the

visitors' centre where there's a lovely selection of well-maintained toys – drawing, LEGO, train set, dressing up and pretend shop. There is a big box of outdoor toys on the grassy area outside the visitors' centre. It's a bit run-down in places, but still worth a visit, particularly because it's free. Suitable for 3+ yrs. "We loved seeing Rocky the Crane and being trains on the old railways," said James.

Opening hours: Site open all year. Visitors' centre – Apr-Oct 11.30-16.00. *Accessibility:* Main area accessible, but some smaller paths are not suitable for wheelchairs. *Eating:* Tea, coffee, juice, crisps and sweets in visitors' centre.

MIDLOTHIAN

Butterfly and Insect World

at Dobbies Garden World, Melville Nursery Lasswade, Midlothian, EH18 1AZ
0131 663 4932
info@edinburgh-butterfly-world.co.uk
www.edinburgh-butterfly-world.co.uk
An attraction for older, bug-mad under 5s who would enjoy the proximity of flapping butterflies and the presence of animals that some younger/more timid children might find scary (eg snakes and spiders). Handling sessions at 12.00 and 15.00. Pushchairs are welcome but it's not completely pushchair friendly everywhere. A massive benefit is the garden centre next door, complete with children's section, pet area (rabbits, budgies and mice) and a great family-friendly restaurant.

Opening hours: Summer – 09.30-17.30, Winter – 10.00-17.00. *Cost:* Adults £6.95, conc £5.95, children (3-15) £4.95, under 3s FREE. Families from £22.95. *Toilets:* To the right of Butterfly and Insect World. Larger toilets in Dobbies next door. *Nappy changing:* In Dobbies' toilets. *Eating:* In Dobbies. *Play areas:* Not in Butterfly and Insect World but a couple in the complex.

Scottish Mining Museum

Lady Victoria Colliery, Newtongrange EH22 4QN
0131 663 7519
www.scottishminingmuseum.com
A must for machine-mad kids of 3+. Wear a "magic helmet" while you walk round the old mine workings, see an old steam train, press lots of buttons to make the model steam engines work, look for the roaring dinosaur, experiment in the Operations Centre with cogs and pulleys, or play with the Thomas the Tank Engine toy railway. If it's dry, play with some traditional Victorian toys in the small outdoor play area. This excellent museum has lots to keep curious children entertained, even if some of the subject matter may be a bit beyond them. I wouldn't really recommend the "Big Stuff" big machines tour for under 5s, however. There is also a small gift shop. Look out for special kids' events during the school holidays.

Scottish Mining Museum Café
A lovely, bright, spacious café seating around 50. Basic meals with a good selection of

sandwiches and rolls, a small selection of warm snacks, home baking, all very reasonably priced. Children's lunchbox with healthy juices. Small table with colouring things and a few toys. Direct access to enclosed outdoor play area.

Opening hours: 10.00-17.00. Cost: Adults £7.50, children FREE, tickets valid for a year. Play area: Small outdoor play area, no extra charge.

FIFE

Deep Sea World

Battery Quarry, North Queensferry, KY11 1JR
01383 411880
www.deepseaworld.com
Situated underneath the Forth Rail Bridge, the aquarium offers you a glimpse of sealife and wildlife from the Amazon to Lake Malawi and our own coastline. The main attraction is the 112m long underwater tunnel where huge sharks and rays swim over your head. We went through it 4 times. There is a timetable at the entrance for shark feeding, seal feeding, animal handling and talks, so it's best to arrive early to plan your visit around these and make the most of the fairly expensive entry price. Check the website for theme days and discounts.

Deep Sea World Café
Bright and spacious, with a great view up to the Forth Rail Bridge. For children there are sandwich lunch boxes and the usual fish fingers, chicken nuggets and hot dogs with chips which are fairly expensive. We enjoyed our reasonably priced baked potatoes loaded with filling and were impressed with the cleanliness on a busy Saturday lunchtime.

Opening hours: 10.00-18.00. Last entry an hour before closing. See website for seasonal variations. Cost: Adult £12.50, child £8.25, family £40, concessions £10.50. Groovy grandparents (2 concessions, 2 children) £36, under 3s FREE. See web for theme days, offers and membership prices. Birthdays/ celebrations: Pirate, Princess, Shark or Under the Sea party themes. Adventure tour, host, meal box, favours, animal adoption certificate. Bottlewarming/Food heating: Self-service microwave. Breastfeeding: Bench in nappy changing room, or staff will show you to an alternative quiet area.

St Andrews Aquarium

The Scores, St Andrews, KY16 9AS
01334 474786
splishsplash@standrewsaquarium.co.uk
www.standrewsaquarium.co.uk
A good wet weather option in St Andrews. The fish tanks were impressive (full of Nemo fish dashing about) and easily accessible to a toddler. A shark is on display in one of the open tanks and there are tanks of starfish and lobsters. It may be that your little one finds the models of open mouthed sharks and octopuses more interesting than the real animals on show! The meerkats are a great attraction too. Feeding times and talks on seals and meerkats are advertised at the entrance. The centre fosters abandoned seals with the idea of returning them to the wild. There is always one resident seal. Nesting seagulls are not part of the official attraction but are visible from the vantage point of the centre. There's a gift shop.

The café has an amazing view of the sea. You can sit outside and have the famous local Janetta's ice cream. With a good kids' menu, the food is simple and reasonably priced.

Opening hours: 10.00-18.00 summer, earlier closing in winter. Shut Dec-Jan. *Cost:* £8 adult, £6 child (over 3); concessions available; family tickets – 2 adults and 2/3/4 children – £25/£29/£33. *Parking:* The Scores is FREE, seasonal pay and display – FREE in winter. *Accessibility:* External ramp access.

St Andrews Museum

Kinburn Park, Doubledykes Road,
St Andrews, KY16 9DP
01334 659380
fifemuseums@fife.gov.uk
A great place to go, rain or shine, for both culture and play. Right in the city centre with FREE parking in front of the building, set in a park with putting in the summer. There is a standing "A-Z" exhibition on the ground floor showcasing the ancient City of St Andrews, complete with dressing up for the under 5s (and over!) and a peephole to put your head under the executioner's axe. Accessed by both stairs and lift on the 2nd floor is a room for rotating exhibitions and – a big bonus – a whole activity room as a play area for kids. The activity room was very well set up on the theme of seas to go along with the exhibition of paintings next door. Activities included art and craft, music, dressing-up and reading. Kids' art work was being exhibited on the walls. The museum is fully accessible with an outside ramp (where staff will unlock the side door). There is a lift inside too. Nappy changing and feeding facilities in the ladies upstairs were pleasant and spacious with nice views! The café downstairs was quite good – cheap and healthy. It was a bit crowded when we went but you can book ahead via a Council service on 0845 155 5555, then dial 451095.

Opening hours: Apr-Sep 10.00-17.00, Oct-Mar 10.30-16.00. *Accessibility:* Outside ramp and inside lift. *Toilets:* Upstairs, accessible by lift.

SWIMMING POOLS & LEISURE CENTRES

Swimming

Most children love the sensation of being in water, although it may take them a couple of visits to get used to it. Learning to swim is not only good exercise but makes sense for safety. There is a wide availability of lessons and adult and baby sessions to help get children and parents into the swim of things.

TOP TIPS

- Remember to check the adult-to-child pool ratios as it varies between pools.
- Always stay near your child in the water.
- If your child is not keen on water at first, don't force the issue, try again in a few weeks' time. Pools can be noisy unfamiliar places, full of strange sensations.
- You should not take your child swimming if you or they have a stomach upset.
- Leave an hour after feeding before entering the pool.
- Small babies get cold quickly so keep pool time short, about 10 minutes to start with.

What to wear

Ordinary nappies are not suitable for use in a swimming pool. Use either disposable swim nappies or reusable lined swimming nappies. Disposable nappies can often be bought at the pool but if you go swimming a lot these can prove expensive. Reusable swimming nappies come in a variety of shapes and colours and can be an integral part of the suit.

You should also consider what you will change your child into. Something warm and easy to get on is best as children lose heat quickly out of the water. It is worth bringing a dressing gown or a poncho towel.

Swimming aids

There are many types. Inflatable ring seats are available for a range of ages and small babies often enjoy floating about in these. However, most of the baby is not in the water in these seats so they are best used where the air temperature is warm. Inflatable arm bands are available in a range of sizes, make sure you choose an appropriate size for the age and weight of your child. There are suits with floats built in or separate float vests worn over a swimsuit. Some pools will only allow you in with British Standard marked arm bands.

Zoodles, bendy foam tubes, can also be a fun option for toddlers who are water confident. Check your floats regularly to make sure they are still safe and in working order.

Many of these options can be bought at pools and floats or bands will be supplied during lessons and also at some fun sessions.

Remember these devices are not a substitute for adult supervision.

Early classes

Early classes aim to give babies water confidence and to give adults techniques to start children on the road to swimming. They get used to moving in the water as well as developing first skills such as reaching out in the water. A range of props such as small toys, watering cans and hoops are used to make sessions fun. Edinburgh Leisure offer these booked in advance or drop in. Pre-school classes are also available. See pages 275 to 279 for more on swimming lessons.

Edinburgh Leisure pools

www.edinburghleisure.co.uk
Check the website for pool opening times and locations. These can be found under pools with each individual pool usually having a "pool timetable at a glance" link.

The ratio for Edinburgh Leisure pools is 2 children under 4 yrs per adult, 1 adult per 4 children between 4 and 8 yrs.

There is FREE swimming for under 5s in all Edinburgh Leisure pools.

Private pools

There are various private pools in hotels and health clubs. Some of these host private lessons and health clubs sometimes have sessions where children are permitted in the pool with adult members.

Accessibility

Edinburgh Leisure pools should be FREE to carers. All pools and leisure centres should have facilities for disabled people. However, these can vary in quality, availability and cleanliness. It may be worth phoning in advance about what equipment is available and if it is in good working order. Most Edinburgh Leisure pools have poolside hoists although you may choose not to use these with smaller children. Other equipment that can be useful includes a height adjustable changing bed (some changing rooms also have pulleys) and a shower chair (some pools only have chairs that double as toilet chairs – with a large hole in the seat area). Most of this equipment is geared towards disabled adults – however, it is often suitable for children too. Find out if shower chairs can be taken to the poolside. If not, ask if you can take a wheelchair to the poolside.

Remember, in all Edinburgh Leisure pools, under 5s swim for FREE. There may be a small charge in non-Edinburgh Leisure pools.
Unless otherwise stated, the Edinburgh Leisure website and email address applies to the swimming facilities below:

www.edinburghleisure.co.uk
mail@edinburghleisure.co.uk

CENTRAL EDINBURGH

Glenogle Swim Centre

Glenogle Road, Stockbridge, EH3 5JB
Pay-and-display on-street parking close to both entrances on Glenogle Rd and Saxe Coburg Pl. Lift access available from the Glenogle Rd entrance.
This beautifully refurbished Victorian pool is a very popular and friendly place to visit. Adult and child sessions and children's lessons available. Changing cubicles are at poolside, one larger cubicle for family changing on left. Hairdryers available. Toilets are in the shower area and also upstairs.
The 23m pool has access steps at each corner. Water level is 30cm below poolside, but there is a bar all around to hold. Upstairs viewing gallery all the way around the pool with benches. Separate small seating area upstairs away from pool. Sauna and steam

room at far end of pool with seating area for relaxation.

Opening hours: Mon-Fri 07.00-22.00, Sat/ Sun 08.00-18.00. Check pool programme for availability.

NORTH EDINBURGH

Pool at Ainslie Park Leisure Centre

92 Pilton Drive, EH5 2HF
0131 551 2400
mail@edinburghleisure.co.uk
www.edinburghleisure.co.uk
A 23m pool with a small sauna. The corner cubicles upstairs are larger. There are playpens both upstairs and at the pool side, and nappy changing facilities. However, with small children it is better to use the downstairs changing as the steps down to the pool can be a bit slippery. There are showers both upstairs and at the poolside. It also has a small gym.
Range of swimming lessons including adult and child lessons and pre-school lessons. Check pool opening times (at the centre or online) as there is no public swimming during lessons.

Opening times: Mon-Fri 07.00-22.00, Sat 09.00-18.00, Sun 09.00-21.00. Parking: On-street parking with restrictions on weekdays, limited metered spaces within s4 permit area. Disabled spaces outside. Pushchairs: Can be parked at reception. Nappy changing: In family cubicles and in both male and female toilets on dry side. Eating: Café and vending machines.

Drumbrae Leisure Centre

30 Drumbrae Terrace, EH4 7SF
0131 312 7957
info.dlc@edinburghleisure.co.uk
Very friendly and welcoming leisure centre.

Facilities include a 25m pool (with fantastic view over the Firth to Fife), gym, multipurpose sports hall, fitness studio, football pitch and café. Range of swimming lessons (including adult and child and pre-school) and Gym Nippers. There is a "Family" pool session at weekends for those with additional needs or young families. Pool changing area is mixed with individual cubicles, including 4 family changing cubicles. Plenty of lockers. There is not always a barrier up between the changing rooms and pool so keep an eye on little ones. Pool has a moveable floor which can be altered to 1m depth.

*Opening hours: Mon-Fri 07.00-22.00, Sat 09.00-19.00, Sun 09.00-21.00. **Accessibility:** Changing facilities near poolside, accessed by a key from reception (deposit required). Spacious with lockers, adapted toilet and shower and a height-adjustable changing bed. Shower chair. Small seat with grab-rail in the communal shower area beside the pool. **Nappy changing:** Four family changing rooms with changing units. **Eating:** Café. Vending machine in reception area. **Birthdays/celebrations:** Some facilities may be available for hire – see Edinburgh Leisure website or call main reception.*

Leith Victoria Swim Centre

Junction Place, EH6 5JA
0131 555 4728
Victorian baths with 23m pool with poolside showers and changing cubicles. Family changing room in one corner with fold-down chair and nappy changing as well as separate male and female changing areas with showers. Disabled changing room and poolside lift. Small sauna at poolside. The centre also has an excellent gym, fitness studio classes and an RPM studio. Adult and baby swim, pre-school lessons and aquafit. Hairdryers in mirrored area between reception and pool. A striking balcony accommodates the spectating area.

*Opening hours: Mon-Fri 06.00-22.00, Sat 09.00-18.00, Sun 09.00-20.30. **Parking:** At Bonnington Rd entrance including disabled and*

*parent and child. **Eating:** Vending machines and part time café and snack area at reception.*

EAST EDINBURGH

Gracemount Leisure Centre

22 Gracemount Drive, EH16 6RN
0131 658 1940
Modern centre with 25m pool, sauna, gym, health and fitness studio and sports hall. Adult and baby sessions, adult and child sessions and children's swimming lessons. Various lessons and classes so public swimming times vary. Check with centre for exact details.

*Centre opening hours: Mon-Fri 06.30-22.00 Sat/Sun 09.00-19.00. **Eating:** Café and internet café. **Breastfeeding:** Private area available.*

Portobello Swim Centre

57 The Promenade, EH15 2BS
0131 669 6888
Lovely refurbished Victorian pool, in a very light and airy building, complete with Turkish baths and a gym/fitness studio. There are two pools; the main 25m pool increases in depth from 1m to 1.3m during public swimming hours (and up to 2m when needed), and is quite cool. The smaller pool is warmer and more suitable for young children. Popular café with great views (see p 175). Plenty of space in the changing rooms – the 3 family rooms have playpens and nappy changing areas. The centre runs a varied timetable of classes, including adult and baby sessions (4 mths +), adult and child sessions, and children's lessons. Staff are friendly.

Opening hours: Mon-Fri 06.00-22.00, Sat 09.00-16.45, Sun 09.00-20.45. Cost: Standard swim, no leisure card £4, under 5s FREE, Family Swim (2 adults, 2 under 5s) £5.70. Parking: On-street. Pushchairs: Secure parking at reception (deposit for lock). Nappy changing: Changing units in the 3 family changing rooms. Eating: Café on 1st floor (accessible by lift). Birthdays/celebrations: Small swimming pool can be hired for parties at weekends.

Royal Commonwealth Pool

Dalkeith Road, EH16 5BB
0131 667 7211
info.rcp@edinburghleisure.co.uk
www.thecommiepool.co.uk
The "Commie" was reopening as we went to press but it promised to offer the following for under 5s: 50m and 25m swimming pools, adult & baby (4 mths-2 yrs), adult & child (2-4 yrs) and pre-school (3½-5 yrs) classes, family swimming on Saturday and Sunday afternoons, a changing village with a family area, Clambers soft play (zoned according to age, with an underwater theme), party room and Refresh Café. If you want to be the first to review the new Commie for Edinburgh for Under Fives, get in touch!

Opening hours: Mon-Fri 05.30-22.00 (closed Wed 09.00-10.00), Sat 05.30-20.00, Sun 07.30-20.00. Soft play open 09.00-18.00.

SOUTH EDINBURGH

Warrender Swim Centre

Thirlestane Road, EH9 1AP
0131 447 0052
A quaint and lovely small pool (23m long, from 0.9m at shallow end to 1.8m at deep end), recently refurbished, very light and airy due to the glass roof. Showers and changing cubicles with family changing available in a separate room. Two further cubicles at the far end of the pool next to showers accessible from poolside. Nappy changing and playpen available as well as highchair style seats. Lockers in the family change area and at the far end of the pool. Good size sauna at poolside although the benches can be hazardously slippery. Good family fun session on Sunday morning with floats. The centre also has a good gym. Adult and baby swim, pre-school lessons and aquafit. Spectator balcony at shallow end with toddler books and toys. No lift access to balcony.

Centre opening hours: Mon-Fri 06.00-22.00, Sat 09.00-18.00, Sun 09.00-20.30. Pool timetable online. Parking: Limited on-street parking with restrictions on week days. Disabled parking outside pool. Accessibility: Ramp access from street with automatic doors, lift to get to pool level. Hoist. Disabled changing room next to the lift. No wheelchair access to spectators' gallery. Pushchairs: Small area to leave at reception. Eating: Vending machines, part time café and snack area at reception.

Dalry Swim Centre

Caledonian Crescent, EH11 2AL
0131 313 3964
An attractive refurbished Victorian swimming pool with sauna and gym, which is clean and well maintained. Check the pool programme timetable for public swimming times, as occasionally the pool is given over to lane swimming only, adults only or to swimming clubs. The centre offers sessions for adult and baby/child and children's lessons and has a programme of activities over the summer holidays. The main changing facilities are upstairs – the large corner cubicles are best – facilities are also available downstairs at pool level. Nappy changing facilities and playpens upstairs and at the poolside. Spectator seating at the poolside, accessed from reception.

Centre opening hours: Mon-Fri 07.00-22.00, Sat 09.00-18.00, Sun 09.00-21.00. Public swimming times vary – check pool timetable on website. *Cost:* Swimming FREE for under 5s, adult £4, family swim (2 adult 2 under 18) £10, family swim (2 adult 2 under 5) £5.70. *Parking:* On-street parking in zone S4 (pay and display) operates Mon-Fri. 2 disabled bays at the main entrance. *Pushchairs:* Good access and space at reception to park.

Kirkliston Leisure Centre

1 Kirklands Park Street, EH29 9ET
0131 333 4700
info.klc@edinburghleisure.co.uk
Facilities include gym, fitness classes, grass pitch, 2G/3G pitches, tennis court, activity rooms and a floodlit training facility.

Wester Hailes Swimming Pool

5 Murrayburn Drive, EH14 2SU
0131 442 2201
admin@whec.edin.sch.uk
www.whec.edin.sch.uk

An older style swimming pool which is really best for older under 5s and older children. There is a 25m free-form pool, a 1m toddler pool with a small slide and a 3.4m diving pool. It is difficult to find privacy in the main changing room where cubicles have low walls and no curtains. There is a separate changing area for parents with under 5s in both the male and female changing rooms and these have playpens, changing tables and high chairs. However at busy times these can fill up. Parents with small children can request access to the disabled changing rooms if unoccupied. Café upstairs with home baking.
Opening hours: Mon, Tues, Thurs, Fri 09.30-21.20. Wed 09.30-18.10 (ladies only 18.00-20.10), Sat 10.30-16.30, Sun 09.30-16.30.

Dunbar Leisure Pool

Castle Park, Dunbar, EH42 1EU
01368 865456
www.enjoyleisure.com
A great option for children of all ages. It has a beached area with water characters for younger children to play on as well as a bubble bed, a wave machine, water jets and a flume. The changing facilities are clean and the pool area is light and bright. The harbour nearby is perfect for exploring while visiting the centre.

Opening hours: Mon, Thurs, Fri and Sat 10.00-17.00, Tues 10.00-21.00, Wed 10.00-14.00, Sun 09.00-17.00. *Cost:* Adult £3.55, concession £2.30, under 5s 45p, family swim (up to 4 people, min 2 children) £9.75. *Eating:* Café sells soup and sandwiches, home baking, drinks and snacks.

Musselburgh Sports Centre

Newbigging, EH21 7AS
0131 653 6367
musselburghsports@enjoyleisure
www.enjoyleisure.com

A modern sports centre, offering a wide range of facilities, such as a pool, health suite and café. Children's swimming classes, including lessons for under 5s, are available – contact centre for details. Also offers children's gymnastics classes. Crèche and Jamboree soft play (see p 123). Good swimming facilities for disabled children, including changing bed, hoist, shower chairs and accessible toilet and shower area.

Opening times: Mon-Fri 07.00-21.30, Sat/Sun 09.00-16.30. Cost: Adult £3.30, concession £1.75, under 5s 45p, family swim (up to 4 people, min 2 children) £7.60.

Bonnyrigg Leisure Centre

King George V Park, Park Road, Bonnyrigg EH19 2AD
0131 663 7579
A modern centre with a leisure pool on two levels. In the lower lagoon there are slides and a small neuk with a bench, the upper lagoon is much shallower and has a small spa pool to one side. There is a flume slide which operates several times an hour and the whole pool can be booked for private parties. Adults may only supervise a maximum of two children under 8 in the pool. For under 5s the centre also offers a soft play room and a range of other activities including gymnastics, martial arts and mini kickers. Contact the centre for current details of activity classes and swimming lessons for under 5s. The centre offers soft play too. There is a playpark just outside the leisure centre, good for children of all ages.

Opening hours: 09.00-21.00, phone ahead to check pool availability before your visit.
Pushchairs: Access to pool is upstairs.
Birthdays/celebrations: Pool, soft play and sports hall can all be booked for private parties.

Loanhead Leisure Centre

George Avenue, Loanhead, EH20 9LA
0131 440 4516
loanhead.LC@midlothian.gov.uk
www.midlothian.gov.uk/info/532/sports_facilities/114/loanhead_leisure_centre
Changing facilities are mixed, with several family cubicles including nappy change table or highchair. The main pool has a small elephant slide which is perfect for under 5s. At set times at the weekend there are large inflatables in the pool which can be great fun for the older ones but leave space a bit limited for the little ones. The baby pool is warm and has a few toys and floats. When the crèche is "closed" it can be used for changing, breastfeeding, leaving pushchairs. Public playpark next to the Leisure Centre.

Opening hours: Mon-Thurs 09.00-22.00, Fri/Sat 09:00-20.00, Sun 09.00-21.00. Crèche Mon-Fri 09.30 or 10.30 for 1 hr. Cost: Adult swim £3.45, children 3+ yrs £1.80, up to age 3 FREE, crèche £1.55. Nappy changing: In swimming pool changing rooms or crèche when not in use. Birthdays/celebrations: You can hire the hall for a Bouncy Fun party for £53.85.

The Penicuik Centre

Carlops Road, Penicuik, EH26 9EP
01968 664066
penicuik.lc@midlothian.gov.uk
www.midlothian.gov.uk
It was wonderful to enter such a spacious and thought-out building – light, airy and great to be able to peek into the swimming pool (this cheered up our two children after our car journey). The library is superb – separated-out children's books into ages, little cosy corners, colouring in tables and Book Bug sessions. I would visit the library as a specific trip. The leisure centre has fantastic classes – for example gym teds (age 3-5) and flex dancing (age 3). Nappy changing facilities were the best I have ever seen with super fold-in doors for our pushchairs. There is a great park directly across

the road through the playing fields and we went to the fantastic Penicuik Arts Centre for lunch. See www.penicuikarts.org.

Opening hours: Mon/Wed 09.00-22.00, Tues/ Thurs 07.00-22.00, Fri-Sun 09.00-20.00. Library (within the centre) Mon/Thurs 09.30-20.15, Tues 13.00-20.15, Wed 09.30-13.00, Fri-Sat 09.30-17.00, Sun 13.00-17.00.

WEST LOTHIAN

Xcite Leisure Pool Livingston

Almondvale Boulevard, EH54 6QT
01506 777870
www.westlothianleisure.com
Formerly Bubbles, this pool is divided into several areas: main pool, teaching pool, toddlers' area and flumes. The water is warm although once you are out the air can be cold. Toddler area has a small slide and a few water features but is shallow so can be a bit cold. The main pool starts off shallow with steps and the depth gradually increases to 1m, ideal for young kids. Under 4s must either wear British Standard flotation device or be accompanied on a 1:1 ratio by an adult. There are two flumes, light and dark. Under 5s are allowed to ride with an adult. They are not open all the time so check with the centre as if your kids are adventurous, this is the best bit. The pool is very quiet during the week until schools are out. The changing area is mixed open plan at the poolside. There are several nappy changing rooms and also several play pens. Very good provision for accessibility. Disabled parking, disabled changing room with shower. Pulley and large changing table in the changing room. Several shower chairs at the poolside which can be lowered into the pool using the hoist. Stretcher board. Unlike Edinburgh Pools swimming for under 5s is not free so it can be a bit pricey. My kids said "We loved the tunnels best".

Opening hours: Mon-Fri 09.30-20.00, Sat/Sun 10.00-17.00. Cost: Adult £4, children £2.50, *family swim £12, various memberships available. Eating: Café.*

Libraries •FREE

0131 200 2000
eclis@edinburgh.gov.uk
www.edinburgh.gov.uk/libraries
Libraries welcome under 5s! In fact, libraries welcome everyone! There's lots for you and your child to enjoy at the library: a huge selection of books, books and music on CD, toys, games, magazines, comics, computers with the internet as well as organised activities and events.

How to join

It's free to join at any age. Just fill out a membership form for your child and they will be given their own library card on which they can borrow 12 items for up to 3 weeks. A welcome letter is sent describing the library service and asking carers to confirm the date of birth of under 16s.

It's also easy to join as an adult. Just go along to any library, give a few details: name, title, date of birth, address, phone number – and that's it! If you would like to borrow audiobooks, CDs or DVDs you will need to provide one proof of name and address, for example a recent utility bill. You can also join online by going to the "How to Join" section at www.edinburgh.gov.uk/libraries and using the membership application form. Your library card will be sent to you by post.

Parents/carers are responsible for books borrowed on their child's card, and for returning them on time. There are no fines on overdue books borrowed on children's cards and it is free to reserve books. There are no charges for damage to board and picture books. Items borrowed can be returned to any Edinburgh City library.

Books – and much more!

All libraries have designated children's areas. They all have kinderboxes with a great range of interactive fun board books, picture books and story books for babies and toddlers. There is also a wide selection of books on CD, cartoons, poetry books, books for beginner readers, books on sensitive topics, chapter books, stories for older children, information books and reference books which are great for homework. Through your library you have access to dual language picture books and books in large print. In all libraries children's books are arranged by subject, interest and reading level. Shelves are clearly marked and there is a leaflet available explaining the system. Staff are on hand to help.

Storytime and Bookbug Rhymetime sessions

Every library in Edinburgh runs Bookbug Rhymetime sessions and many run storytimes for under 5s. Bookbug Rhymetime sessions, aimed at 0-3 yrs and their parents/ carers, incorporate action songs and rhymes, listening to stories and looking at books. They're great fun and they're free! Find out more at: **www.edinburgh.gov.uk/info/469/ libraries_for_children_and_babies**.

Babies can also take part in Bookbug's Library Challenge. A sticker will be added to the Bookbug collector card at every visit, with children collecting a certificate after 4 visits.

Catch the reading bug!

Bookbug

Bookbug

Bookbug works with health visitors and Early Years Services to put books into the hands of babies and their families across the city. Free Bookbug packs are gifted to children at 6 wks, from 13 mths and through nursery at 3 yrs.

Bookbug in Edinburgh works closely with:
Craigmillar Books for Babies
Castlebrae Community High School
2A Greendykes Road
EH16 4DP
0131 621 2621
info@craigmillarbooksforbabies.org.uk
www.craigmillarbooksforbabies.org.uk

Children's Multilingual Picture Book Collections

Dual-language picture books are available in Arabic, Bengali, Chinese, Farsi, French, German, Gujarati, Hindi, Italian, Japanese, Polish, Portuguese, Punjabi, Spanish, Turkish and Urdu. Single language books are available in Arabic, Bengali, Chinese, French, Gaelic, Japanese, Polish and Urdu. The Ethnic Services Library at McDonald Road Library has extensive collections. Smaller collections are available at some community libraries. There are also bilingual rhymetimes running in the city.

Computers and the internet

All libraries have computers with free internet access and word processing and you can call in advance to book time on them. There are PCs dedicated for children's use in all libraries. Most libraries have PS2s and a selection of games for children to use.

Local information

Library notice boards can be a great source of both local and general information and are well worth keeping an eye on. Some libraries keep a diary of forthcoming local events or folders with local information.

Access and toilets

Standards of access vary; new and refurbished libraries usually have good all-round facilities. Every library, apart from the Music Library and Fine Art Library, has wheelchair access, but not all libraries have accessible toilets and a few – notably the Central Children's Library – do not have public toilet facilities at all. The library staff will allow use of staff toilets if possible. Many have nappy changing facilities.

Opening hours

Full-time libraries
Central, Blackhall, Corstorphine, Leith, Morningside, Piershill
Mon-Thurs 10.00-20.00, Fri 10.00-17.00, Sat 09.00-13.00.

Full-time libraries open all day Saturday and on Sunday afternoons
Muirhouse, Newington, Oxgangs, Portobello, Wester Hailes
Mon-Thurs 10.00-20.00, Fri 10.00-17.00, Sat 09.00-17.00, Sun 13.00-17.00.

Part-time libraries
Balerno, Balgreen, Central Children's, Colinton, Craigmillar, Currie, Fountainbridge, Gilmerton, Granton, Kirkliston, McDonald Road (also opens all day Saturday and on Sunday afternoons), Moredun, Ratho, Sighthill, South Queensferry, Stockbridge
Mon, Wed 13.00-20.00, Tue, Thurs, Fri 10.00-17.00, Sat 09.00-13.00.

Mobile Library Service

Edinburgh City Libraries - direct services
343 Oxgangs Road, EH13 9LY
0131 529 5683
access.services@edinburgh.gov.uk
The Mobile Library Service visits about 60 locations in the Edinburgh area ranging from small villages such as Dalmeny, to large urban locations such as Wester Hailes. Other stops include East Craigs, Inch, Barnton, Juniper Green, Buckstone, Cramond, Clermiston, Prestonfield, Liberton and Gracemount. For a full range of stops contact the Mobile Library Service. A wide variety of books are available, including an ever-changing selection of children's books. All mobiles have stairlifts for easier access.

The Book Bus is a mobile library service especially for children and young people. It visits primary schools, nurseries and children's and family centres across Edinburgh.

Listening Books

www.listening-books.org.uk
Listening Books is a charity that provides a postal audio book library service to anyone with an illness or disability that makes it impossible or difficult to hold a book, turn its pages, or read in the usual way. It provides audio books for both leisure and learning – providing important support for the National Curriculum at Key Stages 2, 3, 4 and A Level, as well as a large adult library. The service caters for those with physical disabilities, visual impairment and specific learning difficulties, including dyslexia, for which reading print is frustrating, even impossible. Their catalogues include many titles for children of primary 1 age that might be suitable for slightly younger children.

Details of Edinburgh's libraries are below. You can search for individual libraries' websites at www.edinburgh.gov.uk/directory/12/libraries.

CENTRAL EDINBURGH

Central Children's Library

7-9 George IV Bridge, EH1 1EG
0131 242 8027
Situated next door to the Central Library. Level access. Compact library. If your child needs the toilet you have to leave the building and use the facilities next door in the Central Library.

Edinburgh Central Library

7-9 George IV Bridge, EH1 1EG
0131 242 8000
Comprehensive public reference and information services, major collections of local history material, a large stock of adult fiction and non-fiction, and the largest local collection of books about children, e.g. parenting, play, education etc. Books for young children are available to borrow from kinderboxes in the general lending department. Extensive music, fine art and Scottish collections. Kurzweil reading machine, media aids and PC access software for people with disabilities available in the Resource Centre (0131 242 8136).

Toilets: In basement, access by lift with stairs to negotiate.

Stockbridge Library

11 Hamilton Place, EH3 5BA
0131 529 5665
Stockbridge.library@edinburgh.gov.uk
Local library with main reading area and separate computer suite and meeting rooms. Friendly, helpful staff are welcoming and tolerant of children. Spacious children's area has cushions, low tables and chairs, games, and a separate box of card and pop-up books for very small children – a great place for a quiet half hour, especially on rainy days. The library runs Bookbug Rhymetimes for 0-4 yrs and their parents/carers every Tues at 10.30.

NORTH EDINBURGH

Blackhall Library

56 Hillhouse Road, EH4 5EG
0131 529 5595
blackhall.library@edinburgh.gov.uk

A lovely cosy family library and hub of the local community, which is fairly spacious inside and has a large "Family Collection" of books. Lots of events on throughout the year such as meet the author and other themed events mostly aimed at older children. Bookbug Rhymetimes for 0-4 yrs (and parents/carers) is every Fri 10.30-11.00. There are many useful facilities such as free internet, a learning centre with 8 PCs, Playstation, fax and photocopier and an out-of-hours book return letterbox. Access by ramp at the front from the private car park.

Granton Library

Wardieburn Terrace, EH5 1DD
0131 529 5630
granton.library@edinburgh.gov.uk
Located in a residential area close to Granton Primary School. Library doesn't look the best from the outside but inside has a good selection of books, audio tapes/books, DVDs, magazines and papers. There is free PC/internet access at several computers. Friendly and helpful staff. On-street FREE parking. Bookbug storytelling sessions with snacks for children and adults afterwards – well-run interactive session with traditional and new nursery rhymes aimed at 0-4 yrs, Thurs 11.00-12.00.

Muirhouse Library

15 Pennywell Court, EH4 4TZ
0131 529 5528
muirhouse.library@edinburgh.gov.uk
FREE on-site parking, friendly staff and a good selection of children's books, CDs, and DVDs. Dedicated "Children's Zone" with small table and chairs, soft seating, and other toys to help keep children occupied. The Bookbug programme runs weekly sessions. Songs are led by Bookbug or library staff for the first half hr, then coffee/tea is available for parents/carer, while children can play or take part in colouring

or another activity. The North Edinburgh Arts Centre is located just behind the library, with a café (limited opening days/hrs) if you are looking for lunch or a snack after your visit. Community room, computers, learning centre, photocopier and fax all available.

Toilets/nappy changing: Male/female toilets and nappy changing facilities onsite. At times, tissue and running water/soap are not available, so it's a good idea to have some wipes/hand gel packed in your bag.

Leith Library

28-30 Ferry Road, EH6 4AE
0131 529 5517
leith.library@edinburgh.gov.uk
An open, airy library with a lovely children's section and under 3s play area. My son and I lounged on the sofa and giant soft toys and flicked through some books while my daughter made a soup at the cooker, drove the play car and had a ride on a rocking cow! The children's area also has dual language books, a computer, a TV and games console, sensory bubble light and children's tables and chairs. They offer Bookbug Rhymetime once a week, Friday Craft Club, and under 5s storytime one Sat a month.

McDonald Road Library

2 McDonald Road, EH7 4LU
0131 529 5636
mcdonaldroad.library@edinburgh.gov.uk
There is a nice-sized children's area with only one entrance, which makes it easier to look after little ones. The staff are very welcoming of small children, and very tolerant of their occasional rambunctiousness. They've never seemed to mind the occasional toddler snack or drink in the children's area, and breastfeeding mothers may ask for a quiet, private area. I never feel self-conscious about bringing in my toddler, and

both my children have enjoyed crafts and other activities at the library. They hold children's craft sessions Fri 15.00-16.00 as well as Bookbug sessions and a summer reading scheme.

South Queensferry Library

9 Shore Road, EH30 9RD
0131 529 5576
southqueensferry.library@edinburgh.gov.uk
Excellent selection of books for under 5s. Play area with toys and games, and lots of seating for children. Staff very friendly and welcoming. Plans to use garden area. Bookbug and Storytime sessions.

EAST EDINBURGH

Craigmillar Library

7 Niddrie Marischal Gardens, EH16 4LX
0131 529 5597
craigmillar.library@edinburgh.gov.uk
Very welcoming with an enclosed picket fenced area especially suited to the under 3s. This brightly coloured area has "grass" flooring, cushions, bean bags, soft toys and child-sized furniture. Children can choose their books from the well-stocked child-height boxes. There is a Bookbug session for babies to 4 yrs.

Gilmerton Library

13 Newtoft Street, EH17 8RG
0131 529 5628
gilmerton.library@edinburgh.gov.uk
The children's area caters for a range of ages. Alongside this area there is also a small selection of toys. Free storytelling/singing session for pre-schoolers on the 1st Fri morning of the month.

Moredun Library

92 Moredun Park Road, EH17 7HL
0131 529 5652
moredun.library@edinburgh.gov.uk
Ramp access, photocopier and consoles. There is a children's corner in the library with books for babies and under 5s. Bookbug Rhymetime sessions every fortnight on Thurs from 13.30-14.00 with snacks for children and adults.

Piershill Library

30 Piersfield Terrace, EH8 7BQ
0131 529 5685
piershill.library@edinburgh.gov.uk
This library has a lovely spacious children's area with a good selection of books and toys. Plenty of space to play or sit on the seats or bean bags and share a story. There are weekly rhymetime sessions on Wed afternoons, storytime on Fri mornings, book clubs for older kids and extra events during school holidays.

Portobello Library

14 Rosefield Avenue, EH15 1AU
0131 529 5558
portobello.library@edinburgh.gov.uk
Portobello Library was recently refurbished and is now an excellent place to take young children. They have a great "Cuddle Book Corner" with bright kiddy-sized furniture, toys to play with and a wide selection of books for babies and toddlers. A café area with hot drinks machine has also been added, and there is an IT area with 4 computers, photocopier and fax machine. There are 2 Rhymetime sessions on Wed mornings, and further sessions on Sat and Sun – phone or check the website for details.

SOUTH EDINBURGH

Morningside Library

184 Morningside Road, EH10 4PU
0131 529 5654
morningside.library@edinburgh.gov.uk
Recently refurbished in 2011. Great selection of books, story CDs and tapes, colour-ins and toys to play with during the visit. PS2, PCs, photocopier and fax. Storytime and Bookbug sessions held for the under 5s. Café area with hot drinks machine.

Newington Library

17-21 Fountainhall Road, Midlothian, EH9 2LN
0131 529 5536
newington.library@edinburgh.gov.uk
There was a good choice of books for all ages and the seating was nicely arranged so it was easy and comfortable to read to my 2 yr old. The signage and layout was easy to follow and although I didn't need to ask for help, there were plenty of staff around. The library is down a residential road about 5 mins from the nearest bus stop, a nice area to walk to. Rhymetime for 0-3 yr olds Wed 11.00-11.30 and 13.45-14.15. Free internet.

WEST EDINBURGH

Balerno Library

1 Main Street, Balerno, EH14 7EQ
0131 529 5500
balerno.library@edinburgh.gov.uk
Balerno Library is quite small for an Edinburgh library. It is attached to part of the local primary school. It has a limited selection of books for

younger children and no play area. Although it is perhaps not an ideal place to take younger children, it could be very useful for people who live in Balerno who make use of Edinburgh Council's book reservation service to choose books for children via the internet to collect from the library. In this way it is a valuable part of Balerno's facilities for children. Rhymetime is fortnightly on Fri at 10.30.

Balgreen Library

173 Balgreen Road, EH11 3AT
0131 529 5585
balgreen.library@edinburgh.gov.uk
Small, friendly library situated beside Balgreen Primary, opposite Saughton Park. Two low bookholders and table with crayons/colouring for small children. Monthly Bookbug Rhymetime sessions 1st Thurs each month. Books on shelves, small selection of audio books, PS2 for older children. Photocopier, fax, internet access. Unfortunately no toilets or nappy changing facilities, toilets at nearby Saughton Park. Pushchair friendly but very small library, would be struggling with double pushchair.

Colinton Library

14 Thorburn Road, Colinton, EH13 0BQ
0131 529 5603
colinton.library@edinburgh.gov.uk
This is a well established and well-stocked library for children of all ages. Bookbug and Rhymetime sessions run on alternate Tuesdays (14.15-14.45) and Thursdays (10.15-10.45). Call for confirmation of dates and times.

Corstorphine Village Library

12 Kirk Loan, EH12 7HD
0131 529 5506
corstorphine.library@edinburgh.gov.uk
A great place to call in on a rainy afternoon! The children's section is roomy and includes a selection of toys, and a great supply of pictures to colour in. 3-yr-old Ruth loves making Mummy cups of tea in the toy kitchen while Mummy finds some books to take home! Rhymetime for 0-4 yr olds and their carers is held every 2nd Thurs 10.30-11.00 and 14.00-14.30. Bookgroups on the 3rd Wed of the month (18.45-19.45) and Thurs mid-month (19.00-20.00). Photocopier, fax and PS2, internet access.

Currie Library

210 Lanark Road West, EH14 5NX
0131 529 5609
currie.library@edinburgh.gov.uk
A really welcoming library with a friendly atmosphere. Children's area well-laid out and a very good variety of books. Lots of toys to play with, including farm, truck and dominoes and games for the older ones. Small table and chairs with coloured pens, plenty of seating for reading. My children spent a happy hour here and we went home with 15 books. Bookbug Rhymetime every 2nd Fri at 10.30, alternating with Balerno library. Mother and baby group, please phone for details.

Fountainbridge Library

137 Dundee Street, EH11 1BG
0131 529 5616
fountainbridge.library@edinburgh.gov.uk
Murdoch Terr has ramp access. PS2. Community Room available. Photocopier and fax.

Kirkliston Library

16 Station Road, Kirkliston, EH29 9BE
0131 529 5510
kirkliston.library@edinburgh.gov.uk
A well-stocked library with an appealing children's section with an extensive selection of books for under 5s. Good selection of toys for pre-school children (in fact our 2 yr old was so taken with the toy Dyson it was virtually impossible to interest her in the books!). A computer with children's games is available and there is also a "teen zone" for young people, complete with gaming consoles and DVDs. Bookbug sessions take place on the 1st Tues of the month (except school holidays) 13.45-14.15 and 3rd Fri of the month 10.30-11.00.

Oxgangs Library

343 Oxgangs Road North, EH13 9LY
0131 538 0168
oxgangs.library@edinburgh.gov.uk
A warm, bright and clean library with a huge range of books for children of all ages and a programme of book events for under 5s (Bookbugs, Rhymetimes and Share-a-story). These excellent events are free and are split into 3 age groups, one for babies up to 18 mths, one for toddlers from 18 mths to 3 yrs and one for children aged 2-5 yrs. Visitors should contact the library for the dates of the next relevant session. There are also events for older children (Tiger Tales for ages 4-8 and Chatterbooks for ages 8-11). There is a craft event every Fri from 14.20-15.30 for children of all ages and larger craft events are held throughout the year at Easter, Halloween and Christmas.

Breastfeeding: *Breastfeeding café every Wed, 13.30-14.30.*

Ratho Library

6 School Wynd, Ratho, EH28 8TT
0131 333 5297
ratho.library@edinburgh.gov.uk
The library is best found from the Dalmeny Rd off the A71. There are Bookbug sessions on a Thurs and some Saturdays. Books not as well laid out as some libraries but a great range for a small village like Ratho. Small toy box and designated child section. Toys needed some sorting out. Computers and a photocopier. The picnic tables on their website were not available when we visited!

Sighthill Library

55 Sighthill Road, EH11 4PB
0131 529 5566
sighthill.library@edinburgh.gov.uk
Parent's collection of books, leaflets and magazines. Photocopier and fax. Two PS2s. Learning Centre. Bookbug Sighthill project based at the library running Bookbug sessions and other events for children aged 0-3 and their parents and carers.

Wester Hailes Library

1 West Side Plaza, EH14 2ST
0131 529 5667
westerhailes.library@edinburgh.gov.uk
Access with double pushchair. Community room available on first floor (lift access). Youth Library and Learning Centre. Photocopier and fax. Bookbug Wester Hailes based at the library running Bookbug sessions and other events for children 0-3 and their parents/carers.

TOY LIBRARIES

As their name suggests, toy libraries are centres which lend toys to families, carers, and also to children with special needs. Most of them are run as drop-in centres, and guidance can be given on the toys best suited to your child.

There is generally a small joining fee, and, depending on the centre, toys can be borrowed for little or no charge. It is wise to check with each individual project.

Opening times tend to mirror school terms, but some do stay open during the holidays. The main contact is:

Smart Play Network/National Association of Toy and Leisure Libraries
0131 664 2746
www.smartplaynetwork.org

Contact your local centre for details of opening times. Services are inclusive of everyone – professionals, children and parents/carers.

Casselbank Kids Toy Library

South Leith Baptist Church,
5A Casselbank Street, EH6 5HA
07954 206908
casselbankkids@aol.com
www.southleithbaptistchurch.com
We couldn't say it better than Jacob's mum: "I have been coming to the toy library for the past 2 years, and my son and I love it. There is a huge variety of toys for all ages and lots of yummy food and juice! I have met lots of people and made new friends, as has my son. The highlight for us though is the singing time – which all the children and mums enjoy! Thursday is the highlight of our week!" Jacob, aged 3, says "I love all the toys". Parking available at the large Tesco nearby.

Opening hours: Thurs 09.30-12.00. **Cost:** *Membership £3/yr, 20p-60p/toy.* **Eating:** *Café open in church from 11.30-14.00.*

Gorgie Dalry Toy Library

St Martin's Church, 232 Dalry Road, EH11 2JG
0131 466 6178
www.gdtoylibrary.org.uk

Newington Community Toy Library

Kings Hall, 41a South Clerk Street, EH8 9NZ
07947 589194
newingtoncommunitytoylibrary@gmail.com

Oxgangs Toy Library

0131 441 7318
Currently this toy library doesn't have a venue but the toys are still available and parents/carers should call to arrange a loan.

Play Plus Toy Library

Inch Community Centre
225 Gilmerton Road, EH16 5UF
0131 664 4710

Portobello Toy Box Library

14 Rosefield Avenue, Portobello, EH15 1AU
0131 529 5558
portobello.library@edinburgh.gov.uk
www.edinburgh.gov.uk/directory_record/5073/portobello_library
On 1st floor, accessible by lift. A reasonable selection of toys, most suited to babies/toddlers. Children can play with the toys and then take some away for up to 4 weeks. Membership costs £5/child/year although this is under review with the objective of widening access to disadvantaged families. The service is staffed by volunteers and I was given a warm and friendly welcome. Toys are purchased and donated for use. The team are currently seeking additional funding to purchase more toys, in particular for children with special needs, and storage boxes.

Opening hours: Mon 10.00-11.30 term time only. Opening times under review and likely to be extended to cover school holiday periods too. **Toilets:** Spacious toilet on 1st floor. Key access, key provided at main library reception desk. **Eating:** Coffee, tea, biscuits and children's snacks provided by volunteers (small discretionary donation). Café area with hot drinks machine within the main library area.

P ⬥ ⬥ WC ⬥ ⬥

SPECIAL NEEDS TOY LIBRARIES

Barrie House Toy Library

Barrie House, Canaan Lane, EH10 4FG
0131 446 3120
A division of the Royal Blind School and primarily intended for parents of children who attend the playgroup there, but welcomes other enquirers on behalf of children with visual impairment.

SPLAT Toy Library

Keycomm Resource Centre
1c Pennywell Road, EH4 4PH
0131 311 7130
For children from Edinburgh with special needs. Will also adapt families' toys. Best to phone before visiting to check staff are available.

SOFT PLAY

Soft play is a great way for youngsters to burn off energy when it is too wet or cold for the park. It can be a great social activity too. Soft play centres vary in terms of size and availability of areas for younger children – where some may have great facilities for older siblings, under 3s may be confined to a ball-pit, ideal if they're happy with that, not so good if they're not. It might be wise to avoid planning your first visit to a soft play centre during school holidays or half-days, as they can become extremely busy and the noise and general good-natured mayhem might overawe a young first-timer.

NORTH EDINBURGH

Clown Around

Unit 2 & 3, 109 Restalrig Road, EH6 7NY
0131 553 7676
www.clownaround.me.uk
Clown Around feels more "home grown" than many soft plays. It offers large and small soft play areas, trampoline area and sensory room. There is a small soft play area for under 3s, at the far end of the venue from the entrance, which has its own door to keep children secure inside. Parents accompany children in this area. The larger soft play for over 3s takes up most of the venue space. It is easy to see your child, including from the café. There are some fun touches, such as a bubble machine. The venue also plays child-friendly music, but at a medium/low volume, so it's not intrusive for adults chatting, nor too loud for little ears!

Café has a wide range of hot and cold meals and drinks. Prices are on the cheaper side – £1 for a cup of tea. There are a lot of child-friendly hot food options, plus a healthy lunchbox-style meal.

Staff are friendly. My son thought that under 5s would love the trampolines, and also the swinging rings in the larger soft play section.

Opening hours: 10.00-17.45 (last entry 16.45). Sometimes closes from 16.00 for private parties. *Cost:* Varies by age and length of visit – we paid £3/hr for an older nursery child. Popular session from 10.00-11.00 for pre-schoolers is £1.50, 10.00-12.00 is £2.50. Runs Mon-Fri, term time only. *Birthdays/celebrations:* Large dedicated party room with seating for up to 40 children with a variety of party food. Clown Around do party bags, hats and balloons too. Usual package 1 hr on softplay followed by 45 mins in party room. You can book Clown Around for exclusive use, minimum 15 children, from £10/child.

Molly's Play Centre

Top Floor, Ocean Terminal, Leith, EH6 6JJ
0131 554 0102
info@mollysplaycentre.net
www.mollysplaycentre.net
Large play structure with slides, a corkscrew slide, tunnels, climbing areas and a soft play and ball area for babies and toddlers with their carers. Parents must remain in the area whilst their children are there. You register on entry and then pay for the time you've been there which is a good system. The café supplies basics including drinks, sandwiches etc. It's not a big selection but you can put everything on a tab which was useful. Food and drink from outside not permitted. I went with a 2 yr old and found it was very busy and quite full of older children. There didn't seem to be any supervision in the play structure, so my daughter was knocked over a few times by older kids and the play structure makes it hard to keep an eye on your children for large chunks of time. The older kids were also often in the baby/toddler area. There are picnic tables and sofas to sit on and free wi-fi usage (not tested), but it felt cramped and there is nowhere to put bags or pushchairs. Generally the place could do with redecorating. It's a reasonable rainy day activity if you're at Ocean Terminal but better for older kids than younger ones, particularly after school's out.

Opening hours: Mon-Sat 10.00-18.00, Sun 11.00-18.00. Cost: For 1 hr: 3 yrs+ £3.50 (max age 12), 18 mths-2 yrs £3.00, 12 mths-18 mths £1.50, babies up to 12 mths FREE. Additional play calculated in 15 min segments. Birthdays/ celebrations: For parties you can use the soft play area during usual opening hours for £9.50/ child (10 minimum, 40 maximum) and they can arrange party food and cakes which can be personalised. You also get a visit from Molly the Dog. If you want to hire the soft play exclusively, this costs £12.50/child and includes the cost of 10 laser guns. Exclusive hire Sun 10.00 or Thurs-Sat 18.00 and 19.00.

Rainbow Room

Meadowbank Sports Centre, London Road EH7 6AE
0131 661 5351
info.msc@edinburghleisure.co.uk
www.edinburghleisure.co.uk
A small soft play room with 2 levels. Open for children aged 0-5 yrs, but most suited to 2-3 yrs. The slide ends in a ball pool so children cannot really linger in it to play. Also there is a wall to climb over to get out of the ball pool so younger children will need assistance to get out of it. There is a spacious café next to the soft play.

Opening hours: Mon-Fri 09.00-18.00, Sat/Sun 09.30-18.00. Cost: £2.40. Nappy changing: Small nappy changing room within soft play area without running water. Changing unit in toilets.

EAST EDINBURGH

Portobello Indoor Bowls and Leisure Centre

Westbank Street, EH15 1DR
0131 669 0878
mail@edinburghleisure.co.uk
www.edinburghleisure.co.uk
I never knew this place existed until I had a baby! It is situated right on Portobello promenade. There is a wee soft play which is best suited to under 3s. Their loyalty card entitles you to a free session once you have had 8. They also have Gym Nippers classes for under 5s. There is a really good café.

Opening hours: 7 days, seasonal variations. Cost: £1.80/hr for soft play. Eating: Café provided by Mums Catering (see separate review p 175). Birthdays/celebrations: Soft play and bowling parties available.

Gambado

Fountain Park, Dundee Street, EH11 1AF
0131 257 4412
edinburgh@gambado.com
www.gambado.com/clubs/edinburgh
Part of a chain, you have to register (free) to book a soft play session. A very large play frame, an area for smaller children separate from the main frame and a small climbing wall at the side. The highlight for my children was a column of elastic spider webs which they could fling themselves down. It's in a large room with a spacious café at the side and big windows.

Opening hours: Sun-Thurs 09.30-18.00, Fri-Sat 09.30-19.30. *Cost:* Under 1s FREE, 1-3 yrs £5-6, 4+ yrs £6-7. Adults £1.25. *Birthdays/celebrations:* Toddler Cub parties from £7.95/child. Call 0844 375 9494.

Scrambles at EICA

Ratho, South Platt Hill, Newbridge
EH28 8AA
0131 333 6333
eica@edinburghleisure.co.uk
www.eica-ratho.com
An excellent, well supervised, soft play with a large area for 0-18 mths, separate, multi-level areas for 18 mths-4 yrs and 4-9 yrs including a mini climbing wall. All sections can be viewed from ground level. They have recently started to run supervised sessions on Mondays from 13.00-14.30 and Thursdays from 10.15-11.45 where they look after the 3-5 yr olds for 90 mins while parents/carers can enjoy a bit of grown-up time. Lockers and shoe racks are provided.

Next to Scrambles in EICA is Honey Pot Ceramics that offers pottery, cosmetic and jewellery making and messy arts and crafts.

Scrambles Café
Offers drinks, cakes and snacks. Hot drinks from £1.50, baguettes/rolls from £3, baked potatoes from £3.75 and kids' meals from £2. Seats 120. There is a separate café in EICA if you don't want to use up soft play time, but it is more suited to older children and/or smaller groups.

Opening hours: 09.30-17.30. *Cost:* £4.75/90min, £3.95/60min. Under 12 mths £1.50/90 mins £1/60 mins. *Birthdays and celebrations:* £10/child, hot/cold menu, 1hr 45 mins. Contact parties.eica@edinburghleisure.co.uk.

Timetwisters

Bankhead Drive, Sighthill, EH11 4ES
0131 308 2464
www.timetwisters.co.uk
This is one of the larger soft plays in the city, with an "Ancient Egypt" theme running throughout. It can be quite tricky to find, look out for the "Topps Tiles" sign. There are two main play areas: a small area for under 3s, and a huge structure for 4-12 yrs, although under 4s may use it. Between the two are plenty of chairs and tables, with further seating upstairs (no lift access to upper level). Upstairs seating has some views of the structure for older children. The area for the under 3s has a slide, a tunnel and easy climbing structure, and soft play shapes on the floor. The older play frame has multiple levels with various slides, swings, flying fox and a shooting gallery, and there is also a small indoor football pitch. Older toddlers may find the small play area too basic and the large frame too big, and adults may not accompany children into the "4 and over" frame.

Birthday parties are in rooms upstairs, and the birthday child gets to sit on a throne. There are additional activities during school holidays such as face painting, magicians, and themed events – check website.

The café is on the ground floor between the two main soft play structures. Quite an extensive menu with snacks, breakfasts, main meals, pasta dishes and sandwiches. Almost everything is created on site from scratch and their focus is on healthy, tasty food. Large portions and great value. No highchairs, but booster seats on request.

Opening hours: 09.30-18.00.

EAST LOTHIAN

Jamboree Soft Play

Musselburgh Sports Centre, Newbigging Musselburgh, EH21 7AS
0131 653 5208
musselburghsports@enjoyleisure.com
www.enjoyleisure.com
A medium-sized soft play. A good range of activities for young children and it is all very clean and well maintained. The children's facilities, including heating food or milk and lovely child-sized toilets, are superb. However, there is a lack of seating for adults and only soft drinks are sold within the soft play area, although there is a café in the sports centre. As such, this is probably not somewhere you would want to spend a long time, but if you are in the area, or want to combine it with using the swimming pool or the excellent park across the road, then this is a good indoor play option. The soft play also operates at certain times as a crèche, allowing parents to have a swim while their kids play.

Opening hours: Mon, Wed, Thurs 11.00-16.00 (crèche 09.00-11.00), Tues, Fri 11.15-16.00 (crèche 09.15-11.15), Sat/Sun 09.00-12.00. Cost: £1.85/30 mins. Crèche £3.50/2 hrs, or 50p with an enjoyleisure pass. Eating: Small café downstairs serving snacks and light lunches. Birthdays/celebrations: Soft play can be hired for exclusive use 13.00-16.00 Fri-Sun, £36 for 30 mins (up to 20 children allowed).

Steamy Dreamy Café and Soft Play

32a High Street, Dunbar, EH42 1JH
01368 864970
Bright and cheerful café with multi-level play area which includes slide, tunnel, ropes etc for the older ones and a small ball pit and play corner for babies. No staff supervising but it is visible by parents/carers at café tables. There is the potential for boredom for older under 5s as it is not a huge structure, but as a distraction while having lunch it is ideal. The £3 cost is slightly steep for the structure. My 4 yr old said "I love the super fast purple slide, it's my favourite".

Café sells the usual lunchtime favourites like baked potatoes and toasties, good value, all freshly prepared, and ingredients locally sourced where possible. The kids' lunchbox has standard contents – drink, piece of fruit, sandwich, etc. The kids' menu also included small portions of freshly prepared hot food as well as half sandwiches etc. My 20 mth old tried the cheesy macaroni and gave it the thumbs up. The adults sampled the soups: courgette and brie, and mushroom. Very tasty/hearty with healthy granary bread. Cakes, tray bakes etc also available. Seats 25 indoors, some outdoor tables in good weather.

Opening hours: Mon-Fri 09.00-17.00, Sat-Sun 10.00-16.00. Cost: £3 unlimited play. Membership £60 Sep-Jun unlimited play. FREE play over summer months. Birthdays/celebrations: Parties catered for, at weekends.

MIDLOTHIAN

The Amazone Soft Play Centre

The Kabin, 5 Mayburn Walk, Loanhead EH20 9HG
0131 440 2541
www.thekabin.org

Loanhead's new community building The Kabin includes the Amazone, a fantastic 3-tiered soft play area with a rainforest theme. It can be viewed from the Honeypot Café – a great way for parents and carers to enjoy a cuppa while they watch their charges play (although parental supervision is still required). The Kabin also runs Parents and Tots groups and various other activities for pre-school and older children. The Kabin has also been given a breastfeeding-friendly award.

Opening hours: Mon-Sat 09.00-18.00, Sun 11.00-17.00. Parents and Tots group Mon, Wed and Fri 09.30-11.00. Cost: Amazone £2/ hr. Parents and Tots £1. Eating: The Honeypot Café serves hot and cold snacks and drinks, including home baking.

The Happy Castle

Bankmill, Valleyfield Road, Penicuik
EH26 8LW
01968 675638
07912 753679
www.thehappycastle.co.uk
My daughter had lots of fun in the soft play area – I felt it was a good area for toddlers as it had a really good variety of ball-pools, small climbing steps and a few ride-on toys. The place is perhaps slightly dated but we had fun. There is a larger area for older children too.

Opening hours: Term time – Sun-Thurs 10.00-17.00, Fri-Sat 10.00-18.00. School Holidays – Mon-Sat: 10.00-18.00, Sun 10.00-17.00. Cost: Under 1 FREE, 1-3 yrs £3.50, 4-12 yrs £4.50. Eating: Snacks and drinks available, table and chairs area. Birthdays/celebrations: £9.95/child for parties, which include 1½ hrs in soft play area with endless juice and a buffet option.

WEST LOTHIAN

Playbugs, Linlithgow

Unit 24, Mill Road Industrial Estate
Linlithgow, EH49 7SF
01506 670113
info@playbugs.co.uk
www.playbugs.co.uk
Separate section for young (non-walking) children and a bigger area for kids who are running around. FREE for children who aren't yet walking. Coffee shop-style food. They will provide a tippy cup but don't heat your food. Last entrance is 2 hrs before advertised closing time but have been a couple of times and they have closed early either because not many people in or because they have a party coming in and want to prepare for that. They did advise that this was going to happen when I arrived and they adjusted the entrance fee. Gets busy during school holidays and when raining.

Opening hours: Mon-Fri 09.00-18.00, Sat/ Sun 10.00-18.00. During West Lothian school holidays 10.00-18.00. Cost: Walking child up to 3 yrs – £3.50, 3 yrs and above – £4.50, £9.00 discounted rate for families of 3 – further children in any single family half price thereafter.

Spacebugs

Xcite Leisure Centre, McGinley Way,
Linlithgow, EH49 6SQ
01506 775440
kmcmaster@westlothianleisure.com
www.westlothianleisure.com
Good soft play for kids from 18 mths. Supervised and safe. Good that you can leave your child and go to the gym or for a swim!

Opening hours: 09.00-20.00. Cost: £3. Eating: Costa Coffee in leisure centre.

Arts & Entertainment

Arts & Entertainment

In Edinburgh we're surrounded by arts and entertainment during Festival season, but the city and nearby is pretty marvellous for culture during the rest of the year too. In this chapter we tell you more about where you can go to drink it all in – galleries, theatres and cinemas. We also review arts and ceramics centres, where your little one can develop their own creativity.

ART GALLERIES

Children of any age can be fascinated by paintings and sculpture and Edinburgh offers a wide variety of opportunities to expose the young enquiring mind to art. Holding young children up to see properly and giving constant reminders not to touch can be trying but well worth the effort. Sometimes a gallery may just be a different place to go with a baby and meet friends.

There are also some great examples of art in the environment throughout Edinburgh – the best central location is probably Princes St Gardens. Here you can look and touch! Galleries are generally FREE, but you will have to pay for certain exhibitions.

CENTRAL EDINBURGH

City Art Centre

2 Market Street, EH1 1DE
0131 529 3993
museumsandgalleries@edinburgh.gov.uk
www.edinburghmuseums.org.uk/Venues/
City-Art-Centre.aspx
Hosts up to a dozen temporary exhibitions per year, as well as housing the city's collection of Scottish art. Many of the temporary exhibitions will appeal to children of school age and above, and there are often activities to keep younger brothers and sisters interested too – such as the Art Cart (4+ yrs) full of craft and drawing materials. Keep an eye on local listings or visit the website for details of workshops and other activities. There is access to all floors by lift.

Opening hours: Mon-Sat 10.00-17.00, Sun 12.00-17.00. Cost: Admission to permanent exhibition FREE. Admission to temporary exhibitions varies. Parking: On-street parking outside the building and on other streets close by. Nappy changing: In accessible toilet on ground floor. Eating: Café serving breakfast and lunch as well as coffee, cake, biscuits etc.

The Fruitmarket Gallery **FREE**

45 Market Street, EH1 1DF
0131 225 2583
info@fruitmarket.co.uk
www.fruitmarket.co.uk
Well-presented contemporary gallery with plenty of space to browse comfortably with a pushchair. Would not recommend specifically for toddlers however, given the programme of events. Exhibits mostly at adult eye level and most content not suitable, but worth checking the calendar of forthcoming events prior to a visit. Would recommend this venue more to parents/ carers of babies – the café is an ideal meeting point for mums and offers the opportunity for a bit of culture into the bargain! There is a well-stocked bookshop located at the entrance. Good selection of books (including children's).

Opening hours: Mon-Sat 11.00-18.00, Sun 12.00-17.00. Accessibility: Fully accessible exhibition areas with lift to upper gallery. Nappy changing: In accessible toilet, near entrance. Eating: Café, see p 154.

The National Gallery

The Mound, EH1 2EL
0131 624 6200
nginfo@nationalgalleries.org
www.nationalgalleries.org
Made up of the Royal Scottish Academy (RSA) building on Princes St and the National Gallery of Scotland building behind it on the Mound. They are joined by the Weston Link, which is accessed from Princes St Gdns E. The permanent collection is housed in the National Gallery, special exhibitions are on display in the RSA. The easiest level access is via the National Gallery Entrance on the Mound. Staff are very helpful and will show you the best and most accessible route depending on which part of the building you would like to be in (or help you carry a pushchair up the steps!). They will also show you to a quiet area for breastfeeding if needed. The collection is stunning and always worth a look but there is not much for under 5s. Activities such as Art Cart and Bags of Art occur monthly on Sun. Pushchairs can be borrowed (subject to availability) – they prefer babies not to be carried around in backpack-style carriers.

Opening hours: 10.00-17.00 (19.00 Thurs). Cost: FREE – although a charge may apply for special exhibitions. Toilets: On ground level of Weston Link, designed with accessibility in mind. Eating: Two cafés in Weston Link.

National Galleries Weston Link

Part of the National Gallery Complex
A great place to start for visiting either National Gallery building – there is a large and spacious glass fronted entrance area with excellent views back out towards Princes St Gdns E. Located here are visitor information, cloakrooms, 2 cafés, a shop and toilets with nappy changing

facilities. Beyond the entrance there is an exhibition space with an IT gallery allowing interactive access to the collection (for older children). Access from Princes St Gdns E down a flight of steps or level access at the back of the National Gallery building from The Mound.

Scottish National Portrait Gallery

1 Queen Street, EH2 1JD
0131 624 6200
pginfo@nationalgalleries.org
www.nationalgalleries.org/portraitgallery
The recently refurbished Portrait Gallery is an elegant mix of Victorian and contemporary architecture, with a great glass lift rising through the centre of the building to access each of the 3 floors. The 17 gallery spaces house an impressive collection, illustrating the history of Scotland, its people, and the issues it faces today. This wouldn't be somewhere I would choose to visit with an energetic toddler (although the glass lift alone was a hit when we visited), but the galleries offer a restful place to wander with a sleepy baby, and a series of "Portrait Detectives" trails are great for children 4+. There are 5 themed trails, and they are a fun way to explore for anyone new to the Gallery.

Opening hours: 10.00-17.00 (19.00 Thurs). Cost: Entry and permanent exhibition FREE. Some exhibitions are charged. Eating: Café (see p 159).

NORTH EDINBURGH

Scottish National Gallery of Modern Art One

75 Belford Road, EH4 3DR
0131 624 6200
gmainfo@nationalgalleries.org
www.nationalgalleries.org/modernartgalleries
We regularly enjoy a family trip to the gallery which is home to a fantastic collection of

paintings, sculptures and installations to inspire and excite even the youngest minds. Works by Damien Hirst, Tracy Emin and Andy Warhol among so many others and regular changing exhibitions. Plenty of room to move around and staff are always friendly and helpful. Outside you can enjoy the sculpture trail or a picnic on the "Stepped Serpentine Mound". Make time for a coffee on the terrace while the children have a good run around on the lawn. Gift shop, Bags of Art for 4+ yrs designed to let children explore the gallery's collection and create some artwork. See website for next one. Fun, drop-in art activities one Sun a month.

Opening hours: 10.00-17.00. Cost: FREE but suggested donation of £3. There may be a charge for special exhibitions. Accessibility: Ramp access alongside main entrance. Lift to all floors. Nappy changing: In toilets in basement. Eating: Café in basement (see p 163). You are welcome to picnic on the lawns at the front and rear of the building.

Scottish Gallery of Modern Art Two (formerly the Dean Gallery) • FREE

73 Belford Road, EH4 3DS
0131 624 6200
enquiries@nationalgalleries.org
www.nationalgalleries.org
If you park in the car park, the rear of the building faces you. Here you will find access for disabled visitors which you can also use for pushchairs. Lift access to all levels. This imposing grade A listed building has been transformed by architects, with great features for the under 5s such as a see-through floor and porthole type windows to fire the imagination.

Get the most up-to-date information at www.efuf.co.uk

A lovely setting, with an expanse of grass lawn to the front. Here you'll find several installations – ideal for youngsters to explore on a warm day. The gallery is dedicated to 20th century art, including Dada and Surrealist collections. Highpoints are Paolozzi's Vulcan (the 2-room-high iron man) and the reconstruction of the artist's London studio. Shop sells a range of gifts, cards, books etc.

Opening hours: 10.30-17.00 daily. Cost: FREE entry, some exhibitions may be charged. Parking: Fee applies. Accessibility: Ramp and lift access to enter building. Nappy changing: Downstairs. Eating: Restaurant (see p 163).

Jupiter Artland

Bonnington House, Steadings, Nr Wilkieston EH27 8BB
01506 889900
enquiries@jupiterartland.org
www.jupiterartland.org
Once you have arrived and passed the LOVE BOMB sculpture on your right and the superb landforms created by Charles Jencks (he has a landform structure outside The Scottish National Gallery of Modern Art One), stop in at the gift shop for tickets and be sure to get a map. This provides an indication of what is where, but there is no set route as the aim of Jupiter Artland is to explore and connect with the landscape and the delights to be found in the grounds, which also include horses and sheep. It is a good day out (at least 1½ hrs required) with plenty of opportunity for exercise, exploration and education. Wellies are a good idea if rain has been prevalent. Fuel up before, or end with some wholesome nourishment provided by the silver van. Food is delivered to your table either inside or outside converted stables/farm buildings. Space for children to run around outside whilst food is being prepared. Not particularly pushchair friendly so if under 3 a child must either be willing to walk or be

carried in a sling or pack. There are extra education classes offered in the form of Little Sparks – autumn term classes for pre-schoolers – and Art Sparks for 5+ yrs.

Opening hours: *Mid-May to Mid-Sep,Thurs-Sun 10.00-17.00 (education classes outside these times).* **Cost:** *FREE for under 6, adult £8.50, 6-16 £4.50, family pass (2 adults, 2 children) £23.50.*

THEATRES & ART CENTRES

Theatres are becoming more child friendly and there are often shows for under 5s, particularly during Imaginate in May and the Fringe in August. However, theatres may not be suitable for pushchairs. If a show is advertised as being for children, it's best to check beforehand on age restrictions and its content and duration. Refreshments may not always be suitable for children.

Prices vary by venue and performance. Contact venues or visit their websites for more details. Theatre brochures and festival publications give information on facilities such as parking, toilets and access. For up-to-date information about theatre performances for children and families in Scotland try:

Young Audiences Scotland
c/o Catherine Wheels Theatre Co,
Brunton Theatre, Ladywell Way, Musselburgh
EH21 6AF
0131 653 5255
info@youngaudiencesscotland.com
www.youngaudiencesscotland.com

CENTRAL EDINBURGH

Assembly Rooms

54 George Street, EH2 2LR
0131 220 4348
enquiries@assemblyroomsedinburgh.co.uk
www.assemblyroomsedinburgh.co.uk
Now closed for 18-mth refurbishment project,

scheduled for completion in time for the venue to play a key role in the Cultural Olympiad in summer 2012. See website for updates.

Edinburgh Playhouse

18-22 Greenside Place, EH1 3AA
0131 524 3333 (Admin)
www.edinburghplayhouse.org.uk
A wide variety of shows including opera, musicals, ballet and rock concerts. Occasional children's shows. Some restricted views.

Nappy changing: *In Mezzanine Ladies – closest to bar.*

King's Theatre

2 Leven Street, EH3 9LQ
0131 529 6000
www.fctt.org.uk
Traditional theatre. Occasional children's shows such as pantomimes. Some shows with special low price tickets. £2 tickets for babies under 24 mths may be available for some children's/family shows. A few booster seats available. No lifts, a lot of stairs. Ice cream and refreshments. Closed for refurbishment Feb-Aug 2012.

Royal Lyceum Theatre

Grindlay Street, EH3 9AX
0131 248 4848
www.lyceum.org.uk
Christmas family show. Has also been used as a venue for Imaginate. Lifts to all levels. Very traditional, ornate and plush inside, once you are past the modern glass façade.

Scottish Storytelling Centre

43-45 High Street, EH1 1SR
0131 556 9579
reception@scottishstorytellingcentre.com
www.scottishstorytellingcentre.co.uk
A fantastic place for organised kids' events, including storytelling sessions. You can come in on a rainy day and if the space by the café is not in use, kids can play there while parents can enjoy changing art exhibitions (note: the space is not supervised). Gets very busy at times. Crayons and paper are available. The central feature is the Story Wall made up of lots of story boxes to be discovered and explored.

The centre includes the historic John Knox House and the Netherbow Theatre. Offers a programme of regular storytelling for under 5s – Tiny Tales (6 mths-2 yrs) and Story Space (2-5 yrs). Events monthly. Check dates and times on the website, it's also worth joining the mailing list. During the Fringe they offer a wide range of children's theatre, storytelling and puppetry, some suitable for children 3+. Look out for the Puppet Animation Festival in the spring.

The café is a great place for a coffee. Reasonably priced with cakes (gluten-free too), soup of the day and main dishes including vegetarian. Baby food on sale!

Opening hours: 10.00-17.00. Cost: FREE entry – organised events individually priced. Accessibility: Accessible, excluding upper floors of John Knox House. Pushchairs: Only on lower floors.

Traverse Theatre

10 Cambridge Street, EH1 2AD
0131 228 1404
boxoffice@traverse.co.uk
www.traverse.co.uk
Occasional children's shows including during Imaginate (see p 139). Generous discounts to most performances. The Traverse Bar Café is licensed for children until 20.00 – see p 159.

North Edinburgh Arts Centre

15A Pennywell Court, EH4 4TZ
0131 315 2151
admin@northedinburgharts.co.uk
www.northedinburgharts.co.uk
Purpose-built arts centre offering a variety of performances and other arts activities for children, including the very young. Full programme of theatre and dance performances, plus Saturday workshops for families in a range of art forms. Summer schools and other holiday arts activities. Check website or contact centre for current information.

Café serves reasonably priced food ranging from soups and sandwiches to Indian cuisine provided by various local catering volunteers. Children's play area located in café, and garden area (currently under development) opens off café. A good place to have a light bite after taking in one of the events at the centre.

Opening hours: Tues-Sat 10.00-16.00. Cost: FREE entry, events and some exhibitions charged.

Craigmillar Arts Centre

58 Newcraighall Road, EH15 3HS
0131 669 8432
craigmillarcommunityarts@gmail.com
www.craigmillarcommunityarts.org.uk
Very friendly and spacious old church just opposite the Fort Kinnaird Shopping Centre. Full of free art materials, best suited for artistic parents with babies who would happily sleep in the pram while you express yourselves, or

parents with pre-school aged children who would like to participate. Adults should watch out as the space is fairly crammed with potentially risky objects. Also has scheduled events, such as karaoke, music workshop, photography workshop etc. Check website for details.

Festival Theatre

13-29 Nicolson Street, EH8 9FT
0131 529 6000
www.festivaltheatre.org.uk
Occasional children's shows for 3+ yrs. Although the façade is very modern, the actual theatre is traditional and some seats have a slightly restricted view. Its café, Café Lucia, has had a recent change of management and is becoming increasingly popular, serving everything from great lunch options to cakes.

Nappy changing: In male and female toilets on 1st floor (lift access).

George Square Theatre

George Square, EH8 9LD
0131 651 2189
Used during university holidays for shows, including children's shows. However, as a university lecture theatre it has no specific facilities for young children or babies.

SOUTH EDINBURGH

Church Hill Theatre

33a Morningside Road, EH10 4DR
0131 447 7597
Owned by Edinburgh Council and rented to theatre groups. Some shows are of interest to under 5s – see their brochure. Home of Loopy

Lorna's Tea House – see p 179.

WEST EDINBURGH

St Bride's Community Centre

10 Orwell Terrace, EH11 2DZ
0131 346 1405
www.stbrides.wordpress.com
Children's theatre and film shows, usually in school holidays. Also hosts arts and crafts class, parent and toddler group (see p 302), and after-school club. Café with enclosed play area and reading corner (see p 184). Programme is distributed through local schools and libraries.

EAST LOTHIAN

Brunton Theatre

Ladywell Way, Musselburgh, EH21 6AA
0131 665 2240
boxoffice@bruntontheatre.co.uk
www.bruntontheatre.co.uk
Situated in Brunton Hall on the main street through Musselburgh's West End. Wonderful bistro within the building (see p 184). Theatre has a very varied programme, with shows (many suitable for whole family), dance performances, concerts, films and children's events (shows, pantomimes, films). Many of these have matinee showings. The auditorium is a good size and all seats have a good view of the stage. Licensed bar within foyer and kiosk open during performances. Many workshops also take place in the theatre.

Parking: Big FREE car park to back of theatre, designated disabled parking in front. *Accessibility: Lift and wheelchair gallery at the east entrance.* *Pushchairs: Park in foyer.*

CERAMIC CENTRES

NORTH EDINBURGH

Ceramic Experience

118 Ocean Drive, Leith, EH6 6JB
0131 554 4455
leith@theceramicexperience.com
www.theceramicexperience.com
Great fun for all ages. We were welcomed as soon as we came through the door and were given a full explanation of how it works and what our options were. We were then allowed to just take a look around. All very laid back, relaxed and definitely somewhere we will visit again and again. Cost varies depending on what you do but is reasonable. There are other branches at Crieff, Cupar and Dunfermline – see website.

Opening hours: Mon-Fri 10.00-17.00, Sat/ Sun 10.00-17.30. Parking: In Ocean Terminal for FREE. Eating: Small café. Baby food sold. Birthdays and celebrations: Packages start from £12.

SOUTH EDINBURGH

Doodles

27-29 Marchmont Crescent, EH9 1HQ
0131 229 1399
painting@doodlesscotland.co.uk
www.doodlesscotland.co.uk
I enjoyed the Doodles experience. It was busy when we arrived, but there was plenty of room for us and two pushchairs. We were told to have a look around and then had the process explained to us. It was tricky to get the handprints, but the lady there helped. There is a good area nearby for the children to play in while you finish off/tidy up the pieces. Free tea and coffee for adults. Not too expensive, with about 4 days' wait to pick up painted items.

Opening hours: Mon 10.00-18.00, Tues/Wed 10.30-21.00, Fri/Sat 10.00-18.00, Sun 12.00-18.00. Cost: Items from £1-£60. Parking: Metered on-street (70p/hr). Toilets: Downstairs. Play area: Small area with toys. Birthdays and celebrations: Hire packages and late opening from £10 per person (up to 30 people).

FIFE

Potter About

267 High Street, Burntisland, KY3 9AQ
01592 873680
kathryn@potterabout.co.uk
www.potterabout.co.uk
Decorate your own plates, bowls, ornaments and other gifts. Café serving snacks/home baking with a play corner. Available for party hire and children's parties.

Opening hours: Mon-Sat 09.15-17.00, Sun 10.00-17.00.

CINEMAS

There is a good range of cinemas in Edinburgh, from the independently owned Dominion where the manager greets you in the foyer, or the more "arty" Cameo and Filmhouse, to the sprawling megaplexes, which seem to be showing every film released in the last 6 months. You never quite know how your child will take to their first cinema outing. Remember that the sound volume can be overwhelming, as can the dark. However, there are the chairs, big and plush to little ones, the decor, such as the planetoid carpet of Vue at Ocean Terminal and the ice cream! Some cinemas have children's film clubs – check out your local one for details.

If you are a carer of a disabled child, you may well be able to be admitted free. See www.ceacard.co.uk to apply for a Cinema Exhibitors Association card which some cinemas may ask for in order to admit you for free.

Any information you'd like to add? Email us at info@efuf.co.uk

CENTRAL EDINBURGH

Cameo Cinema – The Big Scream

38 Home Street, EH3 9LZ
0871 902 5723
cameo@picturehouses.co.uk
www.picturehouses.co.uk
The Cameo Cinema is very accessible with the theatres all on the same level. The lights are on low and the volume is also lower than standard screenings. The free coffee or tea completes the whole experience. There are also, sometimes, free Bepanthen samples, as they sponsor the Big Scream. Don't be put off by an unsettled baby – everyone there has a baby, so crying or shouting is totally accepted. A great morning out and about with your baby – highly recommended! One word of warning – it is on early, and buses are tricky if you are using a pram. Be prepared and leave early.

Screening times: Selected Thursdays 10.30-13.00. Cost: £5.00/adult, baby FREE. Parking: Limited pay and display and disabled parking. Pushchairs: Allowed in main theatre. Eating: Café/bar, small coffee kiosk. Birthdays/celebrations: Can be hired out. Breastfeeding: Welcomed in the theatre.

Filmhouse

88 Lothian Road, EH3 9BZ
0131 228 2688 (Box Office)
admin@filmhousecinema.com
www.filmhousecinema.com

For Crying Out Loud
Regular screening sessions for carers and babies. Lights are dim but not too dark and the volume is a little lower. I really enjoyed the film but found that, as there were only a few other mums and babies there, it was a bit "quiet" and felt that I had to shush my little girl. I have not

had this problem elsewhere. If you have a baby that will take a feed and snooze through the film then it is an excellent way to spend a Monday morning! If, however, you have a crawler or an early toddler, then give it a miss. They are very strict if you allow your little one to wander too near the stage or up the steps, even if you are right behind them! Screenings are limited to babies under 12 mths accompanied by no more than 2 adults.

Screening times: Selected Mondays 11.00. *Cost:* Adults £3.50, concessions £2.50.

Weans' World at Filmhouse

Weans' World shows a mix of films for a younger audience, usually on Sunday pm and Monday am, but screenings are not weekly, so check the latest brochure or website for times and dates. Seeing a film here is a real experience, and you can feel the excitement and anticipation when the big red curtain opens!

Cost: £2.50/ticket (child or adult).

Parking: Nearest car parks: Semple St, Castle Terr. *Pushchairs:* Have to be left at the box office on the ground floor. Children must walk or be carried upstairs to cinema 1. *Eating:* Small café/bar. *Birthdays/celebrations:* The cinema can be hired. Call 0131 228 6382.

Newbies at Odeon Lothian Road

118 Lothian Road, EH3 8BQ
0871 224 4007
odeon.lothianroad@odeonuk.com
www.odeon.co.uk
Newbies encourage all parents to bring their babies along to the screening so there is no need to worry about your little one making a noise. A great facility but is probably better suited to younger babies who will sleep through the film. You are made to feel very welcome and the atmosphere is relaxing. The films are slightly quieter and the lights are more raised

than usual. All films are suitable for children. The staff are very friendly and explain what to do clearly – I felt quite happy attending by myself but people did come in groups too. Babies can attend until 2 yrs but I feel this is more suited to younger babies who won't want to move about.

Screening times: Tues late morning/midday (check website). *Cost:* £7.50, however, you can buy a discount card for £2 that will save you £2 every week. *Eating:* Cinema provides a service where you can order food/drinks when seated and they bring it to you.

Sunday Children at Vue Omni Centre

Greenside Place, EH1 3AA
0871 224 0240
www.myvue.com
A great – and cheap – experience for the whole family. Lots of kids and noise as it's a family viewing. The only downside is that you never know what is showing until the weekend.

Screening times: Sun 10.00. *Cost:* £1.25. *Parking:* FREE on Sundays. *Pushchairs:* Secure room for them.

Kids AM at Vue Ocean Terminal

Leith, EH6 6JJ
0871 224 0240
www.new.myvue.com/offers-savings/kids-am
Kid's AM shows films rated either U or PG on Saturday and Sunday mornings, and every day during the school holidays. Films are usually not new releases, but the showings give you a chance to see a film you may have missed at the cinema the first time around! A great, inexpensive rainy day treat for you and your older under 5.

Cost: £1.50 (3D movies £2.75). **Parking:** FREE at Ocean Terminal.

SOUTH EDINBURGH

Dominion Cinema

18 Newbattle Terrace, EH10 4RT
0131 447 4771
directors@dominion-cinema.co.uk
www.dominioncinemas.net
One of the last remaining family-run cinemas in Edinburgh, and long may it continue. A cosy gem of a place that has had a substantial refurbishment to create a 22-seat private cinema. Allow plenty of time to park near the cinema, especially if it's a popular film and/or during the school holidays. At times, may offer parent and baby screenings. Check website.

Parking: Metered 08.00-18.00 Mon-Fri and 08.00-13.30 Sat.

WEST EDINBURGH

Cineworld

Fountainpark, 130-133 Dundee Street
EH11 1AF
0871 200 2000
www.cineworld.co.uk
Access car park via Western Approach Rd or via Dundee St. Yearly passes available. 30 designated spaces for disabled parking.

Large cinema complex located in a purpose-built leisure park in a central location. Underground car park; fee refunded on exit with voucher from cinema or other outlets. Cinema offers booster seats for children. Parties hosted in a special "party" room. Phone or see website for further information and booking.

Movies for Juniors at Cineworld
Shows U or PG films every Saturday morning with tickets from only £1 (children and adults). Films usually not new releases but you may get the chance to see something you've missed. A

fun and inexpensive way to spend an enjoyable morning with your older under 5, particularly on rainy days.

Westside Plaza

120 Westerhailes Road, EH14 2SW
0871 224 4007
www.odeon.co.uk
Eight-cinema complex next to Wester Hailes station. Easy parking, access all on one level. Ice cream, popcorn, etc. Family tickets available. Under 18 mths free if sitting on parent's knee.

Q&A

We asked Rachel Huggins of Monkey Music

Are you a parent? *Yes, to Beatrice aged 4.*

Tell us about Monkey Music: *Monkey Music is the award-winning, pre-school music class for children from 3 months to 5 years, running throughout Edinburgh. Our specially designed progressive curricula offer classes which are action packed, full of fun with original songs, games and playing with a wide variety of percussion instruments. We have 15 children in each class. For 3+ classes there are 10 in a class.*

When our Monkeys are 3 we work with live musicians to develop their understanding of the families of the orchestra, rhythm and graphic notation giving them a really solid base to start learning an instrument. We offer free trials, Monday-Saturday classes and are also available for birthday parties.

How long have you lived in Edinburgh? *I was born and educated in Edinburgh but moved to London for 13 years before returning home in 2008, which is when I started my Monkey Music franchise.*

How do you rate it as a child-friendly city? *It is a wonderful city to bring up children which is why we moved back from London. There is so much on offer on your doorstep or in the surrounding countryside which makes it an exciting, accessible place for parents and children alike.*

Any memorable experiences of Edinburgh as a parent? *There are so many memorable things to do in Edinburgh and part of that is that I remember doing so many of them as a child as well. The Botanics rockery will always be a favourite for hide and seek and nature walks. The Water of Leith is a great place to wander and practise scootering and riding a bike. Cramond is wonderful for feeding the ducks and taking walks out to the island. The New Town still has many hidden treasures and little lanes to explore and investigate and the private gardens are always wonderful to be invited to!*

Recommendations:
- *The Scottish Gallery of Modern Art – Sunday children's sessions*
- *Kiss the Fish Studios*
- *The Imaginate Children's Festival in May*
- *Five Sisters Valley Zoo, West Lothian – so accessible and everything is at the children's level*
- *Porto & Fi for yummy teas*
- *The Scottish Storytelling Centre*
- *The Edinburgh Fringe*
- *Jupiter Artland,*
- *Our Dynamic Earth soft play,*
- *Glenogle Swimming pool.*

Find out more about Monkey Music on pages 272-273. To arrange a free class in the North Edinburgh area, contact rachel.huggins@monkeymusic.co.uk, 0131 260 9667.

Festivals & Events

January-February
Pantomimes and plays
Snowdrop Walk
Model Rail Scotland

March-April
Puppet Animation Festival
Edinburgh Science Festival
The Links Market, Kirkcaldy

May-June
Glenrothes Model Train Exhibition
Imaginate
Balerno Children's Gala
Highland Games
Galas
Plu, Leith Links
The Royal Highland Show

July-August
The Big Tent
National Museum of Flight Airshow
Lifeboat Day, North Berwick
Traquair Fair
The Royal Edinburgh Military Tattoo
Edinburgh Fringe
Edinburgh International Festival
Festival Cavalcade
Pleasance Kidzone
West End Art
Edinburgh International Book Festival
Edinburgh Mela Festival

September-October
Festival Fireworks
Scottish International Storytelling Festival

November-December
Fireworks Extravaganza
Garvald Bazaar
Steiner Christmas Fair
Edinburgh's Christmas
Edinburgh's Hogmanay

Festivals & Events

There are some events which you only have one chance a year to enjoy. Some have a long history, others are more recently established. Some can provide a whole day's worth of entertainment, others can help pass a pleasant hour.

For more information about festivals in Edinburgh, try:
www.edinburgh.org
www.edinburgh-festivals.com
www.edinburghguide.com

Many places to visit in and around Edinburgh have programmes of events. Look out for leaflets, keep an eye out for adverts, sign up for newsletters or check individual websites for details of special themed events for Easter, Summer, Halloween, Christmas, etc.

JANUARY-FEBRUARY

Pantomimes and plays

The panto season extends through winter. While venues such as the King's Theatre and the Playhouse stage traditional pantos, others such as the Royal Lyceum, North Edinburgh Arts Centre, Theatre Workshop and the Scottish Storytelling Centre have offered less traditional shows in recent years.

Although many of the pantos have famous names heading the bill, they tend to appeal to an older audience and are far too long for many under 5s. Probably more suitable are shows such as those from the Singing Kettle (see www.singingkettle.com).

Snowdrop Walk

Hopetoun House, South Queensferry, EH30 9SL
0131 331 2451
www.hopetounhouse.com
Hopetoun House is closed until Easter but opens for this special one-off guided afternoon walk in late February, part of the Scottish Snowdrop Festival. Refreshments are provided. Book ahead. The walk is free but the admission fee to the grounds is charged.

Model Rail Scotland

SECC, Glasgow, G3 8YW
www.modelrail-scotland.co.uk
The annual model railway exhibition takes place over the last weekend of February, Friday-Monday. An absolute delight for any train fan, with over 50 model layouts running and many stands selling and demonstrating equipment. Limited snacks and drinks. Entry fee, family tickets available.

MARCH-APRIL

Puppet Animation Festival

01224 575743
www.puppetanimationfestival.org
The UK's largest annual performing arts event for children, offers children and their families opportunities to be transported to magical worlds of make-believe. Many events are held all over Scotland. Check the What's On diary on website to find out what's on in your local area.

Edinburgh Science Festival

0131 553 0322 (box office)
www.sciencefestival.co.uk
Still one of Europe's largest science festivals, this event takes place every spring in venues around the city. It celebrates Scotland's rich scientific and

technological heritage and, with a large educational element, informs and entertains with its exploration of the fascinating world of science. Providing a family learning experience, with hands-on exhibits, presentations and workshops all developed to give children that "wow" moment when something truly amazing is explained to them in a fun, thrilling way, this event is suited to slightly older children, though under 5s should have fun too. The programme is available at sites including Waverley Station, National Museums Scotland and the Edinburgh Festival Fringe shop on the High St. If you would like one to be sent to you, email **marketing@ scifest.co.uk**. There are free events, but most require purchase of tickets. Check the brochure or website to find out whether you need to book or if you can just turn up on the day.

The Links Market

Esplanade, Kirkcaldy, Fife
www.linksmarket.org.uk and www.fifedirect. org.uk (under Community life and leisure)
This fair dates back over 700 years and is reputedly the longest street fair in Europe. It is held around the third week of April each year and is an open air funfair that caters for all tastes with sideshow stalls, children's rides, helter-skelters and carousels. The Esplanade is closed to vehicles during the market, effectively becoming a pedestrian precinct.

MAY-JUNE

Glenrothes Model Train Exhibition

Lomond Centre, Woodside Way, Glenrothes Fife, KY7 5RA
www.glenrothesmrc.org.uk
Annual exhibition of model train layouts and trade stalls. The 2011 show had 12 layouts and 11 other stalls. The highlight in recent years has been the Lego train layout where children (and adults) can have a go at controlling the engines under the guidance of the friendly layout owner.

Cost: Adult £3.50, child £2, family £9

Imaginate

The Bank of Scotland Imaginate Festival
0131 225 8050
info@imaginate.org.uk
www.imaginate.org.uk
This annual event takes place in Edinburgh and on tour throughout Scotland in May each year. It attracts an audience of children and young people, their teachers, families and carers. A variety of performances, many suitable for the under 5s, are held in child-friendly venues. Check online for more information.

Balerno Children's Gala

www.balernochildrensgala.org.uk
The Balerno Children's Gala takes place each year around the end of May and is a fantastic community event arranged for, and on behalf of, the children and families of Balerno. It encompasses a week long programme of activities which all the children of Balerno are welcome to take part in and culminates in Gala Day, which offers main attractions and a range of other activities along with numerous stalls and sideshows. Some of the events require pre-entry or pre-purchased tickets. Further details, including event times, can be found in the official Gala programme sold in the Balerno area from May. If you do not live in the Balerno area and are interested in receiving a copy then use the website contact form to get in touch.

Highland Games

Various venues around Scotland
www.shga.co.uk
The Highland Games season runs from the end of May to mid September every year.
A great day out for the family to see the colour and vitality of this Scottish tradition. There is something for everyone from lone pipers to massed bands, clever footed dancers to the skill and strength of the heavy events. Food and drink stalls. Ceres and Birnam are both modest-sized events suitable for a young family outing. Birnam hosts the World Haggis Eating Championship and the Mad Kiltie Dash, a 100 yard race for anyone on the field wearing a

kilt. The Scottish Highland Games Association provides a full list of events. Entry fees vary.

Galas

Many local galas in the city and the Lothians take place in June. These may be the principal annual event that draws a community together and they are well worth supporting, although due to changing local demographics, insurance requirements and funding difficulties, many are finding it hard to continue. See local advertising.

Plu

Leith Links
0131 553 2152
info@parentslikeus.co.uk
www.parentslikeus.co.uk/thefestival.html
This 3-day festival, held on Leith Links, is aimed at parents and carers with under 6s and has family shows, activities, storytelling, interactive demos, live music, games, products

and information. Admission to the main arena is FREE – as is almost half of everything on offer throughout the weekend. Reduced-rate therapies, fairground rides and a wide variety of child-friendly food. 2012 dates are 1-3 June. Very popular, so book early.

Royal Highland Show

Royal Highland Centre, Ingliston, EH28 8NB
0131 335 6200
ShowDept@rhass.org.uk
www.royalhighlandshow.org
Scotland's annual farming and countryside showcase runs for 4 days over the last weekend in June. The event provides a marketplace and forum for Scottish agriculture, rural industries and outdoor pursuits. One of the most exciting aspects of the show is of course the animals. If you wander round, you will see over 4500 head of livestock take part in a wide range of competitions and classes. It's not just the best livestock that are judged at the Royal Highland Show though. The finest foods, traditional skills

and show jumping are also assessed with the winners receiving highly coveted prizes. Visit the Royal Highland Education Trust (RHET) Children's Discovery Centre where there are many things to do and see. It is open to anyone and everyone, offering a range of fun, interactive and hands-on activities for children of all ages. There is also a playground for little ones. Advance purchase of tickets is recommended.

Dates and times: Last weekend in June. Thurs 07.00-20.00, Fri-Sat 08.00-20.00, Sun 08.00-18.30. Cost: Adult £25, Concessions £20, Children under 15 FREE. Parking: £5. Accessibility: Electric scooters and wheelchairs for hire. See website for more details. Eating: The Food Hall and a marquee is available to school groups and the public for packed lunches. If the weather is good there is an outdoor picnic area in the Countryside Area.

JULY-AUGUST

The Big Tent

Falkland Estate, Fife
www.bigtentfestival.co.uk
Weekend environmental festival with lots to interest under 5s. Enjoy the whole festival and stay in the campsite which has a dedicated family area. Music, children's activities, food village, stalls, and more. Under 12s go free and further discounts are available if you go green.

National Museum of Flight Airshow

East Fortune Airfield, East Lothian, EH39 5LF
0300 123 6789
info@nms.ac.uk
Held annually every July (check website for actual date) this air display of over 2-3 hrs contains aerial action with military aircraft from the First World War to Wingwalker aerobatics. There are also children's activity workshops, fairground rides, displays, and demonstrations.

Times: Airshow starts at 10.00, car park opens at 09.00. Air display commences 12.00. Cost: 2011 prices: Early bird – adults £16, concessions £14, child 5-15 £8, 0-4s FREE, family £38. Standard (on the day) – adults £19, concessions £17, child 5-15 £10, 0-4s FREE, family £45. Parking: £4. Eating: The Aviator Café, stalls.

Lifeboat Day

North Berwick Tourist Information
01620 892197
North Berwick, last week in July. All kinds of fundraising – fantastic day if the weather is good!

Traquair Fair

Traquair House, Innerleithen
Peeblesshire EH44 6PW
01896 830323
enquiries@traquair.co.uk
www.traquair.co.uk/content/traquair-fair
Taking place in the grounds of Traquair House, this annual fair held 1st weekend in August is one of the longest running fairs in Scotland and is fully focussed on a family audience. With stunning outdoor shows, relaxing music, and dedicated children's entertainment including theatre, puppets, well loved children's entertainers like Mr Boom, workshops and face painting, there is plenty to enjoy. Special entrance prices which include a tour of the house, advance purchase discounts are available and under 5s go FREE.

Eating: Food stalls and restaurant.

The Royal Edinburgh Military Tattoo

The Tattoo Office, 32 Market Street, EH1 1QB
0131 225 1188
administration@edintattoo.co.uk
www.edintattoo.co.uk

141

Against the world famous backdrop of Edinburgh Castle the Tattoo takes place on the Esplanade over the first 3 weeks of August every year. As well as the famous pipes, drums and massed bands a variety of performers from around the world also take part. The Tattoo has never been cancelled due to bad weather, though seats are hard and cold even in August, so a cushion and/or blanket may come in handy.

Performances: Mon-Fri 21.00, Sat 19.30 and 22.30. Cost: £23-57. Under 3s FREE if sitting on adult's lap. Preview tickets half-price.

Edinburgh Fringe

180 High Street, EH1 1QS
0131 226 0026
admin@edfringe.com
www.edfringe.com
In August. Cited in the Guinness Book of Records as the largest arts festival in the world! A myriad of events, such as puppet shows, magic, drama and music at venues throughout the city. The programme lists events by age group. Programme free from the Fringe Office and other venues round the city – bookshops are the best bet for picking one up.

Edinburgh International Festival

The Hub, Castlehill, EH1 2NE
0131 473 2099 (info line)
0131 473 2000 (booking line)
marketing@eif.co.uk
www.eif.co.uk
In August, this festival presents 3 exhilarating weeks of the finest creators and performers from the arts. Edinburgh's major theatres and concert halls, a few smaller venues and some unconventional ones come alive with the best classical music, theatre, opera, dance and visual art from around the globe. Wheelchair users, people with severe mobility difficulties or visual or hearing impairment can buy seats/spaces in

the area of the venue most appropriate to their needs for the lowest (unrestricted view) ticket price for that performance. Their companion's ticket is free. For more information call the Access line on 0131 473 2089 or email access@eif.co.uk. Check website for programme information, available in a variety of formats.

Festival Cavalcade

Procession of floats, pipe bands, groups from Tattoo etc on first Sunday of Festival. Very popular so arrive early. For a seat at the concert by the Chamber Orchestra in Princes St Gdns book early at The Hub (postal ballot, closes May). Small children may not like the noise and crowds around Princes St, George St and The Mound. Bruntsfield Links and Inverleith Park still have great views and if you take a radio you'll be able to hear the music on a local station too.

Pleasance Kidzone

0131 556 6550 (box office)
info@pleasance.co.uk
www.pleasance.co.uk/edinburgh/pleasance-kidzone
A nice selection of toys available for young children to play with. There are shows on during the Festival, some free, so you can take in a show then have a play session. In 2010 there was a babysitting service for 3-9 yr olds to allow parents to see a daytime show. They hope to provide this service again in 2012.

Opening hours: 10.00-17.00 during the Festival. Parking: Limited on-street pay and display. Toilets: Up 2 flights of stairs above bar in main building. Eating: Café with basic food – pre-packed sandwiches, tea and coffee.

West End Art

Craft and Design Fair
www.3d2d.co.uk/festival.html
Usually runs for 3 weeks during the Festival. An open air art, craft and design fair in the grounds of St. John's Church at the corner of Lothian Rd and Princes St. FREE entry and a good variety of stalls selling unique, handcrafted, good quality clothes, accessories, toys, art, pottery, jewellery, etc. There are ramps so you can get around with a pushchair, but it does get busy, especially at weekends. Henderson's @ St John's offers drinks, snacks, and hot food (see p 156).

Edinburgh International Book Festival

Charlotte Square Gardens
0131 228 5444
0131 624 5050
admin@edbookfest.co.uk
www.edbookfest.co.uk
Held in an extensive tented village each August. The world's largest book event and while the majority of sessions are aimed at children 3+ yrs, younger children may also enjoy them. (The programme indicates a recommended audience age.) There are workshops, storytelling from favourite authors and even visits by well-loved characters. Tickets can be booked in advance or on the day, but popular events sell out very quickly. Some are FREE. Excellent children's bookshop with a huge range of titles and an activity corner with chairs/tables for little ones, and hands-on activities including arts and crafts. Website has details about the Children's Book Festival.

Nappy changing: Dedicated tent. Eating: Cafés, ice cream trike.

Edinburgh Mela Festival

North Edinburgh Arts Centre
15a Pennywell Court EH4 4TZ
0131 332 2888
www.edinburgh-mela.co.uk
Usually held at the end of August/beginning of September, presents international artists and performers alongside the best work created by local groups from Edinburgh's diverse communities. It is a showcase of contemporary multi-cultural Scotland and a family event that provides a unique mix of activities, entertainment, arts, a vibrant market place and fantastic food.

Cost: 2011 prices – Day Passes £2 in advance/£2.50 on the day. Under 12s FREE.

SEPTEMBER-OCTOBER

Festival Fireworks

Marks the end of the Edinburgh International Festival, usually at the beginning of September, and is an impressive display of fireworks launched from the castle, with an orchestra playing in Princes St Gdns. Watch from the ticketed areas in Princes St Gdns, visit the free family viewing area in Inverleith Park or choose your favourite spot around the city. It could be too late or too loud for very small children.

Scottish International Storytelling Festival

43-45 High Street, EH1 1SR
0131 556 9579
reception@scottishstorytellingcentre.com
www.scottishstorytellingcentre.co.uk
Scotland's annual autumnal celebration of traditional and contemporary storytelling. Brings together artists and audiences from Scotland and beyond in entertaining and inspiring live storytelling performances, thought-provoking talks, workshops and discussions and fun family

activities. The main programme is for adults, though events designed for children and families are offered including live storytelling which often involves craft and story-making activities. Check each event listing for information on age suitability, or check with the relevant venue.

Cost: Some activities priced, some FREE. Parking: Metered. Eating: Licensed café, serving homemade treats and light meals.

NOVEMBER-DECEMBER

Fireworks Extravaganza

**Meadowbank Sports Centre
139 London Road
EH7 6AE**
Large, well-organised display on 5 November, usually enjoyed by a capacity audience. May prove a bit overwhelming for under 5s. Smaller firework displays organised by local Scout or Round Table groups are advertised locally. See press for details.

Garvald Bazaar

**454/1 Gorgie Road
www.garvaldedinburgh.org.uk**
Held in the Gorgie Rd workshop premises usually on the last Saturday in November or the 1st Saturday in December depending on when the first Advent Sunday falls. Quality handcrafted gifts and food made by the members of Garvald Edinburgh. Santa's Grotto and craft activities for children.

Steiner Christmas Fair

**60 Spylaw Road, EH10 5BR
0131 337 3410
www.steinerweb.org.uk**
This event at the Edinburgh Rudolph Steiner School is a great day out. Lots of lovely stalls, great food and plenty of fun to be had by all.

Edinburgh's Christmas

**0131 529 3785
www.edinburghschristmas.com**
From end November to early January Princes St Gdns transforms into a Winter Wonderland with festive events and activities such as fireworks, lights, funfairs and Europe's largest outdoor ice rink. There is also a German Market (up until Christmas Eve) with quaint wooden stalls selling hot food, mulled wine, crafts and gifts.

Edinburgh's Hogmanay

**Princes Street, EH2 3AB
www.edinburghshogmanay.org**
World famous street party with spectacular events, including carnivals, fireworks and the Torchlight Procession, incredible bands and amazing crowds from every corner of the globe. Lots of fun and games to welcome the New Year, though some events not suitable for under 16s. Check website early November for more details.

Dates: 30 Dec-1 Jan. Accessibility: Full at some events, partial at others. Check website for details.

Eat & Drink

Eat & Drink

When you become a parent it's tempting to think that the type of eaterie that welcomes you has changed. Out go the sleek bistros, in comes "chips with everything". However, armed with the right information you needn't feel pigeon-holed, and the good news is that things are always improving in terms of dining out with children.

The idea of a pleasant meal out is different for different people. To reflect this, we have included a range of cafés, restaurants and bistros in Edinburgh and further afield, which have been tried and enjoyed by our researchers. Cafés and restaurants that appear within larger venues such as stately homes, parks, zoos/wildlife parks and museums, are listed under those venues elsewhere in the book. If it's easy to walk into the café or restaurant without having to visit the venue, we've generally included them in this chapter.

The experience of eating out with young children lies somewhere between fun and chaotic! A newborn will be quite content in a car seat, but in a matter of months a highchair is a priority, then, before you know it, the location of the toilet is the first requisite – the list goes on. Some of the places listed may not be able to accommodate all ages of children, but where there has been a positive attitude towards dining out with a child and enough child-friendly facilities to help you have a pleasant experience, we have included them.

If you are choosing a meal for a special occasion you are always best to book first, mentioning that you have children under 5 (and that you found the restaurant listed in this book!). Check that the facilities you need will be available (highchairs may be reserved, for example). Several hotels and family restaurants have special promotions at the weekend, such as under 5s eating free or special children's entertainment, so it's worth asking.

Licensing

The Licensing (Scotland) Act 2005 came fully into force on 1 September 2009. Licensed premises must now decide whether to "opt-in" to children accessing their premises. Licences are granted depending on whether the facilities are suitable, subject to appropriate hours and areas of access for children, and whether children are accompanied or not. It is now mandatory for nappy changing facilities to be accessible on licensed premises that allow young children. Venues should display their licence/children's certificate. You will also see some venues putting up signs confirming that children are not allowed on their premises as their licence does not allow for this.

Generally speaking, children (under 14) are allowed in licensed premises where a children's certificate is displayed as long as they are accompanied by an adult (for the purposes of eating a meal on the premises). Children are usually permitted on the premises until 20.00, but this can vary by venue and it is worth checking for any specific licensing restrictions in advance if you're planning an evening out.

Let us know!

Please tell us of any other places that you think should be included, and why. Also let us know if you've had any bad experiences in any of the places listed here – management or staff changes can alter a venue for the better or the worse. Facilities change too, so if you discover that our information isn't accurate, please get in touch. You can email us on **info@efuf.co.uk** or via our website **www.efuf.co.uk**.

, and

We've used these symbols throughout this chapter. They're only a rough guide but this is how we've applied them:

 (good value/reasonably priced) – examples: coffee £1.80, cake £2.00, sandwich £2.80, starter £3.00, main meal £5.50, dessert £3.00.

 (mid-price) – examples: coffee £2.50, cake £3.00, sandwich £4.50, starter £6.00, main meal £9.00, dessert £5.00.

 (for a treat) – examples: coffee £3.00, cake £5.00, sandwich £7.00, starter £8.00, main meal £16.00, dessert £7.00.

Menus or sample menus are available online for most of the venues listed – check individual websites for more specific prices.

CENTRAL EDINBURGH

Always Sunday

170 High Street, EH1 1QS
www.alwayssunday.co.uk
Airy, bright, self-service café with friendly and accommodating staff in a super location on the Royal Mile. Wide choice – full breakfasts, home baking, soups, salads and hot dishes. Particularly good on healthy and vegetarian options. No children's menu, half portions upon request. The friendly member of staff gave my little boy a soup sample to see if he liked the options. Clear labelling for special diets. Space available to park 2/3 unfolded pushchairs if quiet. On a nice day there is outdoor seating. 30-40 seats.

Opening hours: Mon-Fri 08.00-18.00, Sat/Sun 09.00-18.00. **Pushchairs:** *When quiet!* **Toilets:** *In basement down steep stairs.*

Aqua Restaurant

Apex City Hotel, 61 Grassmarket, EH1 2JF
0131 243 3400
www.apexhotels.co.uk
Stylish restaurant with views over Grassmarket. Children's portions taken from main menu.

Opening hours: 12.00-14.00, 18.00-21.45 (A la Carte and Fixed Price Menus), 16.00-18.30 (Eat Early Menu) and 18.00-22.00 (Bar Menu).

Atholl Dining Room

The Howard Hotel, 34 Great King Street, EH3 6QH
0131 557 3500
www.thehoward.com
The Howard is a smart but very friendly hotel and although high tea is a formal affair, children are

welcomed with open arms and well catered for. The service is impeccable and when one of my sons developed an urge for non-stop mini Dundee cakes, the staff were all too happy to provide an endless supply. The tea comprises finger sandwiches, light as air scones and jam and a wonderful selection of cakes and patisseries. A definite recommendation for a special occasion.

as they were busy. Large step up to entrance, little space for pushchairs, no lift and the toilets are upstairs via a spiral staircase. Plenty of highchairs though had to help ourselves. Really good range of choices on the children's menu for a reasonable price. Seats 132 indoors only.

Opening hours: 11.00-23.00. Parking: Nearest in George St. Nappy changing: In female toilets, up spiral staircase.

Bar Roma

39a Queensferry Street, EH2 4RA
0131 226 2977
reservations@bar-roma.co.uk
www.bar-roma.co.uk
A very family-friendly place to eat in the West End. We were part of a group of 4 mums and 4 babies in highchairs, and the waiting staff couldn't have been more welcoming and accommodating. Food was excellent and they even thought to keep one of the meals warm because one of our party was busy changing a nappy. Children's portions of pizza and pasta offered. Double doors into restaurant make it easily accessible even for double pushchairs.

Opening hours: Sun-Thurs 12.00-00.00, Fri-Sat 12.00-01.00. Parking: City centre parking. Birthdays/celebrations: Parties welcome. Restaurant can order a cake and decorations are welcome. Pizza-making parties available.

Bella Italia **·££**

9-11 Hanover Street, EH2 2DL
0131 225 4808
www.bellaitalia.co.uk
Busy Italian city centre restaurant with friendly service. Crayons and activity sheet provided. Went on busy Sat evening with no booking, and got a table without a wait, though it was a bit cramped. Main courses took a while to come, but otherwise the service was efficient, especially

BHS Restaurant

64 Princes Street, EH2 2DJ
0131 226 2621
www.bhs.co.uk
Large and spacious self-service restaurant serving canteen-style food at reasonable prices with families in mind. Tends to be quieter than other city centre eateries, especially at the weekend, so you have a good chance of finding a table, a highchair and room for a pushchair! Good choice of meals and snacks and a large children's menu with half portions for under 12s. Children's meals come in decorative lunch bags. There are often meal offers e.g. breakfast for 99p or main course for £2.99. Baby food available. Level access from Rose St or main store via escalator. Seats approx 250 indoors.

Opening hours: Mon-Wed, Fri-Sat 09.00-18.00, Thurs 09.30-20.00, Sun 11.00-17.00.

The Blue Moon Café **·£**

36 Broughton Street, EH1 5SB
0131 556 2788
www.bluemooncafe.co.uk
Famous for its breakfasts, a great place to go after a play at the Barony Community Garden (80 yards up Barony St on the right hand side)! Traditional cooked or veggie, eggs Benedict or Florentine, morning rolls, cheesy beano toast,

then lunch menu after 12.00. Fish and chips, crispy chicken and fishcakes, with NY City cheesecake, banoffee pie, chocolate fudge cake and ice cream sundaes. Seats 30 indoors.

Opening hours: Mon-Fri 11.00-22.00, Sat/Sun 10.00-22.00. No children after 20.00. Parking: Meter parking on Barony St. Pushchairs: Two steps up. With double pushchair, enter through left hand double door. Park in corridor at back. Nappy changing: Downstairs in (closed) bar.

Browns Restaurant and Bar `££`

131-133 George Street, EH2 4JS
0131 225 4442
www.browns-restaurants.co.uk
Lively and large, with a lovely relaxed atmosphere, a firm favourite with many families. Children's meals are excellent quality. A dining experience that doesn't compromise on adult appeal, while remaning child friendly. Attentive and friendly staff. Caters well for family parties with a space at the back of the restaurant.

Opening hours: Daily from 09.00.

Café Andaluz `££`

77b George Street, EH2 3EE
0131 220 9980
One of the big restaurants on trendy George St, Café Andaluz welcomes families with kids. They have a special kids' tapas menu, complete with colouring sheet and word search. Seats 200.

Opening hours: 10.30-22.30. Parking: Paid. Accessibility/Pushchairs: Three steps up to front – internal lift between levels inside. Space for pushchairs. Nappy changing: Dedicated room up 3 steps – or access via disabled lift.

Café Camino `£`

St Mary's Parish Centre, 1 Little King Street, EH1 3JR
0131 523 0102
info@cafecamino.co.uk
www.cafecamino.co.uk
The café and meeting place for St Mary's Cathedral, light and bright with lots of space for pushchairs. It is a fantastic place to have a coffee, sample the baking or enjoy a light lunch. Kids' lunchboxes are available too. Seats around 50.

Opening hours: Mon-Sat 09.00-20.00, Sun 09.00-21.30. Parking: Metered parking outside the café but it is very limited. The easiest place is probably John Lewis car park. Nappy changing: In accessible toilet – you have to get a code and a key from the staff. Birthdays/celebrations: There are 2 spaces for hire behind the café. Café Camino would provide catering.

Café Montagu `£`

12 Montagu Terrace, EH3 5QX
0131 551 5359
www.cafemontagu.com
A bright, welcoming café with the added bonus of a playroom at the rear. Lunch options consist of soup (sometimes, but not always, homemade), baked potatoes, paninis, sandwiches and some hot items such as quiche, pies and nachos. Great coffee is served including a caffeine-free option, plus a small selection of baking. A great place for a cuppa while your under 5 is happy playing with the toys and books. Becoming very popular with locals! Seats 16-20 indoors.

149

Opening hours: 10.00-17.00, 09.00 opening on Tues and Thurs. *Parking:* Limited on-street pay and display on Inverleith Row. *Accessibility:* Assisted access to playroom and toilet at rear (via step). *Pushchairs:* Can leave at back of café next to playroom. *Play area:* Separate playroom at back with toys and books. *Birthdays/celebrations:* Rear room FREE to hire.

5... great places to stop in town for a cake

Scottish National Portrait Gallery Café (p 159)

John Lewis – the Place to Eat (p 156)

Porto & Fi on the Mound (p 158)

Hendersons @ St Johns (p 156)

The Restaurant at Debenhams, Princes St (p 152)

Café Rouge

43 Frederick Street, EH2 1EP
0131 225 4515
www.caferouge.co.uk/location/edinburgh
This French-style café is part of a national chain, and was full of mums and children on the Thurs lunchtime we visited. The friendly staff brought pencils, stickers and an activity book, and a helium balloon as a goodbye present. Simple children's menu, and flexible adult menu including breakfast food until noon, "petit plats", pastries, quick options and a fixed price lunch as well as main courses. There's a popular outdoor seating area, and unfortunately the smell of cigarette smoke drifts into the restaurant on sunny days. Seats 190 indoor and outdoor.

Opening hours: Mon-Sat: 8.30-23.00, Sun: 8.30-22.30. *Parking:* Very limited metered on-street parking. *Accessibility/Pushchairs:* Four steep steps to the entrance and a narrow doorway. Shallower access route from RHS of the outdoor seating area. Spacious inside. *Birthdays/celebrations:* Back of restaurant available. Will serve a cake brought from home.

Centotre

103 George Street, EH2 3ES
0131 225 1550
info@centotre.com
www.centotre.com
Italian restaurant situated on prime venue on George St, pricing as expected for location. Tables both inside and outside. Children's menu with drawing and games and party bag provided. Spacious (enough room for pushchair at table), tables at side/back provide more privacy for breastfeeding.

Opening hours: Mon-Sat 07.30-00.00, Sun 10.00-22.00. *Parking:* Paid parking on George St. *Accessibility:* Several steps up. *Birthdays/celebrations:* Event catering either at venue or elsewhere. Contact events@lovehappyfood.com.

Get the most up-to-date information on
www.efuf.co.uk

Chiquito

29-31 Frederick Street, EH2 2ND
0131 225 4579
www.chiquito.co.uk
Comfortable table service restaurant serving a wide range of Tex-Mex dishes. Friendly, helpful staff. Toilets in this branch were down a flight of stairs.

Chop Chop

248 Morrison Street, EH3 8DT
0131 221 1155
www.chop-chop.co.uk
In 2010, Chop Chop was voted Britain's most popular Chinese restaurant and it has been highly reviewed by the local and national press since opening in 2006. Our experience here was very positive, the staff were very friendly to our 3 children and the food was both excellent and reasonably priced. We had the Unlimited Banquet option at £18.50 per adult, children under 5 dine for FREE and older children are charged £1.70 per portion of dumplings. The banquet gave us a great selection of flavours, a favourite being the pork and coriander dumplings (a house speciality) and was great for giving children a wide range of Chinese food to try out. Staff also brought colouring sheets and pencils to keep the children busy. Seats around 80. See p 164 for Chop Chop in Leith.

Opening hours: Tues-Fri 12.00-14.00, 17.30-22.00. Sat 12.00-14.00, 17.00-22.00. Sun 12.30-14.30, 17.00-22.00.

Circle Café and Bakery

1 Brandon Terrace, Canonmills, EH3 5EA
0131 624 4666
food@thecirclecafe.com
www.thecirclecafe.com

The café is attractively set out – plate glass windows, tall shelves, blackboards displaying the menu. Yummy-looking range of cakes on display, including some more unusual ones. The café serves high quality Brewhaha tea. All food made on premises and sourced from scratch, plus locally sourced where possible. Staff were friendly and service was prompt. The café can't accommodate very many young children at a time – there's limited space for pushchairs and only one highchair. Coming here with your child would probably feel like a bit of a treat for you both. Seats around 40.

Opening hours: Mon-Sat 08.30-16.30, Sun 09.00-16.30. *Accessibility: Low step.* *Pushchairs: Limited space – best to find a table near front window.*

Cuckoo's Bakery

150 Dundas Street, EH3 5DQ
0131 556 62224
hello@cuckoosbakery.co.uk
www.cuckoosbakery.co.uk
Cupcakes and cuckoo clocks are the novelty for adults and children at this café. Although the premises are small, there is a steady stream of parents calling in here. The cupcakes are to be recommended as they are freshly baked on the premises every day, with seasonal themes. Scottish ingredients are used as far as possible. The cakes are tasty and they even have baby cupcakes! The only downside for under 5s still in nappies is that, at the time of visiting at Christmas 2011, there was no room to change a nappy except on the floor of the only toilet. Perhaps of interest to those organising parties – there is a cupcake delivery service, which is by bike! Seats around 16.

Opening hours: Tues-Thurs 10.00-17.30, Fri/Sat 10.00-18.00, Sun 11.00-17.00. *Parking: Paid on-street.*

David Bann

56-58 St Mary's Street, EH1 1SX
0131 556 5888
www.davidbann.com
Has to be Edinburgh's restaurant of choice for vegetarian diners. Vegan options also available, with some menu items vegan on request. The staff are great and children are welcome.

The Restaurant at Debenhams

Debenhams, 4th Floor, 109 Princes Street, EH2 3AA
0844 561 6161
www.debenhams.com
Self-service restaurant with friendly staff and stunning views of the castle. Varied menu including hot food (with children's options cooked to order). Excellent range of cakes. Relaxed and spacious surroundings. There is a comprehensive allergy advice file, provided on request, which sets out all the ingredients in each dish for those with dietary requirements. Seats around 115.

Opening hours: Sun-Wed 09.30-16.00, Thurs 09.30-18.00, Fri 09.30-16.30, Sat 09.00-16.30. Toilets: On same floor as restaurant.

Empires Café   ££

24 St Mary's Street, EH1 1SU
0131 466 0100
www.empirescafe.co.uk
A bohemian Turkish restaurant and tea shop just off the Royal Mile. Persian carpets line the wooden walls and seats, with beautiful hanging Turkish lamps and candle-lit tables. There is an upper loft-style section with low tables and cushion seating for 16 – perfect for an intimate birthday gathering! Delicious food

including Meze platters, and with live music on the weekend. Watch timings – only open in afternoons and evenings. Pushchairs need to be folded. Book in advance. Bring your own bottle. Cash or cheque only. Seats around 25.

Opening hours: Lunch Mon-Sat 12.00-15.00. Dinner Mon-Thurs 17.00-22.30, Fri/Sat 17.00-23.00. Parking: Metered.

Espresso Mondo   £

116 Lothian Road, EH3 9BE
0131 228 3990
www.espressomondobistro.co.uk
Good central place to meet for a drink, snack, or light meal. Menu includes breakfasts, sandwiches, jacket potatoes, pasta and soup as well as pastries, muffins and cakes. No specific children's menu, but half portions are available. Table service. Relaxed seating towards the back of the bistro offers a bit more space and the possibility of parking a pushchair or two. If you are visiting with a pushchair, use the side entrance where there are two small steps, instead of trying to navigate the steeper ones at the front. Seats around 50.

Opening hours: 8.00-23.00 daily. Parking: Castle Terr car park nearby. Accessibility/ Pushchairs: Two small steps at side entrance. Nappy changing: In female toilet.

Filling Station   ££

235 High Street, EH1 1PE
0131 226 2488
Children are welcome in the restaurant area of this bar/restaurant which serves American, Mexican and Italian food and baked potatoes. The staff are helpful, child-friendly and attentive. The food was good for the price. The restaurant has a classic British car themed décor, which

is sure to interest under 5s. They also have a menu for children and a great pack including games, pencils and stickers.

Opening hours: Mon-Thurs, Sun 08.00-22.30, Fri-Sat 08.00-23.00. Accessibility/Pushchairs: There are steps to the bar area, but the restaurant is accessible.

Filmhouse Café/Bar ££

88 Lothian Road, EH3 9BZ
0131 229 5932
cafebar@filmhousecinema.com
www.filmhousecinema.com
Stopped in for a break from Saturday shopping with our 9 mth old in his pushchair Ordered at the bar and food and drink were brought to our table. A good selection of food and beverages to choose from, and vegetarians and vegans are well catered for. Eclectic range of specials plus old favourites such as nachos, jacket potatoes and salads. The falafel with side salad was excellent and staff were very helpful and accommodating. All in all, a relaxed and friendly atmosphere to have a bite to eat with your baby! Seats around 140.

Opening hours: Sun-Thurs 10.00-23.30, Fri/Sat 10.00-00.30. Babies and children welcome until 21.00. Parking: On-street parking. Nearest car park is nearby on Semple St. Toilets: Downstairs and easily accessible.

La Fontana ££

1 Howard Street, EH3 5JP
0131 556 6887
This is one of the restaurants closest to the East Gate of the Botanic Gardens. The Italians love their bambini and this place makes you feel that

you are in a relaxed Continental atmosphere where your children are valued customers too. Run by two friends, this Italian restaurant is a cosy and friendly place. On a Friday at early tea time, a few families like to drop in for a treat at the end of the week. I have seen the waiters entertain the little ones with napkin folding or other tricks!

Once your kids have been here, they will be looking forward to the ice-cream dessert served in a penguin mould, which they can then take home! The food is very tasty, the prices reasonable and service speedy. Lovely Italian wine for the adults on the menu. The lunchtime menu is particularly good value and they do take away pizza, which can be tempting. The seafood specials are often fantastic. Seats around 40. Quote (Bess, 9): "Why is it not in Edinburgh for Under 5s already?"

Opening hours: 12.00-22.00 daily. Parking: Paid. Nappy changing: In female toilet.

The French Fancies £

42 London Street, EH3 6PT
0131 558 1002
thefrenchfancies@gmail.com
Delightful little French café just opened at the foot of Broughton St. Already has nice pastries and tasty French classics like Croque Monsieur and the menu is expanding. Charming place with staff who couldn't be more friendly. For children there are babyccinos and smaller portions on request. In addition to 2 highchairs they have children's stools. A lovely place for a quick, cosy cuppa just off the beaten track. Seats 15-18.

Opening hours: Mon-Sat 08.00-18.00, Sun 10.00-16.00. Parking: Limited on-street. Pushchairs: Space for pushchairs but café down a short flight of stone steps. Play area: Small play corner with children's table, chairs and toy box.

Fruitmarket Gallery Café

45 Market Street, EH1 4DF
0131 225 2583
info@fruitmarket.co.uk
www.fruitmarket.co.uk
Bright and contemporary café offering an eclectic menu (including Turkish, Spanish and Thai food) covering bistro style soup, deli-filled rolls, salads and sharing platters. Very attentive waiter service. All dishes freshly prepared to order and the ambience is relaxed and informal so this is somewhere to sit back, relax and enjoy – not a fast food option! Coffee and cakes strongly recommended. For children there are healthy snacks (soups, pittas and dips) available at reasonable prices. Seats around 36 indoors.

Opening hours: Mon-Sat 11.00-18.00, Sun 12.00-17.00. Parking: Nearest car park Waverley Station. Accessibility: Via ground floor entrance. Pushchairs: Limited space, may need to fold.

Garfunkels

130 High Street, EH1 1QS
0131 220 4445
www.garfunkels.co.uk
Comfortable, casual table service restaurant serving British and American dishes. Salad bar, fish and chips, burgers, pizza. Goodie bag for children.

Opening hours: Mon-Wed, Sun 08.00-22.30, Thurs-Sat 08.00-23.30. Accessibility: Step at front of restaurant. However, restaurant is in the process of arranging a ramp for easier access. Birthdays/celebrations: No specific package but happy to accommodate.

Gennaro

64 Grassmarket, EH1 2JR
0131 226 3706
Traditional, long-established Italian restaurant which welcomes families. Varied menu with children's portions available. No prams allowed, pushchairs must be folded. Seating outside continental style. If not too busy, waiters like to entertain children, allowing parents to enjoy their meal in peace. Carry-out food available.

Hamilton's Bar and Kitchen

16-18 Hamilton Place, EH3 5AU
0131 226 4199
info@hamiltonsedinburgh.co.uk
www.hamiltonsedinburgh.co.uk
This gastro pub offers an all day service, offering breakfasts and a varied and comprehensive menu for lunch and dinner. They cater well for the under 5s with several highchairs, lots of space to manoeuvre pushchairs and nappy-changing facilities in accessible toilet on the ground floor. Staff are very accommodating, there's a children's menu (adapted versions of the main menu, including homemade fish fingers) and dietary requirements are catered for. Due to licensing restrictions, children need to be out by 20.00, but are made to feel welcome at all other times.

With over 70 seats, birthdays and parties can be accommodated – the restaurant section can be closed off if required. FREE WiFi throughout.

Opening hours: From 09.00 daily.

Hard Rock Café · **££**

20 George Street, EH2 2PH
0131 260 3000
Busy and informal family restaurant, with a focus on US and Tex/Mex food. There are small booths available for family gatherings or, if you prefer, some privacy for breastfeeding. Colour-in books, crayons and balloons for children, also plasma screens and fairly loud music to keep them amused. Staff friendly, very attentive, and welcoming to children.

Opening hours: Sun-Thurs 12.00-23.00, Fri-Sat 12.00-23.30. Pushchairs: Very little room to accommodate pushchairs, but staff will make every effort to find space – can be parked in the shop area.

Harvey Nichols
Forth Floor Restaurant · **£££**

30-34 St Andrew Square, EH2 2AD
0131 524 8350
www.harveynichols.com
The main restaurant within Harvey Nichols located on the top floor of the upmarket department store and offers a selection of high quality contemporary Scottish dishes. The Forth Floor Seafood bar also provides a selection of fresh seafood. Despite the initial appearance of an expensive and formal restaurant the place is surprisingly child friendly. The seating is widely spaced and there are a couple of larger round tables towards the back that can accommodate

groups with prams. The menu has a small selection of children's meals but the restaurant also offers all meals on the main menu as half portions, and they also provide colouring pencils for older children. The terrace, which has lovely views across the city, is pretty narrow and therefore not really suited to prams or small children. We found it was a pleasant spot to catch up over a coffee on a quiet afternoon and the staff were helpful in providing highchairs for the babies. The larger child-friendly tables are situated away from the windows so you can't really appreciate the view and the coffee is obviously more expensive than your average Edinburgh café.

Opening hours: Lunch Mon-Fri 12.00-15.00, Sat-Sun 12.00-15.30. Dinner 18.00-22.00. Parking: There is a store car park (fee applies), phone 0131 524 8388 to book. Street parking is available adjacent to the store in St Andrew Sq. Accessibility/Pushchairs: Lift access from the ground floor directly up to the restaurant. Majority of tables were widely spaced.

Henderson's · **£**

94 Hanover Street, EH2 1DR
0131 225 2131 (restaurant)
0131 225 6694 (deli)
mail@hendersonsofedinburgh.co.uk
www.hendersonsofedinburgh.co.uk
Vegetarian café/restaurant. With a lot of space and a number of tables it's a good meeting place once you're down the stairs at the entrance. Food portions are a nice size and healthy, and we found there was a lot of choice for our 2 yr old. Staff were friendly and it had a café feel about it. There is also the Henderson's Deli and shop at 92 Hanover St.

Opening hours: Mon-Sat 08.00-22.00, last hot food 21.30 Mon-Wed, 22.00 Thurs-Sat. Open Sun Aug and Dec only – 11.00-16.00 (restaurant). Mon-Fri 08.00-19.00, Sat 10.00-18.00 (deli). Accessibility/Pushchairs: There are 5 or 6 steep steps to get into the basement, but there is plenty of room once inside.

Nappy changing: In male and female toilets.
Play area: A few toys and books available.
Birthdays/celebrations: Email or phone for details.

folded, the toilets and changing facilities are accessible and nearby. A stylish relaxed getaway, while remaining child friendly.

Opening hours: 09.30-17.30.

Henderson's @ St John's

3 Lothian Road, EH2 4BJ
0131 229 0212
mail@hendersonsofedinburgh.co.uk
www.hendersonsofedinburgh.co.uk/st-johns.php
A cosy café/restaurant in the heart of the city centre located underneath St John's Church on the corner of Princes St and Lothian Rd, serving a range of tasty vegetarian dishes as well as coffee and cake. Children's menu for under 12s.They describe themselves as having a laid back and family-friendly atmosphere and I found this to be very much the case. The food always looks amazing and tastes fantastic – a large array of vegetarian dishes are on offer at reasonable prices. The outside seating (weather permitting!) has a great view of the castle. Access from Lothian Rd is down a steep flight of steps.

Opening hours: Mon-Sat 10.00-17.00, Sun 11.00-16.00. *Parking:* Nearest is George St or Castle Terr. *Pushchairs:* Access OK from Princes St, room enough inside.

The Hub Café

Castlehill, EH1 2NE
0131 473 2067
cafehub@eif.co.uk
www.thehub-edinburgh.com
Relaxed friendly café at top of Royal Mile. Child friendly, spacious and uncluttered (with table service). Separate children's menu and small portions of adult meals too. Good variety of sandwiches, home cooked soups and very nice cakes. Pushchairs can easily be taken in un-

John Lewis
The Place to Eat

St James Centre, EH1 3SP
0131 556 9121
www.johnlewis.com
Large, busy, self-service restaurant and espresso bar on level 4. Fantastic views over the city from large windows. Vegetarian dishes, as well as children's portions and lunchboxes. Small selection of baby food available to buy. Plenty of room for pushchairs. Staff will assist with getting trays to tables. Bibs, bowls and spoons available. Easy access to fantastic baby facilities, "the loos with the views". Children made most welcome everywhere, but the smaller espresso bar with its temptingly low furniture and glass walls is more suitable for babies and older children than lively toddlers.

Opening hours: Mon-Wed, Fri 09.00-18.00, Thurs 09.00-20.00, Sat 09.00-18.30, Sun 10.00-18.00. *Parking:* Paid dedicated car park. *Toilets, nappy changing and breastfeeding:* On same floor in Parent and Child Room.

Leo's Beanery

23a Howe Street, EH3 6TF
0131 556 8403
info@leosbeanery
Fast becoming a hit with mothers in the area who think it is so great that they will only tell their best friends so it doesn't get too crowded – a café with a play area with a train set! The

156

menu is healthy and delicious with options for children on request. If you are sitting in the play area the staff will come and take your order at the table and give you a jug of water while you wait. The decor is very pleasant.

It is a basement café so access is an issue. I visited when I was pregnant and was offered assistance in getting a pushchair up and down the stairs. Seats around 40.

Opening times: Tues-Sun 09.00-17.00. Toilets/Nappy changing: Small with separate space for nappy changing.

Metro Brasserie

Apex International Hotel, 31-35 Grassmarket, EH1 2NS
0131 474 3466
www.apexhotels.co.uk
Chic brasserie in the centre of the city. Open daily for lunch and dinner and snacks in bar area. Children's portions taken from main menu.

MUMS Great Comfort Food

4a Forrest Road, EH1 2QN
0131 260 9806
mum@mumsgreatcomfortfood.com
www.monstermashcafe.co.uk/index.html
MUMS celebrates retro British foods, with a focus on good ingredients. Our waitress was friendly and prompt, but also accommodating, when we asked for slightly different things from the menu choices. Homemade soup was particularly tasty. Portions were good for both adult and child. Great range of puddings.

Bathroom fittings could do with a little update, but the fun visuals, along with good food at good prices, makes this a great place for a family meal. "Tasty" (the macaroni cheese) and "really cool" (copies of the Beano available) showed my son was also impressed. Seats around 45.

Opening times: Mon-Fri 08.00-22.30, Sat/Sun 09.00-22.30. Toilets: Down a fairly steep flight of stairs.

Olive Tree Café

St George's West Church, 58 Shandwick Place, EH2 4RT
0131 225 7001
mail@stgeorgeswest.com
www.stgeorgeswest.com/café
This community-run café serves freshly made soups, sandwiches, baked potatoes, panini and hot meals at reasonable prices. The helpful and kindly staff, many of whom are volunteers, are happy to introduce children to the toybox. If you can avoid the lunch rush, this self-service café is a relaxing place to linger. A couple of high-backed wicker pod chairs are perfect for breastfeeding. Pop into the adjoining Hadeel shop, which sells Palestinian wood and textile crafts and olive oil products. Seats 80-100.

Opening hours: Mon-Fri 9.00-15.00. Last food served at 14.00. Extended opening during the Edinburgh Festival. Parking: Limited metered parking. Accessibility/Pushchairs: Ring the bell at the side door on Shandwick Pl to avoid steps. Ask to be shown the exit button which is slightly unclear. Toilets: Lift access to accessible toilet. Birthdays/celebrations: Café can be hired, but for evenings only. Other rooms in the church are available for parties. Details on the website.

The Orchard Bar

1-2 Howard Place, EH3 5JZ
0131 550 0850
www.theorchardbar.co.uk
Near the East Gate of the Royal Botanic

Gardens is the very welcoming Orchard Bar. It has an excellent separate family room off the main bar, complete with ice cream counter. The children's menu includes cheesy pasta, fish and chips or soup – and half portions from the main menu are also available. For adults, as well as sandwiches they often have game on the menu for pub prices and always have an Anstruther Catch of the Day – and my favourite, goat's cheese soufflé. There are crayons to keep the little ones entertained.

The family room is on street level and I have seen up to 10 pushchairs parked in it! The staff are very friendly and helpful – opening doors on your arrival and giving table service for drinks and food. They are very happy to cater for groups of mums and babies and family parties. There are tables outside on the street if the weather is good enough. It's an excellent place to meet up early lunchtime in the week as you can usually get the family room to yourselves. This pub wins my prize for service with a smile.

Opening hours: Food served 12.00-20.30; kids allowed until 20.30. **Parking:** Paid parking on-street. **Accessibility:** To bar area. Different levels elsewhere. **Pushchairs:** Yes – especially in family room.

Pizza Express ££

32 Queensferry Street, EH2 4QS
0131 225 8863
www.pizzaexpress.co.uk
Also at: 1 Deanhaugh St, Stockbridge, EH4 1LU, Victoria Terr, 59-63 George IV Bridge, EH1 1RN, 23 Northbridge, EH1 1SB, 111 Holyrood Rd, EH8 8AU, Waterview House, Leith, EH6 6QU and 2nd Floor, Ocean Terminal, EH6 6JJ (see p 170). Pizzas with all sorts of toppings (including sultanas!) and dough balls and ice creams that are just a little bit different. Crayons, paper and balloons are available to distract impatient young diners.

Opening hours: Mon-Thurs, Sun 11.30-10.30, Fri/Sat 11.30-23.00. **Birthdays/celebrations:**

Can cater for children's parties if given prior notice.

Porto & Fi on the Mound ££

9 North Bank Street, EH1 2LP
0131 225 9494
A beautifully designed, airy venue with windows opening onto the Mound and Edinburgh views beyond. We were expecting great things when we visited this newly opened branch of Porto & Fi, thanks to the popularity of the original branch in Newhaven, and we weren't disappointed. Food is fresh and delicious, with a tempting selection of breakfast (until midday, all day on Sun), light meals, mains and baking. Children can have smaller portions of adult menu, or cheesy pasta, or fish goujons with curly fries. The menu changes 4 times a year to include the best the season has to offer. Seating also available outside, to the side of the café. Seats around 40 indoors and outdoors. Read about Porto & Fi in Newhaven on p 170.

Opening hours: Mon-Sat 10.00-late, Sun 10.00-18.00.

The Scottish Café and Restaurant ££

The Scottish National Gallery; the Mound (Weston Link), EH2 2EL
0131 226 6524
info@thescottishcafe.com
www.thescottishcafeandrestaurant.com
An airy space situated in a prime location at the Weston Link. It's a haven for a coffee or a meal to be enjoyed either before/after a play outside in Princes St Gdns, a visit at the National Galleries or Academy or indeed any expedition in or near Princes St. The Aberdonian butteries and the Cullen Skink are commendable and

your child can choose from a standard children's menu (made with quality products) or a few of the dishes as a half portion. Not ideal for a "tight budget day", but quality is guaranteed. Seats 175 indoors and 50 outdoors (weather permitting).

Opening hours: Mon-Wed, Fri/Sat 09.00-17.30, Thurs 09.00-17.30, Sun 10.00-17.30.

Scottish National Portrait Gallery Café

1 Queen Street, EH2 1JD
0131 624 6200
pginfo@nationalgalleries.org
www.nationalgalleries.org/portraitgallery
Lovely airy cafe which is just inside the door of the Portrait Gallery so very easy to pop into. A small issue (although I can see why they've done it) is that there's a "no pushchairs" policy, so you park your pushchair in the buggy park (to the right of the entrance, just by the big glass lift) and bring your little one through to sit in one of the many highchairs. This can be tricky if you're on your own with a lively toddler, as I was! Staff will happily help you with food to your table, however. There were healthy and interesting options for a hot lunch, plus soup and very nice sandwiches. You could splash out on a mid-price option for lunch or keep it basic with a reasonably priced soup. The home baking is marvellous and my daughter and I shared a very delicious cheese and herb scone. My latte was lovely. There are interactive screens at the side of the cafe which will interest older children. Seats 40-50.

Opening hours: 10.00-17.00, til 19.00 Thurs.

St Giles Cathedral Café

Royal Mile, EH1 1RE
0131 225 9442
info@stgilescathedral.org.uk
www.stgilescathedral.org.uk
An excellent café, situated behind the Cathedral – you need to walk all the way round to the back to find the entrance, or you can get to it through the Cathedral itself. Very cosily nestled under the Cathedral arches, but decorated in a modern, light style, this is a great place to meet for coffee and cake or something more substantial. Very good selection of hot and cold food, and the range of home baking was particularly impressive. We visited on a rainy day and I can't think of anywhere better to take shelter with a cup of coffee. The lack of baby facilities (e.g. nappy changing) is disappointing but it wouldn't stop me visiting again. Seats around 60.

Opening hours: Mon-Sat 09.00-17.00, Sun 11.00-17.00. Accessibility/Pushchairs: Steps from the Cathedral, or a ramp down if you access from the outside. Even then there are 3 steps down into the café itself, but pushchairs can be left at the top of the stairs. Limited space inside café for pushchairs.

Traverse Bar Café

10 Cambridge Street, EH1 2ED
0131 228 5383
www.traverse.co.uk/bar-café
A large welcoming open bar café, part of the Traverse Theatre. A great place for veggies with plenty of good veggie food on offer. The kids' menu is a bit limiting – half portion of adult sandwiches or soup and not all under 5s will like the selection (hummus/curried mayo/smoked salmon and cream cheese). I asked for a ham sandwich instead and they didn't have any ham on the menu at all. They provided a plain cheese sandwich instead. I also thought the bloomer bread it was served on (no choice) was a bit thick for smaller children. There is a comfy

couch area that is great for wee ones with a really good selection of books and drawing stuff to keep them entertained. I would have liked to see more of this sort of child-friendly thought given to the kids menu. Also, watch for the £2 fee to use a debit card. Seats around 80.

Opening hours: Mon-Wed 11.00-00.00, Thurs-Sat 11.00-01.00, Sun performance dependent. Parking: Limited on-street paid parking/NCP car park 2 mins walk. Nappy changing: Changing room (male and female).

Urban Angel (Forth Street)

1 Forth Street, EH1 2JS
0131 556 6323
info@urban-angel.co.uk
www.urban-angel.co.uk
The newest Urban Angel (the other is at 121 Hanover St) serves high-quality Scottish organic cuisine that can be simple café bistro or full restaurant in style. Also does a great value tapas menu. The restaurant is over 2 floors with a small area upstairs where pushchairs can be left. We found the staff very friendly. We ate from the lunch menu which included some excellent specials from the daily specials board. The atmosphere was relaxed and child friendly and the restaurant had installed a new nappy changing table. Watch the stairs down to the changing facility, however. Seats around 50.

Opening hours: 09.00 til late. Parking: On-street, limited. Pushchairs: Limited space may need to fold. Toilets: Downstairs and fairly tight for space. Birthdays/celebrations: Happy to have parties.

Visit our website for updates:
www.efuf.co.uk

VinCaffè

11 Multrees Walk, EH1 3DQ
0131 557 0088
reservations@vincaffe.co.uk
www.valvonacrolla.co.uk/html/vincaffe.html
A stylish venue for relatively formal dining. Delicious, fresh Italian dishes. Under 5s are welcome. Clip-on booster seats available, but can be quite unstable if your child is wriggly, so may be best to ask for the free-standing highchair (they have one). Seating available downstairs in the café area, upstairs in the restaurant, or outside if the weather is fine, where you can watch the world go by on Multrees Walk. Seats around 80 (indoors and outdoors).

Opening hours: Mon-Sat 08.00-late, Sunday brunch 11.00-18.00. Accessibility/Pushchairs: Not much space for pushchairs although they are welcome. Lift to restaurant upstairs. Birthdays/celebrations: Cakes and decorations can be taken in in advance.

Vittoria

19 George IV Bridge, EH1 1EN
0131 225 1740
www.vittoriarestaurant.com
Vittorias on Leith Walk is a bit of an institution – this was my first time to the George IV Bridge restaurant. Even on a busy Saturday, the staff were excellent and so attentive. The kids menu (up to age 10) was excellent value – £6 for a main (good choice of Italian staples plus salads, sandwiches) plus a drink and ice-cream, with the 2nd child eating for £1 (which was donated to Cash for Kids) where adult is eating a standard main course. Colouring-in and a balloon was given to each child on arrival. The food was excellent – I can't praise this chain highly enough, it is the very essence of a family friendly restaurant in my opinion. Seats around 225 – even on a busy Sat during the Festival we were seated within 5 mins.

basic for nappy changing (located within the accessible toilet) but they are clean. Overall, if burgers are your thing, then this is your place. Seats around 50-60 indoors. No booking.

Opening hours: Mon-Wed 08.00-21.00 Thurs/ Fri 08.00-22.00 Sat 09.00-21.00. **Parking: On-street**, *pay and display.* **Accessibility:** *Step up to entrance.* **Pushchairs:** *Room for pushchairs at the front of the restaurant, plus room by some tables.* **Birthdays/celebrations:** *Negotiable.*

Zizzi

42-45 Queensferry Street, EH2 4RA
0131 225 6937
www.zizzi.co.uk/restaurants/edinburgh-queensferry
A good spot for rounding off a shopping trip, this is a buzzy and family friendly restaurant with typically popular Italian food; pizza and pasta of course but also a nice selection of risotto and meat/fish alternatives. Service is quick and friendly, and crayons are provided for little ones to decorate their own menus. Online discount codes are usually available to make a good value family meal out. See p 173 for Zizzi, Ocean Terminal.

Opening hours: Mon-Sat 12.00-23.00, Sun 12.00-22.30. **Parking:** *Metered parking nearby.*

Opening hours: Mon-Sat 10.00-23.00, Sun 12.00-23.00. **Birthdays/celebrations:** *Has a separate party room. Packages from £17pp.*

Wannaburger

7-8 Queensferry Street, EH2 4PA
0131 220 0036
info@wannaburger.com
www.wannaburger.com
Edinburgh's premier takeaway or sit-in burger restaurant. It's had a quite recent refit and is smart and clean. It is family friendly with a surprisingly large menu (this is a burger place, after all). The kid's options are suitably mini and decently priced. When it's busy, this place can seem cramped but that is deceiving: this is a good size restaurant. The staff are friendly and the food arrives quickly. The facilities are

NORTH EDINBURGH

Anchor Café £

Newkirkgate, Leith, EH6 6AD
0131 554 4750
info@leithcommunitycentre.com
www.leithcommunitycentre.com/anchor_cafe.htm
A bright, spacious café with a view over historic

South Leith Parish Church graveyard. It offers a fairly limited menu of pies, chips, bacon rolls, sausage and beans etc, along with a rotating soup/main/sweet of the day at very reasonable prices. There is no specific provision for children e.g. no plastic plates, sippy cups, children's cutlery etc, but my very picky 2½ yr old was delighted with her beans on toast and cup of milk. There is also FREE internet access available on 4 computers. All in all, a good, cheap spot for a coffee break or lunch if you're out and about in Leith, or if you're using the other facilities in the Community Centre. Seats around 80.

Opening hours: Mon-Fri 09.00-15.00, Sat 09.00-12.00. Accessibility: The whole Leith Community Education Centre is accessible – lift up to 1st floor beside Superdrug.

Brewers Fayre
Newhaven Quay

51-53 Newhaven Place, EH6 4TX
0131 555 1570
www.brewersfayre.co.uk
Large family-friendly pub and restaurant with adjoining soft play area. The emphasis is on kids with a good children's menu (our 19 mth old wolfed down her spaghetti bolognese), lots of highchairs, dedicated nappy changing room and the Fun Factory, great for a post-lunch play. A session for over 3s costs £2.50/hour but the toddler area is FREE. For adults the menu is standard pub fare which suited us just fine. On Sundays they do a popular carvery buffet and there are good value offers during the week. While we were there there was a birthday party in the Fun Factory but the place easily absorbed all the extra people and the kids, and our toddler played very happily in the ball pit without too much disturbance. Not a bad place to stop off in Newhaven for a play on a wet day – the Fun Factory is open 12.00-20.00 most days.

Opening hours: Mon-Sat 12.00-23.00, Sun 12.00-22.30.

The Britannia View
Restaurant (Debenhams)

2nd Floor, Ocean Terminal Shopping Centre, Ocean Drive, Leith
A café canteen in the sky! With a panoramic glass wall facing right over the Royal Yacht Britannia, and the Forth and Fife behind, you can enjoy great views whatever the weather. There is loads of space between tables, a kids table and children's area with armchairs for adults. There is baby food for sale, paper bibs provided and a lunchbox carton with paper and crayons. Excellent for large groups of mums – and dads!

Opening hours: 10.00-17.00. Parking: FREE in Ocean Terminal. Nappy changing: Specific room with chair.

Café Citron

14 Marischal Place, EH4 3NJ
0131 539 7977
mail@cafecitron.co.uk
Café serving coffee, tea, cake, sandwiches. Very welcoming staff who interacted enthusiastically with our 10 mth old. Pleasant, although small, environment. Staff were more than willing to heat our baby's food. Branches also at 24 Viewforth, EH10 4JG (opening hours 07.00-17.00), 85 George St (ESPC showroom), EH2 3ES (opening hours 08.30-16.30) and Exchange Pl, 3, Semple St, EH3 8BL (opening hours 07.00-16.00). Seats 15 indoors and a few outdoors.

Opening hours: 06.00-17.00. **Parking:** *FREE on-street parking – can be busy.* **Pushchairs:** *Access OK but space limited.* **Toilets:** *One very small.* **Birthdays/celebrations:** *Can take away sandwich platters, phone 0131 221 1172.*

Café Modern One

Scottish National Gallery of Modern Art
75 Belford Road, EH4 3DR
0131 332 8600
Access by lift to self-service café in basement. Recently refurbished, this remains a firm favourite for delicious home-cooked soups, filled ciabattas, hot meals, amazing salads and great cakes. Outdoor terrace for fine weather, where children can enjoy the garden. The only downside is that it can be very busy at lunchtime.

Opening hours: 10.00-17.00.

Café Modern Two

Scottish National Gallery of Modern Art Two
(formerly the Dean Gallery)
73 Belford Road, EH4 3DS
0131 624 6200
A lovely café, with very helpful staff who were happy to accommodate our group of 7 babies and mums. The café is situated in 2 rooms, so we were able to take over one end without disturbing others in the room next door. Table service, and plenty of space for pushchairs and highchairs. Excellent food, and delicious baking. Children's options include kids' hot chocolate, babyccino, fruit juice and brownie with milk. Also open to non-gallery visitors. Seats around 80.

Opening hours: Open from 10.00.

Café Revive
Marks & Spencer

Unit 2, Craigleith Retail Park, 40 South Groathill Avenue, EH4 2LN
0131 343 3641
www.marksandspencer.com
A light, bright café. Extensive range of hot and cold food, with children specifically catered for with lunch bags and babyccinos. The café is very child friendly with staff always on hand to carry trays, help with pushchairs, move highchairs etc. Crayons and activity sheets are available. The coffee is particularly delicious. New air conditioning system to avoid the café getting too hot in the summer! Other branches in Edinburgh include Ocean Terminal and South Gyle shopping centre. Seats around 80.

Opening hours: Mon-Fri 9.00-19.30, Sat 9.00-18.30, Sun 10.00-17.30. **Parking:** *Lots of spaces, parent and child and disabled parking all close by.* **Toilets:** *On the same floor. Ladies has a number of cubicles, one of which is large enough to fit a pushchair. Large separate accessible toilet.* **Nappy changing:** *Separate unisex changing area. Also a fold-down changing unit in ladies' loo.*

The Cairn Café
Tiso, Leith

41 Commercial Street, EH6 6JD
www.tiso.com
A café with salads, sandwiches and hot meals. Specials board changes daily and you can also take food away. For children there is a very good selection of soup and sandwiches and lots of nutritious drinks and also baby food on offer. The home-made cakes and biscuits were a particular favourite of my children – Molly, 4 and Kate, 2. The staff were very friendly and helpful. Food is brought to your table once it's been ordered from the counter. There are menus on the table so you could sit and order from there too. Seats around 25.

Opening hours: Mon-Sat 09.00-17.00, Sun 11.00-16.30. *Play area:* Indoor, with a blackboard and some toys.

Channings Hotel and Restaurant **£££**

14 South Learmonth Gardens, EH4 1EZ
0131 315 2226
reserve@channings.co.uk
www.channings.co.uk
A luxury hotel and restaurant near to the Stockbridge/Dean Village area of Edinburgh, which occupies a townhouse once home to Sir Ernest Shackleton. The restaurant is open to non-hotel residents and is located in the basement so you would have to bump downstairs with a pushchair – but there are very willing staff to help out and pushchairs can be stored in the downstairs area. This is more of a special occasion venue where children are well catered for. There is a children's menu and Hipp Organic baby food available. The menu is British food with a fine dining dinner menu and an all-day bar menu. Family events organised occasionally in the spacious conservatory area with children's entertainers and special menus. See website for details of upcoming events. Seats around 60 – 30 in conservatory, 30 in restaurant.

Opening hours: Mon-Sat 11.00-01.00, Sun 12.00-01.00. Children welcome until 21.00. *Parking:* On-street, metered.

Chop Chop **££**

76 Commercial Street, EH6 6LX
0131 553 1818
www.chop-chop.co.uk

Light, open and accessible, this branch of the famous and popular Chinese restaurant is child-friendly and good value. Our 14 mth old enjoyed FREE dumplings while we had the set lunch. Lunch at weekends only. See p 151 for Chop Chop, Central Edinburgh.

Opening hours: Mon-Thurs 18.00-22.00, Fri 18.00-22.30, Sat 12.00-14.00, 17.00-22.30, Sun 12.30-14.30, 17.00-10.00.

Costa Coffee **£**

Ocean Terminal, Leith, EH6 6JJ
0131 555 0824
Extremely accessible, this café opens out on to the ground floor of Ocean Terminal. Self-service style, you can choose from a selection of sandwiches, cakes and coffees, the usual Costa fare. Can be a bit tight to negotiate around the tables with a pushchair but if you sit at the edge there is plenty of room. You can also get coffee to take away. Other branches in Edinburgh include 50 Raeburn Place, 124 Bruntsfield Place, 1 Hanover St, 13a Castle St and 83 George Street.

Cramond Brig **£**

Queensferry Road, EH4 6DY
0131 339 4350
enquiries@cramondbrig.com
www.cramondbrig.com
This is a fantastic, family-friendly place where the only downside is the number of stairs. Although, having said that, the staff were very friendly so would probably assist if required (we visited in a group so didn't need assistance). The children's playroom is definitely the selling point of this venue. Our 1yr old had lots of fun and there were children of all ages in there with him at the same time also having fun dressing up, drawing on the blackboard, playing in the wendy house. The food was really good

and, although we didn't need it, the children's menu looked varied and included more than a couple of dishes that didn't have chips on the side! There are plenty of highchairs and chairs suitable for clip on or fabric portable seats.

Opening hours: Mon, Tues, Thurs 09.00-23.00, Wed 09.00-24.00, Fri 09.00-01.00, Sat 11.00-24.00, Sun 12.00-23.00. Accessibility: Assisted access apart from small area at main entrance. Otherwise numerous steps. Pushchairs: Access is all right, but there are numerous steps inside if going to the Family Restaurant. Nappy changing: In the accessible toilet on the same floor as the main bar but upstairs from the Family restaurant. Play area: Indoor play room with lots of toys for all ages, large blackboard, a wendy house and DVD player. Birthdays/celebrations: Absolutely, especially in the family restaurant. Contact the venue.

Dr Bell's Family Centre ⟨£⟩

15 Junction Place, Leith, EH6 5JA
0131 553 0100
lesley@drbellsleith.org.uk
www.drbellsleith.org.uk
A child-friendly family centre that has a small café, small crèche, parent advice and counselling, summer school, holistic therapies and support groups. The café offers basic sandwich shop style food at very cheap prices – freshly made sandwiches and rolls, soup of the day, jacket potatoes, cakes and hot and cold drinks, including cartons of juice for children and herbal teas. A small gem of a place, especially for those on a low budget, it gets very busy so get there early as there are only 2-3 tables! There is pushchair parking in the foyer entrance and covered overflow area outside – though bring a bike lock for outside. Books for adults to read while in the café are also available. Seats around 12.

Opening hours: Mon-Thurs 10.00-14.00. Nappy changing: There is a separate lockable room with a pull-down changing shelf, running

water and two chairs to sit and breastfeed. *Play area: Free, small area indoors with lots of toys and a sofa for parents. Birthdays/celebrations: The crèche can be hired for birthday parties.*

Drill Hall Arts Café ⟨£⟩

36 Dalmeny Street, Leith, EH6 8RG
0131 555 7100
www.outoftheblue.org.uk
Café located in the Drill Hall space which also houses offices, studios, etc. Nice big open space for children to play though there are people having meetings and working there so they can't be too boisterous. The main space is often used for events and exhibitions. They usually have a few toys. The food is home-made and excellent – mostly vegetarian, organic, free-range and fair-trade. The atmosphere is relaxed and the staff very friendly and accommodating, especially when we had a large drinks spill! There is a lot to look at for under 5s and there are second hand books and CDs for sale. Events and classes on for adults so worth a look. 10 tables and 2 sofas.

Opening hours: Mon-Sat 10.00-17.00. Parking: Plenty of free on-street parking outside.

La Favorita ⟨££⟩

325 Leith Walk, EH6 8SA
0131 554 2430
www.la-favorita.com
Italian restaurant. We had a nice lunch on a weekday. We were welcomed with our pushchair and shown to a suitable table out of the way. It was very quiet though and the tables were close together, at night time I think it could get very busy and difficult for pushchairs. Kids eat for £1 at time of review. Linked to Vittoria.

Opening hours: 12.00-23.00. *Parking:* On-street. *Accessibility:* There's a step in.

Finishing Line Café **£**

Meadowbank Sports Centre, London Road, EH7 6AE
0131 661 5351
info.msc@edinburghleisure.co.uk
www.edinburghleisure.co.uk
Large café that serves a wide range of food including sandwiches, toasties, wraps and rolls and breakfast options. There is a good selection of cakes and buns alongside more substantial hot and cold snacks and main meals. A children's lunchbox is also available with 5 items. I visited the café on a Monday morning with my 2 yr old and 8 mth old to use softplay and have tea and cake. It was very quiet and easy to find a table and highchair. We were able to eat our own snacks as well. My 2 yr old enjoyed the soft play and the bun (which was home made and very tasty). My cup of tea was just a tea bag in a mug but I didn't get to drink it anyway (as is the way with having small children). On one side the café looks out onto the track and an internal gymnasium on the other, both of which provide additional entertainment. In short, a good way to pass an hour or so with your littl'uns in a no-frills but child-friendly venue. Seats around 48.

Opening hours: 10.00-18.00. *Toilets:* On the same level as the café but down a corridor. No space for pushchair. *Play area:* Soft play for younger kids (height restriction applies) that costs £1.80/hr and a small book corner with a couple of toys – free of charge. *Birthdays/celebrations:* Contact events team via mail@edinburghleisure.co.uk

Frankie & Benny's **££**

Ocean Terminal, EH6 6JJ
0131 555 4803
www.frankieandbennys.com
Burgers, pizzas, wraps and great breakfast choices at this all-American restaurant, great for when you need a break from shopping or a treat before the cinema – whatever the time of day happens to be. We visited with three 15 month olds for lunch and we were well catered for with a kids' menu and highchairs. They sell organic baby food for even younger diners. The restaurant feels relaxed and spacious and often has breakfast and lunch deals (we paid £5.95 for one course or £7.95 for two). The kids' menu option is good value for main course, dessert and drink.

Opening hours: Mon-Sat 09.00-23.00, Sun 09.00-22.30.

La Garrigue **££**

88 Commercial Street, EH6 6LX
reservations@lagarrigue.co.uk
www.lagarrigue.co.uk
A very welcoming French bistro where children are well catered for with crayons and even some toys. Tantalising range of food options for adults as well as kids including tasty crepes. Excellent value lunch and early bird dinner menu. Most attentive and friendly staff. Under new ownership/management (used to be Daniel's Bistro). Seats around 70 inside, some outside.

Opening hours: 12.00-22.00.

Guilty Lily

284 Bonnington Road, EH6 5BE
0131 554 5824
www.guiltylily.co.uk
Beautifully refurbished bar on the corner of Newhaven Rd and Bonnington Rd. The inside is comfortable and friendly, with plenty of soft armchairs and sofas, as well as traditional tables and chairs. There is a standard children's menu, choice of pasta, cheese on toast and so on, and ice cream for pudding. A tad limited, but sufficient. The adult menu has a selection of burgers, chips, sandwiches, and mezze, as well as some more substantial specials with fish, meat and vegetarian main course, and a few tasty puddings. Bright and airy, friendly, clean and comfortable. A nice place for a stop off.

Opening hours: 12.00-22.00.

Holiday Inn

107 Queensferry Road, Blackhall, EH4 3HL
0871 942 9025
Inventive children's menu provides plenty of choice (and at time of writing, kids eat FREE); healthy options/"build" your own dinner/kids' cocktail list. There is an outdoor play area for use at Sunday lunchtimes with climbing frame and seesaw.

International Starters

82 Commercial Quay, EH6 6LX
0131 555 2546
edinburgh@internationalstarters.co.uk
www.internationalstarters.co.uk
In some ways ideal for children because of its tapas-style small plates, International Starters felt relaxed and child-friendly. The restaurant prides itself on its eclectic range of dishes hailing from everywhere from Scotland to Asia,

the Mediterranean to the Americas. A lot of the food is exotic and spicy but options like Greek Meze include houmous and pitta bread which were fine for our 15 mth old. Their loaded potato skins and fish and chips would also work well for children. Puddings are more straightforward, with children's ice cream a welcome option. Only open for lunch at the weekends.

Opening hours: Mon-Thurs 17.00-21.30, Fri 17.00-22.00, Sat 12.00-22.00, Sun 12.30-21.00.

Joseph Pearce's

23 Elm Row, EH7 4AA
0131 556 4140
anna@bodabar.com
www.bodabar.com
During the day, this spacious, well-presented pub transforms into a child-friendly Swedish/Scottish restaurant with a play area. Eating utensils for children are provided, as well as a microwave for heating milk and baby food. Kids' menu includes spaghetti (plain or with meatballs), pork noodles, veggie noodles, soup, bread, ice cream. Children may also enjoy the adult menu, such as the Swedish pancakes and Hasselback potatoes. We love the food (the kids especially love the Swedish pancakes!), the play area, and the relaxed atmosphere. It can sometimes get a bit crowded with kids and pushchairs, but that's because it's such a great place to come for lunch! Seats around 20 outside and 30 inside. Booking recommended.

Opening hours: 11.00-17.00 for children. ***Parking:*** *Limited – along Elm Row.* ***Pushchairs:*** *Main dining area is up a short flight of steps, but staff always promptly jump up to offer assistance without being asked, so it is easy to get a pushchair up the steps!* ***Toilets:*** *Up a short set of steps, possibly too narrow for pushchairs.* ***Nappy changing:*** *In male and female toilets.*

Loch Fyne Seafood Restaurant ££

Newhaven Harbour, 25 Pier Place, EH6 4LP
0131 559 3900
www.lochfyne.com
Spacious seafood restaurant in Newhaven, a light and bright room with plenty of space for pushchairs. Some other choices but as expected it is a mainly seafood menu. The 2 course children's menu normally includes a choice such as pasta, fish goujons, sausages, or mussels followed by ice cream. Kids eat FREE at the weekend when adults choose from the a la carte menu. Generally it is worth calling ahead if you plan to go as occasionally the restaurant is closed to other customers for larger private parties. Highchairs are available and there are two booster seats.

Opening hours: Mon-Thurs, Sun 12.00-22.00, Fri-Sat 12.00-22.30. Birthdays/celebrations: Can cater for private parties – you would have to bring your own cake.

Maxi's £

33 Raeburn Place, EH4 1HX
0131 343 3007
rebeccajmaclean@hotmail.co.uk
A great place to go for breakfast, a snack or lunch. Breakfast served til 11.30 and then sandwich/soup/salad lunches and homemade cakes and scones. The food is freshly prepared, you order at the counter and it's brought to your table. A good selection of sandwich fillings for adults and children and also drinks including smoothies and juices. My children (4 and 2) enjoyed drawing and looking at the books in the toy box before they got their sandwiches which were a good size for them. Seats around 34.

Opening hours: Mon-Sat 08.30-17.00, Sun 10.00-17.00. Parking: Paid on-street parking. Pushchairs: Not much space to park them, 2 at a time possible. Better to fold them up, staff will help.

Mimi's Bakehouse ££

63 Shore, EH6 6RA
0131 555 5908
info@mimisbakehouse.com
www.mimisbakehouse.com
A family run café bursting with 1940s character and mouthwatering delights from scones to beautiful cupcakes and an array of all things chocolatey. There is also a varied menu for breakfast, lunch and proper afternoon tea. Booking is recommended and you can BYOB for £4 corkage. We loved the lavish décor and my children polished off their lunch in no time. Very helpful waiting staff provided us with children's cutlery and cool plastic cups and straws. This might be an ideal place to treat a small group of girly pre-schoolers to a cupcake. It was very busy and took a little while to be served, so don't forget your activity bag!

Opening hours: Weekdays 09.00-17.00. Parking: Roadside in surrounding streets. Accessibility: Ramp access but an outer and inner door to gain entry. Nappy changing: Portable folding table on request.

Newhaven Connections Community Café £

7 Craighall Road, EH6 4ND
0131 551 3931
newhavenconnections@n-c.org.uk
www.n-c.org.uk/cafe/café.html
The café serves a good selection of home baking and light lunches. Staff are very friendly and accommodating to children and they ensure a relaxed atmosphere. Food includes home made soup, rolls, toasties and baked potatoes and some delicious cakes. Really great value too. There is a hall next to the café where toddlers could run around to burn off steam, should they wish. A few games and toys are provided.

Opening hours: Tues-Thurs 09.30-16.00.
Parking: FREE, on-street.

Ocean Kitchen Bar and Grill

Ocean Drive, Ocean Terminal, EH6 6JJ
0131 555 6068
Large canteen style café in the centre of Ocean Terminal with fantastic views over the Forth from the floor-to-ceiling windows. Ample seating and space to fit pushchairs and shopping. Choice of sofas for lounging with coffee, or chairs along the windows for eating lunch. Soups, salads, sandwiches and more substantial meals available, as well as coffee and cakes. Pick and mix lunchboxes for children. Lots of organic options, very helpful staff.

Toilets and nappy changing: Ocean Terminal toilets nearby.

Orocco Pier

17 High Street, South Queensferry, EH30 9PP
0870 118 1664
info@oroccopier.co.uk
www.oroccopier.co.uk
This is a very welcoming, roomy restaurant serving Scottish fayre with a relaxed but chic atmosphere. Lovely views of the Firth and the rail bridge for children. The staff – from waiters to managers – are very accommodating and child orientated. Booths are good for families but are further from the views. There is a restaurant and a bistro both offering set menus. Brunch and afternoon tea are also available and there is a good children's menu with healthy fresh options. Booking recommended at peak times. Nice walk down to the harbour afterwards to see the boats with the children.

Opening hours: Mon-Thurs 12.00-15.00, 16.00-22.00. Fri-Sun 12.00-22.00. Children welcome until 19.00. Antico café bar: 07.00-01.00.*Parking:* Limited – on-street. *Accessibility:* Minimal stairs. **Pushchairs:** No/minimal stairs at entrances. Space to park pushchairs. **Toilets:** Accessible toilet on same level as restaurant. **Nappy changing:** Large, clean nappy change in accessible toilet. **Birthdays/celebrations:** Curtained off area available, parties of 10 or more require deposit. Set menu available.

Picnic Café

5 Mid Terrace, South Queensferry, EH30 9LH
0131 331 1346
picniccoffeeshop@hotmail.com
www.picniccoffeeshop.com
This is a little café that we found by chance during a rain storm. Although it is quite small we were given a warm welcome as a family

and noticed that they even had a small play table positioned in one corner. We ordered their excellent fresh coffee and cakes but snacks such as soup and sandwiches were on offer too and takeaway was an option. The café also functions as a gallery and has local artwork for sale on the walls which adds interest. Rain or not, next time we are in South Queensferry we will be popping in again!

Opening hours: Mon-Sat 09.00-16.30, Sun 12.00-16.00. Last hot food order 15.00.

Pizza Express

Waterview House, EH6 6QU
0131 554 4332
www.pizzaexpress.co.uk
This restaurant was crammed with families when we visited one Saturday lunchtime, and it's easy to see why. The staff are very welcoming of little ones and their needs are catered for. We were impressed with their £6.45 4-course children's menu which had doughballs, a selection of pizza/pasta, dessert and a bambinoccino to finish. The adults' food was yummy too. The menu is always great – old favourites that have been going for years, with a good sprinkling of new and interesting dishes to try. Sign up for their frequent offers via the website.

We also visited the newly opened branch on the 2nd floor of Ocean Terminal (0131 555 0606) which we were delighted to find as child-friendly as the Leith branch (staff could not have been more friendly and helpful), with the added bonuses of a little more room, fantastic views across the Forth and easy parking.

Opening hours: Mon-Thurs, Sun 11.30-22.30, Fri/Sat 11.30-23.00.

Porto & Fi

47 Newhaven Main Street, EH6 4NQ
0131 551 1900
enquiries@portofi.com
www.portofi.com
This sea-front café has a number of tables with sea views. The low tables in the window with sofas are quite fun for kids. The kids' menu has a number of choices including fish and chips, fish pie and soups. As well as delicious home baking, there is take-away ice cream. Can get busy at peak times. Downstairs there is a little shop with packaged goods like biscuits, jams and oatmeal. There is a fruit and veg stall too, with lovely seasonal produce. Take it back upstairs to be weighed. Seats around 50. See p 158 for Porto & Fi on the Mound.

Opening hours: Mon-Sat 08.00-20.00 (last orders 19.30), Sun 10.00-18.00 (last orders 17.30). Parking: FREE on Craighall Rd.

Potters Bar and Kitchen

Ocean Terminal, Ocean Drive, Leith, EH6 7DZ
0131 555 6700
edinburgh@pottersbarkitchen.co.uk
www.pottersbarkitchen.co.uk
A large bar and restaurant on the top floor of Ocean Terminal. Dishes include light bites, salads, pasta, fresh seafood and a chargrill selection. It has a nice, friendly and informal atmosphere. It has lovely views over the port and the staff were all very accommodating.

Opening hours: Mon-Sun 10.00-22.30. Parking: FREE in Ocean Terminal. Birthdays/celebrations: Happy to host large parties.

Prezzo

25 Pier Place, EH6 4LP
0131 552 4356
www.prezzorestaurants.co.uk
Italian pizza and pasta restaurant with a fabulous view of the Forth across to Fife. Great on a summer's evening (when it also gets most crowded). We go regularly and always find the staff and the set-up very welcoming to children. There are colouring kits and a good children's menu. The restaurant feels roomy and relaxed. Also at 7-9 North Bridge, EH1 1SB.

Opening hours: 12.00-23.00.

A Room in Leith

1c Dock Place, EH6 6LU
0131 554 7427
www.aroomin.co.uk
Delicious Scottish food in a lovely setting. Darkish when you walk through the door, but go through to the back and there's a nice airy room. From our table we saw ducks swim past the window. They were very accommodating to the 18 mth olds we brought with us and produced children's portions of fish and chips which they enjoyed. Our food, from lamb to risotto to a lovely chicken dish, was fab and filling. We'll be going back.

Opening hours: Lunch 12.00-16.00, dinner 17.30-22.00. **Parking:** *On-street parking.*

Rocksalt Café Deli

46 Constitution Street, Leith, EH6 6RS
0131 554 9873
A relaxed and informal café with a small deli. The café offers a selection of sandwiches, soups and salads and also a small range of larger dishes in a bright and airy building at the northern end of Constitution St. Staff were very friendly and happy to welcome children of all ages. The relaxed and informal atmosphere makes it a good venue for small children. It means you'd probably feel comfortable breastfeeding there too. The children's menu is small but the café would happily adjust portion sizes on the main menu or make specific meals in the deli. The deli can also cater for dietary requirements. BYOB in the evening. A great location in Leith.

Opening hours: Mon-Wed 08.00-16.00, Thurs-Fri 08.00-22.00, Sat 09.30-22.00, Sun 10.00-16.00. **Parking:** *On-street parking nearby.* **Accessibility:** *Majority of seating upstairs but some seating available at ground level.* **Birthdays/celebrations:** *Happy to arrange something special for birthdays.*

Roseleaf Bar Café

23 Sandport Place, Leith, EH6 6EW
0131 476 5268
info@roseleaf.co.uk
www.roseleaf.co.uk
A wonderfully quirky café bar serving mainly Scottish fare which is delivered to a very high standard. Dishes range from chunky cullen skink through tattie scone towers to exotic salads and huge burgers. They also have a great range of coffees and juices. Tailored kids' menu with games also available for little ones. The place is very welcoming for kids – we had two under 1s with us. It can get busy given how good it is so book early. Seats around 30.

Opening hours: 10.00 til late. No children after 19.00. **Parking:** *Limited.* **Birthdays/celebrations:** *Back room can be used for birthdays and they do a special Roseleaf tea party which would be good fun for adults and 3-5 yr olds.*

Tapa

19 Shore Place, Leith, EH6 6SW
0131 476 6776
leith@tapaedinburgh.co.uk
www.tapaedinburgh.co.uk
Spanish style tapas restaurant with good atmosphere and friendly staff. The food was delicious and served quickly by efficient and helpful waiters. We had the special and there was plenty of food to go round even with a hungry toddler picking at our plates! I think this is a great little place to while away an afternoon with your mummy pals and babies. There is also a large toy box for all ages and jars of sweets and lollipops for the older ones. A lot of tables but booking recommended.

Opening hours: 12.00-22.00 – 2 for £10 chef's selection finishes at 17.30.

Vittoria

113 Brunswick Street, EH7 5HR
0131 556 6171
www.vittoriagroup.co.uk
Italian restaurant with a warm family atmosphere. Very extensive range of pizzas and pasta and dishes from the grill. Children's menu includes pasta dishes as well as sausages and beans. Children can eat for £1 for each adult main course on the a la carte menu (terms and conditions apply). Outdoor terrace. Seats around 150.

Opening hours: Mon-Sat 10.00-23.00, Sun 12.00-23.00. Parking: Pay and display. Birthdays/celebrations: Events can be hosted in party room or on outdoor terrace.

Water of Leith Café Bistro

52 Coburg Street, Leith, Edinburgh, EH6 6HJ
0131 555 2613
www.thewaterofleithcafebistro.co.uk
Simply and brightly decorated with the owners providing the service. Menu is great and there is also a good kid's menu which would satisfy most under 5s on solids. Menu for adults is very good with a daily specials board supplementing the usual favourites – simpler morning menu. Food varies from cullen skink, home made pate and fish cakes for starters to burgers, veggie curry, veggie lasagne. Service was great – Ana very laid back and seems to love having kids in the place. Also considers where kids are when placing food, glasses etc on the table. Toddler seat and step in the toilet. The only potential thing to watch out for is the availability of parking on a very sunny day. It's worth pre-booking as the place is only going to get more popular. I would give it a big star! Seats around 30.

Opening hours: 10.00-17.00. Parking: Limited, on-street. Pushchairs: Access OK but folding probably required when busy. Play area: Informal area with some toys and books provided. Birthdays and celebrations: Yes – arrange direct with owner.

The Yard

2 Bonnington Road Lane, EH6 5BJ
0131 554 1314
info@theyardleith.com
www.theyardleith.com
With experience of running Molly's Play Centre these owners know about entertaining kids. There's something for all the family. Enjoy a coffee, brunch, food or drinks. When the sun shines on Edinburgh this place really comes into its own with plenty of outside space and toys to keep the little ones entertained.

Parking: On-street outside. *Birthdays/ celebrations:* Take pride in their birthday parties for children, which they promise will be easy on your pocket too! Contact venue for details.

Zizzi (Ocean Terminal)

1-3 Food Terrace, Ocean Terminal, EH6 6JJ
0131 555 1155
www.zizzi.co.uk/restaurants/leith
The restaurant is on the first floor with views across the Firth of Forth. It was spacious and clean and the service polite and efficient. Kids were well catered for with good quality highchairs as well as a kids' menu. Our baby girl was kept very entertained by the waiters coming out with huge pizzas. Menu is Italian and they regularly have buy one get one for £1 offers. Seats around 100. See p 161 for Zizzi, Queensferry St.

Opening hours: Mon-Sat 12.00-23.00, Sun 12.00-22.30. *Birthdays/celebrations:* Happy to accommodate parties and will provide balloons and party hats plus a cake as required.

EAST EDINBURGH

The Beach House Café

57 Bath Street, Portobello, EH15 1HE
0131 657 2636
www.thebeachhousecafe.co.uk
A lovely, bright café right beside the sea. You can sit indoors and watch the waves through the window, or if the sun is shining there are tables outside on the prom. There is a basket of blankets for you to borrow if you are feeling the cold. The food is mostly locally sourced and good quality including soups, quiches, pizzas, sandwiches

and paninis. There is also a lovely selection of cakes and delicious ice cream. Seats around 50.

Opening hours: Mon-Fri 09.00-17.30, Sat-Sun 09.00-18.00. *Parking:* On-street. *Accessibility:* Fully accessible – level access through the side door, staff will open it for you. *Play area:* Small table with colouring things and a few toys. Enclosed outdoor play area. *Birthdays/ celebrations:* Tables can be reserved.

Café at the Palace, Palace of Holyroodhouse

See p 64.

Café Cassis

Salisbury Hotel, 43-45 Salisbury Road EH16 5AA
0131 667 8991
info@cafecassis.co.uk
www.cafecassis.co.uk
Nestled within the Georgian-style town house of the Salisbury Hotel, this family orientated bistro (formerly Gabbro) offers fantastic food in friendly and relaxed surroundings. The menu is varied with a French influence and offers both food and drinks from locally sourced produce.

Lunch, evening meals, or just a coffee can be enjoyed in the relaxed seating area or outside in the garden. There are stairs into the restaurant but if you contact them before you arrive there is another entrance with easy access for wheelchairs and pushchairs. This entrance is locked but can be opened. Seats around 34.

Opening hours: Tues-Sun 11.00-21.30.

Café Vivo

136 Canongate, EH8 8DD
0131 557 2293
Lovely little Italian café right opposite Canongate Kirk. No children's menu but the friendly staff will accommodate your children's wishes. The pizzas were delicious, the best strawberry milkshake I have ever had (very filling, big enough to share), fantastic coffee. Also paninis, soup with chunky bread, lovely ice creams and cakes. Great quality, excellent value, relaxed friendly atmosphere. Inside is small so you would need to fold pushchairs when busy. Outdoor seating where you can watch the world pass by. A hidden gem on the Royal Mile. Take-away service also available. Does not take cards so you'd need good old-fashioned cash. Seats around 22 inside and 12 outside.

Opening hours: 09.00-17.00.

Elephants and Bagels

37 Marshall Street, EH8 9BJ
0131 668 4404
contact@elephanthouse.biz
www.elephanthouse.biz
This cosy wee café is tucked into a corner in Edinburgh's student area, usually quieter than its partner café The Elephant House. As the name suggests, it is primarily a bagel shop, selling a wide variety of bagels with numerous tasty fillings, but there are also soups, sandwiches, hot drinks, and some nice sweet treats on offer too. It's small, but there is room for a few pushchairs, and in summer additional seating is available outside. There's a great collection of elephant ornaments and pictures to keep children amused for a while, and crayons and paper are provided. Toilets are down a slightly tricky flight of stairs. Seats around 40.

Opening hours: Mon-Fri 08.30-17.30, Sat/ Sun 09.30-17.00. Parking: Metered parking available nearby in George Sq. Birthdays/ celebrations: Possible with prior arrangement.

Engine Shed Café

19 St Leonard's Lane, EH8 9SH
0131 662 0040
admin@theengineshed.org
www.theengineshed.org
Tucked away in a quiet part of St Leonard's but worth seeking out. The café is bright and spacious with lots of room for pushchairs and for active children to roam. The food (all vegetarian) is self service and there's a good choice of hot dishes and some yummy cakes baked on the premises. The staff are very helpful – they custom-made me a coffee to my particularly exacting standards. The café is part of a wider social enterprise (including an on-site bakery and training and conference facilities) which provides employment to people with learning disabilities so a visit is also a good way to support a very important community asset.

Opening hours: Mon-Sat 10.00-16.00. Accessibility: On 1st floor, access via lift.

The Espy

62-64 Bath Street, Portobello, EH15 1HF
0131 669 0082
the.espy.porty@gmail.com
www.the-espy.com
Right on the sea front, this local pub is a great place for refuelling and relaxing after a walk along the promenade. Pub food made to order for breakfast, lunch and dinner. Great choice of delicious burgers. Children's menu, and most things on the menu can be made in smaller portions. Friendly, considerate staff made us feel very welcome. Despite being busy, the atmosphere was still very laid back. We sat and watched the sea view for ages! Seats around 80 indoors and 20 outdoors.

Opening hours: Sun-Wed 10.00-23.00, Thurs-Sat 10.00-01.00. Children allowed until 20.00.

*Parking: On-street, very busy. **Accessibility:** Small step and heavy double doors. **Toilets:** Small. The ladies is up steps. **Nappy changing:** Pull down changing unit in unisex accessible toilet. Ask staff for key. **Birthdays/celebrations:** Takes bookings for small parties.*

Food Chain Café at Our Dynamic Earth 〈£〉

Holyrood Road, EH8 8AS
0131 550 7800
www.dynamicearth.co.uk/visitors/facilities/cafe
A large bright airy self-service café with great views of Salisbury Crags and Arthur's Seat. The café is located to the right of the entrance to Our Dynamic Earth. Good value food range. Children's lunch boxes available for £3.50 (children can pick a combined package of a sandwich, drink, piece of fruit, packet of crisps and a sweet treat). A varied selection of sandwiches and pastries as well as their own homemade soup (which was delicious) and hot options. Friendly and approachable staff. You can visit the Food Chain Café without visiting the Dynamic Earth attraction. Handy place to eat without the hustle and bustle of the Royal Mile. Seats 100+.

Opening hours: Open daily from 10.00-16.45 (closed Mon-Tues during Nov-Mar). Hot meals served 12.00-15.00.

Kitchener's Deli 〈£〉

127 Portobello High Street, EH15 1AF
0131 669 9290
www.kitchenersdeli.co.uk
Café within a well-stocked delicatessen. Not hugely geared up for children but the staff do their best to accommodate your needs. No separate children's menu but they can do half

portions, and no highchairs but they will provide a seat harness. Excellent selection of fresh bread/rolls and fab cookies with smarties on the top which went down a treat with my 3 yr old! 10 tables inside and 3 outside.

*Opening hours: 08.00-17.30. **Parking:** On-street. **Pushchairs:** Access fine, not much room inside. **Toilets:** One unisex, quite narrow.*

Mums Catering 〈£〉

Portobello Indoor Bowling Centre
20 Westbank Street, Portobello, EH15 1DR
07957 700195
mumscatering@yahoo.co.uk
www.mumscatering.com
This is a really good spacious café, lots of room for the kids to run about and overlooks the indoor bowling green which is usually an attention grabber for my little girl! Everything is freshly made, the scones and cakes are particularly good. Look out for the "kiddy" lunchboxes – they regularly change the content so my little girl looks forward to the surprise. The staff are very friendly and accommodating, helping with trays etc if you have your hands full with the wee one. Seats around 80 (plus highchairs). Outside seating available on a lovely balcony overlooking prom and beach.

*Opening hours: Mon-Fri 09.00-17.00, Sat/Sun 09.00-16.00. **Accessibility/Pushchairs:** Lift up to café level. **Nappy changing:** Pull down changing unit in female toilet area.*

Mums Catering 〈£〉

Portobello Swim Centre
57 The Promenade, EH15 2BS
07957 700195

mumscatering@yahoo.co.uk
www.mumscatering.com
This is a great café, we come here every week after my little girl's swimming lessons. It's very family friendly and normally quite busy with mums and kids after the swimming classes. Similar range of food to Portobello Indoor Bowling Centre (above), complete with exciting children's lunchboxes and great scones. The staff are very friendly and accommodating. One of my friends is pregnant and they got in decaf tea for her. Seats around 30-40 (plus highchairs).

Opening hours: Mon-Fri 09.00-17.00, Sat-Sun 09.00-16.00. Parking: On-street. Three disabled spaces. Accessibility/Pushchairs: Unassisted access via ramps and lift. Large pushchair park inside swim centre, limited space to take pushchairs into café. Play area: Table with toys and books, indoors. More suited to toddlers than older children.

Reds `£`

254 Portobello High Street, EH15 2AT
0131 669 5558
contact@reds4families.com
www.reds4families.com
This is one of the most family-friendly restaurants in the city, with an extensive children's menu (plus home-made baby food), two small play areas (one for under 2s and one for 2-7 yrs), and plenty of space for parking pushchairs. The daytime menu is fairly standard bistro fare of sandwiches, salads, baked potatoes and burgers, but the evening menu sees the addition of a few more adventurous dishes like venison and pheasant. It can get very busy – especially on sunny weekends when families are looking for somewhere not too far from the beach. A great relaxing place, which shows you don't have to compromise on the quality of food to make somewhere suitable for children of all ages. Highchairs and booster seats for toddlers are available. Seats around 45,

booking recommended as it can get busy.

Opening hours: Mon-Thurs 10.30-15.00, Fri-Sun 10.30-20.00. Parking: On-street parking. Play area: A great soft play area in the back for younger children, and play-frame for older children – with CCTV screen for parents. There is also a games machine for older kids. Licensed: You can also BYOB, £4 corkage.

The Salisbury Arms `££`

58 Dalkeith Road, EH16 5AD
0131 667 4518
www.thesalisburyarmsedinburgh.co.uk
Recently renovated pub/restaurant very near the Commonwealth Pool and Pollock Halls, it's very different inside to how it looked when I was a student across the road. The menu is standard gastro-pub grub with a Scottish twist – burgers, fish, sausages etc. The children's menu contained the usual: pasta, sausage and mash, fish goujons and grilled chicken. Most came with chips (ready salted, so ask the serving staff if you don't want salty chips for your children). They also serve a range of Light Bites. Service was a little slow, there seemed to be only one waitress serving 10 tables. It is very nicely decorated, and staff are friendly, but I think it was let down by the food which was mediocre. Children are welcome until 17.00. Extensive seating outside and in.

Opening hours: Mon-Sat 12.00-22.00, Sun 12.30-21.30.

5... great cafes with toy areas

Café Montagu (p 149)

Leo's Beanery (p 156)

Ivory & Willow, Corstorphine (p 182)

Water of Leith Café Bistro (p 172)

Loopy Lorna's at the Church Hill Theatre (p 179)

to store the pushchair and a plastic highchair was available for my 1 yr old. A wine cooler was provided with hot water to heat my son's food. Service was friendly if a little slow and the food was fine. There is a heart-shaped fish pond in the back of the restaurant which will no doubt appeal to slightly older children. Disappointingly there was no nappy changing facility. Seats around 140.

Opening hours: 12.00-23.00. **Toilets:** *Down stairs.* **Birthdays/celebrations:** *Celebrations for groups catered for on request.*

SOUTH EDINBURGH

Spoon Café Bistro

6A Nicholson Street, EH8 9DH
0131 557 4567
info@spooncafebistro.co.uk
www.spooncafe.co.uk
An airy and relaxed café/restaurant with exciting and comfortable interior (large tables would be great for big groups). Friendly staff assisted us with the pushchair on the stairlift and were welcoming and knowledgeable. Imaginative and inspiring menu with fresh and seasonal dishes cooked to order. Yummy beetroot cake. Well worth the stair climb and a real discovery.

Accessibility/Pushchairs: Stairlift.

Ti Amo Restaurant

16 Nicolson Street, EH8 9DH
0131 556 5678
www.tiamorestaurant.com
This is a licensed Italian restaurant serving traditional Italian dishes, located directly across from the Festival Theatre. We visited on a very quiet Mon lunchtime and took advantage of the lunchtime special menu. Plenty of space

Buckstone Bistro **£**

Braid Hills Hotel, 143 Braid Road, EH10 6JD
0131 447 8888
bookings@braidhillshotel.co.uk
Families are welcome in the Buckstone Bistro. A wide choice of food in lovely surroundings without being too costly. Table service. No pushchairs.

Butterflies Café **£**

Marchmont St Giles' Church Centre
1A Kilgraston Road, EH9 1TZ
0131 447 4359
butterflies@marchmontstgiles.org.uk
www.marchmontstgiles.org.uk
Popular café in light airy space serving freshly prepared sandwiches, baked potatoes and homemade soups at very reasonable prices. Excellent children's menu catering for very small appetites and slightly larger ones, including breadsticks and cream cheese, toasted cheese and sandwiches. At the end of the café there is space for pushchairs to be left unfolded and for children to play with a selection of toys provided. Also access to a pretty little garden at the rear, if not too cold. Seats around 40.

Opening hours: Mon-Fri 10.00-16.00 (usually closed for some time over Christmas, Easter and in the summer so worth checking). Parking: Within church grounds for disabled badge holders only. Metered street parking in surrounding area. Nappy changing: In unisex accessible toilet, also pull down toddler seat with straps, potty and step stool. Birthdays/ celebrations: Can book church hall for parties with access to kitchen.

Café Blush `££`

219 Morningside Road, EH10 4QT
0131 447 1012
Bright, comfy, decent-sized café with 10+ tables. Parking on-street and limited. The tables are fairly packed in but the staff are happy to help arrange chairs to make space for a pushchair/ highchair. Plenty of atmosphere and lovely service from staff who are very accommodating and cheery. Table service and a good range of cakes and sandwiches to suit all tastes. Not the cheapest coffee or panini in Edinburgh but the ingredients are fresh and good quality. Portions are also decent. Birthdays/celebrations possible – call them!

Opening hours: Mon–Fri 08.30–17.00, Sat 09.00-17.00. Closed Sun. Accessibility: One small step. Whole premises on one level. Nappy changing: In ladies' toilets.

Café Grande `££`

184 Bruntsfield Place, EH10 4DF
0131 228 1188
info@cafegrande.co.uk
www.cafegrande.co.uk
An affordable local for any time of day – breakfast, morning coffee, lunch, afternoon tea, evening meal or snack. Children are welcome and the children's menu is also available in the evening. There are daily specials and homemade cakes. Breakfast is

served until 14.00 Mon-Sat and 15.00 on Sun. The lunch menu is eclectic with international influences, for example the daily specials on this visit included penne carbonara, chicken curry, moules frites and lamb kofta. The dinner menu changes every 4-6 weeks. The bottle of wine, olives and nachos special for £15.50 would go well with the Jazz on Sundays between 19.00-21.00. Seats about 30 indoors and some outdoors.

Opening hours: Mon-Sat 09.00-23.00, Sun 10.00-23.00. Parking: Limited, on-street, paid. Pushchairs: Very limited space inside.

Freemans `££`

2-6 Spottiswoode Road, EH9 1BQ
07595 725248
david@freemansfood.com
www.freemansfood.com
A newly-opened, stylish and child-friendly coffee shop in Marchmont. Rather than being aimed at families, it welcomes and provides for them along with everyone else, giving it a refreshingly "grown-up" feel. There are nappy-changing facilities, highchairs, wide spaces between tables to allow for pushchairs, sofas, children's chairs and some low tables for kids to sit at and a huge chalk board for them to draw on. Half size portions of light meals and snacks (soup, sandwiches) are available as well as a specific children's menu, and there are always jugs of water and glasses out on the side. The coffee and all-you-can-eat toast are very good and the staff are very friendly.

Opening hours: 09.00-21.00. Accessibility: Small single steps – one to enter and one inside. Accessible toilet.

Gillespies `£`

16 Buckstone Terrace, EH10 6PZ
0131 629 9133
enquire@gillespiescoffee.co.uk

www.gillespiescoffee.co.uk
Handy café/coffee shop amongst row of shops at Buckstone Terrace (including Maddie and Mark's Shoes). Extensive snack menu complimented by home baking. Seating includes some comfy sofas. Seats 17 upstairs and 17 downstairs.

*Opening hours: Mon-Fri 08.30-16.30, Sat 09.00-16.30. **Parking:** Limited on-street parking. **Nappy changing:** In female toilets. Sacks provided. Steps for toddlers. **Birthdays/celebrations:** Includes exclusive use/hire of downstairs. Email enquiries@gillespiescoffee.co.uk*

Hellers Kitchen £££

15 Salisbury Place, EH9 1SL
0131 667 4654
info@hellerskitchen.co.uk
www.hellerskitchen.co.uk
Serving breakfast, lunch and dinner, Hellers Kitchen is very popular with parents with young children. The restaurant is light and airy creating a lovely atmosphere and the staff are very friendly especially with kids. Seats around 50.

*Opening hours: Mon-Wed 09.00-21.00, Thurs-Sat 09.00-22.00, Sun 10.00-20.00. **Parking:** Metered on-street parking Mon-Fri (daytime). FREE at weekends. **Toilets:** Down a steep set of stairs. **Birthdays/celebrations:** Yes including baking a cake in-house for the table.*

Loopy Lorna's at the Church Hill Theatre £££

33a Morningside Road, EH10 4DR
0131 447 3042
bookings@loopylornas.com
www.loopylornas.com
Fun and funky child-friendly tea room. Provides delicious teas and home baking, simple soup/

sandwich and mains menu. Children-sized main courses (sandwich/tortilla, wigam/pitta, pizza/beans on toast) and FREE squash available to all children under 12 yrs. Small cupcakes are also available. FREE Hipp Organic baby food. Breastfeeding welcome in main café, comfortable couches available. Cakes are served on vintage stands, and tea is by the pot with individual quirky tea cosies, which my toddler loved – ours was an owl with goggly eyes! We stayed for nearly 2 hrs, and had our teapot refilled with hot water for free at the suggestion of the friendly staff. This feels like a very special grown-up venue, while keeping the little ones happy too. Nigella, eat your heart out! Large venue, but can get very busy. Outdoor seating available. Booking recommended for large parties.

*Opening hours: Sun-Thurs 10.00-18.00, Fri/Sat 09.00-18.00 (kitchen closes 17.30). **Parking:** One disabled badge holder space immediately outside, permit only parking outside (zone S2), metered parking in surrounding streets, directly opposite 16 or 11 bus stop. **Toilets/Nappy changing:** Toilet steps for 2+ yrs. Nappies and wipes available! **Play area:** Toy table area near nappy changing, away from doors/exits. Toys pre-school. Colouring sheets and crayons. Your child can win a cupcake with their name on it if their drawing is particularly creative. **Birthdays/celebrations:** Staff happy to arrange bespoke birthday parties, baby showers, hen parties etc according to individual requirements.*

Luca's Café £

16 Morningside Road, EH10 4DB
0131 446 0233
enquiries@s-luca.co.uk
www.lucasicecream.co.uk
This café is lovely and bright and extremely child friendly. It is very popular therefore quite often busy but you shouldn't have to wait too long for a seat (you can't book). There is a shop

on the ground level selling great sweets and chocolates, as well as their delicious ice cream to take away. The shop sells ice cream birthday cakes which are amazing, you can order a special one but they generally have some in stock, cost approx £16.50 which serves 12-15 people. My little girl especially liked her ice-cream cone which had a teddy shaped wafer on the top! Seats around 40. See p 185 for Luca's, Musselburgh.

Opening hours: Daily 09.00-22.00, last hot food order 21.30. Cost: Coffee £2, sandwich £3-4, cake £3-4, main lunch and dinner £5. Parking: On-street in pay and display bays. Accessibility/Pushchairs: Access fine to ground floor. Main café is upstairs and no lift. Toilets: On ground floor, fully accessible. Nappy changing: In both male and female toilet.

Scott's Deli

10 Gillespie Place, EH10 4HS
0131 228 5200
Great café food – breakfast rolls, wraps, deli platters, good coffee, tea and cakes. Light and airy upstairs to sit with papers provided or browse on the free wi-fi. Downstairs is a proper children's den complete with ball-pools, a climbing frame and slide plus lots of toys and a couple of sofas where you can collapse and relax. There is a good small kids' menu including lovely cake pops. My son loved it and we'll be back. Well worth carrying the pushchair downstairs. No bookings.

Opening hours: Mon-Sun 07.30-18.30. Parking: On-street. Accessibility: No unassisted access. Ground level entry but space between tables limited upstairs. Pushchairs: Some space to leave pushchairs upstairs, otherwise have to carry downstairs but lots of space there. Toilets: Downstairs, no space for pushchairs. Nappy changing: Unisex nappy changing room downstairs. Play area: Great basement play area, FREE and entirely dedicated to kids.

Swanston Golf Club Cafe

111 Swanston Road, EH10 7DS
0131 445 2239
functions@swanston.co.uk
www.swanstongolf.co.uk
Lovely café and restaurant in the Pentland Hills with views over the south side of the city. The club is keen to stress that it is open to walkers and general visitors and that you don't need to have golf membership to visit the clubhouse. Coffee, home baking and light snacks are served from 09.00. The scones are fantastic and are freshly baked every day. It's a perfect place to stop off after a walk in the hills which should really include a trip to see the nearby thatched cottages in Swanston Village. You may see some highland cattle wandering around further up the hillside. For a slightly longer walk you can start from the car park at Hillend or go up as a tourist on the chairlift at Hillend Ski Centre and walk down from there. The children's menu offers the usual range of pizza, pasta, sausage and mash, fish fingers and chicken nuggets. They offer a range of daily specials on main courses, pasta, salads and ciabatta. As for golfing (let's remember its main purpose here!), the club runs a weekly summer academy for children aged 5 – 17 costing £99 for 5 x 3 hour lessons. One to note for the future maybe?

Parking: Nearby car park for walkers in Pentland Hills, separate car park for golfers. Accessibility/Pushchairs: Steps to the front door, lift to bar/restaurant on upper level.

Toast

146 Marchmont Road, EH9 1AQ
0131 446 9873
www.toastedinburgh.co.uk
A lively and popular café, with set times for meals, but drinks, sweet treats and snacks

are available all day. The food is great and half portions are available for children. There's always a good atmosphere, staff are very friendly and helpful, there are plenty of magazines to read at your table, but it is quite cramped and there's not much room for pushchairs. A good place to come with very young babies if you bring them in a sling, and a nice place for a meal with older children, but not ideal for a long amount of time with an energetic toddler. Seats around 30, with an additional table outside in summer.

Opening hours: Mon-Sun 10.00-22.00. Breakfast 10.00-22.00, Lunch 12.00-14.30, Dinner 18.30-21.30. Weekend brunch 10.00-15.00. Parking: On-street parking nearby. Accessibility: Small step, quite narrow doorway and entrance. Toilets: On ground level, with plenty of space to take your child in with you. Nappy changing: Changing mat, no unit. Birthdays/celebrations: Available for bookings for 25 or more people.

5... great places to go for a treat

The Atholl Dining Room, The Howard Hotel (p 147)

Centotre, George Street (p 150)

Harvey Nichols Forth Floor Restaurant (p 155)

Channings Hotel and Restaurant (p 164)

Orocco Pier, South Queensferry (p 169)

WEST EDINBURGH

The Bridge Inn

27 Baird Road, Ratho, EH28 8RA
0131 333 1320
info@bridgeinn.com
www.bridgeinn.com

Under new management and with a full refurb in 2011, this is a very pretty spot and a great place for family dining. The food is definitely into "gastropub" territory, although the kids' menu remains traditional fare (fish and chips, sausage and chips, pesto and pasta, etc, with optional veg) with two roasts for Sun lunch. They try to serve seasonal food and source as much local produce as possible. Special events menus are available for Burns' Night, Easter, etc, and canal boat dining cruises for Sun lunches, Mothers' Day and a special Santa cruise in Dec. Crayons and paper provided. The inn sits beside the bridge over the canal, and so it's a great opportunity to tie in a family meal with a walk by the water. Note that the path is very close to the water and there is no fence.

Opening hours: Mon-Fri 12.00-15.00, 18.00-21.00, Sat 12.00-21.00, Sun 12.00-20.00. Accessibility: Very slight step at entrance, otherwise all on one level. Birthdays/celebrations: Canal boat lunch/dinner cruises can be arranged for a special occasion. Contact Rachel on info@bridgeinn.com

The Caley Sample Room

42-58 Angle Park Terrace, EH11 2JR
0131 337 7204
info@thecaleysampleroom.co.uk
www.thecaleysampleroom.co.uk

With a children's menu perhaps more suited to older under 5s (big portions on big plates), this gastro pub is popular with families on a Sunday lunchtime. Staff are very friendly and there are plenty of seats and plenty of space for pushchairs. Licensed for children until 20.00.

Opening hours: From 11.00 at weekends and midday during the week.

Good Seed Bistro ££

100-102 Dalry Road, EH11 2DW
0131 337 3803
www.goodseedbistro.com/
This bistro is a welcome addition to a part of the city that's quite short on child-friendly cafés. It's ideally placed for a snack or light lunch after a visit to the Gorgie City Farm. Friendly and welcoming, with plenty of space for pushchairs, they offer a good range of snacks and light lunches, with meals served in the evening too. All the food is freshly prepared, locally sourced, and organic, and the Italian chef Andrea is happy to prepare something that accommodates any diet or allergy. If it's a quiet day, he'll often whisk your child off into the kitchen for a look round too, leaving you to sip your coffee or wine in peace for 5 minutes! Seats around 30.

Opening hours: Mon-Sat 12.00-22.00, Sun 12.00-16.00. Birthdays/celebrations: Happy to cater for parties – call in advance to arrange.

Ivory and Willow £

191 St Johns Road, Corstorphine, EH12 7SL
0131 334 4923
info@ivoryandwillow.com
www.ivoryandwillow.com
Large, busy café/restaurant in the heart of Corstorphine which is a big draw for parents of under 5s in the area. Extremely child friendly with plenty of highchairs, a kids' menu (drink, roll and fruit in a lunch box with crayons and colouring sheet for £2.99), playroom, nappy-

changing room, plenty of room for pushchairs and also small toys for sale. General menu includes hot rolls, toasties, bagels, baked potatoes, tray bakes, cakes and muffins. There is a furniture and gift shop attached which is well worth a look, nearest parking is on Manse Rd (accessible by the Old High St, Corstorphine).

Opening hours: Mon-Fri 08.30-17.30, Sat 09.00-17.30, Sun 12.00-16.00.

Kilted Pig £

101b Colinton Road, EH14 1AL
0131 444 1911
oink@kiltedpig.co.uk
www.kiltedpig.co.uk
Pub serving standard pub food just off the canal. They have renewed their menus and have a new "Piglet" children's menu (complete with a drawing on the back), with main courses ranging from homemade fish fingers and chips, sausage/beans/chips, breaded chicken and chips, lasagne and garlic bread and pasta and veg in tomato sauce. The staff are very friendly and although I didn't order for my 9 mth old, the bartender gave us some plastic cutlery which she happily played with while we ate. The pub can get very busy at weekends or evenings with sport on the TV or games at Boroughmuir Rugby opposite.

Opening hours: From 09.00 every day.

Metro West End Bar and Brasserie ££

Apex European Hotel, 90 Haymarket Terrace EH12 5LQ
0131 474 3456
reservations@apexhotels.co.uk
www.apexhotels.co.uk

Staff couldn't be more welcoming to families, and crayons and paper are provided for small children. Look out for good value "Fixed Price" meals. Seats around 40.

Opening hours: 12.00-22.00. *Birthdays/celebrations:* Contact venue.

Mumbie's Café

1 & 5 Gorgie Park Close, EH14 1NQ
07896 212331
07748 258845
mumbiescafe@gmail.com
Facebook: mumbies cafeteria
This relaxed café is based in the Community Centre, part of Slateford Green car-free housing complex, and open on Thurs only. It is run by a Chilean chef and her business partner. They provide a light lunch and snack menu (e.g. home-made and healthy soup, sandwiches, quiches, salads, coffees, juices, pastries etc.). Children's portions and menu available, and portable booster seats. Caters particularly well for parents with babies and toddlers. Although there isn't parking, the café is well served by public transport. Bus routes (3, 33, 38 from Gorgie Rd, 44, 4, 34, 35 from Slateford Rd and 22, 2, 30 from Stevenson Rd) all have stops close by. A great informal place to meet other parents and relax over lunch or a coffee.

Opening hours: Thurs only 10.00-16.00. *Play area:* Extensive soft play area close to dining area so parents can easily supervise children. Large range of toys and equipment available.

The Original Coffee Bean

5-7 Station Road, Corstorphine, EH12 7AA
0131 334 9660
Very friendly café, has recently changed its name from "Caffe Citro" as it's now under new management (actually old management as it's been taken over by the girl who originally owned it 20 years ago). Very welcoming to children – highchairs and a booster seat and crayons available. Lots for little ones to watch as customers come in and out, and they can choose to sit up at the normal tables with comfy leather sofas or on a nicer day out on the back patio (which is covered, so no need to worry about the odd shower!). We love popping in for a coffee and one of their delicious home bakes, but you can also choose from cooked breakfast or lunch menu with soups, baked potatoes, rolls, salads, freshly made savoury tarts, quiches, bruschetta or pizza. They also serve Mackie's ice cream by cone, tub or sundae. Has 6 tables inside and 4 tables on patio outside.

Opening hours: 08.00-16.30. May vary seasonally. *Parking:* Free on-street parking outside. *Accessibility:* Very slight step only at front door, remainder of café all on one level. *Pushchairs:* Pushchair friendly, although at busier times space can be limited. *Birthdays/celebrations:* Can be hired for private functions, or cakes, tarts, quiches etc can be ordered to take away for your celebration.

5... great family-friendly pubs

La Partenope

96 Dalry Road, EH11 2AX
0131 347 8880
www.lapartenope.co.uk
A Neopolitan Italian Restaurant. They serve excellent Italian food made with fresh ingredients and provide a good set lunch menu Tues-Fri. Dinner offers can be found on their website. They are extremely welcoming to children, with very friendly staff, who sometimes even magic up toys to entertain the children.

Although they don't do a children's menu, they do accommodate pushchairs so this is an ideal restaurant to pop into with very small children. Bring their food with you while you enjoy the delightful grown-up Italian cuisine. For older toddlers and children, the food may not all be to their taste but there is pizza and pasta, and of course bruschetta and desserts.

Opening hours: Lunch – Tues-Fri 12.00-14.00, dinner – Mon-Thurs 17.00-22.30, Fri 17.00-23.00, Sat 12.00-23.00.

St Bride's Centre Café

St Brides Community Centre
10 Orwell Terrace, EH11 2DZ
0131 346 1405
www.stbrides.wordpress.com
A friendly, spacious and unpretentious community centre café situated in a converted church. The ambience is relaxed and ideally suited to babies, toddlers and their carers. A small play area, suitable for under 4s, with slide, toy kitchen and baby toys keeps younger children amused while adults can keep a watchful eye as they enjoy a refreshment or light lunch. The play kitchen was particularly popular with my 2 yr old and her 18-mth-old friend! The menu is basic but purse-friendly and healthy. The homemade soup is delicious, famed locally and often prepared using vegetables freshly picked from a regular customer's allotment! A

parent and toddler group is held in the café on Fri 09.30-11.30.

Opening hours: Mon-Thurs 10.00-14.30, Fri 10.00-13.30 (closes for one week after Edinburgh Fringe Festival).

EAST LOTHIAN

Brunton Theatre Bistro

Brunton Theatre, Ladywell Way
Musselburgh, EH21 6AA
0131 653 5250
www.bruntontheatre.co.uk
A very friendly and welcoming bistro within Brunton Theatre in Musselburgh. Main entrance to bistro from foyer. Hearty breakfasts are served until 12 noon, followed by home-made lunches and light bites, all made to order using fresh local produce. Afternoon teas with home-made scones and cakes served from 14.00-16.00. For certain evening shows themed pre-theatre suppers served from 18.00. Children's menu available along with a tasty babyccino! There is a wonderful small play area tucked in the corner with toys, books, jigsaws, children's table and chairs and a chalkboard. Highchairs and booster seats available and can be reserved along with your table. Pushchair park and nappy-changing facilities in foyer. Booking is recommended, especially at lunchtime as it is very popular with locals, and in the evenings, for pre-theatre meals. You can book your show tickets and pre-theatre meal as a package through the theatre box office, or if you wish to book an early bird dinner (without going to the theatre) then call the Bistro direct. A play park has recently been built at the foot of the car park leading to the beach.

Opening hours: 09.00-19.30 – closes 17.00 if no evening show. Parking: Lots, at back of building. Accessibility: Disabled access at the back of building.

Cake `£`

87b High Street, North Berwick, EH39 4HD
01620 894 439
www.cake-café.co.uk
A bright, family-friendly high street café selling soup, sandwiches, salads, cakes, tray-bakes and cupcakes. Very child friendly with great changing facilities and play area. Recently opened in Jan 2011. Sells cakes for all occasions. Wi-fi available. The prices did seem a little expensive for out of Edinburgh. The friendly service was the best bit. My 3 yr old enjoyed the soup and cooking at the child's kitchen. Best scone and jam that I have ever tasted! We would definitely return when in the area. Seats around 34 indoors plus outdoor seating for good weather.

Opening hours: Mon-Sat 09.00-17.00, Sun 10.00-17.00. Parking: High street parking outside café. Pushchairs: Sign saying "Park" for pushchairs, scooters etc outside toilets. Play area: Indoor carpet area to right of food counter. Toys, books and children's kitchen. FREE to use. Birthdays/celebrations: Celebration cakes and cupcakes to order, though café cannot be hired out yet for celebrations.

Lanna Thai `£`

32 Bridge Street, Musselburgh, EH21 6AG
0131 653 2788
lanna_scotland@hotmail.com
www.thaifood-scotland.com
On arriving at the restaurant, we were greeted warmly and seated quickly. First impressions were that it oozed westernized Thai down to the relaxed "café feel" atmosphere and its décor,

including Buddhist statues, fairy lights and the picture of the Thai king. Lunch menu included a good selection of European and Thai dishes, however it was obvious that the dinner and take-away menu held a much more extensive list. We started our meal with spring rolls and sweet potato tempura, which were excellent and exceedingly fresh. Our main dishes were a traditional red curry and quintessential Phad Thai. Both excellent with vegetarian options available. For children there was a small range of European and Thai dishes available. Overall, Lanna Thai, although having minimal children/baby facilities, produced wonderfully fresh dishes at excellent value for money. Has 5 tables of 2 and 6 tables of 4.

Opening hours: Lunch 11.30-14.30. Dinner 17.30-23.00. Carry-out 17.30-23.00. Parking: Free car park behind Brunton Theatre, 80 yds from restaurant. Accessibility: No accessible toilet. Nappy changing: In female toilet.

Luca's `£`

32-38 High Street, Musselburgh, EH21 7AG
0131 665 2237
www.s-luca.co.uk
An East Coast institution. As well as the famous ice-cream to eat in or take out, the cafe serves a full menu from toasties and panini to pizzas and all-day brunches. And who could resist a knickerbocker glory for dessert? Children's portions available. Lovely helpful staff. Kids love it! See p 179 for Luca's, Morningside.

Opening hours: Mon-Sat 09.00-22.00, Sun 10.30-22.00. Accessibility and pushchairs: Easy pushchair access to ground floor, steps to 1st floor.

Merryhatton Garden Centre Coffee Shop

East Fortune, North Berwick, EH39 5JS
01620 880278
lorraine@merryhatton.co.uk
www.merryhatton.co.uk
A very welcoming and relaxing café which serves a good range of food, with a focus on using delicious local ingredients where possible. Get there before noon for a hearty Scottish breakfast, or enjoy freshly made sandwiches, homemade soups or cakes. On the children's menu there is a good selection of sandwiches, soups and baked potatoes in different sizes at a good price. The staff are very friendly and will do anything they can to help out. We asked for a cheese sandwich for our little one, and were given the choice of exactly how she wanted it prepared. She loved the lunch and then played happily in the toy area until we dragged her away. There are about 20 tables of 4 inside and a further 10 outside.

Opening hours: 09.00-17.00. Play area: Small area with good selection of toys and books and a sofa for adults.

Smeaton Tearoom

Smeaton Estate, Preston Road, East Linton, EH40 3DT
01620 860501
mail@smeatonnurserygardens.co.uk
www.smeatonnurserygardens.co.uk
From the A1 take the East Linton A199 exit. Follow signs for Preston Mill through East Linton, turn right on Preston Road. Smeaton Estate is signposted. The Nursery and Tearoom are set in a beautiful old walled garden. The tearoom has been transformed from the original greenhouse and apple store into a wonderful place to eat, drink and relax. It has a traditional feel, plenty of old features inside and a view of fantastic lush gardens outside. Very child-friendly and popular with parents and toddlers during the week.

Serves tasty snacks and lunches. The home-baked cakes are highly recommended! The outdoor seating area allows you to appreciate the nursery and plants around, and gives your little ones a chance to explore. This is a real gem, and definitely worth a visit.

Opening hours: 10.30-16.00.

The Waterside Bistro

1-5 Waterside, Haddington, EH41 4AT
01620 825674
info@watersidebistro.co.uk
www.watersidebistro.co.uk
A recently refurbished privately owned restaurant situated on the banks of the River Tyne that guarantees to use locally sourced (E Lothian) produce where possible. They state they are a child-friendly restaurant and we found the staff very accommodating, pleasant and not put off by little people running about making a mess! There is a fab children's menu (all fresh food) but large portions for under 5s. Babyccinos also available. The bistro has several areas to choose from, an upstairs which is the "family area" with a cool small bar area and toy cupboard with lots to choose from, an outside seating/patio area and downstairs restaurants and bar.

Opening hours: Mon-Fri 12.00-15.30 for lunch, Mon-Thurs 18.00-21.00, Fri 18.00-21.30, Sat 12.00-21.30, Sun 12.30-21.00. Closed on Mon in winter season. Parking: Private car park (small) and on-street parking. Accessibility/ Pushchairs: The Bistro is a listed building so is restricted on accessibility. The Manager says they have regulars who are wheelchair users and access the toilets downstairs but with difficulty as there are steps. There is space to leave pushchairs folded downstairs. Toilets: Both upstairs and downstairs with limited space. Nappy changing: In the upstairs ladies toilet, free wipes. Birthdays/celebrations: The owner has a private catering company "Pink Pastry" which can cater for any occasion.

MIDLOTHIAN

IKEA Café

Straiton Road, Loanhead, EH20 9PW
0845 355 2265
www.ikea.com/gb/en/store/edinburgh
The café has a small play area for young children in the centre. Food is fairly cheap and cheerful but we weren't particularly impressed with the quality, especially of the hot food. IKEA Family Card holders can buy food in the café at discounted prices and can get tea and coffee for free from Mon to Fri. The bistro near the shop exit offers drinks, hot dogs, fries, donuts, ice cream and meatballs.

Opening hours: 09.30-17.00. Breakfast served from 09.30, main meals from 11.00. Parking: Lots, FREE. Accessibility: Lift from main entrance. Birthdays/celebrations: They cater for parties of up to 16 children aged from 3-9 and offer playtime in the crèche followed by food in the private area of the restaurant. Call 0131 440 6630 for more information and to book.

WEST LOTHIAN

The Park Bistro and Restaurant

Linlithgow, West Lothian, EH49 6QY
01506 846666
info@theparkbistro.co.uk
www.theparkbistro.co.uk/park-bistro-home/
The bistro has a warm and cosy atmosphere, and lovely scenery outside onto the Union Canal. Predominantly Scottish food with a varied specials menu, the starters and main

courses were lovely, though, personally, I felt the puddings were a let down. Children's meals are served until 19.00 and are of a good range and quality with the price including juice and ice cream. The staff were incredibly friendly. It is a bit pricey for a frequent outing, but certainly suitable for a special occasion! Seats around 70.

Opening hours: Mon-Thurs 10.30-20.30, Fri-Sat 10.30-21.00, Sun 12.00-20.30. Nappy changing: In the Unisex toilet with separate toddler toilet. Play area: A separate indoors play area with good clean toys. Birthdays/ celebrations: The Wee Room is available by contacting the restaurant direct.

So Strawberry Caffé

3, The Cross, Linlithgow, EH49 7EY
01506 843333
mail@sostrawberry.co.uk
www.sostrawberrycaffe.co.uk
Located very near Linlithgow Palace, the café offers a well-priced and child-friendly selection of food and drink, including light meals, snacks and a range of cakes. We enjoyed a home-baked cake and some nice coffees. Our daughter had some fruit juice. The café also has a selection of toys and books for children – plus a sofa area. Our daughter liked the strawberry theme and reading the books. She particularly enjoyed sharing a large slice of strawberry and cream cake. Seats about 20.

Opening hours: 10.00-17.00. Parking: Car park nearby, free on Sun and pay and display at other times. Some on-street parking also available nearby. Pushchairs: Room for pushchairs but the café entrance does have a step. Nappy changing: Nappy changing unit available on request.

Further Afield

Further Afield

For days when you fancy exploring different surroundings, or if you're looking for family-friendly places to go while on holiday in Scotland, we've put together a selection of venues that are beyond Edinburgh, the Lothians and Fife. As ever, it's always best to check in advance with the venue about opening hours and admission charges – these details can change.

ANGUS

Brechin Castle Garden Centre and Country Park

Brechin, Angus, DD9 6RL
01356 626813
enquiries@brechincastlecentre.co.uk
www.brechincastlecentre.co.uk
Located off the A90, mid-way between Dundee and Aberdeen. Large complex including The Dragon's Lair playpark which has imaginative equipment that has recently been added to. There is also a minature railway which runs, weather permitting, in the summer, plus a large ornamental lake. Garden centre and a shop area, which sells a range of children's books, as well as some clothing, foods, and kitchenware.

Large, airy coffee shop selling a range of snacks and hot food – the portions were huge when we were there. Also provide a children's lunchbox for £3.50. Only food purchased on the premises can be eaten in the grounds.

Cost: Admission to park FREE unless there is a special event

Visit our website for updates:
www.efuf.co.uk

CLACKMANNANSHIRE

Castle Campbell

Dollar Glen, Falkirk, FK14 7PP
01259 742408
www.historic-scotland.gov.uk
A beautiful, wee, quirky castle situated in the stunning Dollar Glen, an hour's drive from Edinburgh through lush countryside. Exploring the castle's rooms will take 45 mins-1 hr. Then there is the neat terraced garden with views across the Glen for a picnic on a nice day. Make sure you bring food or plan to visit one of the coffee shops 5 mins away in Dollar as there is no café. Weather permitting there are also a range of walks in the Glen although it is very hilly. The castle is one step away from being a ruin with the main section having been restored. You need plenty of imagination as the signage is minimal in the castle grounds, and the rooms, although well preserved/refurbished, are not furnished in any way. The souvenir guide does provide information on the rich history of the castle. Beware of the steep spiral staircase with young children. Castle and grounds aren't really pushchair friendly due to cobbles and stairs so probably better for children who can walk unaided, or babies in slings. If the weather has been severe ensure that you call in advance to check the castle is open as it is quite exposed to the elements. This is not the developed tourist centre which many other Scottish castles have been turned into, but take it as it is – a beautiful monument steeped in history and nestled in stunning Scottish countryside.

Opening hours: 09.30-17.30 (Apr-Sept), 09.30-16.30 (Oct-Mar). **Cost:** *Adult £5, child £3, conc £4.* **Parking:** *500m walk from the car park to the castle up a steep hill plus an overflow car park at peak times, a 15 min walk away.* **Accessibility:** *Those with mobility problems can be dropped off closer to the castle – please call in advance. The road from the general car park is very uneven and hilly.* **Toilets:** *One small clean unisex toilet.*

FALKIRK

Bo'ness and Kinneil Railway

Bo'ness Station, Union Street, Bo'ness, EH51 9AQ
01506 822298
enquiries@srps.org.uk
www.srps.org.uk
A perfect place to visit for any toddler or pre-school child keen on steam engines. The Day Out with Thomas special events which take place in May, Aug and Sept are excellent value for money as entertainment is included – puppet shows, magic shows, carousels, bouncy castles, face painting, miniature railway rides and you can get up close to Thomas the Tank Engine and Percy. There are Halloween Weekend trips and Santa Specials too.

The Scottish Railway Exhibition is well worth a visit. You can get up close to historic engines, carriages, trucks and assorted railway memorabilia. It is just a short walk from the main station over the footbridge. Open 7 days in summer, small admission charge.

Opening hours: Vary – check website for latest. **Cost:** *Adult £8, child (5-15) £4, concession £7, family ticket £20, under 5s FREE. Special events – around £9 per person, usually free to babies, check website.* **Accessibility:** *Accessible coach available on most train journeys – phone to check availability.* **Eating:** *Café.*

Callendar House and Country Park

FREE

Falkirk, FK1 1YR
01324 503770
callendar.house@falkirk.gov.uk
www.falkirk.gov.uk/cultural
From M9, turn left along the Laurieston Bypass. At the end, turn left, then right onto A803. Pass the grassy banking of the Antonine Wall and the park entrance is on your left, signposted, at a roundabout. For Callendar House and Stables Tearoom, take first left past the high flats.

A gentle stroll through the beautiful park and woodland by the Antonine Wall (built by the Romans) brings you to a house steeped in history from the conquerors through to the industrial revolution. You enter through the gift shop. Initially there is a lot of reading with the odd, slightly scary, waxwork model, which is of little interest to an under 5. However, on the ground floor, there is a lovely 1825 working kitchen with a roaring fire and costumed interpreters who can tell you about what life was like there in past times. We enjoyed tasting some Georgian biscuits and trying to lift the heavy copper pots and pans. Upstairs you can visit an early 19th century clockmaker's workshop, general store and printer's. They are not always manned by costumed interpreters so you should check availability in advance as this will make your visit much more entertaining. There is also a programme of exhibitions and a contemporary visual art and craft space with workshops, talks and other events, and an art activity box to create your own artwork.

Stop off at Castle Callendar play area just next to the house – an enclosed, dog-proof play park for children of all ages and abilities, which features irresistible spiral slides, unusual tyre swings and a big sand-pit. The house and park are open all year but seasonal facilities include a golf course, mini-golf, bouncy castle, go-karting and a boating lake. The park also has a Stables Tearoom.

Opening hours: Mon-Sat 10.00-17.00 (last admission 16.00), Sun (Apr-Sep only) 14.00-16.00. Accessibility: Access avoiding steps available on request at reception. Lift in the building to access upper galleries. Pushchairs: A few shallow steps up to the main door and space inside, under the stairs, to leave pushchairs. Eating: Refreshments kiosk next to the house and play area. The Stables Tearoom is a short walk from the house.

Falkirk Wheel

Lime Road, Tamfourhill, Falkirk, FK1 4RS
01324 619888
0870 050 0208
www.thefalkirkwheel.co.uk
From the M9 follow brown tourist signs for The Falkirk Wheel, but beware if travelling from another attraction in Falkirk – there are few direction signs in the town itself!

Tickets for boat trips can be booked by phone in advance. Admission to visitor centre is FREE. Pushchairs are not allowed on the boat, nor is there a secure place to leave them in the visitor centre.

The Falkirk Wheel is the world's first and only rotating boat lift. Built as part of the Millennium Link, the canal restoration project reunited the historic link between Edinburgh and Glasgow. The trip on the Falkirk Wheel is made on a pleasure cruiser that departs from the visitor centre. Once on board small children should sit where they can get a good view over the side of the boat as it moves upwards on the lift. At the top of the lift the boat crosses a short aqueduct before passing through a tunnel that is partially illuminated. The boat then turns around and goes back the way it came. The round trip takes about 1 hr. On a hot days the boat's glass roof can make the trip uncomfortable. In the visitor centre there are several interactive displays. Younger children may need help. Remote control boats and playpark. Picnic tables.

Cost: Standard boat trip – adult £7.95, conc £6.95, child £4.95. Eating: Café in visitor centre.

Muiravonside Country Park

The Loan, By Linlithgow, EH49 6LN
01506 845311
Take the A801 south from the M9, J4 (Lathallan Roundabout), then at the roundabout follow the B825 towards Linlithgow and Whitecross. Country Park is signposted on the right.

Set in 170 acres, while the mansion house is long gone there is a stepped garden on its site, with picnic benches and a barked children's play area. While the chute is very high, and the swaying log-walk too advanced for most under 5s, the toddler playpark next to it is much more accessible with bucket swings, a couple of animal-shaped buckabouts and a seesaw.

Main car park is next to Newparks Farm (01506 847726), where children can see an array of animals, including horses, Shetland ponies, guinea pigs and rabbits in abundance, sheep and goats, Tamworth pigs and a Highland bull.

There are industrial relics of the estate's past scattered here and there, so don't be surprised if you come across rusting skeletal tractors. This is a lovely place for stroll. However, the River Avon (said as to rhyme with Gavin) flows alongside some of the paths – and there is a weir and a mill lade, so keep a close eye on children if you take a walk along the lower paths.

There's a visitor centre: park in the small overflow carpark and walk along the road – there are a couple of parking bays for disabled drivers next to it. There are toilets (clean but basic, including accessible toilets) next to the centre, and there's a café on the opposite side of the courtyard. If you go to the visitor centre first you can pick up a really clear map of the entire estate. Contact the Ranger Service at the number above for latest information.

The Pineapple   •FREE

Off A905, then off B9124.
FK2 8LU
www.nts.org.uk/Property/The-Pineapple
Woodland walks and orchard in the grounds of The Pineapple building (National Trust for Scotland). Small car park with path through to walled orchard and various woodland walks. Paths are quite rough and a struggle with a pushchair although three wheelers would cope. Great venue for a family picnic with plenty of space for children to run around safely.

Opening hours: 09.30 until sunset.

Have you any information you would like to add? Email us at info@efuf.co.uk

GLASGOW CITY

A day out in Glasgow

If you feel you've exhausted Edinburgh and the Lothians' offerings for your wee ones, you might want to consider a day out in Glasgow. It's only 50 miles or so away, but can provide a welcome change of scene – and pace. One Edinburgh mum, originally from Glasgow, gives us a tour.

As a Glaswegian native I'd say there are 3 particular areas where Glasgow rivals its more genteel sister city: museums, parks and curry. The good news is that all of these can be enjoyed with your under 5.

If you don't fancy the drive through (albeit an easy hour or so with the motorway taking you right into the heart of the city) you can let the train take the strain. Under 5s travel free and the service from Waverley leaves every 15 minutes. Prams fit onboard pretty comfortably and the children may find the experience part of the adventure (although it was a bit of a disappointment to my son that he couldn't spend the whole journey climbing in and out of the luggage racks).

You may only have time to visit one museum. If so, make it the shiny new **Riverside Museum** (100 Pointhouse Place, G3 8RS, 0141 287 2720 – ample parking for £1 or bus 100 from George Square, every 30 minutes). Incredibly, entry is free and you'll easily pass a few hours here, enjoying the interactive exhibits, the recreated street from the early 20th century and the numerous buses, cars, trams and bicycles – many of which you can climb aboard.

Then take your pick of Glasgow's superlative parks, all of which have ducks to feed, playgrounds to explore and acres of well-maintained grassy space to run across. If you're still in the West End after visiting the Riverside Museum, stop at **Kelvingrove Park** – you could always pop into **Kelvingrove Museum** too, also free, with its own mini museum for the under 5s. If you've not got a pram with you, you might travel back into town on Glasgow's bone shaking "clockwork orange" subway system. Alternatively, if you've headed back into the city centre by other means, an easy 15 minute bus or train ride will take you to **Queen's Park**. If you've got a clear day, from the flagpole you'll get great city views and may manage to catch a glimpse of Ben Lomond.

The other advantage of Queen's Park is that you'll find yourself nicely placed for a lunchtime or early evening curry. Choices abound in this area but I'd recommend the very child-welcoming folk at the family-run **Shimla Pink's** (777 Pollokshaws Road, G41 2AX 0141 423 4488). Please don't feel curry is out of the question even for the pickiest wee one – poppadoms, mango chutney and chicken korma will go down a treat!

The suggestions here are very personal ones, and no doubt other parents will have plenty of good ideas to share – whatever you do, you'll get a warm welcome and lots of the famous Glasgow patter!

HIGHLANDS

Highland Wildlife Park

Kincraig, Kingussie, Inverness-shire, PH21 1NL
01540 651270
www.highlandwildlifepark.org
If you're up North, take a trip to the Highland Wildlife Park. You can view animals there that you won't see anywhere else in Scotland, such as Tibetan wild ass, European elk and bison. There are also smaller animals, such as beavers, otters, polecats and owls, and internationally endangered animals of mountains and tundra. The Japanese snow monkeys by the café are particularly entertaining. Walker, the only polar bear in a public collection in the UK, also lives here.

Opening hours: Jul-Aug 10.00-18.00, Apr, May, Sept-Oct 10.00-17.00, Nov-Mar 10.00-16.00.

194

Landmark Forest Adventure Park

Main Street, Carrbridge, Inverness-shire, PH23 3AJ
01479 841613
admin@landmarkpark.co.uk
www.landmarkpark.co.uk
A great option for entertaining children aged 3 and over. It involves a long journey from Edinburgh (2½ hrs each way) but, should you ever find yourself on holiday in the Aviemore area (and most Edinburgh-based families do at some point), this should not be missed. Landmark is a member of the Aviemore and the Cairngorms group of attractions and visitors to Landmark can get discounted entry to other things on producing their ticket, e.g. 20% off the cost of a Funicular Railway Ticket at the nearby Cairngorm Mountain Railway. Landmark provides a great opportunity to entertain, exercise and educate your children at the same time. For older under 5s the main attractions are the Ant City climbing frame, mini cars, mini diggers, the water slides (toddlers must be accompanied by an adult) and the tree top trail which provides a great opportunity to wander through the forest and maybe even spot some red squirrel in their native habitat. You can also see a working Clydesdale horse and a steam powered saw mill. Older children can enjoy even more thrills and spills with the newly installed Runaway Timber Train roller coaster, tree obstacle courses and the Bamboozeleum optical illusions hall to name but a few of the other attractions. This is not a typical theme park at all and that is to be welcomed. Taking a picnic, as always, saves a small fortune but there is a reasonably priced restaurant and separate snack bar on site offering a good selection of food and a children's menu.

Opening hours: Vary 10.00-17.00 and 10.00-19.00 depending on time of year. Park may close in extreme weather. Call to check before setting out. **Cost:** *Adult (family rate) £12.30, child £10.25.* **Eating:** *Foresters Restaurant and Pinewood Grill Snack Bar.* **Birthdays/celebrations:** *Birthday parties can be catered for outside the school holidays at £14.70/child.*

Colzium Estate

Kilsyth, G65 0PY
01698 266155
countryside@northlan.gov.uk
www.visitlanarkshire.com/things-to-do/
country-parks/colzium-estate/
Colzium Estate has various features worth a visit including seasonal miniature railway, lovely walled garden, large play park, the remains of Colzium castle, ice house and walks which are particularly nice when the spring bulbs are out.

The adventure playground has a small toddler area and attractions for children of a range of ages including a small zip line (watch your children on this – it is not for the faint hearted!).

With quite a few things to look at it is well worth taking a picnic to enjoy the beautiful gardens. There are also events on at certain times of the year.

Opening hours: 12.00-19.00, Apr-Sep (13.00-16.00 Sat/Sun). ***Accessibility:*** *Some paths and areas would not be wheelchair accessible. There are quite steep hills.* ***Pushchairs:*** *Many areas are accessible by pushchair. Some walks would require a sling or are better suited to older children.* ***Eating:*** *Café in summer.*

Palacerigg Country Park

Cumbernauld, G67 3HU
01236 720047
countryside@northlan.gov.uk
www.northlanarkshire.gov.uk
Well signposted from the main road through Cumbernauld. Features a rare breed area with sheep, Tamworth pigs, Zebu cattle, Shetland ponies, peacocks, ducks, swans, chickens and other interesting and unusual variations on farmyard favourites. There are also deer in another part of the park. Visitor centre with wildlife-related displays, café and gift shop. Various walks and nature trails around the park including one with a short tree-top trail. There are also longhouses which are used for various purposes including displaying traditional woodland crafts. There is a play area which has been upgraded to suit a wider range of children and the visitor centre is open quite well into the evenings in the summer.

Opening hours: Apr-Sep 09.00-19.45, Oct-Mar 09.00-16.15. ***Pushchairs:*** *The tree top level is not accessible to pushchairs.*

Active Kids Adventure Park

Burnside Farm, Stanley, Perthshire,
PH1 4QB
01738 827286
play@activekidsadventurepark.co.uk
www.activekidsadventurepark.co.uk
This is a great place for children and young-at-heart parents who'd like to join in too! It has everything: a 3-lane astro slide, 2 sizes of pedal go-carts with separate areas to accommodate younger and older children, trampolines, a giant fort, target football, crazy golf, 2 sizes of jelly belly and farm animals, as well as a good range of outdoor play equipment such as swings and slides. There is also an indoor soft play area for 0-7s which costs extra.

Opening hours: *Soft play/café/toy shop open from mid Mar, outdoor areas from 1 Apr-31 Oct. Open Mon-Sat 10.00-17.00, Sun 11.00-17.00. Cost: £6.75 (child), £4.50 adult, £21 per family, under 2s FREE. Indoor play for under 7s, £3.* **Toilets:** *Child-friendly toilets attached to the café and further toilets in the outside play area.* **Eating:** *Nice, bright café serving home cooked lunches, snacks and home baking. Covered picnic areas outside, and uncovered picnic benches.* **Play area:** *The indoor play area for 0-7s can be used without park entry.* **Birthdays/ celebrations:** *Indoor and outdoor options.* **Bottlewarming/Food heating:** *Microwave in café.*

Auchingarrich Wildlife Centre

Comrie, Perthshire, PH6 2JE
01764 679469
info@auchingarrich.co.uk
www.auchingarrich.co.uk
Directions – about 1½ hours from Edinburgh. Take the M9 past Stirling to A9. From A9 take A822 towards Crieff. At the 2nd exit turn off onto B827 and follow signs to Wildlife Centre.

Set in the hills of Perthshire with a range of birds and animals, the wildlife centre offers a full day out for all the family with lots to entertain all day as there are play areas as well. There are lemurs, emus, meercats, highland cows, ponies, sheep, pigs, rabbits and guinea pigs, cockerels, prairie dogs and wallabies to name a few. Visit the hatchery where you can watch newborn chicks and even get to hold them! Picnic tables can be found in a field with space hoppers and crazy golf. There are peacocks roaming the grounds too, which is quite atmospheric. There is also a gift shop, seasonal events like Easter egg hunts and a falconry centre next door.

Outdoor play area including a sandpit, tunnels, mini tractors, zip wire, swings and a climbing frame. Indoor soft play barn with a separate area for under 2s and under 5s.

The Pine Lodge Coffee Shop has reasonable prices and menu choices that are quite varied and use healthy local food. The children's boxes are good too. Two of the play areas are visible from here with one specially enclosed area for toddlers. You may want to plan feeding time for your bairns to fit in with viewing feeding times for the animals, which are advertised on entry to the park. Around 50 seats inside and 30 outside.

Opening times: *10.00 til dusk all year.* **Cost:** *£8.25 adults, £6.75 children and senior citizens, FREE for under 2s. Family ticket £27.50.* **Birthdays/celebrations:** *From £9.50 each (min 10 children). Adult helpers – 2/10 children. Includes unlimited access to the park, play in the indoor barn or soft play area, outdoor play park and tractor circuit, visit the hatchery, party box with sausage roll, sandwich, yoghurt, crisps, juice and a small sweet.*

Lochleven Castle

On an island in Lochleven
KY13 8UF
01577 862670
www.historic-scotland.gov.uk
Situated off the M90 at Kinross, follow signs from Kinross.

A great day out. Situated on a a tiny island and only accessible by a small motor boat (warm jackets recommended) which takes about 10 mins to cross the loch. Ferry not equipped for wheelchairs. The castle is steeped in history: Mary, Queen of Scots was imprisoned and forced to abdicate here before managing to escape. Access to the castle is across grass. Castle towers are accessed by narrow staircases and therefore unsuitable for those with limited mobility. After exploring the castle and island, follow the footpath opposite the ticket office round the loch for 50m to a great play park. Loch Leven is a National Nature Reserve and an important site for waterfowl.

The ticket office shares premises with a café (independently owned) and a small visitor centre. You could also visit the nearby Vane Farm Nature Reserve (see below) while you are here.

Opening hours: Apr-Sep 09.30-17.30, Oct 09.30-16.30. Castle may close at short notice due to weather conditions. Phone ahead to check. Cost: Adults £5, child £3, conc £4. Includes ferry trip.

Loch Leven's Larder

Channel Farm, Milnathort, Kinross, KY13 9HD
01592 841000
emma@lochlevenslarder.com
www.lochlevenslarder.com
Situated close to the shores of Loch Leven with panoramic views of the surrounding hills, particularly beautiful on approach (choose a fair weather day). Take Junction 7 off the M90 for Milnathort to the well sign-posted tourist attraction boasting 4 Scottish Tourist Board stars. You can reserve a table for any time of the day. Attractive frontage including fresh fruit and veg stalls. Interior is light, warm, spacious and modern. Two main sections: very well stocked farm, houseware and gift shop and the café/restaurant. Table service, well staffed, prompt in bringing highchairs for our 1 yr olds and completely unfazed by sticky fingers and food mess. Great variety of comfortable seating with varying sized tables, well suited to families and pushchairs. Quieter areas with sofas suitable for breastfeeding. Clearly set out menu with healthy options for all. "Cool Kids" menu offers soup, sandwiches, baked potatoes, children's sharing platter (ham, cheese, sultanas, apple) and fresh fruit with good sized portions. Adults: baked potatoes, paninis, sandwiches and a range of specials reflecting seasonal vegetables and produce from the home farm. Plenty of yummy home-baking. "Hearty brunch" menu available 09.30-11.30. Afternoon Tea/specials available from 12.00.

Mid-range prices. Outside decked area great for sunny days with plenty of picnic tables in the garden. Plenty of room to run around without disturbing others – our children loved it! Added bonus is the smaller Summerhouse Café in the garden, selling much of the same menu as the main restaurant combined with an ice-cream shop. Other features include well-marked nature trails with potential visits to local nature reserves. Paths look suitable for pushchairs and you could easily walk to the shores of Loch Leven from the restaurant. You can even visit the animals on the surrounding farm, highland cattle included. "Very nice" pronounced my 3 yr old!

Opening hours: Farm Shop, Food Larder, Deli and Gift Shop 09.30-17.00. Restaurant 09.30-17.00 (last brunch orders 11.30, last food orders 16.30). Summerhouse Café 11.00-16.00 weather permitting. Accessibility: At least 3 motorised "scooters" available for going around the shop and restaurant. Site set on flat or ramped areas all on one level. Play area: Simple and spacious grassed play area with plenty of room for children to run around. Well-built see saw, "house" style slide and stationary sit-on train. Birthdays/celebrations: More than happy to accommodate groups of children and provide a suitable menu.

Noah's Ark

Glendevon Farm, Weston Edge, Perth, PH1 1QE
01738 445568
www.noahsarkperth.co.uk
Fun family centre that caters for a range of ages. The clean, bright soft play area is divided into under 3s, under 5s and under 12s, and features ball shooters, soft roundabouts, slides, trampolines, tunnels, plenty of climbing and interactive games. For an extra £1 there are motor scooters (3-10 yrs), a zip wire, and climbing wall (over 5s). There is also ceramic

197

pottery decorating and, in another part of the building, a 4-lane bowling alley and indoor karting (3 yrs+ can ride with an adult). The large, bright café in the soft play area offers a good range of food, including a children's menu, and newspapers can be borrowed from the reception. Staff were friendly and helpful.

Centre opening hours: Soft play open 10.00-18.00. Bowling and karting open later. *Cost:* 2 hrs soft play £4.25 weekdays, £5.25 weekends and holidays. Under 1s and adults – FREE. *Accessibility:* Reduced entry fee for children with disabilities. The spacious under 3s soft play which has a range of soft shapes can be used by children with limited mobility. Adults can accompany children into the other areas where necessary. *Birthdays/celebrations:* Bright spacious party rooms upstairs.

Perth Leisure Pool

Glasgow Road, Perth, PH2 0HZ
01738 492421
leisure@liveactive.co.uk
www.liveactive.co.uk
Plenty of fun for all the family. The very shallow Monkey Jungle area for under 8s has two slides, exotic birds, a crocodile and monkeys all spouting water; the lagoon is a shallow pool area with a slide and height restriction; there is also a wild water channel, bubble beds, flumes, and a popular outdoor pool which is accessed directly from the indoor pool. A separate children's teaching pool with slide can be used when free, armbands can be borrowed from the poolside, and there are plenty of large floats and foam rings to play with. 6 spacious family changing rooms are a great help.

Café Aqua is a family-friendly café, which is easily accessible to pushchairs and wheelchairs, making it a great place to meet friends and family. It offers a range of hot and cold drinks, light lunches and snacks and tray bakes, a children's menu, children's play area and a baby feeding station.

Opening hours: Leisure Pool Mon-Thurs 10.00-20.30, Fri-Sat 10.00-21.00, Sun 10.00-18.00. Check website for Training Pool and Teaching Pool times. *Cost:* Standard swim adult £4.40, junior/conc £3.40, senior £3.90, Under 5s FREE. Live Active card allows £1 discount for each visit and costs £10/yr for adults, FREE for junior/conc/senior. *Accessibility:* Lift access to changing area, good changing facilities, shower chair to the poolside.

Scone Palace

Perth, PH2 6BD
01738 552300
www.scone-palace.co.uk
In the past, the kings of Scotland were crowned on Moot Hill in the grounds of this impressive looking palace. Young children will enjoy the extensive grounds to run around in, play in the adventure playground and there is a butterfly garden too. The high point of our visit was the Murray Star Maze and the fountain to be found in the middle of it. Peacocks roam the grounds (and can be fed with peanuts purchased from the shop), and there are donkeys, and Highland pony and cattle. The palace interior has little to interest under 5s (apart from two stuffed bears), although primary school age children may enjoy the 'I spy' trail. There is also a gift and food shop and an adventure playground suitable for under (and over) 5s.

The Old Servants' Hall coffee shop serves soup, sandwiches, and light meals, home baking, hot and cold drinks. Highchairs available. A little hard to negotiate with a pushchair, but there are tables outside. There is also a bookable restaurant and a picnic area (by the car park).

Opening hours: Apr to Oct Mon-Fri, Sun 09.30-17.00, Sat 09.00-16.00. Grounds close at 17.45. Nov-Mar Fri 10.00-16.00 grounds only. *Cost:* Palace – Adult £9.60, child

198

£6.80, student/senior £8.60, £27.50 family entrance. Grounds only – Adult £5.50, child £3.75, Student/Senior £4.90. **Accessibility:** Wheelchair users may alight at the gift shop, for chair lift access to the Palace. **Toilets:** Access to toilets including accessible toilet is round the back of the building via the Estate office (not signposted, but staff are helpful). There is also an accessible toilet in the car park.

Vane Farm RSPB Nature Reserve

By Loch Leven, Near Kinross
01577 862355
vanefarm@rspb.org.uk
www.rspb.org.uk
This nature reserve has two nature trails. The Woodland trail (1.6km) is a pretty but steep walk through a birch wood to a viewpoint at the top of Vane Hill. The Wetlands trail is a flat walk alongside Loch Leven and features 3 hides from which you can observe – even identify! – the birds using the colourful displays within the hide. Both trails require appropriate footwear and binoculars (which can be hired from the shop). Children can borrow one of the "explorer packs" containing binoculars plus a variety of spotting, collecting and drawing activities. The café observation area has five telescopes and camera views to observe activity on the loch, and informative displays.

Opening hours: Visitor centre 10.00-17.00 daily. Trails and hides open 24 hrs except 25/26 Dec, 1/2 Jan. Café stops serving hot food at 15.00 and closes at 16.00. **Cost:** *Adults £3, children 50p, concessions £2, family £6. RSPB and Wildlife Explorer members FREE.*

SCOTTISH BORDERS

Dawyck Botanic Gardens

Stobo, Near Peebles, EH45 9JU
01721 760254
dawyck@rbge.org.uk
www.rbge.org.uk
A beautiful hillside garden (part of the Royal Botanic Garden Edinburgh) with mature trees, a burn and several bridges. There are different things to see at different seasons: snowdrops, daffodils and bluebells in the spring, azaleas and rhododendrons in the summer and colourful autumn leaves. The garden is on a slope, steep in places, with one of the paths accessible. The visitor centre situated at the entrance has a gift shop, plants for sale, café and toilets. The café has indoor and outdoor seating and offers homemade lunches and cakes, including a large selection of gluten-free cakes.

Opening hours: 1 Feb-30 Nov. Feb and Nov 10.00-16.00, Mar and Oct 10.00-17.00, Apr-Sep 10.00-18.00. **Cost:** *Adult £5, conc £4, children £1, under 5s FREE, family (2 adults and up to 4 children) £10, Friends of Royal Botanic Garden Edinburgh FREE.* **Parking:** *Gravel car park with disabled spaces.* **Accessibility:** *Ramp access to front door as well as steps. Not completely accessible. Accessible path signposted through the garden.* **Pushchairs:** *Accessible in parts.*

Kailzie Gardens and Tweed Valley Osprey Watch

Kailzie, Peebles, Scottish Borders, EH45 9HT
01721 720007
info@kailziegardens.com
www.kailziegardens.com
The whole garden is a delight all year round but the walled garden has seasonal opening times. To walk through Kailzie at snowdrop time is breathtaking. It is rich with play opportunity with a wonderful children's play area within an enchanted wood. The new area where unusual

The Leadburn Bar, Restaurant and Soft Play Centre

Nr Penicuik, West Linton, Peeblesshire, EH46 7BE
01968 676077
info@the-leadburn.com
www.the-leadburn.com
Opened recently on the site of the original Leadburn Inn, this is a modern, welcoming family-friendly bar, restaurant and soft play area. We were there for 2 hours including lunch and could have stayed longer as my little boy was really enjoying it. Particularly good for older under 5s – plenty to keep them occupied. Mid-priced restaurant, using locally sourced ingredients, in the soft play area, with a good selection of children's food (hot or lunchbox), plus child-sized tables, chairs and cutlery. There is also a soft play-free area where adults and children can enjoy a meal together.

chickens are housed is wonderful. Our children love the magical feel and room to dance and sing. The fly fishing area beside the Osprey Watch can be something else to see – our children enjoyed some poor wee trout being caught and shown to them by a teenage boy. You may need to take extra care with the stream and pond. Small shop selling eggs, crafts and plants and a local information point. Reasonably priced restaurant, light and airy with doors onto a courtyard. Play area with a little static wooden train, little huts, slide, swing and sandpit.

The Osprey Watch is separate, but within the grounds of Kailzie Gardens. Children can play with puppets and enjoy live CCTV footage of osprey and other birds from Easter-end Aug.

Opening hours: Summer (end Mar-end Oct) Walled and Wild Gardens, Woodland Walks Mon-Sun 11.00-17.30, winter (end Oct-Mar) Wild Garden and Woodland Walks only, during daylight hours. Osprey Watch Mon-Sun 10.00-17.00. Cost: Small entry charge depending upon the season and an honesty box for the gardens out of season. The Osprey Watch is £3 for adults. Children under 12 yrs are FREE. Birthdays/ celebrations: Contact the restaurant owners.

The soft play is £2 for unlimited play, with children under 12 mths FREE. Baby/toddler area with slide, ballpit and baby toys, and a multiplay for 4+ yrs with CCTV so that parents can keep watch. Free wi-fi and newspapers for adults.

Very friendly, smiling staff, keen to help. Very busy while we were there. Waiting system which appeared to work well with an area with seating for parents while children play.

Opening times: Mon-Sat 10.00-18.00, Sun 12.00-18.00. Birthdays/celebrations: £6-8 for an hour's soft play and then private area for food. Exclusive use of soft play at set times at extra charge. Party bags/cake for extra charge.

Paxton House

Berwick upon Tweed, TD15 1SZ
01289 386291
info@paxtonhouse.com
www.paxtonhouse.co.uk/
Signposted 3 miles from the A1 Berwick upon Tweed bypass on the B6461 and from the A697 junction with the B6461.

Situated on the banks of the river Tweed, Paxton House was built in 1758 and is a fine example of an 18th century Palladian country house. It lies at the heart of 80 acres of woodland, parkland and gardens, originally landscaped by Robert Robinson, and now incorporates a variety of riverside walks and trails where you can spot the Paxton Teds hiding in the trees and collect rubbings of animal plaques as you go. Lots of wildlife including salmon, heron, cormorants, mute swans, red squirrels, hare and deer and, if you're lucky, a seal. Adventure playgrounds, a putting green and croquet lawn. Nearby picnic tables are the perfect spot for a relaxing bite to eat. Guided tours of the house last approx 1 hr, though access for wheelchairs and pushchairs is limited to the main floor only via a lift. An illustrated guide to the upstairs is provided for anyone unable to access it. The house tour is better suited to slightly older children, though babies and toddlers are welcome. There is a "Paxton Teddy Trail" to interest children during the tour. There is also a gift shop.

Stables Tearoom offers delicious home baking, appetising hot meals and tempting snacks in unique surroundings, with the converted horse stalls a perfect size to house a table and chairs. Children's options are available in the form of smaller portions. Around 55 seats.

Opening hours: Daily 1 Apr-31 Oct. Grounds and gardens 10.00-sunset, house 11.00-17.00 (last tour 16.00), shop and tearoom 10.00-17.00. *Cost:* House and grounds – Adult £7.50, conc £7 children (5-15 yrs) £3.50, under 5s FREE. Family ticket £20 (2 adults and 2-3 children). Grounds only – adult £4, children (5-15 yrs) £2, under 5s FREE, family ticket £11 (2 adults and 2-3 children). *Accessibility:* The grounds, gift shop, tearoom and Ellem Fishing Club Museum are all accessible, as is the ground floor of the house. No access to the 1st floor. *Pushchairs:* No access to the 1st floor.

Traquair House

Innerleithen, Peeblesshire, EH44 6PW
01896 830323
enquiries@traquair.co.uk
www.traquair.co.uk

As I visited with my twin girls, I was unable to tour the House (the doors were not wide enough for my wide double pushchair and the twins don't yet walk) but the grounds were beautiful! I felt a bit disappointed about missing the tour, though still had a lovely day. There is a lovely well-maintained outdoor play area, with toddler area too. There are lots of wildlife activities available from the Gift Shop, and the Maze would be fantastic for older under 5s.

The 1745 Cottage Restaurant (01896 830777) is situated in the old walled garden and serves a whole range of food including delicious home-made soups and lunches as well as tempting scones and home baking. Children can have smaller portions of what is on the menu or if preferred they do a children's lunch box (£4.75). Around 50 seats.

Opening hours: Apr-May, Sep 11.00-17.00, Jun-Aug 10.30-17.00, Oct 11.00-16.00, Nov (weekends only) 11.00-15.00. Closed Dec-Mar. *Cost:* House and grounds – adults £7.60, children £4.10, seniors £6.90, 2 adults and 3 children £21.20. Grounds only – adults £4, children £2.50. *Accessibility:* Difficult to manage. House not fully accessible to wheelchair users. *Pushchairs:* Need to be left outside the House. Access to the restaurant.

Whitmuir
The Organic Place

Whitmuir Farm, West Linton, EH46 7BB
01968 661908
info@whitmuirtheorganicplace.co.uk
www.whitmuirorganics.co.uk

"I like playing on the big spider" – Samuel, 4. Although the main objective of visiting Whitmuir Farm tends to be to stock up on fresh produce and superb meat, there are several other options to keep adults and children entertained. The gallery is an adult zone due to the breakables displayed often at toddler level, but the outdoors area offers 4 different walks, ranging from the duck walk (20 mins) to the cow walk (1½ hrs). The chicken and pig walks are 40-45 mins – wellies are a good idea on these treks, pushchairs really suited for the duck path. There is a big tepee that hosts children's storytelling afternoons, scheduled around seasonal highlights (Halloween, Christmas, summertime) and a percussive steel spider, perched on a hill, which can be played by at least 3 children at a time. There is also a bee education project. This is a perfect place to combine some lovely scenery, fresh air, delicious food and possibly a bit of culture to boot in the gallery, whilst the children are in the play area.

Whitmuir The Organic Place Restaurant
01968 661147
eat@whitmuirtheorganicplace.co.uk
An airy open spaced restaurant with a casual café feel, a great place to go for locally sourced meals. The omelettes are simple but superb as the eggs (indeed most of the fresh produce) are literally from next door. The specials may stray into the exotic (international fare) but the staple dishes (quiche, soups, fish, lamb burgers) are Scottish. Desserts are also homemade and menu changes with the seasons. Children can wander outside or enjoy the play area by the front of the restaurant.

Opening hours: Farm – Mon-Fri 10.00-18.00, Sat-Sun 10.00-17.00. Restaurant – 10.00-16.30. Some evening opening depending on event. Cost: Piglet menu around £4, adult menu main dish around £8, special dishes £12. Play area: Indoor play area by restaurant and a few toy trucks to ride outside.

STIRLING

Bannockburn Heritage Centre

Glasgow Road, Stirling, FK9 0LJ
0844 493 2138
Leave M9 at J9 services and take A872 Stirling, Bannockburn HC, N for 1 mile.
Built near the site of the battle of Bannockburn, when the Scottish army led by Robert the Bruce defeated the English army and drove them out of Scotland. Displays, tableaux, model soldier layouts and audio-visual presentation (15 mins) of the build-up to the famous battle and the battle itself. Some gory bits! On certain days there is an actor who gives a living history presentation for added enjoyment, although some of his weaponry and tales of bloody battles may alarm little ones.

Usually some simple craft activity on offer. Soldiers' helmets and period costumes (including very heavy chainmail for older ones and willing parents) for dressing up as 14th century warriors and peasants! The shop is well stocked with gifts, books and toys for all ages. Drinks, crisps and sweets also available. The hotel next door does have a bistro and a beer garden, however, and is open to non-residents.

The heritage centre is surrounded by grassy parkland that is ideal for children to run about on. A march up to the nearby monument to Robert the Bruce completes the visit. The centre is to be rebuilt for the 700th anniversary of the battle in 2014. Phone to check on facilities.

Opening hours: Heritage Centre – Mar-Oct 10.00-17.00, Apr-Sep 10.00-17.30 (last entry 16.45). Closed Nov-Feb. Cost: Adult £6, family £15.50, one parent £10.50.

Blair Drummond Safari Park

Cuthil Brae, Stirling, FK9 4UR
01786 841456
enquiries@blairdrummond.com
www.blairdrummond.com

We really enjoyed the safari park, the animals had lovely big enclosures that allowed you to drive through and get close! There was also an area to walk around and view the animals from platforms as well as a petting farm where you could touch farm animals, like horses and pigs. The only thing to watch out for is the weather; if it is raining the animals may be hiding! Excellent displays (sea lions and birds of prey) were on regularly throughout the day – just short enough to keep little people amused without getting bored! The best bit was the boat ride out to see the apes on the island. This was great fun and something different to running around or sitting in the car. The play park area is also fantastic, a great space for all ages! It has a fort and a boat climbing frame, surrounded by sand where you can dig for treasure which can be redeemed at the face painting stall. Inside the restaurant there is a little play area near the back with small tables. There are two gift shops.

Emma, 3 yrs, said, "My favourite was the long giraffe and the ice cream!" Poppy, 15 mths, said "Raaaahr!"

The restaurant (01786 841430) is very spacious with plenty of seating both inside and out. There is a wide selection of hot and cold food on offer to suit all budgets. The portion sizes were very generous and the food was tasty. Both of the little ones ate up all their lunches! The feeding and changing room in the lobby was great as it had enough space for more than one child.

Opening hours: Mid Mar-end Oct 10.00-17.30 (last admission 16.30). **Cost:** *Park – adults £12.50, children £9.50, conc £10, children under 3 FREE. Restaurant – £5-£8 for a main meal.* **Eating:** *Lots of little kiosks throughout the park including a fast food café as well as the restaurant. Undercover BBQ areas.* **Birthdays/ celebrations:** *Child £13.50, Adult £9.25. Price includes entrance to the whole park for the day, a choice of two children's menus, balloons and a goody bag. Birthday cake is not provided and parties are not available on Bank Holiday weekends.*

Kings Park

Victoria Place, Stirling, FK7

The park has all sorts of landscape from open space to trees, rough grass and bush – there is lots to explore.

Watch out for the golfers as a large part of the park forms a golf course, although there are good walks round the boundary of the golf course. As well as the tennis courts, skatepark and pitches there is a fantastic playground which includes toddler swings, a water and sand play area, giant swinging tyre and a flying fox, something for all ages. A new play area will boast a number of fun features including a tower/bridge/slide embankment unit, climbing wall, bicycle roundabout, aerial runway and landscape improvements to existing features. There are toilets (plus accessible toilets) and a mother and baby room.

The park is some distance from the nearest shop so best to bring your own refreshments. In good weather there can be an ice cream van at the main gate.

Macrobert Arts Centre

University of Stirling, Stirling, FK9 4LA
01786 466666
www.macrobert.org
Located on University of Stirling campus. Follow
M9 to the Dunblane roundabout then follow
signs to Bridge of Allan. Travel through Bridge
of Allan and the university is on left as you exit
the village.

Fabulous arts centre designed with children
in mind. Lots to interest under 5s. Varied
programme for the whole family including
children's theatre show and films. Panto at
Christmas. Art, dance and theatre workshops
for a variety of age groups and a handy crèche
facility. Spacious foyer area with tables for little
ones, colouring activities and toys.

*Pushchairs: Pushchair parking near main
entrance. Nappy changing: Baby care room
with private feeding area too.*

Stirling Castle

Castle Esplanade, Stirling, FK8 1EJ
01786 450000
hs.stirlingcastle@scotland.gsi.gov.uk
www.stirlingcastle.gov.uk/home.htm
A great day out for toddlers and adults alike.
The castle on its rock can be spotted from
miles away, adding to the excitement, and
is truly impressive as you approach from
the esplanade. There's masses of space to
run about and lots to see, including friendly,
helpful staff dressed in historic costume who
are happy to chat to under 5s about their visit.
The great hall has huge open fireplaces and
a hammer beam roof, and plenty of space for

exploring. The royal apartments have been
restored to their 16th century glory, including
stunning ceilings and wall decorations. The
glorious tapestries in the Queen's apartments
are recreations from the original designs,
woven in the castle workshop. They are full of
animals and stories and the white unicorn kept
my 2 yr old fascinated for at least 10 mins. You
can visit the workshop and see the weavers in
action. The great kitchen has lifelike figures and
exotic food to look at and the palace vaults have
several rooms devoted to interactive exhibits for
children. In fine weather the extensive gardens
and walls are good to explore.

The on-site Unicorn Café provides good
quality snacks and food throughout the day,
including snack packs for children. Plenty of
space in the grounds for picnics on fine days.

*Opening hours: Apr-Sep 09.30-17.00, Oct-
Mar 09.30-17.00. Cost: Adult £13, conc £10,
child 5-15 £6.50. Under 5s FREE. Members
of Historic Scotland FREE. Parking: £4 on
esplanade. On busy days Castleview Park and
Ride is close to the M9 – bus £1.20 return,
child 60p, buses every 25 mins. Accessibility:
Reasonable access to almost all the display
areas. Pushchairs: To most areas – steps and
cobbles.*

Make your business stand
out from the rest – place an
advert in our next edition!
Email business@efuf.co.uk
for more information or visit the
business section of our website
www.efuf.co.uk

Shopping

Shopping

Shopping with small children (or when pregnant) requires a completely different approach from the shopping you may have been used to. Browsing at leisure becomes a distant memory. You have to discover good sources of maternity, baby and children's equipment and clothing, and you will also find that planning, timing, and toilet stops become of the utmost importance!

Edinburgh's large stores

Large shops are becoming increasingly family and child friendly. Automatic doors, lifts, and in-store nappy changing facilities have become standard, as has a café or restaurant with high chairs and often bottle and babyfood warming.

Large stores do alter their layout fairly often, always check the store guide. If you have something to return, ask as soon as you arrive: you may be directed to Customer Services which might save a trek to the wrong department.

Parent and baby rooms

Feeding and changing rooms are now considered a standard requirement in large department stores and shopping centres and are open to male and female carers. Some stores have dedicated rooms for male carers. The standard of parent and baby rooms in the centre of Edinburgh is generally high, but should you find them lacking in facilities, or not clean, tell a manager or supervisor, as it is only through such information that your experience can be improved.

Opening hours

Most city centre shops have late night shopping on Thursday. Many now open longer in the summer and during the Festival, and in the run up to Christmas. We've only included opening hours when they're unusual and the store doesn't have a website for you to check.

Lost children

Generally, stores have procedures for responding to lost children. Try not to panic, then contact a member of staff. Describe what your child was wearing and where you last saw

them. Think of anything that may have attracted them on the way round the store or shopping centre. It helps to carry some ID that identifies you as the carer; a recent photograph is useful. In shopping centres, stores contact the centre's security. Try to teach your child to approach a member of staff in a shop if they become lost.

HIGH STREET STORES

For their range of products, convenience, consistency and a strong online offering, high street shops are often the first port of call. We've listed those most useful for under 5s. Many have locations in the main shopping centres in and around Edinburgh (in which case there's plentiful parking) – full addresses for these can be found in our "Shopping Centres" section, below.

Unless stated otherwise, all have good access for wheelchairs and pushchairs.

Argos/Argos Extra

0845 640 1010
www.argos.co.uk
Catalogue shopping offering a wide range of homewares, furnishings and toys. Most items available in-store to take home, with home delivery for larger items. You can check stock and reserve items online or via telephone or SMS. The handy website www.icheckstock.co.uk allows you to check multiple stores at the same time. All stores have disabled parking spaces.

Craigleith, 0845 165 7256
Fort Kinnard, 0845 165 7416
11-15 North Bridge, EH1 1SB, 0845 165 783
Straiton, 0845 165 7806

BHS

0845 196 0000 (Customer service centre)
www.bhs.co.uk
Catering for the whole family and the home with a wide range of products. Kids' section offers baby clothes and equipment, children's clothes and shoes. With Order & Collect in store you can order online and collect from a participating BHS store when convenient. Stores at:

Cameron Toll, 0845 8410155
Ocean Terminal, 0845 8410218
The Centre, Livingston, 0845 8410224
64 Princes Street, EH2 2DJ, 0845 8410180

Eating: At Princes St store (see p 148).

Boots

101-103 Princes Street, EH2 3AD
0131 225 8331
www.boots.com
Wide range of health and beauty products for all the family. Range varies by store. Although often not as cheap as some other high street chemists, their Advantage loyalty card can earn points redeemable in store. Great for treating yourself! Their online Parenting Club offers advice by weekly emails and extra Advantage card points when shopping from their Mother and Baby department, which stocks baby toiletries, equipment, toys, food and their own brand range of clothing, Mini Mode. Clothing is sized from newborn to 6 yrs and is bright and practical. Mini Mode Miniatures is also available for low birth weight babies starting at 1.4kg (3lbs). Pharmacy, optician and photography services online as well.
Branches include **Craigleith Retail Park, Ocean Terminal, Cameron Toll Shopping Centre, the Gyle, Fort Kinnaird Retail Park, St James Shopping Centre** and locally all over the city. See www.boots.com.

Debenhams

109 Princes Street, EH2 3AA
0844 561 6161
www.debenhams.com
Large department store with clothing for babies and children including own-brand ranges and designer names (including Jasper Conrad and John Rocha). Has a reasonable range of lingerie, including maternity and nursing styles, and some maternity clothing. Online shopping and free personal shopper services available. Also at **Ocean Terminal**.

Toilets and nappy changing: Nappy changing and accessible toilet on 4th floor. Eating: Restaurant (see p 152).

Gap

McArthur Glen Retail Outlet, Livingston
01506 419899
custserv@gap.eu
www.gap.eu
The shop can be a little tight to push a pushchair through, especially a double! As it is an outlet there are plenty of bargains to grab at any time of the year. However, it does seem to be end of season clothes that they primarily stock here. It is easily accessible as it is all on one level and the staff are very friendly and helpful. Gap makes a nice selection of babies'/children's clothes, including outerwear – snowsuits etc. Not cheap but look out for regular sales. Branches also at **the Gyle, Ocean Terminal and on Princes St**.

IKEA

Straiton Road, Loanhead, EH20 9PW
0131 440 6600
www.ikea.com
Unsupervised play area for older toddlers outside and supervised crèche at main entrance (£1 for a maximum of one hour). Shop while your children (3 yrs +) enjoy the soft play, art materials, music or books.

Cots, beds, changing tables, chairs, tables, highchairs, furniture and storage available. Range of smaller items including cutlery, crockery, cups, bathtime accessories, bath and bed linen. Lots of lovely toys and cuddly animals. Most items reasonably priced.

Supermarket-style trolleys, but these aren't allowed in the car park – if you have bulky items, cars must be brought to the pick-up point and loaded there. You can take your child/ren to the car and leave the trolley in one of the secure lock-up points (£1, refundable), but be warned, they don't always work. Staff may "mind" a trolley for you while you collect your car, however.

Parking: Parent and child bays but can be busy. Eating: Café and restaurant (see p 187).

Jenners

48 Princes St
0844 800 3725
jennersedinburgh@hof.co.uk
www.houseoffraser.co.uk
Edinburgh's most famous department store, particularly worth popping into at Christmas for Santa's Grotto and to marvel at the enormous tree that adorns the menswear section. The toy section, in the basement, is a wonderland for little ones. For adults, Jenners houses a branch of Valvona & Crolla – always worth a look. However, in practical terms, it is not terribly pushchair friendly or accessible. Stairs dominate. There are lifts, but the building's quirky layout sometimes means that you have to take more than one to reach the floor you're after. Visit when you have time on your side.

Have you any information you would like to add? Email us at info@efuf.co.uk

John Lewis

St James Centre, EH1 3SP
0131 556 9121
www.johnlewis.com
Scotland's largest department store, offering 5 floors of clothing, homeware, beauty and technology, plus the best nappy-changing room in Edinburgh. The nursery department sells essential items from replacement valves for breast pumps to cotbeds. It offers a free nursery advisor service (no obligation to buy), can set up a baby gift list similar to the popular wedding gift list and runs monthly sittings for Imprints, framed ceramic impressions of your child's hand or foot. A free nursery catalogue can be ordered through the website. Baby and children's clothing (John Lewis and designer) is next to the nursery department. Toys are a level below and well stocked, with some larger outdoor toys on display.

Wide choice of fabrics in haberdashery, from cheap and cheerful prints to sumptuous velvets. Sheeting, quilted fabrics, braiding, ribbons, buttons, motifs, lace etc. Craft materials such as beads, felt, fur fabric, tapestry and embroidery yarns, craft and needlework kits including samplers, dolls house kits, knitting wools and patterns, sewing and knitting machines and craft books. Soft furnishings contains great children's patterns, plus "blackout" curtain lining, blinds and wipe-clean fabric good for tablecovers. The store does not sell maternity or nursing wear.

On the 4th floor opposite the main customer toilets is the dedicated Parent's Room which is spacious, light and welcoming, and attracts customers to the store. It contains a private breastfeeding area, 3 nappy-changing stations with sinks, chairs, bottlewarming, a large toilet cubicle (with mini toilet for small children and another changing table) and water fountain.

You can order items on www.johnlewis.com to be delivered free for collection from the store usually the next day, or free to your home if over £30. There is a pricing policy of "Never Knowingly Undersold", meaning if you see a product cheaper at a high street competitor they will price match. I saw a baby bouncer on offer at Argos (it was sold out) and John Lewis price matched it for me. I have always found the staff friendly and very knowledgeable about products in their department. I would go out of my way to shop there due to the great service and high quality products.

Parking: *Paid car park.* **Eating:** *Café and restaurant (see p 156).*

Marks & Spencer

www.marksandspencer.com
Womenswear, menswear, childrenswear, home furnishings and food hall. Good range of durable baby and children's clothes, many in 100% cotton. Underwear, sleepwear, leisure wear, and party clothes, as well as clothes for outdoors and school. Seasonal dressing up outfits and costumes related to recent film releases. Range of padders, pram shoes and shoes (up to sizes 39/40). Baby range starts from newborn, with clothing for low birth weight babies.

Larger stores include some nursery equipment and toys. Lingerie departments offer nursing bras and an in-store bra-fitting service. Café outlets and nappy changing facilities make stores very child-friendly.

Branches at: **Craigleith Retail Park, Fort Kinnaird Retail Park, Gyle Shopping Centre, Meadowbank (Outlet), Princes St, Slateford Rd, and Straiton.**

Mothercare

www.mothercare.com
Large stores with reasonably priced own-brand clothing for babies and children and a good line of maternity wear. Also stocks various brands of nursery goods and bedding, car seats and pushchairs, as well as a large selection of toys (own-brand, Early Learning Centre, and some other brands). Staff are very helpful. Toilets, nappy changing and breastfeeding areas.

Hermiston Gait, 0131 453 1383
Fort Kinnaird, 0131 657 4050
The Centre, Livingston, 01506 439240

Next

0844 844 8333 (General enquiries)
www.next.co.uk
Fashionable clothing and accessories for men, women and children, including babies (Next Baby Boutique) together with a full range of homewares are available in-store and from the Next Directory, a home shopping catalogue, and website. Directory Order Collection Service is also available. Stores at:

Fort Kinnaird, 0844 844 5060
Gyle Shopping Centre, 0844 844 5640
The Centre, Livingston, 0844 844 5066
107-109 Princes Street, 0844 844 5103
St James's Centre, 0844 844 5012
Straiton Park Way, 0844 844 5677

SHOPPING CENTRES

Edinburgh has a good selection of shopping centres, both in and out of town, if you prefer a range of shops in close proximity (and often under one roof). Many hire out small pushchairs and toddler straps.

Bruntsfield

www.bruntsfieldplace.com
Not technically a shopping centre, but the Bruntsfield area is a very good one for shopping, with plenty of interesting shops to choose from. You can buy children's clothes, shoes, toys and books, as well as lots of useful and luxurious things for grown-ups. There's also a choice of fabulous cafés, and a fishmonger, greengrocer, butcher and baker.

Parking: *Metered street parking.* **Accessibility:** *Variable, many quite small shops.*

 Get the most up-to-date information on
www.efuf.co.uk

Cameron Toll Shopping Centre

Lady Road, EH16 5PB
0131 666 2777
www.camerontoll.co.uk
Two large car parks serve both front and rear entrances. Can be very busy on Friday and at weekends. Keep a tight grip on small children in car parks.

Pedestrian access from Lady Rd but closely set bollards and a roll bar mean large prams and pushchairs need careful manoeuvring.

Self-opening doors and a variety of trolley designs to accommodate various ages of babies and small chidren, although many smaller shops do not allow trolleys inside.

A variety of shops on the main shopping floor, and on the 1st floor there's the foodcourt. The centre usually hosts activities for Easter, Mother's Day etc, such as puppet shows, magicians and other children's entertainers.

Toilets: Ground and 1st floors. *Nappy changing:* Separate room with 2 units and an enclosed area for feeding.

The Centre

87 Almondvale South, Livingston, EH54 6HR
01506 432961
www.shopthecentre.co.uk
Formerly Almondvale Shopping Centre. Get there from M8-A71 or by bus from St Andrews Sq.

Variety of high street shops and places to eat. Situated on one level so easy to navigate. Toilets are near Boots. Two nappy-changing areas and bottle warming facilities in cafés and restaurants. Shopper's crèche for 2-10yr olds. Operates "Little Shoppers" safety scheme throughout, to give peace of mind when shopping with older under 5s. Various coin-operated children's rides around the centre.

Parking: Charged, e.g. 50p/2 hrs, £1/3 hrs.

Craigleith Retail Park

South Groathill Avenue, EH4 2LN
www.craigleithshoppingpark.com
The shops are all on one level and easily accessed via an undercover pavement that runs around the car park. Lots of shops to suit most needs including TK Maxx, Mamas and Papas and Marks & Spencer. There are also 3 options for eating here so whatever your little one fancies there should be something to satisfy! I visit a lot as there is ample and easy parking and the shops are really easy to get around.

Parking: More than 1000 FREE parking spaces. A few parent/child spaces at M&S and Sainsbury's. *Toilets/Nappy changing:* Toilets with space for pushchair as well as accessible, nappy changing and parent and child toilets in Sainsbury's, KFC and M&S. *Eating:* Café Revive at M&S (see p 163), Sainsbury's Café (bottle warming, food heating and highchairs in both) and KFC.

Fort Kinnaird Shopping Park

32 Fleming House, Kinnaird Park, EH15 3RD
0131 669 9090
liam.smith@fortkinnaird.com
www.fortkinnaird.co.uk
A wide range of shops, and several cafés and fast food restaurants. Waterstones has a lovely children's book area and the staff at Café Noir were particularly helpful during our visit. By car just off A1 at Newcraighall junction. LRT bus 30 has a stop in the centre.

Parking: Extensive parking including child and disabled spaces. *Toilets/Nappy changing:* Excellent facilities at Mothercare/Early Learning Centre and Boots. Also in the Management Suite next to Harvey's. Toilets in Marks & Spencer too. *Food heating/Bottlewarming:* In Mothercare and Boots.

Gyle Shopping Centre

**Gyle Avenue, South Gyle Broadway,
EH12 9JY
0131 539 9000
management@gyleshopping.com
www.gyleshopping.co.uk**
Lots of shops including a small Early Learning Centre (loved by younger kids) and a Disney Store (loved by all kids). Can be very busy around Christmas and the sales in Jan, but in general is a nice place to get out and wander about with young kids. Clarks is good for shoe fittings, and M&S is good for clothes for all ages.

Parking: Lots, including parent and child and blue badge. Nappy changing: In female toilets downstairs. Eating: Lots of places to eat in both the food court and around the Gyle. Play area: Two small outdoor play areas, limited facilities.

Hermiston Gait Retail Park

**Off A720 City Bypass, EH11 4DG
www.hermistongait.co.uk**
Range of shops including Tesco, Mothercare, B&Q Warehouse and Halfords. Up to 3 hrs FREE parking. Nappy changing facilities in Mothercare.

McArthur Glen Retail Outlet

**Almondvale Avenue, Livingston, EH54 6QX
01506 423600
enquiries@mcarthurglen.com
www.livingstondesigneroutlet.com**
Jam-packed with shops, cafés and restaurants with easy access as it is all on one level. You don't have to go far to find a toilet or nappy-change facilities. Bright and spacious with lots of space for your little one to run around. Free pushchair or kiddie car hire. The best bit is the huge water fountain/sculpture in the main entrance – fascinating to kids and adults of all ages and can amuse for a good 15 mins! It is

so easy to spend a day here as it has excellent facilities from feeding rooms to restaurants, all the high street shops and more.

Parking: Plenty, currently charged per hour but free after 18.00. Accessibility: Wheelchairs available to hire free of charge. Toilets: Plenty, spacious with space for pushchair. Also accessible and parent and child toilets. Nappy changing: A few unisex feeding and changing rooms. Eating: Various options including Café Nero, Spud u Like, Ashoka Shak, McDonalds.

Meadowbank Shopping Park

London Road, EH7
Includes Marks & Spencer Outlet Store where you can sometimes get reduced toys and books, TK Maxx, and others. Apart from KFC there are no places to sit and eat or feed your child. But there is a big Sainsbury's which has toilets and nappy-changing facilities.

Newkirkgate Shopping Centre

**13 Newkirkgate, Leith
0870 444 1234**
Large car park. Some shops around open square, others in the covered mall.

Ocean Terminal

**Ocean Drive, Leith, EH6 6JJ
0131 555 8888
info@oceanterminal.com
www.oceanterminal.com**
On 3 levels, with great views of the Forth. Many brand name shops, with a few local businesses

too. Quite a lot to appeal to kids including Molly's Soft Play (see p 121) and Build-a-Bear (see p 254). As with all shopping experiences, merchandise on view will have the effect on your little one of wanting to buy everything, or sit at every restaurant, which can be a bit stressful! There are a number of restaurants and cafés popular with families and excellent changing facilities including "parenting suites" on 2 of the 3 floors. Seating areas for breastfeeding. The Vue Cinema (see p 134) is also on-site.

Nappy changing: On all 3 floors, 2 parenting suites (one not marked on map, through department store on ground floor). Play area: Molly's Soft Play, 3rd floor (entrance fee). Birthdays/celebrations: See individual businesses for details.

Princes Mall

Princes Street, EH1 1BQ
0131 557 3759
info@princesmall-edinburgh.co.uk
www.shopprincesmall.com
Refurbished in the early 2000s, this is right next to Waverley Station. Shops such as Bodyshop, Warehouse, New Look, Joy, Whisky Shop and Gleneagles. No one specific big store, but a collection of each of these smaller branches. Not much in the way of children's shopping. On top of the Mall is Edinburgh's Main Tourist Information Centre (see p 34).

Food court with outlets such as KFC, McDonalds, Harry Ramsdens, Costa and O'Briens. There is a general seating area that serves most of these outlets, although Costa has its own seating area at the Mall entrance.

Toilets: Within the Food Court. Nappy changing: Mother and Baby rooms.

St James Shopping

Princes Street, EH1 3SS
0131 524 7989 (customer services)
marketing@stjamesshopping.com
www.stjamesshopping.com
Large central shopping centre housing John Lewis and a range of popular shops from fashion, health and beauty, opticians, banks, jewellers, electrical and entertainment to confectionery and a Post Office. Early Learning Centre, Next and Monsoon Childrenswear. The Food Court on level 1 (accessible via lift) has 3 food counters, toilets, a nappy change room and easy Internet. FREE pushchair or wheelchair hire for £10 deposit + ID (return by 18.00). The centre operates the FREE Child Safe ID wristband which contains your contact details should your child become lost. Both services based at Customer Service desk, under the escalators opposite Game and H. Samuel.

Parking: Paid parking at NCP car parks at Leith St or Greenside Pl. If parking at Leith St, only one floor has access to Centre via the food court, no lift. Accessibility: Entrances via bus station side or Princes St E End, or John Lewis.

Westside Plaza Shopping Centre

Wester Hailes Road
0131 442 3123
www.westsideplaza.co.uk
Indoor shopping centre on 2 levels with lift and escalators. A variety of food, gift, toy, hardware, newsagent and charity shops. Toilets on ground floor with separate nappy-changing area. Railway station, bus terminal and taxi rank nearby.

BABY EQUIPMENT

Also see section on nursery equipment.

Amazon

www.amazon.co.uk
Yes, Amazon has a baby store, with its own separate tab. Fantastic resource for buying absolutely anything for delivery to your door.

Babies 'R' Us

www.babiesrus.co.uk
Babies' equipment section of Toys 'R' Us. Has its own catalogue in-store/online. Very useful if your local Toys 'R' Us is out of stock: it can be faster to order online than ask the store to reserve something next time it's in stock.

BickiePegs

01224 790626 (for bulk orders)
www.bickiepegs.co.uk
A long-established Scottish firm (since 1925). Teething biscuits in Boots and leading chemists. Small mail order brochure in pack. "Doidy" children's training cup and finger toothbrushes.

Boohoo Baby

0845 224 1480
www.boohoobaby.co.uk
Edinburgh-based company offering everything from prams to pushchairs, nappies, highchairs and clothes.

Bundlebean

www.bundlebean.com
Practical and versatile blanket, waterproof nylon shell backed with cosy fleece. Adapts to create a snug pouch which fits onto any pushchair, car seat, bike seat or front-carrying baby carrier, or opens up as a playmat or picnic blanket. Comes in pink, blue and black.

Closer to You

0131 208 4168
info@closertoyou.co.uk
www.closertoyou.co.uk
Run by an Edinburgh mum, Closer to You provides a wealth of information about the various types and styles of slings available. Slings for sale online or in person by booking a "sling shopping appointment".

Glasgow Pram Centre

0141 552 3998 (sales advice)
sales@glasgowpramcentre.co.uk
www.pramcentreonline.co.uk
Great website, good range of baby and toddler equipment, and discounted prices.

The Great Little Trading Company

0844 848 6000
enquiries@gltc.co.uk
www.gltc.co.uk
Wide range of helpful, interesting, practical products for parents and children. Also sells children's clothes. No quibble returns policy.

Groovystyle

01442 872888
sales@groovystyle.co.uk
www.groovystyle.co.uk
All types of baby equipment from top brands.

Kiddicare

0871 781 7000
hello@kiddicare.com
www.kiddicare.com
Online baby superstore offering a wide range of products and accessories.

Little Green Earthlets Ltd

0845 072 4462
01435 811555
www.earthlets.co.uk

Amazingly wide range of environmentally friendly and ethically sound baby equipment, products, nappies and clothing.

Safetots

01438 728888
info@safetots.co.uk or customerservice@safetots.co.uk
www.safetots.co.uk
For a range of safety equipment.

Show Me Slings

susan@showmeslings.co.uk
www.showmeslings.co.uk
Baby sling consultant Susan Ansell, trained with Trageschule UK and a British Association of Babywearing Instructors member. Provides information about the safety and comfort of slings and how to use them. Slings can be tried. Stocks a small range of slings for purchase.

Slingjax

0870 042 4028
www.slingjax.co.uk
For sling sales and hire.

Totseat

0131 226 6064
happy@totseat.com
www.totseat.com
A great "highchair" for little ones from 8-30 months. Made of fabric and fits into a travel pouch. Couldn't be handier. See ad, p 147.

BABY EQUIPMENT HIRE

Tom Thumb Baby Equipment Hire

0131 667 1159
07910 929650
www.tomthumbbabyequipmenthire.co.uk
One-stop shop for the hire of essential items for babies and pre-school children.

Books

Even in these days of Amazon, e-readers and online book sales there is nothing quite like looking round a real bookshop. It's often only by browsing in person that you spot that quirky, unusual or unjustly overlooked tale that will become a favourite with your under 5. Whether you're looking for new, second-hand, or a title from your childhood, Edinburgh is well provided for.

Most shops now have some sort of distraction for toddlers and young children, such as boxes of toys, tables and chairs or reading books. Better stores have staff who are well trained, specialise in children's books and can give invaluable advice and recommendations.

If you can't find the book you want, most bookshops will be happy to order it for you. In addition to books and audio books, you can also order large print books and books in languages other than English.

Some bookshops offer a free search service for out-of-print titles. Others may be able to guide you towards companies which specialise in searching and locating them – it's always worth asking! Alternatively, start trawling second-hand bookshops, where you can still find hidden jewels.

Pages and stages

Despite television and DVDs, books are still extremely popular with under 5s. There is a tremendous choice, superbly illustrated in many different styles, which are entertaining for parent and child alike. They can be introduced at the baby stage, where the focus is on bold patterns, pictures and robust pages. By 9 mths most babies will happily sit on your knee and look at a book for at least a few moments. The bedtime story for a toddler is an ideal way to wind down after a hectic day and to spend 10 minutes or so with your child. Books introduce children to words and language they would not hear in normal conversation and greatly increase language development. They can also help introduce children to concepts, ideas and situations out of their normal, everyday life, helping to stimulate their imagination. There are titles which can help young children come to terms with some of the more traumatic aspects of growing up, such as going to hospital or losing a grandparent.

Literary city

We have tried to list the best stocked and most friendly bookshops below. Children's books are also sold in supermarkets, department stores, toy shops and some stationers. Don't forget to visit charity shops, NCT Nearly New Sales, church book sales, second-hand and jumble sales. Libraries also host sales where you can find great bargains.

It almost goes without saying that Edinburgh has inspired and been home to many writers. Witness such talent in action by looking out for any storytelling or author sessions during holidays in your local library or bookshop.

Barefoot Books

0800 328 2640
www.barefootbooks.com
Books about our planet, cultures and ourselves. Creative and imaginative stories your little ones will enjoy.

Blackwell's Bookshop

53-62 South Bridge, EH1 1YS
0131 622 8222
Edinburgh@blackwell.co.uk
bookshop.blackwell.co.uk
A nice contrast to the Waterstone's behemoth. The South Bridge branch is a labyrinthine shop, and the children's section is in the basement. Easy access through main door on South Bridge and then via the lift. Run by the friendly Julie Gamble (interview p 258), the children's section is impeccably tidy and organised. Not the biggest in town but one of the finest, with a great selection of titles for all ages. There are child-sized tables and chairs for colouring and reading. A very welcoming shopping experience.

Accessibility: Relatively good, for every step there is a ramp. Eating: Café Nero.

The Book People

0845 602 3030
www.thebookpeople.co.uk
An easy way to buy books. Many familiar authors for pre-school and older children, as well as a wide range of books to support school studies and learning to read, plus activity and puzzle books. Particularly good value are their multiples sets e.g. 10 children's books for £10. A cost effective way to find quality items for party bags, or to source items for other children's birthdays. Gift card and party invitation sets available at times. Would also be suited to book groups or purchasing for nurseries and playgroups. Registered users can earn points towards future purchases, and there are regular opportunities to get discounts on delivery costs. Special delivery discounts for OAPs, registered disabled, registered carers, foster parents and registered childminders: further details online.

Cost: Delivery – single item £1.95, multiple items £3.95. FREE delivery for orders over £25.

Booksdirect

0870 165 0299
bca_customersupport@thewebbgroup.co.uk
www.booksforchildren.co.uk
Fifteen catalogues/year. Editor's recommended selection for each of 5 specific age groups sent automatically. Covers books from 0-12 yrs. Members must buy 4 books in the first year.

The Edinburgh Bookshop

219 Bruntsfield Place, EH10 4DH
0131 447 1917
vanessa@edinburghbookshop.com
www.edinburghbookshop.com
This shop feels how you would want a bookshop to feel; homely and welcoming, with friendly staff and a pleasant relaxing atmosphere. No garish

displays. Everything gives the impression it has been thought through with some sense but also with regard to what is being sold; a bookshop for book lovers. The children's section is cute and comfortable, with cushions and activity sheets, and a good selection of titles on offer. A great shopping experience. Really good website too.

Pushchairs: Perhaps not on a busy day, as it is not a large shop!

Green Metropolis

customersupport@greenmetropolis.com
www.greenmetropolis.com
A great idea – recycling books in a sustainable way. Find your books a new home, get some fresh stories and make some money. You help the environment and money from every book sold goes to the Woodland Trust.

Linton Books

Deanfoot Road, West Linton, EH46 7DY
01968 660339
derek@lintonbooks.plus.com
www.west-linton.org.uk/linton_books.html
My daughter and I had a lovely browse around this small, very quaint book store – there was a good range of books but I did find it difficult to squeeze around the tightly packed shelves with a pushchair! My daughter particularly enjoyed saying hello to the owner's friendly cat! There were some good Scottish children's story books which we enjoyed looking at and my daughter chose a fun Scottish sticker and book set. So we had a good visit. West Linton is a lovely village and we made a trip to the small play area which was just further along from the book store.

Nic's Barefoot Books

31 Hillview Terrace, EH12 8RG
07867 856900
nicola@currie-mullan.com
www.nicola-currie.barefootbooks.com

Children's books and CDs which aim to offer an authentic alternative to the commercialisation of childhood, with an emphasis on make-believe, other cultures and our planet. For babies and children to 12+ yrs. Buy online, directly from Nicola or arrange for a Barefoot Books stall at your playgroup or fundraiser.

The Red House Children's Books

0870 191 9980
www.redhouse.co.uk
Mail order and online children's book shop. Hardback and paperback books, audiotapes, CD-ROMs, videos, games and activities plus character merchandise. Good deals available.

Waterstone's

128 Princes Street, EH2 4AD
0843 290 8313 (West End branch)
www.waterstones.com
Children's books area is a spacious area with tables, chairs and colouring. There is a café and toilets, but no nappy-changing facilities. Other branches at **George St, Cameron Toll, Fort Kinnaird and Ocean Terminal**.

Parking: *Depends on branch, FREE parking at Ocean Terminal, Fort Kinnaird and Cameron Toll, paid parking for central branches.* **Accessibility:** *Lifts in branches where children's book area is not on ground level.* **Toilets:** *In West End branch.* **Eating:** *Some branches have cafés.*

WHSmith

Gyle, EH12 9JR
0131 317 1771
Branches also throughout Edinburgh and surrounding areas. There are 2 branches in the Gyle, one is specifically a book store. Quite well laid out, with easy access with a pushchair, wide aisles and labelled areas so you can find what

you're looking for. A good selection of children's books, but nowhere for kids to enjoy them.

Visit our website for updates:
www.efuf.co.uk

CAKES & COOKERY

3D Cakes

20 Roseburn Terrace, EH12 6AW
0131 337 9990
enquiries@3d-cakes.co.uk
www.3d-cakes.co.uk
Award winning cake designer specialising in 3D wedding and novelty cakes.

Cost: Examples of cakes with costs on website.

Creative Cookware

89 Rose Street, EH2 3DT
0131 226 2117
lin@creativecookware.co.uk
www.creativecookware.co.uk
This independent cookware shop sells pans, bakeware, utensils, knives and kitchen essentials. We liked the cookie cutters, colourful silicon bakeware and children's crockery too. Small shop with internal steps so tricky with a pushchair, but the friendly staff helped entertain my children when we visited.

Accessibility: There are 3 steps up to the shop and 2 further steps inside.

The Finishing Touch

17 Patrick's Square, EH8
0131 667 0914
More than 40 novelty tins to hire, plus numbers, letters, squares, hexagons, etc. Good instructions. Also every imaginable utensil and ingredient for cake decorating. Lots of party paraphernalia too including party toys, masks, wigs and an extensive range of ribbons.

Lakeland

55 Hanover Street, EH2 2PJ
0131 220 3947
www.lakeland.co.uk
Successful chain of cookware stores with wide selection of bakeware, including tins, decorations, parchment and cases, cake and jelly moulds and cupcake stands. Also sells household and garden goods, specialist foods and gifts. Colourful mail-order catalogues.

Accessibility and pushchairs: Use accessible entrance from George St. Lift to basement.

CARDS & CRAFTS

Duff Doodles

0208 748 5986
www.duffdoodles.com
Supply greetings cards and illustrations. Commissions taken for any occasion.

Phoenix Trading Greeting Cards and Giftwrap

0131 449 6331 (Julia Grindley)
www.phoenix-trading.eu/web/joannawatson
or **www.phoenix-trading.co.uk/web/julia-grindley**
www.phoenix-trading.co.uk
UK's leading direct card-selling company. Very wide range of greetings cards, invitations, thank you notes and giftwrap at up to 50% less than shop prices. Call for free brochure or order online (delivery FREE). Julia Grindley, one of the Edinburgh traders, is available for coffee mornings, parties, fairs and fundraising events.

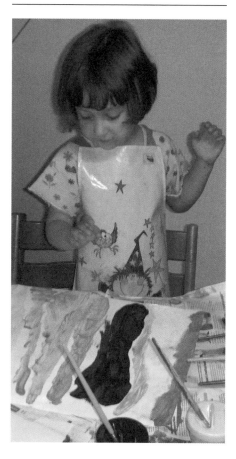

Yellow Moon

0844 826 8677
www.yellowmoon.org.uk
Website with arts and crafts focus but huge product range, including travel items, novelty gifts, educational toys and much more. Lots of decorate-it-yourself items ranging from colour-in Christmas cards to complicated model sets. Many items come in multiples, great for making birthday or Christmas presents, or for party bags. Some tie in to school topic themes, such as Egyptians, Romans, Native Americans, also lots of themed items for Halloween, Christmas, Mother's Day etc. Many products are fundraisers for Children in Need. Nurseries and other groups can also act as agents and fundraise for up to 20% of value of items, at given times of the year e.g. before Christmas. Registered users are emailed when there are special offers, making it even more cost effective.

Cost: £3.45 standard UK delivery. Free delivery if you spend over £45.

CLOTHING

Most department stores, large supermarkets and some chemists stock babywear, children's clothes and maternity wear (also see High Street and Supermarkets sections).

Sizing is a problem with buying children's clothes – there are many different systems so the age range given is only a rough guide. If using real nappies, it's worth buying the next size up in vests and trousers. Some smaller shops will make-to-measure at little or no extra charge for children with specific needs.

More stores now offer maternity clothing which are comfortable, fashionable and even flattering, with adjustable waists which "grow". Even after the birth you may find that you keep wearing maternity clothes for a while, so you may well get many months' wear out of them. Some stores also stock breastfeeding tops.

Babipur

01766 770644
shop@babipur.co.uk
www.babipur.co.uk
The name is Welsh for "Pure Baby". Offers ethical and environmentally friendly clothing and baby products online.

Bishopston Trading Company

0117 924 5598
www.bishopstontrading.co.uk
A workers' co-operative set up to create employment in a South Indian village. Clothes for adults and children from birth made from natural fabrics, mostly organic cotton. Catalogue and online ordering, also available in One World in St John's Church (see p 257).

Blessings and Blossoms

132 St John's Road, EH12 8AX
0131 334 8322
sales@blessingsandblossoms.co.uk
www.blessingsandblossoms.co.uk
Very stylish selection of boutique and baby clothes, although prices do match the incredible high quality! Great for special occasions – definitely not for everyday wear!

Blue Peach

0131 467 4911
07834 418374
info@bluepeach.eu
www.bluepeach.etsy.com
Online supplier of quality childrenswear handmade in Scotland.

Boden

0844 873 0000
www.boden.co.uk
Mini Boden is logo-free. Very good quality and stylish clothes for children up to 14 yrs, made mostly of natural fabrics.

Bright Sparks

01683 300648
sheila.brightsparks@tiscali.co.uk
www.brightsparksknitwear.co.uk
Handknitted childrenswear made in Scotland.

Cambridge Baby

01223 572228
helenandnick@cambridgebaby.co.uk
www.cambridgebaby.co.uk
Natural clothing, fairly traded and eco-friendly.

Clever Togs

01568 750673
info@clevertogs.com
www.clevertogs.com
Fun and educational, hand-embroidered babies' and children's appliquéd t-shirts. Eco-friendly and fair trade! Made in Scotland.

Clothkits

01243 600301
01243 533180
www.clothkits.co.uk
Funky outfits and accessories supplied in kits for you to make. Easy-to-follow instructions.

CozyBear Scotland

0843 289 4910
enquiries@svenicoll.com
www.cozybear.co.uk
Colourful baby, toddler and children's fleece clothing and gifts.

Cute Toots

07794 886672
cutetoots@hotmail.co.uk
www.cutetoots.co.uk
Brilliant bandana bibs handmade in Edinburgh. They look great and they're eco-friendly too.

Earth Matters

94 High Street, North Berwick, EH39 4HE
01620 895401
earthmattersltd@fsmail.net
www.earthmatters.org.uk
Combined Fair Trade and eco-shop stocking a wide range of baby/children's clothes and toys.

Parking: FREE on-street. Accessibility and pushchairs: Small step.

Fabric of the Universe

0131 258 9221
info@fabricoftheuniverse.co.uk
www.fabricoftheuniverse.co.uk
Based in Edinburgh selling gorgeous organic ethically made babywear.

Frugi

01326 572828
info@welovefrugi.com
www.welovefrugi.com
Lovely organic clothing for children and babies.

Greenfibres

01803 868001
mail@greenfibres.com
www.greenfibres.com
Organic cotton and wool clothes for babies and children, washable nappies, cotton toys.

JoJo Maman Bebe

9 Multrees Walk, EH1 3DQ
0131 558 8052
edinburgh@jojomamanbebe.co.uk
www.jojomamanbebe.co.uk
A shop as well as an online and mail order company. The shop stocks maternity and nursing clothing, baby wear from tiny baby up to 5 yrs, plus a small selection of feeding, travelling and bathing accessories. A catalogue is issued quarterly with free P&P, returns can be made to the store. The big bonus is that there is a customer toilet with nappy-change facilities!

Joules

0845 250 7170
www.joulesclothing.com
Style, colour and quality for little ones.

Kitschy Coo

general@kitschycoo.co.uk
www.kitschycoo.co.uk
Edinburgh-based clothing for children. Unique and funky clothes – every item is a one-off.

La Redoute

0844 842 2222
www.redoute.co.uk
Fashionable children's clothes at reasonable prices, along with teenage and adult ranges. Personal account option. There are often "free p&p" options with online orders. Free returns.

Little Green Radicals

0207 733 6402
info@littlegreenradicals.co.uk
www.littlegreenradicals.co.uk
Childrenswear that is organic and fair trade. Ranges for babies and children.

The Merry Go Round

Main Street, Gullane, East Lothian, EH31 2AP
01620 842222
www.the-merry-go-round.co.uk
Lovely shop with gorgeous clothes for wee ones.

The Natural Collection

0845 367 7003
www.naturalcollection.com
Organic cotton clothing, bedding and washable nappies as well as many other eco and/or ethical-friendly products.

NCT Bra Fitting

Naomi Crowley 0131 332 2191
Frankie Taylor 0131 664 3710
www.nctedinburgh.moonfruit.com
Offers a wide range of beautiful, practical and comfortable maternity and feeding bras in all sizes from a 28 to 44 back size and an A to L cup size. Edinburgh has two trained NCT volunteer fitters who will be happy to arrange a free, no obligation fitting in their own home. Edinburgh NCT will get 10% commission on any purchases and this will go to help train breastfeeding counsellors and antenatal teachers.

NCT Shop

0845 8100 100
www.nctshop.co.uk
Baby clothes, accessories, gifts, books, leaflets and videos. Also stocks maternity clothing, sleepwear and a good range of maternity/ breastfeeding bras in a wide range of sizes.

Nippers

131 Bruntsfield Place, EH10 4EB
0131 228 5086
mail@nippersforkids.com
www.nippersforkids.com
Lovely merchandise and some good party costumes make this shop worth a visit even though the shop floor is cramped to negotiate with a pushchair.

Visit our website for updates:
www.efuf.co.uk

Nordic Kids

0208 736 0580
cs@nordickids.co.uk
www.nordickids.co.uk
Funky baby clothes and cool children's clothing.

Polarn o Pyret (Jenners)

48 Princes Street, EH2 2YJ
0131 260 2324
www.polarnopyret.com
Popular Swedish brand of clothing which is functional as well as stylish.

Pretty Pregnant

www.prettypregnant.co.uk
Online store that has a good range of maternity clothes for work and formal events (not so much casualwear). The clothes are priced at the top end, e.g. jeans at £55-£85. Very good range of nursing tops, casual and formal, plus dresses. Bras, swimsuits and tights.

Rainbow Babies

0207 099 5705
info@rainbowbabies.co.uk
www.rainbowbabies.co.uk
Trendy, simple, colourful, affordable clothing.

Tatty Bumpkin

01732 812212
sales@tattybumpkinshop.com
www.tattybumpkinshop.com
Specialists in organic and bamboo kids' clothing.

The Treasure Trove

23a Castle Street, EH2 3DN
0131 220 1187
shop@selfaidsociety.co.uk
www.selfaidsociety.co.uk
The Treasure Trove is exactly that, a small shop selling unique, quality handmade goods. Lovely baby knitwear is located in drawers by size, each one different in colour and pattern. Knitwear for older children and adults is hung along the wall, together with small selections of handmade jewellery, cards, toys, gifts, crochet and Shetland shawls. The counter tempts you with cakes and preserves. Goods can also be made to order from your own pattern or using your own material. The goods are all made by members of The Royal Edinburgh Repository and Self Aid Society, which assists those of limited means to achieve an independent livelihood. There is commission, ensuring funds go directly back to the individuals who have invested their time and effort, so a very worthy cause! If you are not lucky enough to know someone who can knit for your child and want something different from the high street then this is the place to go! We have received many compliments on my daughter's snuggly cardigan, see photo!

Vanilla Bloom

6 William Street, EH3 7NH
0131 220 2502
contact@vanillabloom.com
www.vanillabloom.com
Upmarket boutique for maternity lingerie and fashions, baby/children's clothes, equipment and toys. Brands include HOTmilk, Mama Mio, Maternal America, Inch Blue and Catimini.

Accessibility/Pushchairs: One step into shop, lift into basement.

VertBaudet

0844 842 0000
www.vertbaudet.co.uk
Sizeable catalogue selling babies', children's and maternity clothes, and nursery goods. Also bedding and children's bedroom accessories. Personal account facility. Free returns. Range of low birth weight baby clothing.

DRESSING-UP CLOTHES

Hopscotch Dressing Up Clothes

0208 696 1313
www.hopscotchmailorder.co.uk
Dressing up outfits 18 mths-9 yrs. Cloaks, clowns, princesses, animals, astronauts, etc.

The Magic Wardrobe

Dressing up Clothes for Kids
0131 667 4813
cherryledlie@blueyonder.co.uk
www.themagicwardrobe.btck.co.uk
Local recycling project which turns used and unwanted fabrics into children's dressing-up clothes. All profits go to Edinburgh NCT. Costumes can be bought from stalls at school fairs, or direct at any time. Check website for upcoming stalls, or phone to discuss a commission or private viewing. Ideal Christmas and birthday presents for imaginative kids. Donations of fabric, trimmings, old patterns, etc, always welcome!

SCHOOL UNIFORM

Many department stores and supermarkets stock skirts, pinafores, shorts, trousers, blazers, shirts and socks in traditional school colours. Their stock is extensive in May, June and July but most have a reduced stock in other months. Other suggested retailers:

Aitken and Niven

234 Queensferry Road, EH24 2BP
0131 467 8825, and
6 Falcon Rd West, Morningside, EH10 1AQ
0131 477 3922
www.aitken-niven.co.uk
Long-established Edinburgh retailer, which stocks schoolwear and sportswear including uniforms for Edinburgh's independent schools. Also stocks school shoes.

Clan House

45 Grove Street, EH3 8AF
0131 229 6857, and
28-30 Morningside Road, EH10 4DA
0131 447 3414
www.clanh.com
Stockists of uniforms, sportswear and equipment. Also stocks most Edinburgh school badges to sew on.

DANCEWEAR AND SWIMWEAR

Some of Edinburgh's department stores stock dance and keep-fit wear. However, it does pay to shop around. Some dance teachers also sell shoes and/or leotards, so it's worthwhile asking if your child is starting a class.

Dancewear

182 Rose Street, EH2 4BA
0131 226 5457
sales@dancewear-edinburgh.co.uk
www.dancewear-edinburgh.co.uk
This wasn't the obvious location to review with my heavy footed 2 yr old, but the staff were very friendly and knowledgeable. Whether you are looking for "Hip hop" shoes or sequinned skating dresses this shop has each dance genre covered, from 2 yrs. Specialises in point shoe fittings, also has the uniform list for several local dance schools and does mail order.

Dancia International

42 South Clerk Street, EH8 9PS
0131 668 9444
www.dancia.co.uk/dance-shop/edinburgh
Full range of dancewear for children, covering all specialities, and also all types of shoes. Full fitting service.

Splash About

info@splashabout.net
www.splashabout.net
A wide range of products to keep little ones warm and safe in the water or sun. Includes

neoprene swim suits, SPF 50+ sun-suits for the beach, waterproof and leakproof swim nappies (Happy Nappies), and various flotation devices. Website includes articles about what to consider if looking for baby swim lessons. Products extensively tested and trialled in France.

KILTS

There are several specialist kilt shops in Edinburgh, although shops such as Aitken and Niven, Ortak and John Lewis stock kilts, tartan wear and/or accessories.
Proper kilts are expensive because of the amount of material used. A reasonable alternative is the "half kilt", in which not all pleats are full (as they are in a proper kilt) but it still swings well and looks good. Many shops also sell kilted skirts off the peg.
Shops which sell made-to-measure kilts usually have books of tartan (you may need to choose a small set for a small kilt). These stores can help link your surname to a specific clan.
If you only need a kilt for a special occasion, a good alternative is to hire one.

Davison Menswear & Kilt Hire

31-33 Bruntsfield Place, EH10 4HJ
0131 229 0266
077665 52930 (24 hr contact)
sales@qualitykilts.co.uk
www.qualitykilts.co.uk
Friendly staff, run by the Davison family, which makes for a pleasant shopping experience.

Accessibility: One step into shop, if customers phone ahead arrangements can be made for easier access.

Hector Russell

95 Princes Street, EH2 2ER, and
137-141 High Street, EH1 1SG
0131 225 3315
sales@hector-russell.com
www.hector-russell.com

224

These stores stock boys' kilts and trews and girls' kilted skirts, as well as: kilts, socks, sock flashes, belts, sgian dubh, shirts, and shoes. Also offer a made-to-measure service for children and dancers. Online mail order service also available.

Highland Laddie

6 Hutchison Terrace, EH14 1QB
0131 455 7505
Complete outfits sold. All accessories available: jackets, shirts, brogues and shoes, sporrans etc.

Cycling Equipment

A quick tour through the different types of equipment you can buy to accommodate little passengers while cycling and get them started on their own bikes. See pages 39-42 for more on getting around Edinburgh by bike.

Child seats

Most shops will fit a child seat for nothing, or for a minimal charge, if you have bought from them. Don't lose any of the nuts and bolts, as some are unique and irreplaceable. A child seat will affect the handling and stability of your bike, and place a greater strain on it, so keep it well maintained, especially brakes and wheels.

Rear child seats
The best rear child seats are made from high-impact, rigid moulded plastic, with headrests to support a child who has fallen asleep. They should also have a safety harness, footguards and straps to prevent feet getting caught in the rear wheel. If you have a sprung saddle, cover or replace it so that little fingers don't get caught. Suitable for children from around the age at which they are able to sit unsupported (usually 6 mths) until they get too heavy for the seat. This aspect varies with manufacturer recommendation, but it's usually 22kg, approx. up to 3-4 yrs.

Front child seats

These aren't recommended. The child feels colder than in a rear-mounted seat, shielded by your body. Also, if they fall asleep, you must use one arm to support them and ride one-handed, which is unsafe.

Child trailers

Two-wheeled pushchairs that attach to the rear fork of an adult bike. The fixing device allows the adult bike to be laid on its side without tipping the trailer up, but it is a good idea to fit a stand to the adult bike. Most can carry two children from 9 mths to 5-6 yrs, with the limiting factor being their weight – the maximum combined weight is usually 50kg. A very young child can also be carried when strapped into a child seat, although this will leave no room for a second child. Most trailers also have a luggage space at the back. Trailers usually come with a rain-and-sun cover and a visibility flag. The best also have quick release wheels and can be folded down for easy carriage in trains, buses and cars. They are fairly expensive, but they do tend to have a high resale value. They also make useful luggage or shopping carriers, long after families have grown up! Makes include Adams, Burley, Bike Trax.

Compared with a child seat, the child misses the view, feels the bumps more and is right at exhaust height on any road. However, a single adult can take two young children at once, the balance of the adult bicycle is less affected and the trailer may stay upright if the adult bicycle falls over. The children also stay cosy and dry in all weathers.

Trailercycles

Also known as Tag-A-Longs, these consist of a special frame, without front wheels and with forks, which attach to an adult bike (or tandem), either at the seat post or rear rack. The child can help with the pedalling, but braking and steering are left to the adult. They are excellent for taking children out cycling in situations where either it would not be safe to let them cycle independently, or where a child wouldn't be able to cope with the distance or hills. It's also a great

way for a child to learn about observing traffic, signalling and road positioning while being safely in the control of an experienced adult. Some models have gears so children can learn how to change gear without having to worry about steering at the same time. The great advantage of trailercycles is their versatility. You can buy a "seconds" tow hitch, which allows the trailercycle to be quickly swapped between adult bikes. A trailercycle can also be carried easily on trains by simply detaching and storing alongside the adult bike in the cycle storage area.

Trailercycles are suitable for children from 3-4 yrs up to around 9 yrs. Makes include Bike Trax, Adams and Ally Cat.

Trailgator

A special bar which attaches to an adult bike and converts a regular child's bike to a trailercycle by lifting up the front wheel. Obviously, these are much cheaper, but are really only suitable for small bikes. Larger children's bikes tend to fall over too easily.

Tandems

A "junior back" style tandem has a frame designed for an adult "pilot" at the front and a child "stoker" at the back. A potentially good solution if you are to do a lot of cycling, but they're not very versatile. Makes include Dawes, Orbit, Thorn and Swallow.

Ordinary tandems are fitted with "kiddy cranks" or crank shorteners. More versatile than a junior back tandem, as they can easily be converted back to ordinary tandems again.

Tricycles

A tricycle fitted with one or two child seats at the back can also be a good way of getting the family on the move. Suitable for children from 12 mths to 5 yrs.

Cycling solo

Balance bikes or "runners" are becoming more popular. These bikes without pedals (available with and without brakes) are a great way to get little ones cycling and learning to balance. Most of the bicycle shops listed have at least one type of balance bike for sale. Try them out for size. Probably suitable from 2-3 yrs or when children can sit on the bike and reach the ground with the balls of their feet. Wooden versions are also available from toyshops. Otherwise check out children's bikes with stabilisers or tricycles, especially those with a handle that lets adults push/control the trike comfortably.

Helmets

A helmet should be an essential piece of equipment for all cyclists. It is important to take your child to the shop to have them fitted properly so they don't wobble. Look for one that has a European or American standard, preferably both, as these standards have superseded the British one. To make them more acceptable for children, go for the coolest looking one you can afford! Children who are putting a lot of effort into pedalling will also appreciate one with plenty of ventilation. Makes include Met, Hamax, Cateye, Specialized, Giro, Bell. Helmets are all "first impact" so should be replaced after a serious bash or if they are damaged.

General safety

- Under no circumstances should you cycle with a baby in a backpack or sling.
- Keep children's shoelaces short and tucked away. The same applies to scarves and other loose clothing.
- Dress children in brightly coloured clothing, so that they are visible to motorists.
- Think twice before carrying a very restless child.
- Beware of very cold and wet weather.
- Make sure that the adult bike is kept in good mechanical order. Especially ensure that the brakes are always working well to cope with the additional weight that the bike will be carrying.

A good tip!

Try out some of the more expensive items like trailers or trailercycles before you buy, to make sure that you are happy with the handling and that it's the right bit of gear for you. Try and borrow from another family, or consider hiring for a weekend – you could save yourself an expensive mistake! Go to a bike shop specialising in trailer bikes or tandems for advice on the best and most suitable equipment to buy.

BICYCLE SHOPS

Alpine Bikes

48 Hamilton Place, EH3 5AX
0131 225 3286
www.alpinebikes.co.uk
Adult and child bikes, child seats and helmets, trailer bikes and child trailers. Also stocks Gore bikewear, Altura clothing and panniers. Bike spares and repair service with 24 hr turnaround. Hires out trailer bikes, child trailers and mountain bikes. Also stocks demo bikes.

BG Cycles and Blades

48 Portobello High Street, EH15 1DA
0131 657 5832
www.bgcycles.co.uk
Bikes, trailer bikes, child seats and helmets, plus in-line skates. Also repairs and spares – can uplift or deliver bikes for repair or service within a 15-mile radius, small charge.

Bicycle Repair Man

111 Newington Road, EH9 1QW
0131 667 5959
bicycle.repair.man@unicombox.com
www.bicyclerepairmanedinburgh.com
Bikes, child seats and helmets, trailer bikes and child trailers. Spares, same day repair service.

The Bicycleworks

29-30 Argyle Place, EH9 1JJ
0131 228 8820
www.thebicycleworks.co.uk
Repair and wheel building shop with a wide range of spares and accessories. Sells child seats. Instant puncture repairs or tyre replacement. Fast turn around on all other repairs/servicing.

The Bike Station

250 Causewayside, Newington, EH9 1UU
0131 668 1996
www.thebikestation.org.uk
Scotland's largest seller of reconditioned/recycled second-hand bikes – all fully refurbished and with a 3 mth warranty. Offers many other services to encourage more people to start cycling and support those already cycling. Examples include Dr Bike – mobile mechanical service; training sessions; mechanical courses.

Bike Trax

11 Lochrin Place, EH3 9QX
0131 228 6633
info@biketrax.co.uk
www.biketrax.co.uk
Bikes, child seats and helmets, trailer bikes, child trailers and folding bikes. Dawes, Ridgeback, Trek, Brompton etc. Free aftersales service. Will repair any make of bike, including children's bikes. 24 hr turnaround where possible. Free estimates. Free advice on cycle matters, local cycle routes etc. Also hires out bikes and equipment. Hire before you buy, charge deducted from purchase price.

Cycle Scotland

29 Blackfriars Street
0131 556 5560
info@cyclescotland.co.uk
www.cyclescotland.co.uk
Bikes, child seats, trailer bikes, child trailers, tandems. Repairs/servicing. Also hires out a large selection of adult and child bikes, tandem,

trailer bikes, child trailers, child seats etc. Organises cycle tours, holidays and days out.

Edinburgh Bicycle Co-operative

8 Alvanley Terrace, Whitehouse Loan, EH9 1DU
0131 228 3565
www.edinburghbicycle.com
Fantastic range of children's bicycles, trailers, trailer bikes, child seats, helmets, reflectives, accessories and clothing: all selected with the same attention to detail that the Bike Co-op lavish on their famed adult range. The child-friendly staff will happily offer advice to ensure your child gets fitted with, for instance, the correct size of helmet and the right size of bike.

Freewheelin

91 Slateford Road, EH11 1QR
0131 337 2351
info@freewheelin.biz
www.freewheelin.biz
Bikes, child seats and helmets. Can also order trailer bikes, child trailers and tandems. Spares, servicing and repair service with same/next day turnaround.

Halfords Stores and Superstores

www.halfords.com
Good selection of children's sit-and-ride toys, trikes, pedal cars and bikes – Apollo and Raleigh. Child seats, spare parts and accessories. Free aftersales service. Usually repair bikes bought here, but may occasionally do small outside repairs. Major repairs in-store. Free fitting of child seat if bike bought at Halfords. Branches at **Hermiston Gait Retail Park, Seafield Rd East, and 11 Straiton Mains**.

Leith Cycle Co

276 Leith Walk EH6 5BX
0131 467 7775, and
1 Cadzow Place, EH7 5SN
0131 652 1760
www.leithcycleco.com

Bikes and full range of safety accessories including child seats and helmets. Hire before you buy, charge deducted from purchase price. In basement, Recycling (0131 553 1130) offers reconditioned bikes guaranteed for 3 mths.

MacDonald Cycles

26-28 Morrison Street, EH3 9BJ
0131 229 8473
www.macdonaldcycles.com
Also at **35 High St, Musselburgh, EH21 7AD.**
Good selection of children's trikes and bikes – Raleigh, DiamondBack, Giant and Dawes. Cycle parts, child seats, children's helmets, children's cycle capes, spare parts and safety accessories. Free aftersales service. Will repair any bike, if parts available. Usually 24 hr turnaround, sometimes quicker. Will fit child seat free if both bike and seat are bought here.

Theraplay Ltd

0141 876 9177
info@theraplay.com
www.theraplay.com
Tricycles for children with additional needs. You can request a rep visit to assess the kind of trike that will suit your child. The Imp model comes in child-friendly colours and is suitable for children from 2½.

Velo Ecosse

25-27 Bruntsfield Place, EH10 4HJ
0131 477 2557
sales@veloecosse.com
www.veloecosse.com
Bikes, child seats and helmets. Trailercycles, trailers and a large range of cycle clothing. Spares and accessories. Repairs and servicing in 24-48 hrs. For serious cyclists, they stock Giant, Pinarello and Shimano amongst others.

FOOD & DRINK

Babylicious

01494 432902
www.babylicious.co.uk
Wholesome frozen babyfood.

The Chocolate Tree

07790 214280
0131 228 3144
freddymatthis@gmx.de
www.the-chocolate-tree.co.uk
Hand crafted organic chocolate. Yum. Need we say more?

East Coast Organic Boxes (ECOBox)

24 Boggs Holdings, Pencaitland, EH34 5BD
01875 340227
www.eastcoastorganics.co.uk
Organic vegetable boxes as well as organic fruit, eggs and bread. Free delivery service available – phone or check website for details. Collection points throughout Edinburgh or collect direct from farm.

Knowes Farm Shop

Knowes Farm, East Linton
01620 860010
knowesfarmshop.co.uk
Feeding the hens is the best bit. Ask beforehand and the shop will give you bread. The shop itself is a large farm shop. The staff toilet can be used by a mother in distress. There is a riverside walk nearby. It's a public right of way and pushchair and dog friendly. My 3-yr-old daughter loves feeding the hens and the walk by the river.

Accessibility/Pushchairs: Small step at entrance/exit of shop.

Mama Tea

0131 336 1936
info@mamatea.com
www.mamatea.com
From the Morning Mama to combat morning sickness, to the Ready Mama for labour and birth, and the New Mama for breastfeeding – Mama Teas have something for everyone. Based in Edinburgh.

Pillars of Hercules Organic Farm

By Falkland, Fife
01337 857749
bruce@pillars.co.uk
www.pillars.co.uk
Organic vegetable boxes as well as organic fruit and eggs. Free catalogue. Delivery to Edinburgh and Fife areas.

Real Foods

37 Broughton Street, EH1 3JU
0131 557 1911
info@realfoods.co.uk
www.realfoods.co.uk
This long-established wholefood shop specialises in natural, organic, fair-trade and vegetarian goods. Many products such as flour and oats are sold loose and in bulk, at very reasonable prices. Stock includes dried fruit and nuts, honey and nut butters, speciality flours and grains, eco cleaning products and skincare. We like their jumbo raisins, which are gratifyingly big. The staff are knowledgeable and friendly. An extensive online shop offers free delivery for orders over £5. Also a Tollcross branch at **8 Brougham St**.

Pushchairs: Several steps to the entrance, and narrow aisles, but pushchairs do fit.

So Baby

01829 772555
yourthoughts@so-baby.co.uk
www.so-baby.co.uk
Menu of meals suitable for every stage of weaning and feeding from 6 mths-2 yrs.

The Whole Shebag

07931 738767
01501 785436 (tel/fax)
bags@thewholeshebag.com
www.thewholeshebag.com
Wholesome frozen babyfood. Delivers fresh and tasty organic fruit and vegetables throughout the central belt every week. Great selection, bag contents can be adapted to suit your tastes. Each bag contains a newsletter with handy recipe suggestions.

Haircuts

Edinburgh has a good selection of hairdressers who are relaxed with children, patient, and have a calm approach. Having a haircut can be traumatic for some young children, although others love it.

Many hairdressers have special seats for children and books and toys for while they are waiting. Some show DVDs. If your child is shy, it might be worth asking if they can sit on your knee while their hair is being cut. Timing is important – choose a time when your child is usually on good form, perhaps early in the day or after a nap. If possible, go for a quieter period at the hairdressers.

If it's your child's first visit to a salon, you could make the appointment with them in person, so s/he can get used to it. If you are looking for a hairdresser for your family, why not have a haircut first yourself, to chat to the stylist and how keen s/he is to cut children's hair, or if there is another stylist that specialises in children's cuts. Some salons offer reduced rates for children when a parent has a haircut.

Another option is to have a hairdresser come to your home. Check out www.yell.com or local press.

Emma Hall Hair Design

19A Haddington Place, EH7 4AF
0131 557 4888
mail@emmahall8.orangehome.co.uk
www.emmahallhair.co.uk

A lovely, all-organic hair salon with reasonable prices, friendly staff, and best of all, a play area for little ones. The staff are very welcoming towards children. It's so nice to be able to schedule a haircut without also having to arrange a sitter!

Cost: *Children from £8, ladies' cut and style from £36, gents' cut and style £19.* **Parking:** *1hr FREE outside the shop. Otherwise paid parking on the surrounding streets.* **Pushchairs:** *You need to descend a flight of stairs to the shop, so it may be easier to leave the pushchair at home. Staff are happy to help with pushchairs on the stairs.*

Kids' Stop

36 Morningside Road, EH10 4DA
0131 446 0123
Extremely child-friendly salon, which also welcomes adults! Special child's seat provided (horse, rabbit, bike), video during haircut, play area with toys, video and books. Sliding scale of rates, dependent on child's age. Make-over parties also available – please call salon for more information.

Toilets: *Down a flight of 12 stairs.* **Nappy changing:** *In toilet, downstairs. Mat and wipes provided.*

Kute Kutz

4 Meadow Bank Avenue, EH8 7AP
0131 661 1339
www.kutekutzedinburgh.com
Kids' hair salon with quad bike or a pink scooter seat which the kids love! TVs help to keep the children focused while getting their hair cut. Certificate and lock of hair for first haircuts.

Accessibility/Pushchairs: *One step into shop, and limited space inside.* **Toilets:** *Staff toilet can be used.*

Madison Hairdressing

36 Duart Crescent, Drumbrae, EH4 7JP
0131 339 1118
www.madisonhairdressing.co.uk
Hair salon for women, men and children. No appointment necessary.

Mizzumi

73-75 High Street, Musselburgh, EH21 7BZ
0131 665 1212
A stylish salon for adults which also has a dedicated kids' area painted in bright colours with TV and videos to entertain little ones while they have their hair cut.

HOLIDAYS

Access Travel

01942 888844
www.access-travel.co.uk
Holiday destinations picked with disabled people in mind – wheelchair access, special aids for hire, adapted vehicles and car hire. Nursing and care services in some resorts.

Baby-Friendly Boltholes

08454 890140
www.babyfriendlyboltholes.co.uk
Great recommendations for baby-friendly holiday accommodation to take the stress out of travelling with babies and toddlers.

The Calvert Trust

01434 250232
www.calvert-trust.org.uk
Activity holidays for disabled people with well-established sites at Exmoor, Keswick and Kielder.

Tourism for All

0845 124 9971
info@tourismforall.org.uk
www.tourismforall.org.uk
A national charity dedicated to making tourism welcoming to all. Great website containing information about hundreds of accessible hotels and attractions in the UK, plus special offers on getaways. Also provides information sheets on destinations beyond the UK.

LABELS & PERSONALISING

Able Labels

www.able-labels.co.uk
sales@able-labels.co.uk
0844 371 2423
Ways to label a whole range of items, from pencils to wheelie bins, bags to nametapes for clothes. Includes gift ideas such as photo jigsaws, personalised towels, and much more. If you need to label items for nursery/school, includes labels for shoes and dishwasher-proof labels for lunch boxes. Possible to add pictures/

use different fonts, and make labels that are easily recognisable.

Cash's Name Tapes

02476 466466
www.jjcash.co.uk
Classic maker of name tapes for over 160 years. Woven, iron-on and stick-on labels, but also travel items such as personalised luggage straps. Choose from a range of colours, fonts and pictures to make your labels special; good if you or someone you know makes or knits clothes. If you want to include a rather special bookmark alongside a book as a present, there is a Beatrix Potter series of woven bookmarks.

Easy2Name

01635 298326
www.easy2name.com
Labels to sew, iron or stick on, including shoe labels. Also ink stampers to label items, and EasyTags, a button type label which is very quick to attach. The site also has labels to identify food allergies, for lunch boxes, and identity wristbands for trips/holidays. There are additional practical items like reusable food labels for the freezer, or fun fabric patches for disguising e.g. holes in trouser knees. You can also gain 20% commission if distributing the labels to a group like a nursery or playgroup.

Identity Direct

0845 450 5098
www.identitydirect.co.uk
A wide range of items which can be personalised, including clocks, toys, bedding and gift items. Baby items such as quilts, bibs and babygros. Books personalised to your child, with their name and details about them, for a special gift. Lots of focus on familiar characters from Disney and other TV shows. Iron-on and stick-on name labels, with a particularly wide range of vinyl labels. Includes stretchable labels for harder-to-label items like swimming goggles. Also personalisable gifts for older family members, including football themed mugs and posters.

Mini Label

www.minilabels.co.uk
All types of label for clothing, backpacks, and dishwasher-proof labels for packed lunch equipment. Iron-on labels that actually stay on (the writer can confirm this!).

Personal Presents

01494 877260
Personalisable presents for special "firsts", such as Christening, Christmas, first day at school. Items include plates and cups, bibs, candles. Some name labels and stickers but also wooden stamps to use with ink pads, and personalised ribbons for wrapping presents. Named pencils and stationery sets. Lots of personalised gift items for occasions such as Father's Day, Easter, Christmas, sports gifts etc.

Stuck on You

0845 456 0014
www.stuckonyou.biz/unitedkingdom
A focus on stick-on/bondable labels, but includes lots more, including embroidered gift items such as towels, bibs, baby clothes etc. Personalisable items such as calendars, books and diaries. Iron-on and stick-on clothing labels, including colour-paired labels for socks. Wide range of icons to accompany labels. Fun shaped tags for school bags, pencil cases, keyrings etc. Labels for kitchen food stuffs, and personalised note pads for letter writing. Vinyl labels are waterproof, dishwasher and microwave proof and UV resistant. Schools and other groups can also fundraise through distributing labels.

MAKE YOUR OWN

Edinburgh has an excellent choice of wool and fabric shops. The shops listed below are those which have something special to offer, and those which are more "out of the way".

John Lewis (see p 208) and The Cloth Shop probably have the largest choice of pattern books and paper patterns for everything from maternity wear to pyjamas, dressing gowns and dressing-up outfits. There are usually patterns for soft toys and "teen" dolls.

Most of the city's wool shops stock baby wools. Pingouin and Rowan have children's knitting patterns and Pingouin has a baby/toddler magazine. Paton's has a wide range of knitting patterns, starting at 14" for small babies.

The Cloth Shop

169 Bonnington Road, EH6 5BQ
0131 554 7733
Large warehouse-style shop, with a fantastic selection of dress, curtain and upholstery fabric, and all the haberdashery that goes along with it. Stencil kits and cushion pads available, along with some great tulles and seasonally printed fabrics for dressing-up clothes.

David Drummond

77-81 Haymarket Terrace
0131 539 7766
Sewing machines, including service and repairs. Haberdashery and wool. A treasure trove.

The Dress Fabric Company

38 Bruntsfield Place, EH10 4HJ
0131 221 0464
dressfabric@hotmail.co.uk
Stocked full of lovely fabrics – the hard part is deciding which one to choose.

Opening hours: Tues-Sat 10.00-18.00.

The Grassmarket Embroidery Shop

19 The Grassmarket, EH1 2HS
0131 226 3335
sueblack101@yahoo.co.uk
www.edinburghembroideryshop.co.uk
Easy access and looked like it had a good stock of embroidery stuff. Staff helpful.

Kiss the Fish Studios

9 Dean Park Street, EH4 1JN
0131 332 8912
www.kissthefishstudios.com
"Look at all of the things to paint!" Samuel, aged 4. This is the rainy day dream for children 3+ who have even the slightest inclination to paint, glue, model and create. They can choose a simple pre-determined object (boxes, animals) to decorate in a variety of ways. Super idea for homemade gifts from your child if your own home isn't kitted out with a fully stocked arts and crafts box. Gifts, cards and arts and crafts kits sold on site. Toddler classes and workshops depending on season. Not recommended for under 3s and it's a good idea to check space at weekends, as it is popular for birthday parties.

Cost: Starting from £2 up to £14 – includes varnish and materials. Accessibility: Room for wheelchair but toilet a squeeze. Birthdays/ celebrations: Parties for all occasions.

Mandors

131 East Claremont Street, EH7 4JA
0131 558 3888
www.mandors.co.uk
Good range of dressmaking fabrics for everyday wear through to bridalwear, faux fur etc. Plenty of fun fabrics for children's projects and fancy dress outfits, and some nice fabrics for children's bedroom curtains etc. There's also a good stock of haberdashery, such as ribbons and finishings, and a selection of patterns. Staff are happy to welcome children. Part of the shop is downstairs but no-one minded me leaving my pushchair at the top of the stairs.

McAree Brothers

19 Howe St, EH3 6TE
0131 558 1747
sales@mcadirect.com
www.mcadirect.com
A haberdashery shop, very useful for buying materials and accessories for your knitting or sewing. Plenty of knitting patterns that either you or your under 5 can use to create dolls, animals, bags, etc. Online shop (see website) which offers home delivery.

MARKETS

Edinburgh Farmers' Market

Castle Street
0131 652 5940
www.scottishfarmersmarkets.co.uk
There is lots to tempt here: raspberries from Perthshire; Scottish cheeses; meats like venison, poultry, game, pork or beef; fish; wine; juice; home baking; jams and soap and much more. Edinburgh Farmers' Market is a bit of an institution among those who like to get up early and get something good for dinner on Saturday night or a special Sunday lunch. The stallholders are often very chatty if there is not too long a queue behind you. It can be a bit bleak in winter, but rain or shine every Saturday the stallholders set up from 08.00 and the market is in full tilt by 09.00. At busy times, it can be harder to get a pushchair through. There is a seating area to enjoy a coffee or juice along with what's on offer from the vans at the market: the hog roast and porridge producers have been there for a few years. I found it not too pricey, considering the quality and variety of seasonal, local produce. The producers are mainly Scottish, although one or two travel up from England. Some of the local organic vegetable producers attend, who can arrange a weekly delivery service. The whole shopping experience outside is very refreshing – it is lovely looking up at Edinburgh Castle rather than at shopping aisles.

Opening hours: Sat 09.00-14.00. *Parking:* Multi-storey opposite, free parking until 08.30, metered afterwards. *Toilets:* Downstairs. *Eating:* Vans and stalls.

Stockbridge Market

Saunders Street and Kerr Street, EH3 6TN
0131 551 5633
www.stockbridgemarket.com
Running on Sundays from 10.00-17.00, this is a relatively new market which concentrates on providing quality foodstuffs through its farmers' stalls. There are also some craft stalls.

MISCELLANEOUS

Stardust Ceilings

stardustceilings@blueyonder.co.uk
www.stardustceilings.com
See stars indoors at night with this clever paint effect. Almost invisible by day, the paint charges up on daylight levels. As light fades in the evening, starlight patterns are revealed, fading again as daylight levels return. Products are created by a small family firm based in Edinburgh. Free consultation/quotations for ceiling prices. Posters also available in large sizes and can be posted FREE to UK addresses. A magical effect in a child's bedroom, but may also be suitable for public settings such as play/therapy rooms for special needs groups.

Thingimijigs

0844 844 5262
www.thingimijigs.co.uk
Wide range of character lunch boxes, but lots more, including character clothes for dressing up, and other character items such as sunglasses, umbrellas, bedding etc. Gifts for grownups too, and seasonal items for Christmas and Hallowe'en. Includes a bargain section where items are £1.99.

MOBILITY

In this section you'll find providers of, and advisers on, mobility equipment. Speak to your child's occupational therapist or physiotherapist about what would be most useful. Some equipment is free at www.edinburgh.gov.uk/info/922/equipment_and_adaptations_to_the_home. Information on the equipment, and a form to fill in to get it, is on the site.

For wheelchairs there should be a referral to ETC – Enabling Technology for Children. Get more information at www.smart.scot.nhs.uk/index.php/services/wheelchairs-and-seating, and contact ETC on 0131 537 9433.

Cyclone

0800 180 4850
www.cyclonemobility.com
Manufactures wheelchairs, including a sports-style wheelchair for children.

The Disabled Living Foundation

0845 130 9177
www.dlf.org.uk
Great website containing a wealth of information and resources about equipment. Fact sheets on all aspects of living with a disability.

G & S Smirthwaite

01626 835552
www.smirthwaite.co.uk
Market leaders in the design and manufacture of equipment and furniture for children from 8 mths with additional needs. Covers seating, standing, toileting, bathing, changing and showering, plus ranges for therapy and sensory integration.

Go Kids Go!

0870 121 0050
01482 887163
roy@go-kids-go.org.uk
www.wheelchairchildren.org.uk
The leading provider of wheelchair skills training across the UK and Ireland. Courses are FREE and equip young wheelchair users with the skills to become independently mobile.

JCM Seating Solutions Ltd

01733 405830 ext 1
www.jcmseating.co.uk
Equipment for children which includes seating systems, car seats and sleeping systems.

Lomax

01382 503000
www.lomaxmobility.com
Dundee-based manufacturer of wheelchairs. Kidactive chairs come in lots of different colours.

Nottingham Rehab Supplies

0845 120 4522
www.nrs-uk.co.uk
Wide variety of daily living equipment and aids, including a Learning, Development & Play range.

Sunrise Medical

01384 446688
www.sunrisemedical.co.uk
Stock wheelchairs for adults and children – the Zippie brand has a funky-looking children's range.

The Whistling Tortoise

42A Hamilton Place, EH3 5AX
0131 225 6365
www.whistlingtortoise.co.uk
Although this mobility equipment shop mostly caters for elderly people and primary schools, it has a wide range of suppliers and is happy to order in equipment for younger clients.

Whizz Kidz

020 7233 6600
kidzservices@whizz-kidz.org.uk
www.whizz-kidz.org.uk
Provides essential mobility equipment including tricycles and manual and powered wheelchairs, offers wheelchair skills training and campaigns to ensure that disabled children get the mobility equipment they need at the right time.

NAPPIES

Modern cloth nappies are not only very fashionable, they're easy to use: no pins, boiling, or complicated folds. And, if you use a nappy laundry service, there's no washing! They're effective, comfortable and convenient, can save you money and are good for the environment as they can be used again and again, and for more than one child!

235

Listed below is a selection of mail order nappy suppliers. A more extensive list can be found on the Changeworks website: **www. changeworks.org.uk**. Companies including Greenfibres and The Natural Collection sell nappies by mail order. Department stores and other stores including John Lewis, Mothercare, the Musselburgh Pram Centre and SeeSaw stock a selection of nappies and accessories. Selected branches of Boots, Tesco, Sainsbury's and Waitrose also stock a limited range of cloth nappies and accessories.

Babykind

www.babykind.co.uk
Committed to using products that are environmentally friendly, and by making great nappies as available and affordable as possible hope more people will switch to and stay with reusable nappies. Agents offer parents an informed choice about the nappy system they choose for their baby by showing you a range of products, how they are used, discussing your own requirements and the pros and cons of the different types. If you feel that you want to go ahead and order some nappies, your agent can do this for you too, and arrange delivery to your home.

Anna Cox (0131 553 3991 and 07790 884095) covers Edinburgh and Scottish borders and Sandra Vick covers Midlothian and possibly borders nearby. Both can be contacted via the Babykind website.

Dulce Cor

enquiry@dulcecor.com
www.dulcecor.com
Offers a wide range of real nappies and accessories. Free advice, demonstrations and group nappuccinos. Offers gift vouchers and online gift lists so family and friends can help with the cost of nappies. Second-hand sales service and special offers also available.

Lollipop

0845 601 7308
hello@teamlollipop.co.uk
www.teamlollipop.co.uk
Suppliers of reusable cloth nappies. Provide an online nappy guide if you are unsure about which are right for you and your baby. Outlets from high street stores to nappy advisors. Use the "Advisor near you" link to find nearest retailer/nappy advisor.

The Nappy Lady

0845 652 6532
info@thenappylady.co.uk
www.thenappylady.co.uk

Plush Pants

01865 408040
christine@plushpants.com
www.plushpants.com
Nappies and related natural products.

The Real Nappy Project

0131 555 4010
realnappies@changeworks.org.uk
www.changeworks.org.uk
Encourages parents in Edinburgh and the Lothians to use real nappies. To help you choose, there's a comparison chart with different types of nappy, absorbency and cost. Links to online videos which give useful tips on different nappy styles and folding. Provides Trial Packs and Lending Kits to help you try out real nappies with your baby as well as incentives including vouchers for low income families. Free, relaxed, informal coffee mornings ("Nappuccinos") are held regularly to give you a chance to try the nappies and speak to parents who are using them. They also hold free information sessions for community organisations, will attend ante-natal classes or any kind of parent/baby group and can tailor the session accordingly.

236

Tots Bots Ltd

0141 778 7486
hello@totsbots.com
www.totsbots.com
Shaped towelling nappies made in Scotland.
Winner of numerous awards.

Twinkle Twinkle

0118 969 5550
info@twinkleontheweb.co.uk
www.twinkleontheweb.co.uk
Comprehensive selection of washable nappies,
potty training, bedwetting aids, natural toiletries,
slings. Free advice, downloadable guide on
using nappies.

NURSERY EQUIPMENT

**Many shops in Edinburgh sell well-known
brand name equipment. If you decide to buy
second-hand or an uncommon make, bear in
mind that second-hand equipment can be in
very good condition, but it may not conform
to current safety standards. Cot and moses
basket mattresses should always be bought
new. The same applies to car seats: you can't
be sure if the seat has been in a traffic accident
– there may be stress damage that you can't
see, but which could endanger your child**

After-sales service should be considered; ask
about servicing and repairs before you buy. Most
of the outlets listed will do both, and many will lend
you a temporary replacement if necessary. Retain
your receipt for a while, as this is usually required
before repairs are undertaken. Talk to friends
before you buy – you only discover the pros and
cons of equipment once you've lived with it.

Shops usually keep one demonstration pram
in stock. Ordering your style and colour can take
from 6-20 weeks! No shop will make you buy a
pram if you discover you don't need it (if you have
twins, for example!) and most will store it until you
need it.

Which? Magazine and Practical Parenting
often have reports on nursery equipment and it is
worth checking back copies in the library, even if
it's just to see what to look out for.

High street stores listed above are worth
visiting for nursery equipment. Other stores to
consider are listed below.

The Foam Centre

176 Causewayside, Newington
0131 667 1247
www.foamcentre.org.uk
Different foams cut to any size and shape. Can
be made to fit cot, moses baskets, booster
seats etc. "Beans" to top up or make your own
beanbags. Maternity wedges, lumbar supports
also supplied.

Mamas and Papas

Craigleith Retail Park,
South Groathill Avenue, EH4 2LN
0845 268 2000
www.mamasandpapas.com
Sells top quality clothes and accessories.
Must admit, I found the usefulness of the store
limiting for my twins, as the double pushchairs
were impractical and a bit flimsy, when cheaper
alternatives were far superior. Furniture is
incredible quality, and the clothing is adorable.

*Pushchairs: Fine for single pushchairs, difficult
for side-by-side doubles.*

NCT Shop

0845 810 0100
www.nctshop.co.uk
A wide range of nursery equipment, furniture,
car seats, slings, pushchairs and accessories
available from the catalogue and website.

Raeburn & Corstorphine Pram Centre

115-117 St John's Road, Corstorphine,
EH12 7SB
0131 334 6216
info@pramcentre.net
www.pramcentre.net

Independent specialist pram and nursery centre which offers a wide range of products including prams and pushchairs, nursery furniture and bedding, car seats, highchairs and accessories. Pride themselves on customer service and providing 100% impartial advice, and their prices are very comparable with the other big names in prams and nursery furniture. The shop is naturally busiest at weekends when space can get a bit tight, so dropping in mid-week would guarantee you get maximum staff time.

Parking: FREE parking around the corner in Station Rd. Accessibility: Small step up into the shop.

OUTDOOR AND SKI SHOPS

There's no such thing as bad weather, only unsuitable clothing – a mantra repeated by many an Edinburgh resident! Keeping the small members of the family warm and dry is essential to everyone's enjoyment while outdoors. There is a good selection of dedicated outdoor shops in Edinburgh, and many offer clothing and equipment for under 5s. As with most things, you get what you pay for. Keep your primary usage in mind, and keep comfort as a priority.

Baby carriers/backpacks allow you to go off the beaten track with your child safely away from mud, wet grass, sheep droppings, etc. They can be equally useful in the town, but try before you buy – remember you/your partner may be carrying it considerable distances. Also ensure your child is happy being carried in this way – not all children are. Consider whether you will be using it more in the country or the city and choose an appropriate model. If both parents will be using it and are different heights, get an easily adjustable one.

Blacks Outdoor Leisure Ltd

24 Frederick Street, EH2 2JR
0131 225 8686

and
13-14 Elm Row, EH7 4AA
131 556 3491
www.blacks.co.uk
Stores stock children's boots and socks. Ski wear available at Frederick St store.

Go Outdoors

Oxcraig Street, Unit D, 65 West Harbour Road, Granton, EH5 1PW
0845 113 0294
www.gooutdoors.co.uk/edinburgh
A spacious well-equipped shop with a good selection of children's gear to inspire you to get outdoors! Camping, hiking, cycling and skiing gear. Our kids enjoyed having a look in the various tents on display indoors and outdoors.

Eating: Vending machines, tables and chairs.

Millets

12 Frederick Street, EH2 2HB
0131 220 1551
www.millets.co.uk
On 2 floors, stair access. Main children's department at rear of ground floor. Clothing (from 12 mths), boots (from size 10), rucksacks, camping gear all available in a variety of styles and patterns. The Kids Eurohike range of children's outdoor explorer equipment, e.g. compasses, torches, binoculars, etc, is fun and can make trips out easier for everyone.

Nevisport

19 Rose Street, EH2 2PR
0131 225 9498
www.nevisport.com
Stocks Deuter and Littlelife baby carriers and has a good range of waterproof clothing for toddlers upwards, fleeces, lightweight boots and children's rucksacks. For skiers there is a range of children's clothes/equipment. Skis from 70cm, boots from size 16 (mondopoint sizing).

Pushchairs: Access through doorway big enough for tandem pushchair but children's dept is on 1st floor. Staff will help get pushchairs upstairs. Toilets: Staff toilet available for emergencies.

Sports Warehouse

24-26 Coburg Street, EH6 6HB
0131 553 6003
Sales – sales@sportswarehouse.co.uk
Orders – shop@sportswarehouse.co.uk
www.sportswarehouse.co.uk
Visited on a Saturday afternoon – pretty quiet though. Varied sports equipment on sale, from camping gear to specialised cricket attire, as well as the usual sports/outdoor wear and shoes. A selection of childrenswear/shoes for all ages. Staff were helpful – one offering to bring down a coolbox from the second floor as stairs were too steep for pushchair (no lift). Ended up carrying my son up – bit tricky – but he had a ball crawling in and out of tent displays so it was worth the effort!

Tiso Edinburgh Outdoor Experience

41 Commercial Street, Leith, EH6 6JD
0131 554 0804
edinburgh_oe@tiso.co.uk
www.tiso.com
Excellent outdoor equipment shop which sells everything from camping equipment to children's carriers, outdoor shoes and wellies to children's waterproofs. Staff are very friendly and knowledgeable. There is a "boot path" which toddlers enjoy scrambling on. Room4Health is a clinic upstairs which offers therapies including baby massage and yoga classes. Also a branch at **123 Rose St, EH2 3DT** (0131 225 9486).

Accessibility: Direct access from pavement. Doors are quite heavy though. Eating: The Cairn Café (see p 163).

Trespass

27-29 Frederick Street, EH2 2ND
0131 225 7456
www.trespass.co.uk
Good range of outdoor clothing and boots for children 2+ yrs. Winter stock includes sledges, ski wear and more substantial waterproofs. Store is on 2 floors, children's department at rear of ground floor. Also branches at **Gyle, Craigleith Retail Park, Fort Kinnaird and Ocean Terminal.**

PARTIES

In this section we've included a few bits and pieces to help you when planning a children's party, from venues to bouncy castles, fancy dress to entertainers. For shops for cakes or baking equipment, see "Cakes & Cookery" section, above.

PARTY VENUES

Parties, whether at home, in a local hall or at an all-inclusive venue, need forward planning. If you're booking a venue most places recommend doing this at least 8 weeks in advance. Many church halls, public halls, schools, community centres and sports clubs will hire out their premises for an afternoon. Remember weekends will be busier.

Soft play centres also offer birthday packages, often with the use of a party area: the actual soft play structures are usually open to everyone. However, younger children may get nervous if it is too crowded. Some offer times for booking the soft play for exclusive use.

We've listed a few suggestions for party venues below, but many of the venues listed elsewhere in the book offer party packages – look out for this symbol!

Bonnyrigg Leisure Centre

King George V Park, Bonnyrigg, EH19 2AD
0131 663 7579
Soft play, suitable for children up to 6 yrs, followed by use of large hall for birthday tea (bring your own food) and use of a large bouncy castle. Max 20 children.

Broxburn Swimming Pool

East Main Street, Broxburn, West Lothian
EH52 5EQ
01506 775680
www.westlothianleisure.com
Soft play parties are hosted in the "Spacebugs" soft play area. Max 20 children. Party price includes exclusive use; just bring your own birthday tea.

The Children's Party Cruise

The Bridge Inn, Ratho
0131 333 1320
info@bridgeinn.com
www.bridgeinn.com
A children's party on board a cruising canal boat restaurant. A CD player is provided, take your own CDs. A disco or entertainer can be organised at extra cost. There is plenty of space to play. Food can be supplied by the Bridge Inn. Max 36 people.

Cramond Kirk Hall

0131 312 6911
07979 795331
www.cramondkirk.org.uk
Variety of hall and room sizes available for parties and events. Ideal for bouncy castles, sports and games, dancing, singing, arts and crafts.

Edinburgh Leisure Centres

mail@edinburghleisure.co.uk
www.edinburghleisure.co.uk
Bouncy castle parties available at Ainslie Park, Drumbrae, Gracemount, Jack Kane, Kirkliston, Meadowbank and Queensferry High. Soft play parties available at EICA Ratho, Kirkliston, Queensferry Recreation Centre, Meadowbank and Portobello Indoor Bowls. Mini-Kickers party (great for those budding little football stars!) available at Gracemount.

Linlithgow Leisure Centre

McGinley Way, Linlithgow, EH49 6SQ
01506 775440
A soft play party followed by a birthday tea. Max 20 children.

Livingston Leisure Centre

Almondvale Parkway, Livingston
01506 777870
"Space bugs" soft play party, for children up to 7 yrs, includes 2 hrs of fun on slides, chutes, ball pool and a birthday tea; just bring the cake. Invitations, party bags and thank you cards (voucher for free admission) are provided.

Party Planet

36 Baileyfield Road, EH15 1NP
0131 669 1231
parties@partyplanetonline.co.uk
www.partyplanetonline.co.uk
Specialist party venue offering a wide range

of party themes. We attended for a 6 yr old's birthday party, and our 2 and 4 yr old had a great time dancing, bouncing, having their faces painted, and singing on stage with a microphone. Children are whisked away to the "Party Room" where staff keep them entertained for about an hour, and parents can enjoy a drink and snack at the small café in the front (additional cost). Children reappear later to eat party food and staff clean up all the mess after them! The venue itself is small, but serves the purpose. Staff were enthusiastic and interacted with the children well on the day of the party, but are very busy, and seem unable to speak on the phone when making general enquiries. Best to try and contact them on e-mail if you are hoping to arrange a party or find out more details.

Opening hours: Open 7 days. Times vary depending on party schedule. Cost: Generally around £12 a head. Contact venue for exact cost.

The Play Planet

Donibristle Industrial Estate, Dalgety Bay
01383 822288
www.theplayplanet.co.uk
Situated 5 mins from Forth Bridge. Party lasts 2 hrs and includes 1 hr in soft play (3 separate areas for 0-2, 2-5 and 5-12 yrs) and 1hr in themed party rooms. Live appearance by Zimmy the alien, birthday tea, complimentary

coffee vouchers, personalised invitations and party bags are all provided.

The Spartans Community Football Academy

94 Pilton Drive, EH5 2HF
0131 552 7854
jackbeesley@spartanscfa.com
www.spartanscfa.com
Football-based parties that include use of the pitch and a fully qualified coach, party food and room hire. The basic Bronze package is £10/child but for £12.50 you can get the Silver package which also includes a Spartans gift for the birthday boy or girl, and a commemorative photo. For £15/child, the Gold package includes a feature in the Senior team match-day programme, Spartans gifts for all attendees and the chance to be a mascot for a Spartans Seniors' game. In addition, Spartans mascot "Sparry the Squirrel" can be hired for photos and carrying the cake.

St Ninian's Church Hall

St Ninian's Road, Corstorphine, EH12 8AY
0131 539 6204
Venue only. Two large halls, one with adjoining kitchen, which can be hired separately or together. Max 30 children.

241

BOUNCY CASTLE HIRE

Bennetts Bouncy Castles

9 Meadowplace Road, EH12 7TZ
0131 334 4545
bennettshire@blueyonder.co.uk
www.bennettshire.co.uk
Bouncy castles delivered and set up. All sizes, for indoor use or in your garden with a shower cover. Specialised designs for under 5s.

Bouncin' Castles

0131 478 2541
www.bouncincastles.co.uk
A range of bouncy castles, delivered within the Edinburgh area.

Sir Bouncealot

07900 827813
sir.bouncealot@yahoo.co.uk
www.sir-bounce-a-lot.co.uk
Inflatable ball ponds, bouncy castles, inflatable fun runs and a 50ft obstacle course available for under 5s.

CATERING

Food by Cat

cat@foodbycat.co.uk
Professional chef and mum, all home-made children's party catering. Sandwiches, colourful cupcakes, wibble-wobble jellies, dinosaur chocolates, flapjacks, fritters, mini-meals and lots more. Organic, low-sugar and dietary requirements available. Can supply child-friendly crockery and cups.

DECORATIONS, FANCY DRESS & ACCESSORIES

Party Mania

30 West Nicolson Street
0131 667 6020
www.partypartyparty.co.uk

Tableware, party bag fillers, decorations, poppers, confetti, wigs, hats and helium balloon table decorations. Helium gas tanks can also be hired to fill your own balloons.

The Party Shack

140 North High Street, Musselburgh
0131 665 2200
www.thepartyshack.net
Specialises in items for themed parties. Stocks lots of party accessories, balloons and children's fancy dress.

ONLINE PARTY ACCESSORIES

There are hundreds of online companies out there who provide everything – invitations, tableware, hats, party bags, balloons, and pinatas! Most have all the latest themes such as the Disney Princesses, Thomas and Friends, and Spiderman. If you search for "children's party supplies" you get thousands of results! We've listed a few tried and tested ones to get you started.

Kidsparties4U

www.kidsparties4u.co.uk

Kids Party Shop

www.kids-partyshop.co.uk

The Little Things

www.thelittlethings.info

Party Godmother

www.partygodmother.com

Party Pieces

www.partypieces.co.uk

ENTERTAINMENT

When discussing a party with an entertainer, tell them the age span of the children (not all are suitable for under 5s, although those below are) and whether you have seen them before (many entertainers have several routines). Some may even run the whole party if you want.

Don't forget many of those who run regular classes and weekly sessions are also happy to provide their services for parties. See the "Activities and Classes" listings for The Drama Studio, Jo Jingles, Monkey Music and others.

Beano the Clown

Unit 275, 44-46 Morningside Road, EH10 4BE
07948 070569
beanosab@hotmail.com
Beano.theclown.free.fr
Songs with guitar, magic show with glove puppet and balloon animals, taking an hour which is usually enough for under 5s. Longer sessions also available with extra games. Beano also does shows where he starts by putting on his make up in front of the children so they are not afraid of the clown face. Beano has been a clown for over 15 years and can do shows in both English and French when required. He is a member of Equity and Clown International.

Carriesmatic Theme Parties

07952 945749
clownzabound@live.co.uk
www.edinburghentertainers.co.uk
Carrie provides themed parties, using dance, song, stories, puppets, balloons and face-painting to give an interactive and educational experience. Some favourite themes are: princesses and knights, animals, pirates and mermaids, bugs and butterflies, circus and clowns, teddy bears' picnic and ballet, but you can choose your own theme or have no theme.

Carrie is a dance and drama teacher and special needs specialist, and can carefully plan parties to suit children with special needs.

Doodle & Splat

Contact: Lynda and Pamela
0794 282 514
doodle@doodleandsplat.co.uk
www.doodleandsplat.co.uk
Through a combination of imaginative play and organised art and craft activities, your child (2+ yrs) and their friends will have great fun exploring their creative side, painting ceramic figures, making birthday crowns or having lots of messy fun. Parties can be customised with lots of options to choose from. The children can take home their individual masterpieces. Doodle & Splat parties last for over an hour. They provide all materials, floor mats, aprons for children, and clean up at the end.

Flotsam and Jetsam Puppets and Stories

2 Summerhall Square, EH9 1QD
0131 662 9834
07813 705840
info@flotsamandjetsam.co.uk
www.flotsamandjetsam.co.uk
Lively puppets and stories designed to appeal to younger children (2+ yrs). Puppeteer and storyteller will come to your party wearing her magical "story dress". The dress has many pockets and in each one are puppets and props waiting to come out and tell their stories. Lots of joining-in fun and a special surprise for the birthday child. Call for a brochure and current prices. Shows based around the seasons are also available to playgroups and nurseries.

Gary James and Stone the Crow

46 Easter Drylaw Bank, EH4 2QN
0131 332 8321
07932 728675
g.james@blueyonder.co.uk
www.stonethecrow.co.uk
Magic fun shows for all events. Full-time professional entertainer.

Gordon's Magic and Puppet Show

0131 652 2189
gordonhunt1@btinternet.com
www.gordonsmagicandpuppets.com
Entertainment for birthday parties and other events with puppets, magic, balloon animals and organised games. Packed with chances for party guests to participate in the action.

Jango the Clown

07932 087445
mail@clowncompany.co.uk
www.clowncompany.co.uk
Jango is multi-talented and puts on a real show to entertain kids of all ages. We've seen him cope with a party for 100 under 5s and they all loved every minute.

Jimmy Craig

26 Muirfield Street, Kirkaldy, KY2 6SY
01592 261706
This experienced fun magician provides prize-winning fun-filled magical entertainment for children. He specialises in shows suitable for children of playgroup age and up.

Mr Boom

The Old Repeater Station, Libberton, South Lanarkshire
01555 841168
info@mrboom.co.uk
www.mrboom.co.uk
The children's one-man band from the moon has been visiting planet Earth for some 26 years now. He's written a wealth of science-based songs well known to several generations of youngsters. He's a popular draw at fundraising concerts, and visits schools and nurseries with his enchanting singing and dancing show for young children. Sing along all together now! Dance in a pixie ring! Be a planet going round the sun! If Mr Boom's there, you'll have lots of fun.

Stina Sparkles Entertainments

Discos, face painting and more...
Kids/adult parties and corporate events

We can offer a wide range of entertainment to cater for all your party needs.
Whether it's a party for your little angel, or a karaoke girl's night out.

For more information contact
Christina on 07724 814 117
ww.stinasparkles.net

 Find us on
Facebook

Stina Sparkles

07724 814117
www.stinasparkles.net
Face painting, glitter tattoos, balloon modelling, discos, children's entertainment and games, and even Sparkie the Dog! Stina has it all for parties of all kinds.

Tricky Ricky

10 Drum Brae Avenue, EH12 8TE
0131 339 8500
ricky@trickyricky.com
www.trickyricky.com
Edinburgh's multi-award winning children's entertainer and magician. Magic, songs and balloon modelling. A riot of fun and laughter, including Bingo the real puppet dog!

 Any information you'd like to add? Email us at info@efuf.co.uk

PHOTOGRAPHY

Department stores and shopping centres often have visiting companies which specialise in photographing young children. The following companies are experienced in working with under 5s.

Studio, on-location and underwater photography for families, babies and kids.

www.clearphotography.co.uk t.0131 538 0501

Clear Photography

22 Laurie Street, EH6 7AB
0131 538 0501
info@clearphotography.co.uk
www.clearphotography.co.uk
I took my son to have studio portraits taken by Susan at Clear Photography when he was 4 mths old. The photoshoot was very relaxed, Susan had such a lovely manner with my son and really knew how to get the best smiles out of him. The photos were available for me to view online very quickly and I was impressed by the quality and number that had been taken despite the shoot lasting only 30 mins. The ordering process was quick and easy and the prints very reasonably priced. The photos are absolutely beautiful and I've had so many lovely comments about them. I was so impressed that when Clear advertised that they were doing underwater shoots I booked my son in for one. Again, the experience was outstanding and I got a brilliant shot of my son looking straight at the camera. Highly recommended.

Cost: Photoshoots from £25, prints from £11.
Birthdays/celebrations: Vouchers available.

Helen Pugh Photography

07837 533051
info@helenpughphotography.com
www.helenpughcreative.com
A professionally trained photographer covering the Edinburgh area and beyond, photographing people in their own environment or at a favourite location. Maternity sessions need to be booked 2 mths before due date. Newborn sessions should be booked whilst still pregnant, agreeing a rough diary date based on due date, with the shoot taking place within baby's first 2 weeks.

Cost: 1 portrait session £45, 2 sessions £70, 3 sessions £90 and 4 sessions £100. Products £75 - £600. Prints £18 if they are duplicates of chosen framed images.

Klaklak Photography

Ashley House, 1F Ashley Terrace, EH11 1RF
0131 208 2484
studio@klaklakphotography.co.uk
www.klaklakphotography.co.uk
Studio or location portraits taken by an award-winning children's photographer. As well as children's sessions, they offer a service called Bump to Baby where photos are taken of your baby over the course of a year in 3 sessions.

Cost: Studio – 1hr £45, Location – 2 hrs £100. Prints – £25-45.

245

Leo Friel Photography

0131 220 5661
07778 639787
studio@leofrielphotography.co.uk
www.leofrielphotography.co.uk
Fun, natural child and family portraits taken at your home, family event, or special location. Leo's unobtrusive approach makes you and your child feel comfortable in front of the camera, resulting in photographs full of personality.

Birthdays/celebrations: Will attend any event to photograph.

Moments-Preserved

68 St Stephen Street, Stockbridge, EH3 5AQ
0131 226 3589
www.moments-preserved.com
Specialises in children's and family portraits.

Cost: Normal studio session (45 mins to 1½ hrs) £150, though look out for discounted offers. Framed prints from £135, canvas wraps from £295, acrylics from £395.

Nipper Snappers

07515 521357
info@nippersnappers.co.uk
www.nippersnappers.co.uk
East Lothian based photographer offering a mobile service, shooting on location at the client's home or garden or, weather permitting, a venue such as a local park. Covers Edinburgh, East Lothian and Midlothian and happy to travel further. Also photographs parties, christenings and weddings.

Cost: Photo shoot – £60 (includes an unframed A3 size print). Prints – £5-40. Canvas prints from £68.

PHOTO express

7 Melville Terrace, EH9 1ND
0131 667 2164
info@photoxp.co.uk
www.photoxp.co.uk
Family portraits taken either in the studio, your own home or on location. Studio SE of the Meadows.

Cost: Portraiture sitting – £40, individual prints £9.50-£105 (depending on size). Framed prints £86-£130.

Picture House

2 Swanfield (off Bonnington Road), EH6 5RX
0131 553 1177
info@picturehousestudios.co.uk
www.picturehousestudios.co.uk
An independent portrait studio run by award-winning photographers. Offering a variety of packages including the Cherubs Programme – portraits of your new baby over the course of their 1st year (3 mini-shoots, 3 folio prints and 1 contemporary display folio).

Opening hours: Appointment necessary. Cost: Cherubs Programme £55, Photoshoot Packages - £155-325. Extra prints from £30.

Rachel Hein Photography

07973 779223
rachel@rachelhein.com
www.rachelhein.com
Edinburgh-based lifestyle photographer specialising in natural portraits of babies, children and families taken on location or in your own home.

Sarah Elizabeth Photography

0131 448 0111
info@sarahelizabeth.co.uk
www.sarahelizabeth.co.uk
Female photographers who specialise in baby and children portraits and weddings. Sessions take place in their custom-built studio or on location.

Venture Photography

Unit 1B, Meadowbank Retail Park
17 Earlston Place, EH7 5SU
0131 652 8130
edinburgh@venturephotography.co.uk
www.venturephotography.com/uk
Experienced photographers of family portraiture
and weddings. Portrait sessions begin with a 1
hr Venture Experience in their state-of-the-art
studio. Located just 5 mins from the centre of
Edinburgh, park close to the steps at the West
side of the car park as the shop entrance is
situated on London Rd.

Parking: 4 hrs FREE.

P

 Visit our website for updates:
www.efuf.co.uk

PORTRAITS

Genuine European Portraits

Freepost RRYZ-EHGU-ZXSB
EH10 0BR
0131 202 6229
customercare@portraits.org
www.portraits.org
Specialises in hand-drawn portraits on a
parent preview basis for nurseries, playgroups,
toddler groups etc, which receive commission
for each portrait, so it is a good fundraiser.
Individual drawings from photos can also be
ordered through the website.

Pencil Portraits

07773 398749
gardiner.aimee@yahoo.co.uk
www.aimeegardiner.co.uk
Pencil portraits by artist Aimee Gardiner, who
can draw life-like portraits from photographs.

*Cost: 6"x6" £65 for children or animals, £85 for
adults. 9"x9" £90 for children or animals, £110
for adults.*

SECOND HAND

Greenside OMNI Car Boot Sales

The largest car boot sale in Edinburgh. Located
in the city centre at the NCP car park on
Greenside Row, EH13 3AA, under the OMNI
centre. Trading Sun from 09.00 to 13.00.

NCT Nearly New Sales

www.nct.org.uk/branches/events/nearly-
new-sales
Good quality second-hand nursery equipment,
toys, prams, carriers and clothes for babies
and young children. Held every few months at
venues in Craiglockhart and Cramond, also in
Linlithgow. Check website for details.

Polwarth Nearly New Sales

**Polwarth Church, Polwarth Terrace,
EH11 1LU**
www.nearlynewsale.org.uk
There are 3 sales each year, usually in Apr, Sep and Nov. They can sell babies', children's and maternity clothes, toys, and baby and nursery equipment. The seller receives the money from the sale minus the price of the tickets which they are required to buy to sell their goods, with any proceeds going to local charities.

Relove

17 St Stephen Street, EH3 5AN
0131 226 4141
reloveedinburgh@gmail.com
Facebook page – Relove Edinburgh
This family-run business sells second-hand baby, children's and maternity clothes, toys and baby equipment. Aimed at "parents on a budget, designer mums looking for a bargain and grannies needing a highchair for the weekend". Specialises in real nappies. Expect to pay more than in local charity shops or nearly-new sales, but the stock is high quality and in good condition. Large items can be delivered.

Pushchairs: Small shop, but pushchairs are welcome.

SHOES

Most children's shoe departments aren't situated on the ground floor of shops for safety – a few steps to check the fit could take junior out into the street! Many stores now operate a ticketing system – take a ticket before looking around.

Don't be shy where your child's feet are concerned. If you don't think a shoe fits, ask to have it checked by another more senior fitter. Several shops selling nursery equipment also sell soft shoes for babies and toddlers. Also try Aitken and Niven for school shoes and John Lewis for children's shoes.

Charles MacWatt Homemade Boots and Shoes

0117 921 4247
www.shoe-craft.co.uk
Made to measure and to order shoes, boots and sandals for children and adults.

Children's Foot Health Register

01295 738726
cfhr@shoeshop.org.uk
www.shoe-shop.org.uk
Lists shops in the UK that are members of the Children's Foot Health Register. Members are committed to the highest standard of shoe fitting for young, growing feet and guarantee to provide comprehensive training for staff and offer children's shoes in whole and half sizes and in up to 4 width fittings. Website contains lots of useful information about the growth of babies' and children's feet.

Clarks

www.clarks.co.uk
Children's shoes at: **79 Princes St, Craigleith Retail Park, Cameron Toll Shopping Centre, Fort Kinnaird and Gyle Centre**.

We visited the shop on Princes St, where there is a good selection of pre-walking shoes. Here, the children's department is down a flight of stairs, with no lift, however, pushchairs can be left behind the counter on the ground floor. The First Shoes experience means that your child's feet will be measured by a trained staff member, and you will receive a photo of your child in their shoes, a great memento! Staff are consistently helpful as your child's feet grow, and will honestly tell you if the shoes are not fitting well (even if this means the pair of pink sparkly ones your 2 yr old has her heart set on need to be exchanged for something else!). Odd Shoe service available at an extra 25% if your child has different size feet. Ordering service.

It's worth saving old shoes and donating them to the Shoe Biz appeal collection point in selected stores, where they are then recycled to raise funds for education projects worldwide.

invest in the future of your child's feet with us

Childrens feet have to last their entire life, that's why we ensure all our staff are expertly trained to find the perfect fit. We have styles to suit all shapes and sizes of feet, as well as every season and occasion - from cruisers right up to size 41 (UK 7).

Our footwear is funky and stylish as well as being durable and beautifully crafted. With brands such as Startrite, Angulus, Ricosta, Geox, Ecco and Lelli Kelly, there's always a great choice.

Maddie & Mark's Shoes -
nurturing little feet is our nature.

EDINBURGH − Blackhall * Bruntsfield *
Buckstone * GLASGOW − Silverburn
www.maddieandmarks.co.uk
email: info@maddieandmarks.co.uk

Daisy Roots

sales@daisy-roots.com
www.daisy-roots.com
Baby booties and toddler shoes for 0-4 yrs.

Maddie and Mark's

1 Craigcrook Place, EH4 3NG, 0131 315 3322
205 Bruntsfield Place, EH10 4DH, 0131 447 9779
14 Buckstone Terrace, EH10 6PZ, 0131 445 4425
info@maddieandmarks.co.uk
www.maddieandmarks.co.uk
Friendly staff who really know their shoes and will take time to find the pair that fits your child based on width, length and potential growth. Plenty of room for style and variety at this independent retailer. They stock shoes from the UK and Continent including Angulus, Start-rite, Ecco, and Ricosta − not Clarks due to distributing regulations. If one child needs shoes and another doesn't there is the play area or indeed all of the colourful shoes and accessories to look at. Also a store at Silverburn, Glasgow (0141 880 4333).

Nappy changing: Changing mats, wipes and bags in toilets.

Robeez

00800 15718100 (toll free number)
info@robeez.eu
www.robeez.co.uk
Shoes for different stages from 0-6 yrs.

Russell & Bromley

106 Princes Street, EH2 3AA
0131 225 7444
www.russellandbromley.co.uk
Excellent range of shoes for babies and children of all ages, from those starting to "cruise" upwards. The children's section is on the 1st floor, accessible by stair or escalator (no lift). This necessitates leaving pushchairs in a clearly marked area on the ground floor, and carrying

smaller children upstairs. The staff are all trained and feet are measured using Start-rite gauges. Shop can be busy (a ticket system operates at busier times) so it is best to visit early on in the week. Children will enjoy looking at the carousel horses while waiting!

Vincent Shoes

67 Comely Bank Road, EH4 1AW
0131 315 4856
www.vincentshoes.co.uk
Functional and stylish shoes for children 6 mths to 8 yrs. A Swedish Company, these reasonably priced shoes come in fun and funky designs. Regular sales and special offers.

Wee Masons

90 The High Street, Haddington, EH41 3ET
01620 825600
www.mason-shoes.co.uk
Small, friendly shop with experienced staff and hardly any queues. Toys and videos are available to amuse other children while another is being fitted. Good range of Start-rite, Primigi and GEOX. Gym shoes, wellies and gift vouchers are also available.

SUPERMARKETS

A big supermarket shop with young children can be tricky, however stores do try to help. Most have car parks with wide Parent and Child spaces near the entrance. Tell Customer Services before you start a shop if you think you'll need a hand with shopping, then ask at the check-out if you need help getting bags to the car.

Baby cradle trolleys are suitable for babies up to 9kgs (20lbs) and toddler trolleys to around 3 yrs. Some trolleys can be used with a car seat. Safety instructions are printed on each trolley. Do report any faults.

Most stores offer shopping online, charging a delivery fee (around £5). Or if you can make it to the supermarket but can't get shopping home, many stores will deliver it, also for a charge.

Trolleys for disabled children are often kept in-store. Ask your local store to buy one if it doesn't already have a trolley like this, which usually has a large box seat with padding and a five point harness – suitable for children who don't need extra seating support. Trolleys do exist with extra support but are rarely seen! If you need help, some supermarkets may supply a member of staff to go round the store with you, particularly at quieter times.

Asda

www.asda.com and
www.direct.asda.com
As well as 5 stores in the area (listed below), Asda online has a dedicated babyshop as well as baby and children's clothing in the George section.

Chesser Supercentre, 3 Newmarket Road, EH14 1RJ (0131 442 6750). George clothes and Post Office. In Store Collection.

Edinburgh Superstore, 100 The Jewel, Brunstane, EH15 3AR (0131 669 9151). George clothes, Café, Pharmacy and Post Office. In Store Collection.

Leith Superstore, 2 Sandpiper Drive, EH6 6QL (0131 561 2300). George clothes and Café. In Store Collection.

The Centre (Almondale Centre, Livingston) (01506 835980). George clothes, Café and Post Office. In Store Collection.

Straiton (0131 465 1500). George clothes and Café.

Nappy changing: FREE nappies in all branches. Eating: Café in some stores. FREE jar of baby food if you spend £1 or more in the café.

The Co-operative Food

customer.relations@co-op.co.uk
www.co-operative.coop/food

Owned, not by a small group of shareholders, but by more than 5 million consumers, Co-operative Food is well known for stocking a high range of Fairtrade products. Branches at:

2B Church Newton Rd, Danderhall EH22 1LT, 0131 660 1284

Clayknowes Rd, Stoneyhill, EH21 6UW 0131 653 3193

114 Dairy Rd, EH11 2EZ, 0131 337 6376

43 Pennywell Rd, Mainsway, EH4 4DR 0131 332 9666

49 Shandwick Pl, EH2 4SD, 0131 221 5280

M&S Simply Food

www.marksandspencer.com
Useful stores which these days often go beyond being "Simply Food" by stocking greetings cards, newspapers, small gifts – even underwear. This can mean that you can end up getting a biggish shop when you only popped in for one or two items. Food ranges from fruit, veg, bread and milk to high-quality ready meals, deli items and wine. Prices at the higher end but look out for offers and meal deals such as "Dine in for £10" which are good value. Branches include: **Craigleith Retail Park, Lower Straiton Retail Park, Morningside Road, Ocean Terminal.** See website for all branches.

Morrisons

www.morrisons.co.uk
Supermarket chain that where possible sources locally and manufactures in own sites. All meat 100% British sourced. Dedicated baby section on its website, though does not offer an online/home delivery service. All branches but Livingston Carmondean have cafés and the Livingston stores have pharmacies. Branches at:

Bathgate, 2 Linkston Way, Bathgate, EH48 7XN, 01506 813852

Ferry Road, EH5 2HF, 0131 315 4970

Granton, Waterfront Broadway, Granton, EH5 1SA, 0131 551 2742

Gyle, South Gyle Broadway, Gyle, EH12 9JU, 0131 317 1197

Hunters Tryst, 30 New Swanston, EH10 7JA, 0131 445 5647

Livingston, Retail Park South, Almondvale Road, Livingston, EH54 6DB, 01506 465641

Livingston Carmondean, Carmondean Centre, Livingston, EH54 8PT, 01506 433224

Moredun, Gilmerton Road, Moredun, EH17 7JH, 0131 664 9868

Portobello Road, 4 Piersfield Terrace, Portobello Road, EH8 7BQ, 0131 661 5661

Sainsburys

www.sainsburys.co.uk
Shopping in-store and online. Lots of their everyday food, like fresh chicken, eggs and milk, are 100% UK sourced. Dedicated Baby and Toddler online club (www.sainsburys.co.uk/littleones). Cafés are owned and operated by Sainsbury's serving a wide selection of food and drinks throughout the day and a children's menu for 4-8 yrs. All children's main meals come with a FREE piece of fruit. Ella's Kitchen baby food sold at cafés too. Main stores only listed below.

Blackhall, 185 Craigleith Road, EH4 2EB, 0131 332 0704. Kids Clothing (TU), Toys, Click & Collect, Café.

Cameron Toll, 6 Lady Road, EH16 5PB, 0131 666 5200. Kids Clothing (TU), Toys, Click & Collect.

Livingston, Unit 1, Almondvale Retail Park, Almondvale South, Livingston, EH54 6RQ, 01506 413699. Kids Clothing (TU), Toys, Click & Collect, Café.

Meadowbank, Unit 9-10 Moray Park, EH7 5TS, 0131 656 9377. Pharmacy, Click & Collect.

Murrayfield, 39 Westfield Road, EH11 2QW, 0131 347 8560. Kids Clothing (TU), Toys, Click & Collect, Café.

Straiton, Straiton Mains, Loanhead, EH20 9PW, 0131 448 2181. Kids Clothing (TU), Pharmacy, Click & Collect, Café.

Scotmid Co-operative

customerservice@scotmid.co.uk
www.scotmid.com
Community-based food stores with branches throughout Edinburgh that sell food and grocery items as well as sweets, snacks, soft drinks, alcohol, magazines, fresh produce and tobacco products. They also sell mobile top up cards and stamps. Many branches accessible. No toilets.

Tesco

www.tesco.com
Supermarket chain that offers shopping in-store and online. Dedicated online baby section. Most stores have a café. Main stores listed below.

Bathgate, Blackburn Road, Bathgate, West Lothian, EH48 2ES, 0845 677 9033. Clothing, Direct Collection, Café.

Colinton, Colinton Mains Drive, EH13 9AH, 0845 677 9249. Direct Collection, Café.

7 Broughton Road, EH7 4EW, 0845 677 9245. Pharmacy, Direct Collection, Costa Coffee.

Hardengreen, Bonnyrigg Road, Dalkeith, Midlothian, EH22 3PP, 0845 677 9205. Clothing, Direct Collection, Café.

Hermiston Gait, Cultins Road, EH11 4DG, 0845 671 9450. Clothing, Direct Collection, Café.

Leith, 76 Duke Street, EH6 8HL, 0845 026 9637. Clothing.

South Queensferry, Ferry Muir, South Queensferry, EH30 9QZ, 0845 677 9643. Clothing, Direct Collection, Café.

Waitrose

customersupport@waitrose.co.uk
www.waitrose.com
A chain of supermarkets (part of John Lewis) offering in-store and online shopping. Branches at: **38 Comely Bank Rd, EH4 1AW (0131 332 6312)**, which also has a pharmacy, and **145 Morningside Rd, EH10 4AX (0131 447 6899)**. Both offer Shop Online, You Collect – not to be confused with Ocado, which is a separate business.

Toilets: Comely Bank branch.

TOILETRIES & COSMETICS

The Body Shop

Princes Mall, Princes Street, EH1 1BQ
0131 556 2641
www.thebodyshop.co.uk
Lots of enticing lotions and potions, all ethically/ environmentally sourced and produced, something they are keen to promote. Includes a baby range of products, Buriti Baby, with cloths and towels as well as shampoos/bubble bath etc. At the high end of the cost scale for similar items in other high street shops but would make beautiful gifts. Other branches in Edinburgh – see website for details.

Crabtree and Evelyn

4 Hanover Street, EH2 2EN
0131 226 2478
www.crabtree-evelyn.co.uk
Wonderful array of soaps, bubbles, lotions and creams for women and men, all beautifully presented and packaged. Gift sets available.

Greenbaby

0800 023 4289
www.greenbaby.com
Lovely organic skincare for wee ones.

Lavera

01557 870266
info@pravera.co.uk
www.pravera.co.uk/lavera-natural-cosmetics
Organic natural cosmetics, skincare and bodycare products for the whole family.

Lush

44 Princes Street, EH2 2BY
0131 557 3177
customercare@lush.co.uk
www.lush.co.uk
We visited on a busy Saturday afternoon. Although it is a small-ish shop, its layout was easily accessible with a pushchair. Staff were very friendly and helpful and spoke directly to my 1-yr-old son. Wide selection of colourful, handmade cosmetics and lots of gift ideas. The items stacked on lower shelving may prove too tempting for those little ones on their feet and ready to explore.

Accessibility: Step at front door.

Milk & Honey Organics

0845 299 8758
www.milkhoney.co.uk
Luxurious natural and organic gifts for prenatal and postnatal, and new baby gifts. Beautifully wrapped and delivered to your door.

Pharmacy2U

www.pharmacy2u.co.uk
Offers a complete range of high street pharmacy products and services online, including an "ask our pharmacists" service.

TOYS, GIFTS & CARDS

Argos, Asda, BHS, The Disney Store, IKEA, John Lewis, Mothercare and Sainsbury's and others also offer a selection of toys. When buying for playgroups etc it is always worth asking whether discounts are available.

The Baby Stork Company

1st Floor, Ocean Terminal, EH6 6JJ
07731 786728
thebabystorkcompany@yahoo.co.uk
www.thebabystorkcompany.co.uk
Small family-run shop offering good range of unique toys, gifts and clothing for babies and small children from quality suppliers such as Kaloo, Olive & Moss, Jellycat, Sophie the Giraffe, Inch Blue, and many more. Great place to purchase an extra special gift for a birth, birthday, christening, etc.

Bliss

5 Raeburn Place, Stockbridge, EH4 1HU
0131 332 4605
Interesting, quirky shop with lovely baby clothes and accessories. Good selection of gifts for babies and toddlers, plus cards. Ideal for those looking for something a bit different for a gift.

Bohemia

33a Morningside Road, EH10 4DR
0131 447 7701
info@bohemiadesign.co.uk
www.bohemiadesign.co.uk
A chocolate box boutique of unusual and unique gifts, jewellery, bags, women's clothes, baby and children's wear, toys, cards, books and home furnishings. Online store also available.

Bright Minds

0844 412 2250
www.brightminds.co.uk
Presents for babies and children up to school age. Lots of developmental/educational items – more England and Wales focused in terms of school curriculum references. Also sells personalised items.

Build-A-Bear Workshop

119 Princes Street, EH2 4AA
0131 226 5789
and
98/8 Ocean Drive, Ocean Terminal, EH6 6JJ
0131 554 8377
www.buildabear.co.uk
Children just love this place. What is more exciting than seeing your very own bear being built – and then choosing outfits and accessories, from surfboards to rollerboots to biker jackets and sun shades. While you watch your bear being filled, you can add a "heart" – a sound, a song – the list goes on. The average bear is £15 and accessories about £5 each so this is for a special occasion and it is very addictive! I would recommend this for 3 + yrs.

Birthdays/celebrations: Special birthday parties for up to 6 children at a time – food not included. Contact stores for more.

Clementine Home and Gifts

141 Bruntsfield Place, EH10 4EB
0131 477 2237
info@clementinehomeandgifts.co.uk
www.clementinehomeandgifts.co.uk
Packed with a huge selection of pretty home accessories and gifts, we spent ages browsing all the beautiful items. I especially loved the baby leggings complete with pictures on the bottoms! The rocking horse was a favourite for my little girl.

Cloudberry Gifts and Café

193 Whitehouse Road, EH4 6BU
0131 538 0168
info@cloudberrygifts.co.uk
www.cloudberrygifts.co.uk
An exciting new boutique style gift shop with café in Barnton offering perfect gifts for everyone. It is (they claim) the perfect shop for people who love beautiful and quirky bits and bobs. Fantastic gifts for all occasions, excellent

selection of cards and wrapping paper. Scottish sourced local gifts, handmade (to order) door signs and plaques. Quirky unusual small gifts. Well worth a visit. Café has around 12 seats.

Digger Gift Shop

35 West Nicholson Street, EH8 9DB
0131 668 1802
A charming gift shop you could spend hours in, selling all sorts of things including home knitting, earrings and fab cards (starting at £1.99). Friendly staff.

Early Learning Centre

Unit 61, St James Centre, EH1 3SJ
0131 558 1330
www.elc.co.uk
The St James branch is a spacious shop with great merchandise and easy access for pushchairs. Staff were helpful but wouldn't let my friend's 2½ yr old use their staff loo even though it was urgent and she had a baby with her. However, John Lewis is nearby. Join the Birthday Club – no charge – and get a discounted purchase around your child's birthday. Plenty of toys open for the kids to try out and play with while you browse. I had trouble persuading my toddler to leave. Other branches in and around Edinburgh – see website.

Eero and Riley

7 Easter Road, EH7 5PH
0131 661 0533
info@eeroandriley.com
www.eeroandriley.com
Bright and cheerful gift shop selling contemporary design and crafts, many from small Scottish companies. With homewares, jewellery, accessories, kids' stuff and gift cards, it should inspire any present buying. Exclusive personalised baby blankets would be a great new baby gift. A bit tight for pushchairs, but very friendly staff made us feel comfortable to browse. If you can't visit the shop, see their brilliant website!

The Flower Stork

0800 161 3363
www.theflowerstork
Baby gifts, particularly clothes/bibs etc, packaged and arranged in the shape of blossoms; others in shape of cupcake, slice of cake etc. Also has gifts for mum. All baby clothes sized 3-6 months, for boys/girls or in neutral colours. Quite pricey for individual items but would make beautiful gifts.

Flux

55 Bernard Street, Leith, EH6 6SL
0131 554 4075
bea@get2flux.co.uk
www.get2flux.co.uk
A lovely eclectic collection of gifts, cards and things to make your house look pretty! Staff are very friendly and helpful, especially with pushchairs. A number of children's toys/gifts that are quirky and a little bit different. Items within easy reach of children.

Good Gifts Catalogue

0207 794 8000
www.goodgifts.org
The original source of "donate a cow" type gifts. Over 200 items, many with a development focus but some with environmental themes like regenerating meadowland. You get a keepsake card to send or keep (including a Christmas cracker version!), which you can personalise via the website. Prices from £5, but can pick and mix 5 or more smaller gift items. Includes wedding lists and in memoriam gifts, plus schools resource pack on themes of social justice and charity.

Green Gift Company

07808 400773
www.greengiftcompany.com
Quality gifts, including jewellery, bags, home and bath items and Christmas items. Attractive and unusual bags; affordable jewellery. Christmas presents at pocket money prices. Every item is in one or more of the following categories:

fair-trade, recycled, organic, sustainable, or locally produced. Can also do hosted parties in Edinburgh/central belt with incentives for hosts, or as fundraisers.

Gulliver's Toys and Gifts

165b Bruntsfield Place, EH10 4DG
0131 629 9424
info@gulliverstoys.co.uk
www.gulliverstoys.co.uk
Traditional and wooden toys, games and puzzles. A small backroom has new baby gifts and christening wear. Online shop.

Halibut and Herring

108 Bruntsfield Place, EH10 4ES
0131 229 2669
wendy.beaumont@btconnect.com
www.halibutandherring.co.uk
An Aladdin's cave of wonderful and quirky gifts waiting to be discovered. A chest of wonderful treats that will leave you walking away with more than you intended to go in for. Small gifts ranging from £2 to stylish, handmade handbags for about £30, there is something for everyone in this boutique. Run by Wendy Beaumont, once an interior designer, whose boundless love of the quirky, the unusual and the charming manifests itself in this cosy nook of a shop, tucked away in the heart of Bruntsfield.

Hawkin's Bazaar

0844 557 5261
www.hawkin.com
A very wide selection of items, including unusual presents, fun toys, kids crafts, gadgets, games, books. Craft items from £2.50. Party bag items which you can buy as individual items, from 10p. Low-cost art supplies. Plenty for older kids too. Includes a big retro section, with gifts covering several decades. Shop in St James Shopping Centre (0131 446 4030).

Helios Fountain

7 Grassmarket, EH1 2HY
0131 229 7884
www.helios-fountain.co.uk
Toys, books, gifts and craft materials. Wooden toys from various countries, as well as traditional toys such as kaleidoscopes, marbles and spinning tops. An intriguing collection of soft toys, ranging from the seriously cute to the slightly bizarre. The craft materials are especially useful to encourage creativity in children and include a large selection of Fimo, as well as candle-making and card-making supplies.

Holz Toys

0845 130 8697
www.holz-toys.co.uk
Lots for babies upwards, including stacking/ sorting toys, make believe, vehicles and puzzles. Lots of wooden toys, ethically and environmentally made, supporting Fair Trade. Site searchable by price, age or a gift finder tool. Pocket money section with £0-£5 and £5-£10 categories. Particularly beautiful wooden puzzles and marble runs.

Insect Lore

01726 860273
www.insectlore-europe.com
Ideal for budding naturalists and admirers of creepy crawlies. Buy live insects and butterflies for hatching, homes for bugs etc. Some items for play including wooden food playsets, child's gardening items. Also books, posters, puppets and other items to expand awareness of a particular topic. Gift vouchers available. Great for unusual presents or to fire interest in science and the outdoors.

Letterbox

0844 557 5263
www.letterbox.co.uk
Items for outdoor play, traditional toys, personalised presents, bedroom decoration, dressing up, home and travel. Ranges like Peppa Pig, Charlie and Lola. Site searchable by age, price, girl/boy. Toys can also include name/ initials. Further personalised items including named pencils, pens, pencil cases, name tapes. Quality toy shop feel and prices; good to point grandparents to for birthdays/Christmas.

Mulberry Bush

01403 790796
www.mulberrybush.co.uk
Traditional toys parents and/or grandparents will know and like. Includes dolls' houses, push and ride toys, wooden toys and trains. Toys for babies upwards, including rattling balls, hammer pegs, trucks with bricks etc. Quality advent calendars (wooden/magnetic) for many years' use. Stocking filler/pocket money items.

Nic Nac Noo

0131 664 1724
www.nicnacnoo.com
Family-run online toy store, specialising in natural, wooden and organic toys, also with an ethical/handcrafted focus. Categories include baby and toddler, books, pretend play, educational toys, music, outdoors. One of the largest suppliers of wooden organic educational toys in the UK. The design of the website rather anticipates you know what you are looking for – lots of items in each category, but you can also search by manufacturer. Includes pocket money prices section.

Ollie and Forbes

0131 208 0405
www.ollieandforbes.com
Edinburgh-based gifts company, covering categories of new baby, early years, pre-school, books and clothes. Good quality. Nice rubberwood sets of animals on different themes: forests, arctic, etc. Ethical, fair-trade, eco-friendly and environmentally sustainable items, many unique to these traders.

One World Shop

St John's Church, Princes Street, EH2 4BJ
0131 229 4541
info@oneworldshop.co.uk
www.oneworldshop.co.uk
Lovely shop in beautiful grounds just off Princes Street. Compact but packed with goodies, including clothes, bags, jewellery, food and cards, all Fair Trade. There is also an excellent selection of Fair Trade children's clothes and toys. We particularly loved the world music CDs for children.

Playsongs

0208 776 6286
www.playsongs.co.uk
Songs for babies and toddlers. Book comes with CD, no requirement to read music. Songs include actions suitable from very young ages, such as peek-a-boo, bouncing on the knee, finger play etc. Attractive illustrations and suggestions on how to adapt and extend activities as the child gets older. "Action songs" is the most well known of the collection, but there is also one with songs about baby/toddler daily routine, and another with songs for bedtime/naptime. Many songs are written by the company and performed to high standards for the CD.

Poundstretcher

www.poundstretcher.co.uk
Budget/value store stocking a selection of inexpensive toys, craft and party supplies, small gifts, sweeties and children's toiletries. Selection varies somewhat by location and size of store. If travelling with a pushchair, be aware that a lift may not be available at multi-level locations (such as Shandwick Pl).
     Branches at: **42 Shandwick Pl, 42 Lothian Rd, 65 West Harbour Rd, 100-106 Southbridge, Fort Kinnaird, 245-249 Gorgie Rd, Meadowbank Shopping Centre and West Side Plaza (Westerhailes).**

Spirit of Nature

01258 837848
www.spiritofnature.co.uk
Eco items for family and home including baby and child, nappies, toys, household, body and skincare, gifts and items for men/women. Can search by brands and within price categories. Clothing, jewellery and accessories, and lots of wooden items for babies/older children. Site includes a blog on eco topics, featuring different products.

Studio One

10 Stafford Street
0131 226 5812
www.shopstudio1.co.uk
A delightful and unique gift shop with jewellery, accessories, candles, toys, and dining, living room and bath items. The good-sized toy section suits a variety of ages and contains a lot of items that probably won't be found elsewhere in Edinburgh.

Pushchairs: Steep steps, staff happy to help.

Supertramp Trampolines

01884 821419
www.supertramp.co.uk
Over 25 years' experience of making trampolines. Range of sizes and shapes, including mini trampolines for indoor fitness for mum and dad. Also sell accessories and spare parts. Prices include free shipping to mainland UK addresses. If you order before 14.00, Mon-Fri, despatched for delivery next business day. Investment item prices but many come with warranties of several years.

Toys Galore, Morningside

193 Morningside Road, EH10 4QP
0131 447 1006
donaldnairn@yahoo.co.uk
Very well stocked. Toys for all ages and from very cheap to more expensive. Prices seemed in line with other shops. Staff were very helpful

and asked if they could help as soon as I went in – important as there is so much stock it can be hard to find the exact thing you are looking for quickly. Range includes: Lego, wide range of jigsaws, Sylvanian Families, wooden toys, Playmobil, pocket money toys.

Toys Galore, Stockbridge

13 Comely Bank Road, EH4 1DR
0131 343 1244
My kids love this shop. It has a good selection of different toys for all ages e.g. Lego, Playmobil, soft toys, Sylvanian Families, games, craft items, models, etc. There are also plenty of "pocket money" or "party bag" toys. Shop is happy to get items not in stock from the bigger Morningside store if required or order items they may not have. Children are encouraged to try stuff out and the staff are helpful too.

Accessibility: One step up into shop.
Pushchairs: Quite narrow but possible to get a pushchair round.

Toys 'R' Us

Kinnaird Park, Newcraighall Road, EH15 3RD
0131 657 4121
www.toysrus.co.uk
Huge range of pre-school toys, soft toys, dolls, games, Lego, Playmobil, outdoor toys and so on. A store directory points to the different areas and there is a pick-up point for bulky items and electrical toys. Climbing frames, chutes, swings, sandpits and Wendy houses available with samples on display. There is no play area and as such a vast array of toys may prove tempting, parents may find it easier to shop without their offspring. The Babies 'R' Us area stocks baby food, toiletries and nappies in bulk quantities, as well as nursery equipment. Reward card scheme.

We asked Julie Gamble, Children's Book Buyer for Blackwell's Bookshop ...

How long have you worked at Blackwell's Bookshop? *I've been here for almost 10 years.*

What do you like/dislike about your job? *I love finding books that are just right for our little customers. I get to see most books about 2 months before they arrive in the shop! There isn't really much I don't like about my job.*

How long have you lived in Edinburgh? *For 10 years.*

How do you rate it as a child-friendly city? *It is extremely child friendly, there are loads of activities city-wide for kids to get involved in all through the year.*

Any memorable experiences of Edinburgh? *This year I watched the Hogmanay fireworks from a roof in the Old Town. We were right in the centre of everything and it was made even more magical as we saw all the lanterns people had lit floating across the sky.*

Recommendations: *The Storytelling Centre on the Royal Mile. They have special storytelling sessions for under 5s and a lovely café. You can check times and events on their website.*

You can find out all about bookshops on pages 214-217.

Activities & Classes

Activities & Classes

There is a plethora of options for taking your little one(s) to activity sessions and classes. They vary from blocks of sessions booked in advance to activities where you can drop in when it suits you. Often there will be an opportunity to attend a taster session. Below we cover activities and classes for babies and children, but at the end of the chapter there is a short section on activities and classes for adults.

As elsewhere, we've included the most up-to-date prices we can but they may have changed since publication.

 These activities can also be good for parties and it's always worth asking if the teacher would be interested in a private booking.

ARTS & CRAFTS

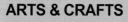

Doodle & Splat

Contact: Lynda and Pamela
07942 825114
doodle@doodleandsplat.co.uk
www.doodleandsplat.co.uk
Art and craft and messy play for 1-2½ yr olds and 2-5 yr olds with classes at various locations in

Edinburgh and Fife. Parents/carers stay with their child, creating works of art to take home and share with their families without having to worry about the mess! A great way to meet up with friends in a safe environment where children have the opportunity to have fun and be messy. The class is divided between planned art and craft activities and imaginative play areas which include Play Doh and cutters, chalk boards, colouring pictures and rubbing plates plus a messy tray of water, slime, shaving foam and sand. Each week there are different activities set out to explore, which helps children to build their confidence, use their imagination and express themselves visually. Classes run for 45 mins during school term time. Sessions available for toddler groups and nurseries plus birthday parties for up to 7 yr olds.

The Imagination Workshop

136 Marchmont Road, EH9 1AQ
0131 466 0148
nicki@theimaginationworkshop.co.uk
www.theimaginationworkshop.co.uk
Offer craft workshops for 2+ yrs. Arty parties also available.

 Visit our website for updates: www.efuf.co.uk

Messy Art Class for Mums and Toddlers

Ratho Community Centre, 1 School Wynd
0131 333 1055
Messy cookery classes for under 3s and parents/carers. Get involved in fun and messy cooking with young children and encourage healthy eating.

Messy Munchkins

Murrayfield Parish Church
Inverleith Parish Church
Gambado, Fountainpark Complex
and North Merchiston Club
07876 542492
juliet@messymunchkins.co.uk
www.messymunchkins.co.uk
Free-play 1 hour sessions for your 8 mth-5 yr old to explore and learn through messy play. Each class is built around a "theme", and several messy play activities are set up for you and your child to discover. On the day we attended in Murrayfield there was a "weather" theme, with artificial snow play, "rainbow rice" to scoop, stand, and sit in, sunshine custard to ooze everywhere, autumn shredded paper, as well as a chalkboard and painting/gluing. The class leader facilitates the session and learning outcomes for each activity are clearly identified. My 3 yr old enjoyed the freedom to make a mess, and I enjoyed the knowledge I wouldn't have to clean it up! A great way to let kids be kids!

Cost: Trial session £5 (refundable on booking block of 10 classes). Block of 3 classes – £19.50, block of 6 classes – £39, block of 10 classes – £55. 50% discount for each additional child. Birthdays/celebrations: Contact Messy Munchkins for details, but generally £100/10 children and £5 each additional child.

BABY CLASSES

Here are a few suggestions for early classes with your little one, but as the weeks progress you'll find the possibilities keep widening. Check out individual sections later in the chapter, such as music fun, swimming, yoga and gymnastics, for lots more classes and activities you can enjoy with your baby.

Baby Nippers

www.edinburghleisure.co.uk
A recent addition from Edinburgh Leisure, these classes concentrate on encouraging babies' development and basic skills such as crawling, aided-walking, rolling, hopping, jumping, throwing and catching. Sensory equipment, hand apparatus and music are used in the class, which is for babies from 8 wks-18 mths. Classes at: Portobello Indoor Bowls Centre, Meadowbank Sports Centre, Craiglockhart Leisure Centre and Gracemount Leisure Centre. Contact individual venues for details.

Baby Sensory

edinburghcentral@babysensory.co.uk
www.babysensory.com
I really enjoyed this class. There are over 100 different ones, so you could go for months and never do the same thing twice! It is very intense with lots of visual, auditory and textual stimulation. My 10-mth-old little girl always had a fantastic nap immediately afterwards. Although structured, it is a very relaxed atmosphere. There is no obligation to join in either – if you feel your child is not enjoying an activity, you can just watch. My daughter's favourite class was the water-themed one – she loves splashing about and getting wet! CDs and a goody bag available for sale, although I bought the goody bag and found it overpriced. For 0-13 mths.

Cost: £65/10 wk term. Birthdays/celebrations: Yes – at your own home or private venue.

Edinburgh Baby Massage

Contact: Anne Nash
07879 448181
edinburghbabymassage@gmail.com
www.edinburghbabymassage.co.uk
5-week baby massage courses for babies from 6 wks until crawling. Courses are available in Anne's home in south Edinburgh or at your own home. Pregnancy and postnatal massages for mums available as well.

Scents of Wellbeing

Reflexology

Indian Head Massage

Aromatherapy Massage

Hot Stone Fusion Massage

Fertility / Maternity Reflexology

Pregnancy / Postnatal Massage

Baby Massage Classes

Anne Young BSc RN CBMI MIFPA
Tel: 0131 552 4830
Mob: 07811 073 202
www.scents-of-wellbeing.co.uk

Are you following us yet? We're @EdforUnder5s on Twitter or you can be our friend on Facebook – look for Edinburgh Ed.

Scents of Wellbeing

25 Inverleith Row, EH3 5QH
0131 552 4830
0871 107 3202
anne@scents-of-wellbeing.co.uk
www.scents-of-wellbeing.co.uk
Baby massage classes to promote wellbeing in babies and bonding between parent and child. Classes can either be at 25 Inverleith Row or at your own home. Anne ran a class for 4 mothers and babies in my home last year. Babies were 3 mths old and all enjoyed being massaged, during the classes and then as the massage became part of our nightly preparations for bed. Anne provides oils and laminated notes to help parents remember the techniques. She is a very reassuring teacher who completely understands babies – just the thing for a bunch of nervous new mums!

BALL SPORTS

3v2 Soccer Academy

07872 448788 (Roddy Maughan)
info@3v2socceracademy.co.uk
www.3v2socceracademy.co.uk
Football classes for children – the "Mini Stars Programme" for 3-5 yr olds and the "Micro Stars Programme" for 2-3 yr olds.

Coerver Football Coaching

0844 808 0442
scotland@coerver.co.uk
Classes run at various locations – after school, weekends, and holiday camps. For pre-school.

Edinburgh Accies Mini-Rugby

minis@edinburghaccies.com
www.edinburghaccies.com
Mini-rugby for 4+ yrs.

Enjoy-a-Ball

0845 226 2694
office.team@enjoy-a-ball.com
www.enjoy-a-ball.com
Ball sports lessons, held indoors at venues across Edinburgh. Small age-range groups; small classes, ranging from 8 max for youngest children. Skills move from basic ball skills up to learning the 8 sports of basketball, baseball, football, hockey, volleyball, tennis, rugby and cricket. Includes specific ball-sport instruction (appropriate to age), how to use equipment safely, but also fun activities to warm up and wind down. Sport is mixed with chances to socialise with other children, and practise turn-taking, listening skills and good sportsmanship. There are reward stickers, and trophies which can be won week by week. My son adores it! Venues vary, but are church hall/community centre type locations, sometimes with toys to play with for waiting younger siblings. Children attending classes are encouraged to bring a drink. Parents are on a rota: one sits in per week, but it's possible for others to be off-site during the lesson, returning in time for collection. Age range: 3-9.

Class times: Check with each centre. Some daytime classes; after school classes for older children. Some instructors work in schools and nurseries. Holiday clubs at Easter and in the summer. Cost: £5/lesson, payable in termly/half-termly blocks; may shift to direct debit to spread costs. No refunds for missed lessons. Free trial session. Birthdays/celebrations: Can be booked for parties for 4 yrs +. The 90 mins session includes break for food and drink. Parents arrange the venue, food and drinks.

Golf

0131 652 2178
www.edinburghleisure.co.uk
Coaching for 3+ yrs at Craigentinny Golf School. Coaching camps and individual lessons on offer.

Mini Kickers

0131 652 2178
www.edinburghleisure.co.uk
Classes for 3-5 yr olds from Edinburgh Leisure. The football programme enables children to learn and enjoy the basics of football through a range of fun practices and games. The classes, delivered by SFA coaches, will help develop good co-ordination and build their communication skills. Also at Bonnyrigg Leisure Centre – 0131 663 7579.

Play2Learn Sports Coaching

07952 147577
07766 143918
shane@play2learn.info
www.play2learn.info
Football and multi-sports sessions for nurseries and playgroups across Edinburgh and the surrounding areas. Also offer holiday camps and parties.

Playball

0131 652 2178
www.edinburghleisure.co.uk
Edinburgh Leisure classes based on fun, movement and play. Allows children 3-5 yrs to try a range of sports including basketball, football, rugby, golf and tennis.

Rugbytots

0845 313 3252
kirsty@rugbytots.co.uk
www.rugbytots.co.uk
A weekly play session for boys and girls 2-7 yrs. All classes are led by SRU qualified coaches. Sessions available in Edinburgh, Lothians and the Borders. Classes cover all the motor skills by using rugby as a medium with the main emphasis on fun. Book online.

The UK's first rugby specific play programme for young children

For children aged 2-7

- Weekly play session for children between the age of two and seven
- Designed to enhance your child's social and physical skills
- All sessions are fully insured and led by an RFU level one coach who has been first aid trained and CRB checked
- Classes now available in Edinburgh and Lothians area

Socatots

07923 005534
j.smith@socatots.com
www.socatots.org/edinburgh
A soccer-specific physical play programme for children 6 mths-5 yrs. Sessions are held in various venues in Edinburgh and East Lothian and feature parent/carer participation.

Tennis and Tots Tennis

0131 443 0101
0131 652 2178
www.edinburghleisure.co.uk
Edinburgh Leisure runs these classes which teach children 3-5 yrs basic hitting, movement and co-ordination skills for tennis. Run by qualified and experienced coaches in a fun and encouraging environment. Parents/carers must be present during the session.

Waverley Tennis Club

0131 667 9517
waverley@waverleysports.co.uk
www.waverleysports.co.uk
Offers a thriving Juniors section with excellent coaching from 4 yrs.

Wee Dribblers

0131 652 2178
www.edinburghleisure.co.uk
Parent and toddler sessions run by Edinburgh Leisure. Fun play with all types of balls as an introduction to football.

DANCE

Classes for younger children (2-4 yrs) usually teach music and movement – nursery rhymes and simple dancing: hopping, skipping, toe-pointing, mime and moving in time to music. Socialising (learning to wait your turn for example) are key elements in all dancing classes. Footwear can be light shoes, available from any decent shoe shop, more often ballet shoes. In addition to the classes listed here, you can find others through recommendations and ads in local libraries, community centres, shop windows and the local press. When choosing, consider such factors as the teacher's qualifications, class content and studio facilities.

Angela Watson School of Dance

0131 661 9590
angela4dance@yahoo.co.uk
Ballet, modern and tap classes in Colinton, Fairmilehead and Firrhill. From 3 yrs.

Baby Loves Disco

www.babylovesdisco.co.uk
Monthly disco class for children (from 6 mths) and parents. Classic disco music. Chill-out area, snacks and a bar for adults.

Boogie Babies

0131 652 2178
www.edinburghleisure.co.uk
Hip hop and pop dance classes for under 5s at Edinburgh Leisure Centres.

Buckstone Youth Dance

0131 478 0745
www.buckstoneyouthdance.org.uk
Ballet (RAD) from pre-school year. Modern and tap (ISTD) from Primary 1.

CeilidhKids

0131 667 8898
ceilidhkids@ceilidhkids.com
www.ceilidhkids.com
Fun and fitness for you and your child. For children 3-5 yrs and their parents or carers. Book a block of classes or pay as you go. Ceilidh Kids also offer family ceilidhs for celebrations, parties or fundraisers.

Creative Dance

0131 652 2178
www.edinburghleisure.co.uk
Classes for 3-6 yr olds with Edinburgh Leisure.

Dance Base

14-16 Grassmarket, EH1 2JU
0131 225 5525
dance@dancebase.co.uk
www.dancebase.co.uk
Scotland's National Centre for Dance – fully accessible building offering state-of-the-art facilities, with 4 dance studios. Lots of classes on offer, including drop-in sessions. Toddler music and movement classes, pre-school and primary dance sessions.

Dance for All at the Theatre School

106 St Stephen Street, EH3 5AQ
0131 226 5533
jennylewis@danceforall.freeserve.co.uk
www.danceforall.co.uk
2-4 yrs – general nursery dance; a fun introduction to dance steps, rhythm and co-ordination, mime, songs and creative dance. 4-5 yrs – pre-primary ballet; a gentle introduction to more structured dance steps and sequences, alongside free expression and creative dance, rhythm and co-ordination exercises. Tap dancing classes and jazz classes from 4 yrs. After-school classes and all day Sat. Phone for full details.

The Edinburgh Dance Academy

4-6 Coltbridge Avenue, EH12 6AH
0131 337 3402
edinburghdance@aol.com
www.edinburghdanceacademy.co.uk
Ballet from 3 yrs. Classes are held in venues throughout Edinburgh and the Lothians. Contact for current details, venues and requirements.

Feet Foxes Dance Class

Out of the Blue, 36 Dalmeny Street,
Calton Centre, 21 Montgomery Street, and
Lifecare Centre, Cheyne Street, Stockbridge
07515 060272
chellemurdoch@hotmail.com
Feet Foxes Facebook Page
One of the best mum-and-toddler dance classes I have attended, and I've been to lots of them! It is well-paced, with a comfortably predictable schedule of songs, story breaks, and dancing. No activity lasts too long, and there's a good balance of structured and unstructured activity. 'Chelle', as the kids call her, has a lovely, relaxed teaching style. My 2 yr old adores this class! Although the age range is 2-5, younger children are welcome and there are several infants who regularly come along. My 6 yr old has also attended on occasion during school holidays.

Class times: Out of the Blue class – Thurs 10.00-11.00, Calton Centre class Thurs 15.00-16.00. Lifecare Centre class – Wed 15.00-16.00. Cost: £4-5/family. **Birthdays/celebrations:** *Arranged on request. Contact Michelle.*

Lothian Dance Academy

0131 669 9073
contact@lothiandance.com
www.lothiandance.com
Pre-school ballet, tap, jazz and creative music classes for 3-5 yrs, and also for older children. The main studio is in Portobello but classes are also held in other locations throughout the city. Phone for current prices and locations.

Manor School of Ballet

0131 334 0399
enquiries@manorschoolofballet.co.uk
www.manorschoolofballet.co.uk
Music and movement for ages 2-4 yrs. Ballet, jazz, tap and Highland classes. Venues across Edinburgh. The youngest pupils wear normal clothes, plus ballet shoes, which the school sells at a reasonable price. Children start to wear leotards from 3 yrs. The school employs several teachers who are all RAD, ISTD and UKA registered.

Mhairi Hogg School of Dancing

0131 449 3035
Tap, Highland, and Modern Dance Classes for all ages held in Colinton Mains Community Centre and Oxgangs Neighbourhood Centre. Nursery Tap classes are held for 3-5 yrs. A class leotard is worn, plus Highland, tap, ballet or jazz shoes.

Morag Alexander

01875 853027
moragalexander@btinternet.com
www.moragalexander.co.uk
Classes in East Lothian and Midlothian. Ballet, jazz and tap. From 3 yrs.

Morningside Dance Academy

0131 477 4344
0131 668 4977 (also fax)
morningsidedance@btinternet.com
www.morningsidedance.co.uk

Ballet, tap, modern and jazz dancing from 3 yrs. RAD and BTDA syllabus to Examination Standard.

The Royal Academy of Dance

0207 326 8000
The RAD has a registration system for teachers – contact them for a list of local registered teachers.

Steps School of Dance

0131 339 2315
Alex55555@btinternet.com
Ballroom, Latin, disco, and rock 'n' roll. From 4 yrs.

Tap and Ballet with Mrs P Allam

01259 742973
Nursery ballet from 3 yrs. Classes, accompanied by a pianist, are held in Blackhall. Fully qualified staff.

Waterfront Dance Studio

07772 504958
niki@waterfrontdancestudio.co.uk
www.waterfrontdancestudio.co.uk
Ballet, tap and modern dance. From 3 yrs.

The Calton Centre

Activities and classes take place in all sorts of places in and around Edinburgh. We take a look at the new Calton Centre.

121 Montgomery Street, EH7 5EP
0131 661 0880
07413 521336
info@caltoncentre.co.uk
www.caltoncentre.co.uk
A fantastic, brand-new dance studio/meeting space just beside Montgomery St Park! Although the centre has only been open for a few weeks at the time of writing, it already boasts a diverse and eclectic offering for both adults and children.

The current schedule includes such activities as a Spanish Amigos language club, a mum-and-baby playgroup, a Feet Foxes toddler dance class, and ballet and hip-hop classes led by Morningside Dance Academy, with even more new classes to come. The venue is beautifully renovated and fully accessible. Although there are no eating facilities, it does have a kitchen.

Opening hours: Mon-Sat 10.00-22.00. Sun by special arrangement. Cost: Class prices vary, as do prices for booking various halls. See website for more. Parking: Pay and display outside the Centre. Free parking on the east side of Easter Rd and other surrounding streets. Accessibility/Pushchairs: Entrance ramp and accessible lift. Plenty of space for pushchairs inside the building. Toilets: Male, female and accessible toilets on both floors. Birthdays/celebrations: Dance halls can be booked for children's parties.

DRAMA

The Drama Studio

0131 453 3284
info@thedramastudio.com
www.thedramastudio.com
Drama workshops for 3+ yrs in various venues across Edinburgh. Also run holiday workshops and birthday parties.

Helen O'Grady Drama Academy

0131 667 0939
midscot@helenogrady.co.uk
www.helenogrady.co.uk
Children's drama programme for 3-5 yrs. Story telling, dramatic play, creative movement, songs and language development activities.

Lyceum Playtime

Royal Lyceum Theatre Edinburgh
0131 248 4848
www.lyceum.org.uk
Creative Learning programme offers fun drama workshops for parents and children aged 2-4 yrs. Times and dates vary. See Lyceum website or call.

Orcadia Creative Learning Centre

3 Windsor Place, Portobello
0131 669 1075
Classes for children from 4 yrs with special needs and learning disabilities. Includes dance, music, mime, puppetry, mask and creative movement.

Sparkles Arts

07717 706778
info@sparklearts.co.uk
www.sparklearts.co.uk
A fun mix of drama, dance and music with professionally qualified teachers. Also offer parties tailored to your child's age group. For 2+ yrs.

Stagecoach Theatre Arts

0131 449 9507
edinburghnorth@stagecoach.co.uk
www.stagecoach.co.uk
Classes and holiday workshops at numerous venues in Edinburgh. Stagecoach teaches acting, dancing and singing.

GYMNASTICS

Gymnastics classes accommodating under 5s are generally available in Edinburgh. When choosing one it is well worth checking the teacher's qualifications for teaching pre-school children, the facilities and the insurance cover.

All British Amateur Gymnastics Association (BAGA) coaches will charge a set fee to children who attend their classes. This is paid to the Association for insurance purposes, irrespective of the cost of the course. Anyone working with young children, i.e. nursery groups etc., might be interested in taking the Scottish Gymnastics Coaching Award for pre-school gymnastics and movement.

Gymbabes

Cluny Centre,1 Cluny Drive, Morningside, EH10 6DN
01875 819966
joletelier.lobos@virgin.net
www.tumbletots.com
Part of the "Tumbletots" programme, Gymbabes is a great way to encourage your baby to be active from an early age and for them to explore and test their abilities in a safe environment. The class starts with a song and warm-up massage, and ends with more singing. For the 30 mins or so in between, babies are encouraged to try out the various pieces of equipment around the room (such as trampolines, slides and tunnels) and the "circuit" is changed every couple of weeks. There is a very good ratio of staff to babies and they are on hand to help guide your baby through the equipment, but the format is very informal and unstructured. Age range: 6 mths to walking.

Class times: Mon/Fri 11.35. Cost: Registration/ annual membership £22, then £5.50/class.

Gym Nippers

Weekly classes delivering structured fun, movement and co-ordination lessons using large and small apparatus. Split into two sections. Parent and Toddler is for 18 mths-3 yrs, aiming to improve co-ordination and motor skills through song, dance and movement. Coaches are all pre-school qualified at working with this age group. Second section is 3-5 yrs. Develops self-confidence and social skills. Landing and shaping, dance, rotation and rebound are covered. Young gymmasts also learn about levels and direction, balances and shapes, swing and turns and twists.

Ainslie Park Leisure Centre
92 Pilton Drive, EH5 2HF
0131 551 2400
mail@edinburghleisure.co.uk
www.edinburghleisure.co.uk/detail-525
We've been attending Parent and Toddler classes here for the past year and they have been excellent. We've attended with my other daughter who is only 9 mths and the coaches couldn't have been more helpful and happy for us all to come to the class which has been great. There are two circle times, one at the start and one at the end of the 40-minute class where singing and movement to music happens. The rest of the time is spent on all of the great gym equipment, but the coaches are always on hand to give you help and advice on how to use the various items. My daughter has learned lots of skills – forward rolls and tumbling round a bar! We've loved every minute – but the best bit has been seeing my daughter's progress. She's certainly put everything she's learned into practice at playparks and softplays!

Cost: £4.40 per class, book per term.

Scottish Gymnastics Association

www.scottishgymnastics.org
Contact the assocaton for information on coaching awards, a copy of the syllabus, and advice on gymnastics classes.

Toddler Gymnastics

Wester Hailes Education Centre, 5 Murrayburn Drive
0131 442 2201
Classes for 3-5 yrs. Block booking – a waiting list applies. Contact the centre for more details.

Tumble Tots

www.tumbletots.com

Edinburgh East contact: Jo Letelier-Lobos
01875 819966 or 07747 776088
joletelier.lobos@virgin.net
Covers Fairmilehead, Haddington, Marchmont and Morningside.

Edinburgh West contact: April Wallace
0131 336 1234 or 07977 235327
Covers Corstorphine, Cramond, Murrayfield, Murieston, Ravelston and Trinity.
www.tumbletots.com/edinburgh//www.tumbletots.com/edinburgh-west

This specially designed programme helps develop co-ordination, balance, agility and climbing skills. Follows on from Gymbabes from walking to 5 yrs (Gymbobs sessions for 5+ yrs). Supervision is by specially trained staff. Tumble Tots are for children from walking confidently to 2 yrs, for 2-3 yrs and for 3-5 yrs. Children with additional support needs are welcome to attend classes suited to their developmental stage. Sessions are based around activity stations.

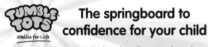

The springboard to confidence for your child

Tumble Tots is Britain's leading National Active Physical Play Programme for children from 6 months to 7 years

www.tumbletots.com/Edinburgh or call Jo on **01875 819966**
www.tumbletots.com/Edinburgh-West or call April on **0131 336 1234**

HORSE RIDING

Edinburgh and Lasswade Riding Centre

Kevock Road, Lasswade, EH18 1HX
0131 663 7676
lasswaderiding@btconnect.com
www.lasswadestables.com
Half-hour pony treks for under 5s. Small Shetland ponies and older, quieter ponies are used. For children from 2 yrs – as long as the child is happy to sit on the pony s/he can be taken on a small trek. The ponies are on leads and one person is allocated to each child. Children should wear welllies/boots. The Centre also hosts children's parties and these include a pony trek, the opportunity to feed and groom a pony and then party food and grassy play area.

Riding for the Disabled

Riding for children from 3 yrs with teams of enthusiastic and dedicated volunteers. Eligibility applies to all conditions except for arthritis or severe epilepsy (not controlled). At:

Drum Riding, Gilmerton
0131 664 5803
drumrda@hotmail.co.uk

Muirfield Group, East Lothian
01620 842 502
muirfieldrda@aol.com

Ravelrig Group, Balerno
0131 449 7994
ravelrigrda@tiscali.co.uk

Thornton Rose Group, Midlothian
0131 654 2993 or 07985 591612
RDA.ThorntonRose@j5863.fsnet.co.uk

West Lothian Group
0845 450 6952
rhonamf@btinternet.com

Each centre's contact number is the home number of the contact for the organisation. Consider putting your child's name down as soon as you can as waiting lists are very long. A medical information form will need to be completed for your child and countersigned by a medical professional who knows them.

LANGUAGES

Allemann Fun

0131 447 2013
allemannfun@arcor.de
www.allemannfun.org.uk
Group meeting at Gillespie's High School for children 3+ yrs who are bi-lingual in German. Child must have a German-speaking parent.

Gaelic Parent & Toddler Group

0131 529 2415
For 0-3 yrs. Groups meet in Corstorphine, Fountainbridge and Leith.

Le Petit Monde

07910 045743
info@lepetitmonde.co.uk
www.lepetitmonde.co.uk
Puppet shows, classes and workshops in French and English for schools and nurseries. 3+ yrs. Other venues considered.

Mini French

Contact: Felicity
07800554328
minifrench.edi@gmail.com
www.minifrench.co.uk
Fun French sessions for babies, toddlers, preschoolers and parents. The aim of this class is to introduce French to pre-school children, while they are most open to learning new languages, in a fun, welcoming atmosphere. Action songs, traditional nursery rhymes and props used. Parents improve their French along the way – your level of French is no obstacle. CD to use at home is provided as part of block. Classes last an hour including social time. Venues in Leith and Marchmont (potential additional venues in 2013).

Spanish Amigos

0131 510 0328
kirsty@spanishamigos.co.uk
www.spanishamigos.co.uk/clubs/edinburgh.htm
Mama and Toddler club in Craiglockhart Leisure Centre and the new Calton Centre. Other types of class available, contact Kirsty for more.

MARTIAL ARTS

The Edinburgh Judo Club

0131 554 8330
edinburghjudo@aol.com
www.edinburghjudo.com
Evening and weekend classes from 3 yrs.

Junior Judo

0131 555 4578
george@juniorjudoclub.co.uk
www.juniorjudoclub.co.uk
Classes start from 4 yrs. Highly experienced and long-running judo tuition for youngsters.

Shishi Kai Judo

0131 447 7859
jim@shishikai.co.uk
Judo classes for children aged from 4 yrs. All coaches qualified, registered and child protection vetted. Contact club for prices and more information.

MISCELLANEOUS

Community Courses

Balerno High School
5 Bridge Road, Balerno, EH14 7AQ
0131 477 7733
Easter and Summer Holiday programme of activities for pre-school children at Balerno High School. Contact Denise Young on the above number for further information.

Relax Kids

01993 810 811 (Head office)
relaxkids@theseaoftranquillity.co.uk
www.relaxkids.com
Classes from pre-school (4+ yrs) where children learn how to use various relaxation techniques in a fun way.

Talking Tots

07803 820 677 (Jen Cadger)
jen@talkingtots.info
www.talkingtots.info/Edinburgh
Fun, interactive classes for pre-school children, aged 1-5 yrs, that help develop confident communication and social skills. Classes last around 45 mins and are held at various locations across the city. Talking Tots also runs nursery sessions, private parties and Summer Tots.

MUSIC FUN

Young children love music. However, most under 5s are not yet able to specialise in a particular instrument. Most of the music classes below, therefore, teach listening skills and moving in time to music. It is highly advisable to book in advance for all of them.

Baby Music

0131 229 3667
info@pregnancyandparents.org.uk
Action songs, rhymes and lullabies for babies-1 yr, from 1 yr- toddlers and now for 3yrs +. Class includes time for tea/coffee and socialising with other parents. Very popular classes, so please call for venue, times, cost and to reserve a place. Concessions available.

Baby Singing with Laura

Butterflies Café, Marchmont St Giles,
1a Kilgraston Road, EH9 2DW
0131 476 9228
nctlaura@googlemail.com
www.babysinging.co.uk
Friendly, gentle music and singing for babies (newborn-12 mths) with parents/carers, held in a light and welcoming room by café. Includes action rhymes and songs to acoustic guitar, parachute games and hands-on resources with traditional and new songs. All on ground level, pushchair parking space and toilets/nappy changing. New folk welcome to drop in.

Class times: Mon 11.00-12.00. Cost: £6/adult/ session, or £20/4 week block.

Musical fun and games
Butterflies Cafe, Marchmont
www.babysinging.co.uk

Daisy's Music Time

0131 661 2106
betty@ednet.co.uk
Fun music sessions for babies and toddlers aged 3 mths-3 yrs in the Trinity area. Singing, rhythm activities, movement, listening and playing percussion instruments. Lots of props. Classes run during term time by an experienced teacher. Phone for current times and further information.

Edinburgh Young Musicians

St Thomas of Aquin's High School,
2-20 Chalmers Street, EH3 9ES
admin@e-y-m.org.uk
www.e-y-m.org.uk
Held at St Thomas of Aquin's High School, nr Tollcross, in central Edinburgh on Sat mornings. Musical play classes for children, starting in their final pre-school year, leading to instrumental tuition, choirs, orchestras, chamber groups and musicianship classes for older children. The pre-school classes provide a general introduction to music, aiming to develop children's sense of rhythm and pitch, listening skills, co-ordination and imagination. The school staff room is available as a waiting room for parents and children, where there is a self-service coffee shop set up.

Class times: Sat mornings during school term time. Cost: From £3.90 to £10.70/week depending on class taken.

Hullabaloo!

01875 341679
07966 434591
charlotte_mcmillan@sky.com
Music classes in Pencaitland and Haddington for 4 mths-2 yrs and toddlers to pre-school. Singing and movement to popular rhymes and songs.

Jack and Jill Music Fun for Tots

St Catherine's Argyle Church
61-63 Grange Road, EH9 1TY
0131 667 9664
info@jackandjill-music.co.uk
www.jackandjill-music.co.uk
Live, interactive music classes for babies, toddlers and pre-school children (3 mths-5 yrs) with accompanying adults, taught by qualified and experienced musicians. Live music, singing, dancing and playing of simple percussion instruments, with the content based around themes such as farm animals, transport and countries.

Jill, a qualified teacher and music therapist, welcomes children with special needs at her music classes. She tries hard to make sure that all children are included in the activities.

Class times: Wed – 09.30-10.15 12-24 mths, 10.30-11.15 24-36 mths, 11.30-12.00 3-12 mths. Fri – 09.30-10.15 18-27 mths, 10.30-11.15 27-36 mths, 11.30-12.15 3-5 yrs. Cost: £5.50/class.

Jo Jingles

www.jojingles.com

Edinburgh East & Midlothian
Contact: Susan
0131 620 3282
jojingles@thejamesons.co.uk

Edinburgh West & West Lothian
Contact: Joanne
0131 443 4196
jojingles@goodall5.co.uk

Music and movement classes for various age ranges from 6 mths-5 yrs. Includes action songs, nursery rhymes and playing musical instruments. Some songs are familiar, others are new, so there's something to keep the participating parent/carer on their toes. Also available for birthdays. Classes held in various venues throughout the city.

Mini Music Makers

0141 287 2943
catherine.williams@nycos.co.uk
www.nycos.co.uk/mini-music-makers
Run by the National Youth Choir of Scotland and available in venues centrally and in Leith during term times, this group for 0-3 yr olds is aimed at engaging children and parents in singing activities at the very earliest age. The class is really good fun. There are songs with participation from puppets and toys with percussion instruments also used. The songs often involve the children's names and then doing fun actions which really encourages participation. They absolutely love the sessions – our baby girl gets excited on a Friday when she knows she is going. A really good weekly session.

Monkey Music
(Heigh Ho class)

Main Hall, Lifecare Centre, 2 Cheyne Street, Stockbridge, EH4 1JB
0131 260 9667
info@monkeymusic.co.uk
www.monkeymusic.co.uk
Introducing children to music through accessible songs and activities, Monkey Music originated in London in 1993 and has now franchised all over Britain. The venue is superb; the Lifecare Centre in Stockbridge is easy to get to, get into, and is very spacious. The good thing about Monkey Music is that it allows the wee ones access to instruments. The Edinburgh North classes are run by Rachel Huggins and Helen Balfry (great, contrasting styles). A great treat for your little maestro.

Class times: Wed & Sat – 10.25-10.55. *Cost:* £70/10 weeks.

Monkey Music
(Morningside & Pentland)

Venues at: Fairmilehead Parish Church, Juniper Green Parish Church, Morningside (Eric Liddell Centre) and Newington (Mayfield Salisbury Church)
alison.rankin@monkeymusic.co.uk
www.monkeymusic.co.uk
Run by experienced musicians with a passion to pass on their love of music to young children, Monkey Music classes centre around "Monkey" who plays the instruments and does all the actions along with the children. My son has attended Monkey Music classes from 5 mths until nearly 3 yrs old and really enjoys them, concentrates well during the sessions listens to the CDs in the car all the time! I believe it has developed a real love for music in him. My 1 yr old loves trying to do the actions and play the instruments. Classes are grouped by age, developing skills appropriate to the age group. Contact Alison to book a complimentary trial class.

Cost: £6.60/class payable at the beginning of each term. Sibling discount available.

Morningside School of Music

0131 447 1117
morningside@polarflamemusic.com
www.morningsideschoolofmusic.com
Private and group instrument lessons from 4 yrs.

Music Bugs

0844 822 1156
hilary@musicbugs.co.uk
www.musicbugs.co.uk
I can't praise Music Bugs enough. A welcome change from more formal classes, the relaxed atmosphere promotes learning through interactive fun. Tons of different props and colourful instruments which the wee ones are

all rhythm and no blues!

Tel: Alison on 0131 669 6004
(Edinburgh South)
Tel: Rachel on 0131 260 9667
(Edinburgh North/West)

Music classes for babies and young children!
Action songs and rhymes
Music and movement
Fun with percussion
Musical games

Since 1993 thousands of children across the UK have grown up with Monkey Music. Our unique teaching curriculum was written by classically trained musicians, and introduces music to very young children in a way they can easily understand and enjoy.

Rock 'n' roll – from 3 months
Heigh ho – from 12 months
Jiggety jig – 2 & 3 year olds
Ding dong – 3 & 4 year olds
It's fun, formative and a great way of making friends!
www.monkeymusic.co.uk

encouraged to explore. A mix of old favourites and new songs plus knee-bouncers and action rhymes that have become favourites at home. My son chants "Bugs, bugs, bugs!" gleefully all the way there. Various venues. Age 6 mths-4 yrs

Cost: £5.50 per session, first taster free. Siblings under 12 mths free. Twin and sibling discounts. **Birthdays/celebrations:** Birthday parties can be arranged – enquire via website or at class.

Music for Fun

0131 620 0685
ninacraighead@blueyonder.co.uk
Songs, dance, percussion playing, confidence building and more with a former primary school teacher in her own home. Parents relax in the kitchen while children enjoy musical fun in the living room. Age 3-5 yrs.

Music for Little People

0131 440 2362
ann.heavens@googlemail.com
www.musicforlittlepeople.co.uk
Offers parents/carers and children the opportunity to explore the foundations for music in a fun and interactive way. Classes according to developmental age from 0-5 yrs.

Music with Mummy

0131 316 9076
07971 045384
musicwithrachel@btinternet.com
www.music-with-rachel.co.uk
Lively approach to music for children up to 3 yrs. Structured programme that encourages listening skills, sense of rhythm through music and games – and having fun! Has been running since 1992. Weekly sessions – please phone for current times.

Portobello Music School

0131 669 1120
info@portobellomusicschool.com
www.portobellomusicschool.com
An exciting music initiative offering comprehensive music education to children from pre-school to primary school age. Classes take place at Towerbank Primary School, Portobello, on Sat. Creative music classes, group instrumental instruction, junior choirs, and children's composition classes.

Sing and Sign

07779 605614 (Judith Watson)
edinburghsingandsign@gmail.com
www.singandsign.co.uk
Classes are for babies and toddlers 7-18 mths and run in a course of 10 wks (during term times). Signs are taught through songs and rhymes which are specially written or adapted to target signs relating to babies' routines and interests. Musical instruments, props, puppets and pictures are used to capture the babies' attention and the aim of the classes is to enhance parent-

baby communication by using signs (as well as having a bit of fun along the way).

Song Circle

0131 332 7067
07919 954334
stockbridgemusic@blueyonder.co.uk
Singing sessions for under 5s. Class for babies and a session for 2-5 yrs old. Nursery rhymes, action songs, poems and lullabies.

SPORTS

Athletics

0131 458 2100
www.edinburghleisure.co.uk
Coached Edinburgh Leisure classes from 3 yrs. Focuses on the fundamental skills of running, jumping and throwing.

Edinburgh Leisure Holiday Camps

0131 458 2100
www.edinburghleisure.co.uk
Edinburgh Leisure run camps during school holidays at various centres across Edinburgh. Activ5 programmes for under 5s offer sports activities and arts and crafts too.

Edinburgh Southern Orienteering Club

enquiries@esoc.org.uk
www.esoc.org.uk
If you are looking for a new activity to enliven a walk why not try orienteering? Edinburgh Southern Orienteering Club (ESOC) has set up permanent orienteering courses in various easily accessible parks, and woodland areas around Edinburgh, including The Hermitage of Braid, Cammo Estate, Corstorphine Hill, Bonaly, and Hillend. Orienteering involves following a course on a specially drawn map, finding your way between control markers in the right order. On a permanent orienteering course

the control markers are posted with numbers and letters and young children usually love the fun of looking for the next post. Once you have bought the map pack (£1.50) you can do as much or as little as you like. There are suggestions in the map packs for courses to suit everyone and when you have completed your course you can send off for a certificate. For more details about permanent courses and other information about orienteering see the ESOC website. Age range – 3+

Cost: £1.50 per map pack. Accessibility: Please check ESOC website for most suitable courses for wheelchairs.

Ice Skating

Murrayfield Ice Rink
0131 337 6933
info@murrayfieldicerinkltd.co.uk
www.murrayfieldicerinkltd.co.uk
Beginners' learning-to-skate classes and private coaching available from 4 yrs. Parent and toddler classes on Thurs mornings.

SWIMMING CLASSES

Edinburgh Leisure offers classes in their pools. In addition to the classes listed below there are a number of private swimming teachers in Edinburgh. For children with additional needs there are council-run classes for smaller numbers. Phone the venue in advance to check on its facilities and layout – you could also request a trial session to ensure you're happy with a class before booking a block of sessions.

Adult & Child Water Activities Programme

www.edinburghleisure.co.uk/list-217
Edinburgh Leisure classes at venues across the city. Adult and Baby for 4-12 mths, Adult and Child for 12-40 mths.

Learn to Swim

www.edinburghleisure.co.uk/detail-285
Edinburgh Leisure pre-school classes at venues across the city. Book individually with the venue that suits you best. Learn to Swim is a Scottish Swimming programme used from 3½-5 yr old beginners, onwards.

Dipping a toe in

Pre-school swimming lessons, Glenogle Swimming Baths
www.edinburghleisure.co.uk/detail-285

Once your children are 3½ they are old enough to attend Edinburgh Leisure pre-school swimming lessons. Children go into the water without their parents, leaving you free to spectate or if you can manage it, to take advantage of the Why Wait reduced price gym visit. Classes last 25 minutes and are usually run around 15.30 to fit in with school times. Glenogle, where we go, has a good spectator area but it is very warm! There is a small area with toys for smaller children if they are spectating with you. There is no public swimming during lessons.

The teachers are really friendly and encouraging. Songs and games are used to keep the children motivated as they are taught water confidence, breath control and floating. A lead teacher is often on the side of the pool and assistants may be on the side or in the pool. Buoyancy aids are provided. The children have the opportunity to progress through classes.

The lessons are very popular. There is one booking date for rebooking followed by a later date for new bookings. Course run in 3 terms and in order to get a good chance of getting into the class that you want, find out in advance what the new booking date is and phone up first thing. Term dates are available on the Edinburgh Leisure website.

Swimming classes are run at all Edinburgh Leisure Pools. 25-minute lessons cost £4.20 per class for most venues but you must pay for the whole term at once. Term lengths vary from 8-12 weeks. See individual pool listings (in Under Cover chapter) for more contact details.

Lothian Waves Swimming Club

Braidburn School, 107 Oxgangs Road North
Lothian Waves provides a safe environment for children with special needs who want to enjoy the water and learn to swim. Under the guidance of 2 qualified swimming teachers, children work with a team of volunteers to ensure each swimmer has a minimum of one-to-one support. Class sizes are relatively small to allow lessons to be tailored to each child's needs. Three separate sessions take place on Thursday afternoons starting at 16.20 and finishing at 18.00. Please register your interest with Carol Douglas (07768 142466) or Janice Borthwick (07913 984309).

SwimEasy

0131 466 0764
info@swimeasy.co.uk
www.swimeasy.co.uk
Classes begin with SwimBabies (4-24 mths – see below) followed by SwimTots (2-3 yrs) for young children accompanied by an adult. SwimEasy's Core Programme starts from 4 yrs with the "Pre-school Stage".

SwimEasy provides a progressive swimming lessons structure in accordance with the "British Long Term Athlete Development Plan". There are seven progressive stages of swimming ability: Pre-school; Non-Swimmer; Beginner; Learner; Improver; SwimWell; SwimFast/ SwimFaster.

SwimEasy's aim is for children to move through the stages as quickly as possible, while learning, and mastering, the basic underlying swimming skills on all four strokes. This is a long-term, multi-year swimming programme. All children are encouraged to complete all seven stages, enabling them to learn many important skills along the way, which will equip them to become strong, safe swimmers. Call to discuss your little one's needs.

SwimBabies with SwimEasy at Oaklands

Oaklands School, 750 Ferry Road, EH4 4HQ
0131 466 0764
info@swimeasy.co.uk
www.swimeasy.co.uk
SwimBabies covers babies from 4-24 months. The classes are designed to get young babies accustomed to being in the water, teaching them some basic safety and also the right technique to aid their progress as swimmers in later years.

Our class is based at the Oaklands pool which is designed for disabled access with the added benefit of very warm water for little ones. They last between 30 and 45 minutes.

Exercises range from breathing, gripping the poolside and kicking strokes to fun activities including songs and slides. Our daughter really enjoys the songs and just being in a large warm pool where she can thrash about!

SwimBabies says of its programme: "SwimBabies classes are specially designed, allowing parent and baby to enjoy water activities together while developing skills and experiencing new methods of aquatic learning. Progressive learning for babies is essential and therefore total submersion is not encouraged until many other aquatic skills are practised by both parent and baby."

Also available at Braidburn School, Edinburgh, and Donaldsons School, Linlithgow.

Cost: £79.80 per block of lessons.

 Make your business stand out from the rest – place an advert in our next edition!
Email business@efuf.co.uk for more information or visit the business section of our website
www.efuf.co.uk

Swimming Nature

0870 094 9597
bookings@swimmingnature.com
www.swimmingnature.co.uk
Swimming Nature is a programme which aims to teach children to develop good technique naturally without arm bands. Fun games, songs and rewards are used to maximise childrens' enjoyment of water. The modular course is easy for parents to follow. Lessons are either one to one or in very small classes with instructors in the pool. Classes are booked and paid for a term at a time. 5-day intensive courses are available throughout the school holidays. Contact the provider for details of times and locations.

Get the most up-to-date information on
www.efuf.co.uk

Waterbabies

182a Ferry Road (Head Office), EH6 4NW
0131 554 6682
woggle@waterbabies.co.uk
www.waterbabies.co.uk
I have taken my son to Waterbabies for 2½ yrs and he loves going to the classes, loves swimming and is confident in the water. The classes are fun and really develop confidence in the water and going under the water from an early age which has been a really special experience.

This is how Waterbabies describes itself: "Multi-award winning classes for babies from birth onwards. Taught by fully qualified STA instructors, with babies swimming above and below the surface. Vital water confidence and safety skills are taught with an overall aim to teach you to teach your baby to swim.

"Classes run in terms - roughly in line with the school calendar - are small and held throughout Edinburgh in private, warm water pools. Contact Water Babies for term dates and prices."

TUITION

Kumon

www.kumon.co.uk
After school classes from 3 yrs. For all levels of English and Maths abilities.

Whizzkids

0131 447 5893
hello@whizzkids.uk.com
www.whizzkids.uk.com
Fun and educational computer classes for children aged 3+ yrs. Computer-based activities are used to teach pre-school children basic language and maths skills. Classes are held on an individual or small group basis and are booked in monthly blocks.

YOGA

Yoga for Baby

Avril Berry
0845 0949 729

07990 744044
avril@yogaforbaby.com
www.yogaforbaby.com
An excellent way to introduce your little one to yoga and you don't need any previous experience yourself. Provides a great opportunity for you and your baby to socialise in a relaxed and supportive environment. Classes suitable from 6 wks until toddling (see Yoga for Toddlers).

Yoga with Babies

0131 229 3667
info@pregnancyandparents.org.uk
Friendly and relaxed classes. Yoga with Newborns – to help mothers renew strength in the first few months after birth, to ease babies' transition into the world and to facilitate the developing mother/baby relationship. Yoga with Babies is from 4-10 mths and changes pace to follow the needs of the developing baby and those of parents to be stronger and more active. Twins are welcome.

Yoga for Children

Aditi Yoga Centre
5 Alva Street, EH2 4PH
0131 226 2601
info@aditiyogacentre.com
www.aditiyogacentre.com
For children 2-5 yrs. Classes are a blend of active and passive poses, and are a combination of playful yoga postures, animated breathing exercises and imaginative relaxation and meditation activities. Classes need sufficient numbers in order to run.

Yoga for Toddlers

Avril Berry
0131 225 2012
avril@yogaforbaby.com
www.yogaforbaby.com
Follows on from Yoga for Baby classes withAvril (see above). Suitable from 18-20 mths to 3 yrs. Parents/carers are fully included as the classes include yoga practice for you and your toddler. Experienced yoga teacher who clearly enjoys working with under 3s.

For Adults

Making time for yourself as well as your children is very important. There are many possibilities open to parents with under 5s, thanks to evening classes, open/flexible learning opportunities and a wealth of community-based initiatives to help parents extend their horizons and have a break from childcare. Here are a few starting points.

Community Education Centres

Community Education Head Office
0131 469 3250
These provide a broad range of formal and informal activities and classes. There are opportunities to study for qualifications, keep fit, or learn a new craft or skill. Many provide a crèche. The majority of these centres are schools, community schools or resource centres.

Many centres run programmes under the management of the City of Edinburgh Council's "Adult Community Education Programme". Classes start in September, January and April. Contact the head office for further information on classes, or contact your local centre direct.

You can find your nearest centre by visiting: **www. edinburgh.gov.uk/directory/24/community_ centres**

Education, training and career development

Edinburgh offers a huge variety of education, training and "new direction" courses. There are also opportunities to learn a practical skill, craft or sport through the Community Learning and Development Programme run by the City Council at schools throughout the city. Crèches are available at some venues.

If you're not sure what you're looking for, use the following web address as a starting point: **www.edinburgh.gov.uk/info/284/adult_and_ community_education**

If you'd like to talk to someone or make an enquiry you can phone the council's Community Learning and Development team on **0131 469 3250** or email **community. learninganddevelopment@edinburgh.gov. uk.**

Here are a few more organisations that could provide help if you're looking for a new direction:

Women Onto Work (WOW)

Norton Park, 57 Albion Road, EH7 5QY
0131 475 2622
www.womenontowork.org
Provides courses for women who have been out of employment for 6 mths or more, and who live in an eligible area. WOW can also help women look at options for employment or further study. WOW also provides courses for women from an ethnic minority or with a disability. Full childcare provided. Courses in Craigmillar, Greater Pilton, Wester Hailes, South Edinburgh and citywide.

Beeleaf Coaching

07954 433659
sam@beeleafcoaching.co.uk
www.beeleafcoaching.co.uk
Specialises in supporting women in the workforce. Offers support through workshops and coaching, and provides advice on returning to work and flexible working.

Skills Development Scotland

0808 100 1050
www.myworldofwork.co.uk
Provides information, advice and guidance on careers and learning as well as skills development. Offers services to individuals of any age who may be thinking of furthering their education, changing careers or trying to get a job. There are local Skills Development Scotland centres in Central Edinburgh, Wester Hailes, Musselburgh and Dalkeith.

Pre-School Play & Education

Options and Timeline From 0-5 Years
Toddler Groups
Playgroups
Nurseries
Gaelic Education
Accessible Pre-school Play and Education

Pre-School Play & Education

There are many opportunities for under 5s to meet with others of the same age. Informal groups can provide a welcome break from the home, offering a large range of toys and space to play. This is a great way for you to meet others too. There are also more structured pre-school options.

You can read about some of the options for pre-school play and education in this chapter. This time we haven't included comprehensive information on nurseries – the well-established and popular Edinburgh Nursery and School Guide will provide this for you, as well as a handy checklist of things to consider when looking round nurseries. You can get copies in bookshops and in many supermarkets in Edinburgh. See www.nurseryandschoolguide.co.uk for more information.

OPTIONS AND TIMELINE FROM 0-5 YEARS

After becoming an expert on birthing options, travel systems, cots and weaning, you will now find that you have to acquire a deep knowledge of the education and childcare available for your little one(s)! It can be overwhelming for the busy parent/carer, so we have tried to provide some useful information to help get you started.

BEFORE BIRTH

Nurseries can have long waiting lists! Consider submitting an application for a private nursery if you know you will need childcare upon returning to work.

Visit our website for updates:
www.efuf.co.uk

0-1

Parent and baby groups
These are informal groups that are generally held in health centres or in someone's home. Your health visitor, clinic or NCT can put you in touch with other parents in your area. This is a good way to meet others in a similar situation to yours, and find support and friendship for you and your baby. You'll also be very welcome at **parent and toddler groups**, most of which are open to young babies, see details below.

Private nurseries
Many offer childcare from 3mths and are usually open between 08.00 and 18.00, Mon-Fri, all year, and are therefore useful for parents/carers who work outside the home. Spaces for under 2s can be hard to find, so try and register as soon as possible. Fees will be higher for under 2s, as the staff/child ratio is higher. All private nurseries should be registered with the Care Inspectorate, and are inspected once a year. Nurseries that provide education to pre-schoolers will also have an HMIE (Her Majesty's Inspectorate of Education) report available.

1-2½

Parent and toddler groups
These groups are generally set up by local parents and are held in church halls, community centres, or schools, and cater for babies and toddlers. The parent/carer stays for the session. Some groups separate the babies and the toddlers by age and have specific days for specific age ranges. Facilities and standards

vary, but most have a selection of toys and puzzles, books, crayons and some larger pieces of equipment, such as climbing frames, chutes, play cookers, ball pits, wendy houses, etc. It is best to check personally for atmosphere and safety standards, particularly of outdoor equipment. Prices range from nothing to £5-7+ per term. There is often a small charge for tea, coffee, juice, biscuits and so on. It's not unusual for groups to have a rota for making tea etc, and carers help set up and tidy away the toys.

Nurseries

See above (0-1) for information on private nurseries. If you are planning to send your child to a council nursery, you should submit an application form around the time your child turns 2. On the application form, you will be asked to list, in priority order, up to 3 nursery choices (there are no catchment areas, meaning that you can send your child to any nursery in the city if a place is available). A nursery place will be offered as soon as possible after your child becomes eligible.

2½-5

Important! Beginning at age 3, all children are eligible for a free, part-time place in nursery (term beginning after 3rd birthday).

This is funded by the Scottish Government, up to a total of 475 hours/year, which usually means up to 5 x 2½ hour sessions/week. If claiming a funded part-time place through a Partner Provider Centre, complete a Pupil Information Form from the Centre in the term before your child becomes eligible for funding.

Playgroups

These are voluntary, non-profit-making groups, which provide more structured play/education. They may be open mornings or afternoons, or both. Charges are usually low and parents may be expected to help on a rota basis. Many playgroups operate in partnership with the City of Edinburgh Council (through a "Partner Provider"), meaning that you can receive a refund of all or part of your fees once your child is eligible or that the place may be provided free. All groups that are Partner Providers are

registered and inspected by the Scottish Care Inspectorate and HMIE. Some playgroups require your child to be toilet-trained.

City of Edinburgh Council Nurseries (3 yrs +)
These are nursery schools and nursery classes based in primary schools across the city that are run by the City of Edinburgh Council. All provide free part-time places usually from the term after your child's 3rd birthday – 5 morning or afternoon sessions a week. If you need longer hours, wraparound care or full-day care, you may be able to purchase these at the nursery your child attends.

Private nurseries
If the nursery is a Partner Provider, you will be able to receive a refund of all or part of your fees once your child is eligible.

Independent school nurseries
These are independent schools that have a nursery department. Most offer a morning, afternoon or whole-day placement. Fees are payable. If the nursery is a Partner Provider, you will be able to receive a refund of all or part of your fees once your child is eligible.

4

Register for primary school – usually in mid-November of the year before your child begins school. Look for local advertisements advising of exact registration dates and birthdate eligibility.

4½-5

The entry date for children starting primary school (P1) in Scotland is August. In general, children starting P1 in August must have either celebrated their 5th birthday in the preceding 6 months (from 1 March onwards) or are due to celebrate their 5th birthday in the following 6 months (up to 28 February). You should contact the Council if you have just arrived from England or Wales, where the admission ages differ.

See below for more on toddler groups, pages 304-315 for more on playgroups and pages 316-320 for more on nurseries.

TODDLER GROUPS

PARENTS' PICKS

Baby and toddler groups can be a lifeline – you meet new people and get advice and tips from other parents and carers, and occasionally you finish a cup of tea while it's still warm! However, it can be nerve-wracking just turning up to a group when you don't know what to expect, particularly if you're a very new parent. Listings (in tables, later) give you basic information but there's nothing like word of mouth to give you an idea of what a group is like, so read on – we hope it will encourage you to try a new group soon!

Little Leithers
Thursday, 10.30-12.00, FREE

Destiny Church, 12 Castlebank Street
EH6 5HA
0131 555 2707
www.destinyedinburgh.com
A group for carers with children under 12 mths. It provides a huge choice of toys suitable from birth and includes a sing-song at the end. My 8 mth old loved playing with her friends and different toys. The coffee and cake was a real treat, and it was great to enjoy a hot drink and chat with new mums. A great place to escape the house and make lots of new mummy friends! Best bit for me – being able to have a hot cup of coffee without it going cold! Best bit for my daughter – singing songs! The group is in a church but if you are not religious, don't be put off! They do not promote Christianity in the group. It is very much just about playing and meeting other mums. This group is FREE but donations are welcomed. Runs term-time only.

Parking: Limited, on-street. *Accessibility:* Step into hall. *Nappy changing:* FREE emergency nappies and wipes! *Eating:* FREE cakes, biscuits, coffee, tea and juice provided.

St Mary's Episcopal Toddler Group, Friday, 10.00-11.30, £1

Walpole Hall, Chester Street (between Manor Place and Palmerston Place), EH3 7RA
0131 225 6293
office@cathedral.net
www.cathedral.net
The strength of this playgroup is the size of its venue: Walpole Hall is a lovely (and long) old church hall, completed in 1933, and in great condition. Run by Alison Howard, this group is ideal if you have an energetic youngster who likes to run around! There are lots of toys for play, the group are friendly and inviting, and the atmosphere is relaxed and enjoyable. The end of the session is capped by a brief sing-song, and an enthusiastic run around the hall. Also, this is one of the only groups to run every Fri, even during holiday times. £1 entry.

Parking: Street parking, pay and display. *Pushchairs:* Steps into hall, lots of room inside for pushchairs. *Toilets/Nappy changing:* Available on request. *Eating:* Hot drinks provided for adults, snacks brought along on rotational basis by regulars.

St Paul's & St George's Church Babies & Toddlers Group
Thursday, 10.00-11.30 and 14.00-15.30, £2

10 Broughton Street, EH1 3RH
0131 556 1335
office@pandgchurch.org.uk
www.pandgchurch.org.uk
This is possibly the most professionally run playgroup in the city. The church has had an overhaul and its facilities are impeccable. The play area is superbly organised and divided by age groups. There is a separate area in the large hall for food and drink (snacks and juice are provided for the wee ones whilst biscuits and hot drinks are laid on for the adults). The on-

duty staff are fantastic, friendly and helpful. The end-of-session sing-song is incredible; taken by Maria, she is a force of nature who grips adults and little ones alike with her enthusiastic leadership. Highly recommended, but do phone before you go – highly popular too! Cost: £2.

Parking: Street parking, pay and display.

Palmerston Place Church Baby & Toddler Playgroup
Monday, 10.00-11.30, £1

Annan House, 10 Palmerston Place (left of church), EH12 5AA
0131 220 1690
www.palmerstonplacechurch.com
This is an excellent, friendly playgroup. Your host is Ruth Sinclair, wife of the church's minister, Colin. The group is very relaxed and welcoming and, whilst not the biggest of venues, it is surprisingly spacious. There are boxes of toys, mats, a couple of slides, plus a changing area; enough to cater for the very tiny baby or the growing toddler. Tea and coffee are served along with juice, water and biscuits, in an allocated area. The group ends with an enjoyable sing-song led by Ruth. Highly recommended. £1 entry.

*Parking: Street parking. **Accessibility:** Ramp with secure entry.*

PEEP Baby & Toddler Group,
Monday 13.30-14.30, FREE

Duncan Place Resource Centre
4 Duncan Place, EH6 8HW
0131 555 2707
A fantastic group for carers and babies! It provides an opportunity for playing and interacting with other babies (to 12 mths) and a place to meet other carers. It is free and the

selection of toys and resources is varied and provides stimulation for your baby. Baby snacks, tea, coffee and biscuits are provided after class. My little girl loved the messy play and story telling the best! I enjoyed seeing her painting and experiencing the sensation and texture for the first time – and I enjoyed the biscuits too! Term-time only.

Q&A

We asked Ruth Sinclair...

Are you a parent? *We have 4 "children", now ranging in age from 15-27! We now have a 7-month-old grandson, so have moved seamlessly from children to grandchildren without a break!*

Your group: *Palmerston Place Church Baby & Toddler Group.*

Tell us about it: *Large carpeted room in our suite of halls. Free play and conversation with refreshments available. Tidy up at 11.10, then sing-song often with piano. Birth to 3-4. Capacity of 25.*

How long has your group been running? *Approx 11 years*

Were you involved in the creation of the group? *Yes – we wanted to offer an "open door" welcome to the community – a safe place in a Christian environment.*

How long have you lived in Edinburgh? *15 years.*

Any memorable experiences of Edinburgh as a parent? *Feeding squirrels in Botanic Gardens, "mystery walks" round Blackford Hill, with picnic.*

Recommendations: *Tumble Tots was a great success with our youngest, who was our only "baby" in Edinburgh.*

Toddler Groups
Do phone ahead to check days and times as these details can change.

Name	Address	Phone Number (0131 +)	Contact Details/ Web Address
CENTRAL EDINBURGH			
The Acorn Club	Inverleith Church, Ferry Road EH3 5PR	476 2067	Kath Drainer
Croileagan (Gaelic Parent and Toddler Playgroup)	Tollcross Community Centre, Tollcross Primary School, 117 Fountainbridge EH3 9QG	529 2415	Norma Martin, norma.martin@ edinburgh.gov.uk
Inverleith Church Toddler Group	Inverleith Church, Ferry Road EH3 5PR	552 7615	Ann Tracy
King's Tots	The Kings Centre, 11 Gayfield Street EH1 3NR	629 6119 (church office)	www. kingschurchedinburgh. org
St Mary's Episcopal Toddler Group (Walpole Hall)	Chester Street (between Manor Place and Palmerston Place) EH3 7RA	225 6293	office@cathedral.net, www.cathedral.net
Stockbridge International Playgroup	St Stephen's Centre, St Stephen's Street, Nr Howe Street EH3 5AB		
St Paul's & St George's Church – Babies & Toddlers Group	10 Broughton Street, EH1 3RH	556 1335	office@pandgchurch. org.uk, www.pandgchurch. org.uk

Day(s)	Time	Drop in?	Cost	Rota	Age Group	Other Information
Mon	09.15-12.00	Yes	£2/family	Yes	0-5	Term time only. Tea, coffee, snack. Craft-based.
Wed/ Fri	09.15-11.00	Yes		No	0-5	The group is open to any to join. Gaelic speaking play leader in place for language input. See also Corstorphine and Leith groups.
Wed	10.00-12.00	Yes	Small charge	Yes	0-3	Tea, coffee, home-baking. Snack for children.
Tues	10.00-12.00	No	50p/family/ week	No	Babies-pre-school	Term-time only. Waiting list – please contact before visiting.
Fri	10.00-11.30		£1 entry			Hot drinks provided for adults, snacks brought along on rotational basis by regulars. Sing-song at the end. Runs during holidays. See p 284 for more.
Mon/Fri	10.00-12.00	Yes	£2.50/ family/ session	Yes, casual	0-4	Large play area with quieter areas for babies. Lots of toys, activities and books.
Thurs	10.00-11.30, 14.00-15.30		£2		Baby to todder	Snacks and juice for wee ones, biscuits and hot drinks for the adults. End-of-session sing-song. See p 284 for more.

Name	Address	Phone Number (0131 +)	Contact Details/ Web Address

NORTH EDINBURGH

Name	Address	Phone Number (0131 +)	Contact Details/ Web Address
Blackhall Mother and Toddler Group	St Columba's Church, Columba Road EH4 3QU	332 4431	Su Lawrence, blackhalltoddlers@ yahoo.co.uk
Comely Bank Toddlers	St Stephen's Comely Bank Church, 10 Comely Bank Rd EH4 1DW	Mobile 07785 386782	Emma Scott Bell, comelybanktoddlers@ yahoo.co.uk
Croileagan Gaelic Medium Parent & Toddler Group (Leith)	Leith Community Centre, 12a Newkirkgate EH6 6AD	529 2415	Norma Martin, norma.martin@ edinburgh.gov.uk
Davidson's Mains Parish Church Toddler Group	1 Quality Street EH4 5BB	476 3519, 312 6282 (church office)	Moira Harvey, dmainstoddlers@ btinternet.com
Dean Church Parent and Toddler Group	Dean Church, 65-67 Dean Path EH4 3AT	225 5998	Jill Murray, jill.murray@gmail.com
Dean Tots	Dean Church, 65-67 Dean Path EH4 3AT		

Day(s)	Time	Drop in?	Cost	Rota	Age Group	Other Information
Tues	09.30-11.30	No	£15/term	Yes	0-3	Tea, coffee. Snack for children.
Thurs	09.30-11.30	Yes	£2.50/visit plus 50p for additional children or £1.50/visit plus £5 hall hire fee if joining for a term.	Yes, organised on the day.	From newborns to pre-school age	One room for under 2s, one for over 2s. Tea, coffee, cakes for adults and healthy snacks/ juice for children. Drama session once a month and arts and crafts session weekly. Group has been running over 30 years.
Mon	09.30-11.30	Yes	FREE		0-5	
Thurs	09.30-11.30	No	£15/term	Yes	0-4	Lots of toys and activities. Snack is provided for children and coffee and biscuits for grown-ups on a rota system. Please bring a cup/ beaker for your child.
Mon	09.30-11.30	Yes	£2/week for 1 child. £3/ week for 2 or more children	Yes, organised on the day	3 mths-4 yrs	Snacks and drinks for children and adults.
Thurs	09.30-11.30	No	£1 for child up to 1 yr. £4 for over 1 yr. £6 for 2 children	No, but help tidy at end	0-4	Playleader sets up toys, snacks and leads singing.

Name	Address	Phone Number (0131 +)	Contact Details/ Web Address
Early Years Centre (Muirhouse)	Craigroyston Community Centre 1a Pennywell Road EH4 4QP	332 3855	Diane Hope
Edinburgh Twins Club Bumps & Babies/Toddler Group	St Stephen's Comely Bank Church, 10 Comely Bank Road EH4 1DW		www.edinburghtwins. co.uk
Forthview Primary School	West Pilton Place EH4 4DF	332 2468	Tracey Berry
Holy Cross Mother & Toddler Group	Holy Cross Church Hall, Quality Street, Davidson's Mains EH4 5BP	336 2311	Laurie Hawksey
Holyrood Abbey Church of Scotland Baby and Toddler Group	Marionville Road, on corner with London Road EH7 5TT	661 4230	Ann McTaggart
Little Leithers	Destiny Church, 12 Castlebank Street EH6 5HA	555 2707	www.destinyedinburgh. com
Parent and Toddler Group, North Leith Parish Church	Madeira Street, Leith EH6 4AW	554 4980	Eileen Doig
Parent & Toddler Group, Cramond	Cramond Kirk Hall, Cramond Glebe Road EH4 6NS	336 2036, mobile 07594 566083 (Joanne)	Joanne Parkins
Parkgrove Parent & Toddler Group	The Munro Centre, 6 Parkgrove Street EH4 7NT	539 7179	

Day(s)	Time	Drop in?	Cost	Rota	Age Group	Other Information
						Phone to check days and times available.
Mon	10.00-11.30		£2/family/session			Only for parents or carers with twins or more.
Thurs	09.00-12.00	Yes	FREE	No	0-4	Term time only, run by a homelink teacher. Coffee/tea. Snack for children.
Mon	09.30-11.30	Yes	£1		0-4	Coffee/tea for carers.
Mon	10.00-11.30	Yes	60p/family	No	0-3	Fruit and biscuits for children. Coffee/tea and biscuits for adults. Waiting list.
Thurs	10.30-12.00		FREE though you can provide a donation.		0-12 mths	Term-time only. Coffee and cake and singing songs.
Mon/Thurs	09.30-11.30	Yes	£5/quarter	No	0-4	Term time only. Snacks and drinks for children included, adult snacks and drinks can be purchased.
Tues	10.00-12.00	Yes	£2/family	No	0-4	Singalong and crafts.
Thurs	09.15-11.30	Yes	£2	No	0-4	

Name	Address	Phone Number (0131 +)	Contact Details/ Web Address
PEEP Baby and Toddler Group	Duncan Place Resource Centre, 4 Duncan Place EH6 8HW	555 2707	www.destinyedinburgh.com
Pilmeny Group	Pilmeny Youth Centre, 44 Buchanan Street EH6 8RF	554 0953	dlmh@live.co.uk
Ripple Project Parent and Toddler Group	McLaren Halls, Restalrig Road South EH7 6LE	554 7400	
South Leith Parent Toddler Group	South Leith Church Halls, Henderson Street EH6	Mobile 07538 325288 (Eve), 07985 219527 (Nicola)	Eve and Nicola, eve.anna@blueyonder.co.uk
South Queensferry Under Fives Childminders' Group	South Queensferry Community Centre, Kirkliston Road, South Queensferry EH30 9NZ	331 2113	Community Centre Office
South Queensferry Under Fives Mother and Toddler Group	See above	See above	See above
St Andy's Teeny Tots	St Andrews Church Hall, 410 Easter Road EH6 8NT	553 8839	standysteenytots@gmail.com
Toddler Group, St Christopher's Church	Craigentinny Road EH7 6RL		
Toddler Group – Craigentinny Primary School	Craigentinny Primary School, Loganlea Drive EH7 6LR	661 3109	
Trinity Toddler Group	Holy Cross Primary School, School Buildings, Craighall Road EH6 4RE	551 1046	Anne Tyson, http://trinitytoddlers.co.uk/index.html

Day(s)	Time	Drop in?	Cost	Rota	Age Group	Other Information
Mon	13.30-14.30		FREE		0-12 mths	Term-time only. Messy play and storytelling. Baby snacks, tea, coffee and biscuits. See p 285 for more.
Tues/ Thurs	09.30-11.30	No	£1/child	No	0-3	
Tues	09.30-11.15	Yes	£1			Tea, coffee, snacks, juice.
Tues	09.30-11.30	No	£1	No	0-4	Waiting list, please phone.
Thurs	09.30-11.30	Yes	Yes	No	0-4	
Mon/ Wed	09.30-11.30	No	Donation	No	0-4	
Wed	13.30-15.30	No	£1	No	0-3	Waiting list. Pop in or email for details.
Thurs	09.30-11.30	Yes	£1.50	No	0-3	
Tues	12.30-14.15		Small contribution for snacks		0-3	
Mon-Fri	10.00-12.00	No	£1/session plus £5/ quarter	Yes	0-4	Coffee and tea. Snack for children.

Name	Address	Phone Number (0131 +)	Contact Details/ Web Address
EAST EDINBURGH			
Braidwood Tots	Braidwood Centre, 69 Dumbiedykes Road EH8 9UT		
Greengables Toddler Group	8a Niddrie House Gardens EH16 4UF	669 9083	Jane Watson
Inch Community Centre Play Plus Toy Library	225 Gilmerton Road EH16 5UF	664 4710	
Liberton Kirk Baby and Toddler Group	5A Kirk Gate EH16 6RY	664 8264	
Niddrie Baby and Toddler Group	Niddrie Community Church, 12 Hay Drive EH16 4RY	669 9400	Lizzie Aylett
Northfield and Willowbrae Toddler Group	Northfield and Willowbrae Community Centre, 10 Northfield Road, Northfield EH8 7PP	661 5723	
Parent and Toddler Group, Magdalene Community Centre	Brunstane Primary School, Magdalene Drive EH15 3BE	669 8760	Rab Hogg
Prestonfield Toddlers	Cameron House Community Education Centre, 34 Prestonfield Avenue EH16 5EA	667 3762	Susan Ferguson

Day(s)	Time	Drop in?	Cost	Rota	Age Group	Other Information
Thurs/ Fri	Thurs 13.00-15.00, Fri 10.00-12.00		80p		0-5	Snacks for children and adults, free play and songtime.
Tues/ Thurs	Tues 12.45-14.15, Thurs 10.30-12.00	Yes	FREE	No	0-3	Term time only.
Tues	09.00-12.00	Yes	FREE		0-3+	
Tues	13.30-15.00		£2		0-5	
Mon	10.00-11.30	Yes	Yes	No	0-4	
Mon/ Wed/ Fri	09.45-11.30	Yes	£1.50	No	0-3	
Wed/ Fri	10.00-12.00					
Wed/Fri	10.00-12.30	No	50p			Centre membership required.

Name	Address	Phone Number (0131 +)	Contact Details/ Web Address
St Martin's Church Parent and Toddler Group	St Martin's Church, Magdalene Drive EH15 3DB		
St Peter's 0-5s	St Peter's Church, Lutton Place EH8 9PE	667 6224	
St Philip's Church	Brunstane Road North EH15		
Toddler Group – Brunstane Primary School	Brunstane Primary School, 106 Magdalene Drive EH15 3BE	661 3109	
Toddler Group – Parson's Green Primary School	Parson's Green Primary School, Meadowfield Drive EH8 7LU	661 3109	
Valley Park Community Centre	37 Southhouse Road EH17 8EU	664 2210	

SOUTH EDINBURGH

Name	Address	Phone Number	Contact Details
Barclay Viewforth Church Toddlers	Barclay Viewforth Church Hall 1 Wright's Houses Bruntsfield EH10 4HR	229 6810	Katherine Ellis
Blackford Toddler Group	Reid Memorial Church, West Saville Terrace, Blackford EH9 3HY	662 1203	
Fairmilehead Toddler Group	Fairmilehead Parish Church, Frogston Hall, 1a Frogston Road EH10 7AA	Mobile 07810 718163	Rona Welsh, fairmileheadtoddlers@googlemail.com, www.fhpc.org.uk
Marchmont Mum & Toddler Group	Marchmont St Giles Church, 1A Kilgraston Road EH9 1TZ	447 4359	www.marchmontstgiles.org.uk
Morningside Parish Church Baby and Toddler Group	Morningside Parish Church Hall, Cluny Gardens EH10 6DN	447 6745	www.morningsideparishchurch.org.uk/
Next Step Parent & Toddler Group	Edinburgh Steiner School, 60 Spylaw Road EH10 5BR	337 3410	

Day(s)	Time	Drop in?	Cost	Rota	Age Group	Other Information
Thurs	10.00-11.15					
Mon/ Thurs	09.30-11.00	Yes	80p		0-4	Well established group. Small charge for refreshments.
Fri	10.00-11.30					
Thurs	13.00-14.45		Small contribution for snacks		0-3	
Wed/ Fri	09.30-11.15	Yes	Small contribution for snacks		0-3	
Tues/ Thurs	am		FREE		0-3	Phone to check times and waiting list.

Day(s)	Time	Drop in?	Cost	Rota	Age Group	Other Information
Tues	10.00-12.00	Yes	50p	No	0-4	Coffee and tea. Snack for children.
Wed	10.00-11.30					Snack and drinks for sale at nominal cost.
Mon/ Tues/ Thurs/ Fri	10.00-11.30				0-5	
Thurs	10.00-12.00	Yes	50p		0-4	
Mon/ Wed	10:00 – 11:30	Yes			0-3	
Mon-Fri	10.15-12.30		£5		0-4	

Name	Address	Phone Number (0131 +)	Contact Details/ Web Address
The Old Schoolhouse	140 Morningside Road EH10 4PX	447 7833	
St Catherine's Argyle Church	61 Grange Road EH9 1TY	667 7220	www.stcatherines-argyle.org.uk

WEST EDINBURGH

Name	Address	Phone Number (0131 +)	Contact Details/ Web Address
Balerno Toddlers	Balerno Parish Church Hall, Johnsburn Road, Balerno EH14 7DN	Mobile 07866 362780	Kate Gibb, katejag@aol.com
Broomhouse Mother and Toddler Group	St David's Church, Broomhouse Crescent EH11 3RH	443 1207	Call Slateford Green Community Centre for details
Carrick Knowe Parent & Toddler Group	Carrick Knowe Church Hall, 118-132 Saughton Road North EH12 7DR	334 1505	
Carrickvale Parent and Toddler Group	Carrickvale Community Education Centre, 2 Saughton Mains Street EH11 3HH	443 6971	
Colinton Toddler Group	St Cuthbert's Church Hall, 6 Westgarth Avenue EH13 0BD	Mobile 07730 102327	Ally
Craiglockhart Mother & Toddler Group	Craiglockhart Church Hall, Craiglockhart Drive North EH14 1HS	444 0852	Rachel Carlyle
Craigmount Tots	Craigmount Community Wing, Craigs Road EH12 8DH	339 8278	

Day(s)	Time	Drop in?	Cost	Rota	Age Group	Other Information
Thurs	09.30-11.30		£2		0-4	
Tues	10.00-12.00	Yes	50p		0-5	
Thurs	09.45-11.30	Yes	£1/session and £4/term	Yes	0-5	Term time only. Coffee and tea. Snack for children.
Tues	09.00-11.00	Yes	Donation	No	0-3	
Thurs/ Fri	10.00-11.30	Yes	Donation	No	0-4	Runs during school holiday.
Mon/ Tues/ Thurs/ Fri	09.30-11.00	Yes	Donation	No	0-4	
Mon	09.15-11.15	Yes	£2.50/ session or £1.50/ session if paid/term in advance	No	0-5	
Mon	10.00-11.45	Yes	£2/session (snack included)	Yes	0-4	All welcome.
Mon/ Wed/ Fri	Mon 14.00-16.00, Wed/Fri 09.30-12.00	Yes	£1	Yes	0-5	

Name	Address	Phone Number (0131 +)	Contact Details/ Web Address
Croileagan Gaelic Medium Parent and Toddler Group	Corstorphine Youth and Community Centre, 14 Kirk Loan EH12 7HD	529 2415	Norma Martin, norma.martin@ edinburgh.gov.uk
Dads Rock	Gate 55, 55 Sighthill Rd EH11 4PB	Mobile 07511 533 432 (David), 07813 461 571 (Thomas)	Twitter (@ DadsRockEdin) and Facebook (Dads Rock)
East Craigs Mother & Toddler Group	East Craigs Church Centre, 2 Bughtlin Market EH12 8XP	339 8336	Katie Petrie, petrie37@ btinternet.com
Edinburgh Twins Club Bumps & Babies/Toddler Group	Oxgangs Neighbourhood Centre, 71 Firrhill Drive (off Oxgangs Crescent) EH13 9EU	441 7558	
Gorgie Salvation Army Toddler Group	431 Gorgie Road EH11 2RT	346 2753	Mrs Barber, Children's Development Officer
Gorgie Tots	Destiny Church, 52 Gorgie Road EH11 2NB	555 2707	Destiny Church Leith
Happy Faces Toddler Group	Colinton Parish Church, Dell Road, Colinton EH13 0JR	441 9055	Nichola Pearce
Jack and Jill Mother and Toddler Club	St Anne's Church Hall, Kaimes Road EH12 6JT	334 2039	Frances Tennant
Kirkliston Project Parent and Toddler Group	Kirkliston Community Centre, 16-18 Queensferry Road EH29 9AQ	333 4214	Community Centre Office
Mem Drop-In Toddler Group	Gorgie Memorial Hall, 338 Gorgie Road EH11 2QU	337 9098	

Day(s)	Time	Drop in?	Cost	Rota	Age Group	Other Information
Mon	09.30-11.30	Yes		No	0-5	The group is open to any to join. Gaelic speaking play leader for language input. See also Tollcross and Leith groups.
Sat	10.00-11.30	Yes	FREE	No	0-5	Scotland's only father and child play/music group. Visits from art clubs and museums, free healthy snack. See p 24 for more.
Tues/ Thurs	09.30-11.30	Yes	Yes	No	0-4	Open during school holidays and term time.
Thurs	10.00-12.00		£2		0-4	Only for families or carers with twins or more.
Tues	09.30-11.00	Yes	£1	No	0-4	
Thurs	10.30-12.00	Yes	Donation	No	0-3	
Tues	09.30-11.30	Yes	£1	Yes	0-4	Coffee and tea.
Wed	09.30-11.30	No	Yes	Yes	0-4	
Mon/ Wed	09.00-11.30	Yes	Donation	No	0-4	
Mon-Fri	Mon-Fri 09.30-12.15, Wed/ Thurs 12.30-15.00	Yes	£1	No	0-4	

Name	Address	Phone Number (0131 +)	Contact Details/ Web Address
Messy Monsters	Dreghorn Barracks, Caledonian Community Centre, Redford Road EH13 9QW	310 2730	Community Development Workers
Murrayfield Parish Church Baby & Toddler Group	Ormidale Terrace EH12 6EQ	346 4166	Beverley Kerr/Clare Berroya
Oxgangs Brae Toddlers	Oxgangs Neighbourhood Centre, 71 Firrhill Drive (off Oxgangs Crescent) EH13 9EU	441 7558	Elizabeth Brash
Palmerston Place Church Baby & Toddler Playgroup	Annan House, 10 Palmerston Place (left of church) EH12 5AA	220 1690	www. palmerstonplacechurch. com
Polwarth Parent, Baby and Toddler Group	Polwarth Parish Church, 36-38 Polwarth Terrace EH11 1LU	346 2711	www. polwarthtoddlergroup. org.uk
Ratho Under Threes Group	Ratho Community Centre, 1 School Wynd, Ratho EH28 8TT	333 1055	
Slateford Green Community Centre	1-5 Gorgie Park Close EH14 1NQ	443 1207	
St Bride's Centre Toddler Group	10 Orwell Terrace EH11 2DZ	346 1405	
St Mungo's Minis	St Mungo's Church, St Mungo's Ministry Centre, 46B Bavelaw Road, Balerno EH14 7AE	449 9903	Kate Yates
St Nicholas Toddler Group	St Nicholas Church, 122 Sighthill Loan EH11 4NT	Mobile 07954 407309	Shelley Illingworth, shelley.23@hotmail. co.uk
St Ninian's Church Baby & Toddler Group	St Ninian's Church, St Ninian's Road EH12 8AY	334 7301	
St Thomas Church Toddler Group	Gyle Hall, 79 Glasgow Road EH12 8LJ	316 4292	

Day(s)	Time	Drop in?	Cost	Rota	Age Group	Other Information
Wed	10.00-12.00		£1		16 mths-4 yrs	Go to barracks and ask the guard for the community centre.
Fri	10.30-12.00	Yes	£1/session	No	0-3	Coffee and tea.
Tues	10.00-12.00				0-4	
Mon	10.00-11.30		£1 entry		0-3	Tea and coffee, juice, water and biscuits. The group ends with a sing-song. See p 285 for more.
Tues/Thurs	Tues 10.00-12.00, Thurs 14.30-16.30	Yes	£2	Yes	0-4	Term time only.
Tues/Thurs	10.00-12.00	Yes	50p for members, £1 for others	No	0-3	
Wed	09.30-11.30	Yes	Donation	No	0-3	
Fri	09.30-11.30	Yes	FREE	No	0-4	
Tues/Wed	10.00-11.30	Yes	50p	No	0-4	Coffee and tea. Snack for children.
Tues/Fri	09.30-11.30	Yes	Small charge	No	0-5	Run voluntarily by local child minder.
Tues/Fri	10.00-11.30	Yes	£5/term	Yes	0-3	
Tues	10.00-11.30	Yes	FREE	Yes	0-3	

Name	Address	Phone Number (0131 +)	Contact Details/ Web Address
Stableroom Toddler Group	Colinton Parish Church Hall, Dell Road EH13 0JR	441 3313	Fi
Stableroom Tuesday Toddler Group	See above	441 9853	Marylyn Osbourne

MIDLOTHIAN

Name	Address	Phone Number (0131 +)	Contact Details/ Web Address
Loanhead Parents 'n' Tots	The Cabin, 5 Mayburn Walk EH20 9HG	440 2541	Paula Jackson, www. lclc.org.uk/activities. htm

PLAYGROUPS

PLAYGROUP INFORMATION

Scottish Pre-School Play Association (SPPA)

0141 221 4148
www.sppa.org.uk
At time of publication, there is no Lothian/East of Scotland office. For Edinburgh and West Lothian help and advice, you can contact the above number, Mon-Fri 09.30-16.00.

Playgroups

Name	Address	Phone Number (0131 +)	Contact Details/ Web Address
CENTRAL EDINBURGH			
Edzell Nursery Ltd	St James Scottish Episcopal Church, 57b Inverleith Row EH3 5PX	Mobile 07909 672377	Penny Short, edzellnursery@gmail. com

Day(s)	Time	Drop in?	Cost	Rota	Age Group	Other Information
Thurs	09.30-11.15	No	£20/term in advance	No	0-3	Coffee and tea. Snack for children.
Tues	14.00-15.30	Yes	£20/term in advance	No	0-3	Coffee and tea. Snack for children.
Mon/ Wed/ Fri	09.30-11.30	Yes	£1		0-4	Term time only.

The list of playgroups below is as comprehensive as possible. Listings are not recommendations – we encourage you to make contact and see if the group fits your child's needs. All the details were correct at the time of checking. However, details do change, so please let us know if you come across any information that needs updating for the next edition. And if you come across any playgroups that aren't listed below, please tell us – we haven't left any out intentionally!

Day(s)	Time	Cost	Age Group	Other Information
Mon-Fri part time; term times	09.00-11.50	£170/term; £105/ term part-time (3 mornings)	2½-5½	

Name	Address	Phone Number (0131 +)	Contact Details/ Web Address
Nari Kallyan Shangho Project	Darroch Avenue, 7 Gillespie Street EH3 9NH	221 1915	nks@nkshealth.co.uk, www.nkshealth.co.uk

NORTH EDINBURGH

Name	Address	Phone Number (0131 +)	Contact Details/ Web Address
Blackhall Nursery	Ravelston Park Pavilion, Ravelston Park, Craigcrook Road EH4 3RU	332 8296	admin@ blackhallnursery.co.uk, www.blackhallnursery.co.uk
Blackhall Playgroup	St Columba's Parish Church, Columba Rd EH4 3QU	332 4431	www.blackhallstcolumba.org.uk
Craigentinny/Lochend Playgroup	Craigentinny Community Centre, 15 Loaning Rd, Restalrig EH7 6JE	661 8188	Paula Grieve
Cramond Playgroup	Cramond Kirk Hall, Cramond Glebe Road EH4 6NS	07913 819 085	cramond.playgroup@ hotmail.co.uk
EPNS Funtime Playgroup	Royston/Wardieburn Community Centre, Pilton Dr North EH5 1NF	552 5700	Elma Guthrie, elma@ blueyonder.co.uk, www.ep-ns.co.uk
Leith St Andrew's Playgroup	St Andrew's Church, 410-412 Easter Road, Leith EH6 8HT	07792 493359	Christine Anderson, www.leithstandrews.org
Prentice Centre Playgroup	West Granton Community Trust, The Prentice Centre, 1 Granton Mains Ave, Pilton EH4 4GA	552 0485	Janet Campbell, prenticecentre@ hotmail.com

Day(s)	Time	Cost	Age Group	Other Information
Mon-Fri	08.30-12.45, 12.45-16.45	Under 2: full day £21.25, full week £106.25, half day £11.25. Over 2: full day £14, full week £60, half day £8. 30p/day for snack	0-5	
Mon-Fri	08.55-11.30, 12.10-14.45	FREE – weekly donation of £1.50 towards food etc.	3-5	28 children max.
Mon-Thurs	Mon/ Wed/Thur 09.30-12.00, Tue 12.00-14.30		2½-5	
Mon-Fri	09.15-11.30	£25/week, £6/ session	2½-5	
Mon-Fri	09.05-11.55	£9/session, £3/ month snack	2-5	
Mon-Fri	09.15-11.45	£12.50/week	2½-5	Term time only.
Mon-Fri, min 2 days/wk	09.30-11.30	£6 – morning snack included	2-5	
Mon-Thurs (crèche available Fri)	09.30-11.30, 12.30-14.30	£1	2-5	9 children max.

Name	Address	Phone Number (0131 +)	Contact Details/ Web Address
Reindeer Playgroup	Holy Cross Church Hall, Quality St EH4 5BP	07906 518747	Ruth McKenzie
St Mary's Playgroup	St Mary's Primary School, 63 East London St, Murrayfield EH7 4BW	556 1634	Gail Dempster
Tom Thumb Nursery	The Vennell Hall, Smithsland, South Queensferry EH30 9HU	331 4273	Debbie Urqahart, www.tomthumb-nursery.co.uk
Trinity Nursery	Wardie Church, Primrose Bank Rd EH5 3JE	551 3847, mobile 07576 334935	Pam Johnston, pam.johnston@blueyonder.co.uk
Wardie Nursery	Wardie Residents Club, 125 Granton Road EH5 3NJ	552 2446	Suzanne, wardienursery@googlemail.com

EAST EDINBURGH

Name	Address	Phone Number (0131 +)	Contact Details/ Web Address
EPNS Gilmerton Project Playgroup	Gilmerton Community Centre, 4 Drum St, Gilmerton EH17 8QG	664 2335	Elma Guthrie, elma@blueyonder.co.uk
Northfield/Willowbrae Nursery Playgroup	Northfield & Willowbrae Community Centre, 10 Northfield Road, Northfield EH8 7PP	661 5723	Mrs Jill O'Malley, jill.om@btinternet.com
Portobello Toddlers Hut Playgroup	28 Beach Lane, Portobello EH15 1HU	669 6849	Ms Karen Wilson/Ms Catherine Abbot
St James' Playgroup	Parish Church Hall, Rosefield Place, Portobello EH15	07807 602329	Emma Milton

SOUTH EDINBURGH

Name	Address	Phone Number (0131 +)	Contact Details/ Web Address
Bruntsfield Community Nursery	Montpelier EH10 4NA	228 1526	nursery@bruntsfieldnursery.co.uk, www.bruntsfieldnursery.co.uk

Day(s)	Time	Cost	Age Group	Other Information
Tues-Fri	09.15-11.45	£8/morning	2½-5	
Mon-Fri	09.00-12.00	£6 day – yoga included	2½-5	
Mon-Fri	09.00-11.30 (pre-school), 12.15-14.45 (playgroup)	Morning – funded; afternoon – £5.20 for playgroup	2 yrs 3 mths-5 yrs	
Mon-Fri	9.00-12.00	£12.50/morning	2½-5	Partner provider.
Mon-Fri	09.00-11.00	£1.30 top up	2½-5	
Mon-Fri	09.00-11.30	£17.50	2½-5	
Mon-Fri	09.15-11.45	Funded places for over 3s; under 3s £30/week plus £2 snack	2 yrs 8 mths-5 yrs	24 children max.
Mon/Tues/ Thurs/ Fri	Mon/Fri 09.00-11.30, Tues/ Thurs 13.00-15.30	£6 per session	2½-5	Waiting list.
Mon/Tues/ Thurs/ Fri	09.00-12.10	£30/week	2½-5	21 children max.
Mon-Fri	Mon-Thurs 09.00-11.45, Fri 09.00-11.30	Funded places; extra for snack/art fund	3-5	

Name	Address	Phone Number (0131 +)	Contact Details/ Web Address
Duncan Street Pre-School Playgroup	Baptish Church Hall, 13 Duncan Street EH9 1SR	667 8097 (10.00-17.00)	duncanstreetplaygroup @googlemail.co.uk, www.duncanstreet.co.uk
Greenbank Pre-School	Greenbank Church, Braidburn Terrace EH10 6ES	447 8068	Mrs Kate Humphrey, greenbankpreschool@ gmail.com, www. greenbankpreschool. org
Holy Corner Community Playgroup	Christ Church Hall, 6A Morningside Rd EH10 4DD	228 2768	Alison Kirkwood
Marchmont Playgroup	Marchmont St Giles Parish Church, 1a Kilgraston Road EH9 2DW	Mobile 07504 035420	Mrs Donna Cunningham, marchmontstgilespg@ gmail.com, www. marchmontstgiles. org.uk
Mayfield Salisbury Playgroup	Mayfield Salisbury Church, 1 Mayfield Road EH9 2NG	667 1522, mobile 07753 163168	Freda Mitchell, www. mayfieldsalisbury.org
Nile Grove Community Playgroup	Greenbank Church, Braidburn Terrace EH10 6ES	Mobile 07505 366580	Vanessa Charlton, nilegroveplaygroup@ gmail.co.uk, www. nilegroveplaygroup. co.uk
St Fillan's Playgroup	8 Buckstone Drive EH10 6PD	Mobile 07790 067927	Mary Wong, fun@ stfillansplaygroup. org.uk, www. stfillansplaygroup. org.uk

Day(s)	Time	Cost	Age Group	Other Information
Mon-Fri	09.00-11.45	Funded. Snacks 30p/day	3-5	
Mon-Fri	09.00-11.35, 12.35-15.10	£2 per week towards snacks	3-5	30 children max.
Mon-Fri	09.10-11.45	£7; funded places	2½-5	2-5 mornings a week. Term-time only.
Tues-Thurs	09.30-12.00	£21/week	2 yrs 3 mths-4 yrs	
Mon-Fri	09.10-11.40	£6/session	2-5	
Mon-Fri	09.15-11.45	£8/session plus £8/term for maintenance and £5/term for snacks	2 yrs 3 mths-5 yrs	Places available at time of writing.
Mon-Thurs	09.15-11.45	£7.50/session, deposit required	2-5	Waiting list.

Name	Address	Phone Number (0131 +)	Contact Details/ Web Address
WEST EDINBURGH			
Balgreen Playgroup	Balgreen Bowling Club, Pansy Walk, Balgreen Road EH11 3AT	313 5097, mobile 07972 352591	Kelly Thacker, balgreenplaygroup edinburgh@gmail.com, www.balgreenplaygroup. wordpress.com
Compass Playgroup	Deanpark Primary Pre-School Centre, 1 Main St, Balerno EH14 7EQ	449 4530	
Corstorphine Village Playgroup	Corstorphine Old Parish Church Hall, High Street EH12 7ST	Mobile 07707 695426	www.corstorphinevillage playgroup.co.uk
Craigsbank Church Playgroup (A)	Craigsbank Church, Craigs Bank EH12 8HD	334 1190	Liz Walls
Craigsbank Church Playgroup (B)	East Craigs Church Centre, Bughtlin Market, East Craigs EH12 8XP	339 8336, mobile 07770 364912	Siobhan Schulberg
Currie Playgroup	Currie Baptist Church Hall, 16 Kirkgate, Currie EH14 6AN	449 2016	Amanda Gillespie, info@currieplaygroup. co.uk, www. currieplaygroup.co.uk
Dreghorn Pre-School Playgroup	25-27 Dreghorn Gardens EH13 9NW	441 5974	Helen Mullen, e415@ btinternet.com
EPNS The Patch Project Crèche	Sighthill Primary School, Calder Park EH11 4NF	Mobile 07804 323064	Elma Guthrie, elma@ blueyonder.co.uk, www.ep-ns.co.uk
EPNS The Patch Project Playgroup	See above	See above	See above

Day(s)	Time	Cost	Age Group	Other Information
Mon-Thurs	09.00-11.30	£6.50/session, paid a month in advance	2-5	15 children max
Mon-Thurs	09.00-11.45	Phone for details	2-5	18 children max.
Mon-Fri	09.15- 11.45	£5.75/ session and paid on a termly basis. Inc snack and drink.	2½-5	24 children max.
Tues-Fri	09.15-11.10	£5/session	2 yrs 3 mths-4 yrs	
Mon-Fri	09.15-11.15	£5/session	2-4	24 children max.
Mon-Fri	09.00-11.45	£6/session	2-5	Lunch club available at extra cost.
Mon-Fri	09.00-11.30 or 13.00 with wraparound care and lunch	£8.50/day or £14/ day incl lunch for 2-3 yr olds. Partner provider funded places for 3-5 yr olds.	2-5	Term time only. Graded excellent by care inspectors.
Mon-Fri	Mon-Fri 09.30-11.45, Mon-Thurs 12.30-14.45	£4/session bookable and payable in advance	From 4 mths	Term time only.
Mon-Fri	Mon-Fri 09.30-12.00, Mon-Thurs 12.30-15.00	Morning £15/week, afternoon £12.50/ week	From 2 yrs	Term time only.

Name	Address	Phone Number (0131 +)	Contact Details/ Web Address
Forrestine's Playgroup	Forrester High School/St Augustine's High School, 208 Broomhouse Rd, Sighthill EH12 9AD	334 9262 ext 345, mobile 07914 076782	Sandra Davidson, forrestinesplaygroup@ gmail.com
Fox Covert Nursery	Fox Covert Primary School, Clerwood Terrace EH12 8PG	467 7264	Janie Wallace, fcnursery@hotmail. co.uk
Gylemuir Community Playgroup	Gylemuir Community Centre, 10 Westerbroom Place, Corstorphine EH12 7RT	Mobile 07704 140071	
Harrison Playgroup	North Merchiston Club, 48 Watson Crescent EH11 1EP	Mobile 07580 154391	Tor Bretherton, info@harrisonplaygroup. co.uk, www.harrisonplaygroup. co.uk
Juniper Green Community Playgroup	1 Juniper Park Road, Juniper Green EH14 5DX	453 4427, mobile 07948 554889	junipergreenplaygroup@ hotmail.co.uk, www. junipergreenplaygroup. vpweb.co.uk
Kirkliston Playgroup	The Pavillion, Allison Park, Carmel Road, Kirkliston EH29 9DD	333 4525, mobile 07876 510917	Fiona Knapp, fionalknapp@hotmail. com
Littleflyers Playgroup	Kirkliston Leisure Centre, 1 Kirklands Park Street, Kirliston EH29 9EY	333 4700, mobile 07749 234098	Michelle Stevens
Riccarton Playgroup	59a Curriehill Road, Currie EH14 5PT	Mobile 07814 568635	
Stableroom Playgroup	Colinton Parish Church, Dell Road EH13 0JR	477 9494, 312 2264	Kerena Mitchell
The Village Playgroup	7-11 Main Street, Balerno EH14 7EQ	451 5756	Ms Alice Anderson

Day(s)	Time	Cost	Age Group	Other Information
Mon-Fri	09.15-11.45 (Mon-Fri), 12.00-14.30 (Mon-Wed)	£4.75/session (payable 2wks in advance)	2-5	20 children per session.
Mon-Fri	08.55-11.30 (pre-schoolers), 12.20-14.55 (ante-pre-schoolers)	Funded places	3-5	Term time only. For children planning to attend either Fox Covert ND or RC Primary School.
Mon-Fri	09.00-11.45 (11.45-12.30 lunch club)	£6/morning	2 yrs 3 mths-5 yrs	
Mon-Fri	09.15-11.30	£15 admin fee upon joining, £6/session full time, £6.50/session part time, 2nd child 50p discount.	2-5	Places available at time of writing.
Mon-Fri	09.15-12.00	£8/session, paid a month in advance	2-5	
Mon-Fri	09.15-11.15	£4.50/day	2-5	Term time only.
Wed-Fri	09.30-11.30	£7.75/session	2-5	
Phone for details	Mornings	Phone for details	Pre-school	
Mon/Wed/Fri	09.15-11.45	£7/session	2½-5	Partner provider.
Mon-Fri	Mon-Thurs 08.00-12.00, 13.00-16.00. Fri 08.00-13.00	£10/session	2-5	34 children max.

NURSERIES

This edition we haven't included a full list of nurseries.

You can get useful, up-to-date information online from the council including a list of council-run nurseries at this address: **www.edinburgh.gov.uk/downloads/download/1798/pre-school_nurseries_list**.

Also check out the comprehensive **Edinburgh Nursery and School Guide**, updated yearly and available for £3 from bookshops and supermarkets around Edinburgh, and at: **www.nurseryandschoolguide.co.uk**.

Nursery choice

Things to consider

When choosing a nursery, it is sometimes hard to know where to start! If possible, get recommendations from other parents. Visit several alternatives, ideally with your child, so that you can get an idea of how s/he feels about them too. Make a list of questions to ask. Then, in order to get a realistic picture, drop in unannounced on more than one occasion at different times of the day. Ultimately, the choice is a personal one, and depends on your individual family needs. However, we have provided some points you may find helpful to consider when making your decision.

What kind of nursery place?

• Do you require a private nursery or a nursery class in an independent school? If so, enquire as soon as possible, as waiting lists can be long.
• Do you require a nursery place in a council nursery when your child turns 3? If so, submit a nursery application form around the time your child turns 2.
• Does your workplace offer nursery care? If so, is there a waiting list?
• Does your college or university offer nursery care? If so, is the care year-round or term-time only?

• Does your child require additional support? If so, you should discuss your needs with the head teacher or staff centre manager to make sure these needs can be met.

Activities

• How is the day structured? Ask to see the daily planner. This should give you an idea of the activities and experiences offered to the children.
• Are the children happily occupied during your visit?
• Did you feel the atmosphere is chaotic or calm and what do you think will best suit your child?
• What activities are available during free play periods?
• Do children have access to a TV, or is a radio on during your visit – and how do you feel about this?
• Are outside trips/visits/activities/classes provided? Is there an additional charge for these? How are they supervised?
• How much outside time is provided during the day, and when/where does this take place?
• Are there specific activities you would like your child to take part in and are these available?

Facilities

• Does the nursery seem friendly, inviting, and light?
• Is it brightly decorated with children's artwork?
• Is there room for a variety of activities?
• Where are naps taken, and what sleeping facilities are provided?
• Do you feel confident about the security measures in place?
• Are there activity areas for children of different ages? Does this arrangement benefit your child?

Feedback and communication

- What sort of report do parents receive at the end of the day (nappies, sleeps, meals, activities) and is this verbal or written?
- Is your child assigned a key worker with whom you can discuss daily matters and general progress?
- What opportunities do parents have to discuss their child's needs and other matters with the nursery staff and management?

Staff and education

- Who is in charge of the nursery, and are they available during your visit?
- What qualifications are held by staff?
- Are staff/child ratios being complied with?
- How do staff members manage challenging behaviour?
- Does the nursery follow the "Curriculum for Excellence"?
- What does the HMIE report say about the nursery?
- What does the Care Inspectorate report say about the nursery?

Financial considerations

- Does the weekly charge include meals, milk, nappies, wipes, etc.?
- Are any free settling-in sessions provided?
- Are there any discounts available for students, families on low incomes, companies and siblings? Remember, if you spend money on childcare while you work and you qualify for the Working Tax Credit, you might be entitled to financial help with childcare costs.
- Does the nursery accept childcare vouchers?
- If it is a private nursery and your child will still be attending at age 3, is the nursery a Partner Provider?
- How are nursery fees collected?
- If your child attends on a part-time basis, are you able to purchase "extra sessions" if necessary?

Practicalities

- Is there a waiting list, and, if so, how long is it?
- Does the nursery welcome expressed milk?
- Are meals and/or snacks provided? If so, ask to see a week's menu to make sure you are happy with the range of food on offer.
- What are the food preparation facilities like?
- What provision is made for vegetarian children or those with allergies etc?
- Are real nappies accepted?
- For part-time places, is there a minimum number of sessions your child has to attend?
- What sort of settling-in process does the nursery adopt, and is this sufficient for your child?
- Does the fee for part-time sessions include snacks and meals?

Timetable

- Do opening times fit in with your schedule? Remember, at private nurseries you are paying for the service, and shouldn't have to drop off at precise opening times if it doesn't suit your schedule.
- Are pick-up times flexible?
- Is there an after school club for older children?
- Is there parking available at busy times?

This is not an exhaustive list of questions, but we hope we have given you a good starting point. As a final consideration, don't ignore your instinct when choosing a nursery – chances are that if you get a "good feeling" from your visit at a nursery, your child will too. Good luck!

FURTHER NURSERY & SCHOOL INFORMATION

The City of Edinburgh Council Early Years Team

0131 529 2103
earlyyears@edinburgh.gov.uk
www.edinburgh.gov.uk/info/851/nurseries_ and_playgroups
Provides information on nursery entitlement, what to look for when visiting a nursery, arranging a nursery visit, and how to apply for a nursery place. Relevant forms and guides can be downloaded from the website.

East Lothian Council Department of Education & Children's Services

01620 827827
customerservices@eastlothian.gov.uk
www.eastlothian.gov.uk

The website provides information about nursery education, and about moving from nursery to primary school. Follow the links from "Education and Learning", and then to "Nurseries and Playgroups" to access relevant information and specific contacts.

Edinburgh Nursery and School Guide

www.nurseryandschoolguide.co.uk
Annual publication that provides information about fees, facilities and achievement results for independent and state school as well as daycare nursery providers – all in one handy guide. Also provides information about clubs and classes for a range of ages. Available for sale (£3) in select shops around Edinburgh (such as Sainsbury's, Waitrose, WHSmith and Blackwell's) or online.

Edinburgh Schools

www.edinburgh-schools.co.uk
A directory of education in Edinburgh. As well as detailed information on each state and private school, there are listings of nurseries, extra-curricular activities and days out. There is also a brief guide to nannies, au pairs and childminding options.

Her Majesty's Inspectorate of Education (HMIE)

01506 600200
www.hmie.gov.uk
Inspects and reports on the quality of pre-school education. Reports can be accessed via the website.

Midlothian Council Education and Children's Services

0131 270 7500
education.services@midlothian.gov.uk
www.midlothian.gov.uk
Provides information about nursery education offered by Midlothian Council, as well as childminders and pre-school education options. Follow the links from "Education and Learning" to "Nurseries, Playgroups and Childcare" to access relevant information.

National Day Nurseries Assocation Scotland

0141 248 8694
scotland@ndna.org.uk
www.ndna.org.uk
A national charity organisation that aims to enhance the development and education of children in their early years. The website provides information to parents about finding and choosing a nursery as well as information about nursery inspections.

Scottish Council of Independent Schools

0131 556 2316
info@scis.org.uk
www.scis.org.uk
Represents over 70 member independent, fee-paying schools in Scotland. Provides information about schools with nurseries, choosing a school, special needs education, financial considerations, etc. You can also find out information about fees, exam results, pupil numbers, and so on.

Social Care and Social Work Improvement Scotland (SCSWIS)/Care Inspectorate

0131 653 4100
0845 600 9527
www.scswis.com
From Sep 2011, The Care Commission changed its name to The Care Inspectorate. The Care Inspectorate is the independent regulator of social care and social work services in Scotland. All childcare services, including nurseries and childminders, must be registered with the Care Inspectorate. Childcare premises are inspected regularly to ensure that health, safety and quality standards are being met, and reports are compiled after the inspection. These reports are compiled with the childcare provider in mind rather than the potential parent, so they may seem dry, but you can access them via the Care Inspectorate website. The Care Inspectorate updates the registration list regularly and if you cannot find suitable childcare provision in your preferred area, it is worth phoning them.

Are you following us yet? We're @EdforUnder5s on Twitter or you can be our friend on Facebook – look for Edinburgh Ed.

GAELIC EDUCATION

Gaelic Education

Waverley Court, Business Centre 1/4
4 East Market Street EH8 8BG
0131 529 2415
www.edinburgh.gov.uk/info/20084/gaelic_
language_and_cultural_support/863/gaelic_
in schools
There are three Gaelic toddler groups that operate in the city (Tollcross, Corstorphine and Leith – see toddler group listings), and an established nursery class at Tollcross Primary School (see below).

Gaelic Nursery and Primary School Education

Tollcross Primary Head Teacher
0131 229 7828
0131 529 2415 (Norma Martin)
There is a Gaelic medium unit at Tollcross Primary School which caters for nursery and primary pupils from all over the city. There is no requirement for the parents to have any knowledge of Gaelic.

ACCESSIBLE PRE-SCHOOL PLAY AND EDUCATION

It can be more difficult to find childcare for children with additional needs. However, don't give up!
    Start by contacting any of the organisations listed above, and in our "Childcare" section, pages 324-330, and ask about the provision they make for children with additional needs.
    Your local Child and Family Centre may be able to help by offering group care and pre-school education. You can find out more at www.edinburgh.gov.uk.
Here are a few organisations in Edinburgh specifically dedicated to the development and education of children with additional support needs.

Barrie Nursery Early Years Playgroup

43-45 Canaan Lane, EH10 4SG
0131 446 3120
canaan@royalblindschool.org.uk
Situated at the Royal Blind School Canaan Lane Campus, this group meets once a week. It includes a toy library (see p 120), access to a hydrotherapy pool at weekends and the services of a parent counsellor.

Bright Sparks Playgroup

The Cockpen Centre, 1b Cockpen Road
Bonnyrigg EH19 3HS
0131 270 5662
0131 270 5665
A playgroup for children with additional support needs, providing the normal range of play facilities including sand, water, art and crafts, books, construction and pretend play. There is also a range of more specialised toys for children with special needs.

Westerlea Early Education Centre

11 Ellersly Road EH12 6HY
0131 337 9876
This is an early learning support centre for young children (0-3) with additional support needs, offering support for families and childcare professionals too. Managed by Capability Scotland, it offers one-to-one, group, music, hydrotherapy and sensory sessions.

 Make your business stand out from the rest - place an advert in our next edition! Email business@efuf.co.uk for more information or visit the business section of our website www.efuf.co.uk

Edinburgh Visiting Teaching & Support Services

0131 469 2850
www.vtss-edin.ik.org
The pre-school home visiting support team can support you and your child in the home with activities that promote his or her growth and development, and resources that encourage your capacity to educate your child. The team can also provide information to help and support your child's transition to nursery school.

Q&A

We asked Lesley Walpole of St Andy's Teeny Tots Group...

Are you a parent? *Yes.*

Tell us about St Andy's Group: *We meet every Wednesday 13.30-15.00 at the Easter Road Hall in Leith St Andrews Church (door on Lochend Road). Carers bring children (from birth to pre-school age) along to play with our wide range of toys (suitable for small babies up to 3 year olds) and play with play dough, draw and glue. We have a healthy snack, run races and sing songs. Tea, coffee and biscuits are available for carers. Everyone who comes along has commented how friendly our group is. We are also becoming known for the number of dads who attend with their children.*

How long have you lived in Edinburgh? *I have lived in the Edinburgh area since birth, moved away for 8 years and returned in 2008.*

How do you rate it as a child-friendly city? *Generally Edinburgh is VERY child friendly. There are plenty of places for nappy changes, and cafés and restaurants have highchairs and children's menus. Buses can sometimes be tricky with pushchairs but are usually OK. I usually walk and find few problems getting around. There are many playparks and places to go for walks, along with a huge range of playgroups. Most of these seem to be in the morning however. Libraries are also great places to go not just for book lending, but for activities and playing with toys. Friends with children in other cities can't believe the huge range of things to do in Edinburgh!*

> *"Friends with children in other cities can't believe the huge range of things to do in Edinburgh!"*

Any memorable experiences of Edinburgh as a parent? *Picnicking in the Botanics is always great. We've done it in sun, snow and rain. There's always room to run around outside to tire children out, very good facilities, indoor areas for the more unpleasant weather trips, and ducks, fish and squirrels to see. We've been there at least once a week since the birth of my daughter and expect to continue now I have a 2nd on the way. It's very easy to get to (I have a half hour walk, but buses are regular and parking is easy). We just love it there.*

Recommendations: *St Paul's & St George's Babies and Toddlers Group on Thursdays is excellent. Very friendly helpers and well organised.*

Monkey Music is also brilliant. I've taken my daughter since she was about 5 months old and she loves it – singing, dancing, and playing instruments.

Swimming class at Leith Victoria pool is quite a small class but very enjoyable.

Find out more about St Andy's Teeny Tots Group on page 292.

Practical Information & Support

Childcare
Healthcare
Help & Advice
Benefits & Social Security Information
Media Listings
Social Work Services
Support & Assistance
Other Guides to Edinburgh

Practical Information & Support

This section is meant to be a starting point if you are looking for help or advice. It is not all-encompassing, but we have listed some organisations that can provide information and support to parents and carers.

CHILDCARE

The search for, and selection of, the right type of childcare can be time consuming and you may have to make compromises and decisions you might not have considered previously. If involving extended/immediate family is not a viable option, choices include taking your child to a childminder, employing someone to come to you, or enrolling your child in a nursery (see our "Pre-school" chapter for more on nurseries).

Give yourself as much time as you can to check out the options so that you don't feel pressured into making a decision. Talk to others about their experiences. Keep an open mind and have faith in your instinct for what will suit you and your child. There are various good solutions and at least one of them will make sense for you.

If you feel happy and relaxed about your childcare arrangements, then you can use your time away from your child much more effectively. While your child may seem so vulnerable, remember that other adults outside the family can be a very positive part of their life.

For impartial and comprehensive advice on all forms of local childcare, contact:

Edinburgh Childcare Information Service

Waverley Court Level 1.2, 4 East Market Street, EH8 8BG
0800 032 0323 (Freephone)
0131 529 2110
childcareinformation@edinburgh.gov.uk
www.scottishchildcare.gov.uk

As part of the Government's National Childcare Strategy, the City of Edinburgh Council runs the Childcare Information Service which aims to provide free and impartial information about registered childcare. Parents and carers can contact the service to find out about the most suitable childcare for their family's needs.

Information is available on all different types of registered childcare – whether provided by the independent, voluntary or statutory sectors, including: childminders; independent nurseries; local nurseries; out-of-school care; playgroups; crèches and holiday play-schemes. Lists and profiles of childcare provision can also be tailored to meet each family's specific needs, such as services for a particular age group or geographical area. Information is regularly updated.

For information and support about returning to work, your local NCT branch may have a working mothers' group, or you could contact:

Working Families

1-3 Berry Street, London, EC1V 0AA
0207 253 7243
0800 013 0313 (low income familes help)
advice@workingfamilies.org.uk
www.workingfamilies.org.uk
Helps children, their parents and employers with information about childcare and flexible working including advice on workplace violence, maternity rights and tax credits, as well as benefits, tax credits and childcare for parents of children with disabilities.

AU PAIRS

An au pair is a single person aged 17-27 who has come to the UK to learn English, and wishes to stay with an English-speaking host family while they study. They will expect board, lodging (a room of their own) and an allowance in return for helping in the house or childcare of up to 25 hrs a week. They are not required to have any childcare experience/ qualifications, however many families find that au pairs are a great solution. Given that they come to the UK to learn English, there may be language barrier issues, at least at first.

There are many agencies that can guide you through the process of finding and hiring an au pair, and keep you informed of any legal requirements in terms of immigration and employment. The long established magazine The Lady is also a good place to start. Au pairs can also be found through contacts with the language departments of local schools, colleges and universities.

Please note that UK immigration rules are changing so check with the Home Office UK Border Agency website:

www.ukba.homeoffice.gov.uk/workingintheuk

Au pairs should have the opportunity to study, and in return for board and lodging with a room of their own and a reasonable allowance (£80-100/wk) they should help in the house (including light housework and childcare) for up to 5 hrs/day, 5 days/wk. So they should have at least 2 full free days/week (including evenings). There should be 1 week's paid leave for every 6 mths worked. If you go on holiday without them they must be paid in your absence, and they are entitled to paid public holidays.

An au pair is not a nanny and should be left in sole charge of the children only at your discretion. However, they can be perfect as a help around the house or for part-time care for older children.

Get the most up-to-date information on
www.efuf.co.uk

Au Pair Ecosse

6 Park Place, King's Park, Stirling, FK7 9JR
01786 474573
ruth@aupairecosse.com
www.aupairecosse.com
This company can provide au pairs to anywhere in Scotland. Au pairs come from throughout the EU as well as Canada and other countries. Placements can be arranged from 3 mths to 1 year. One-off placement fees apply. The company can also arrange short term holiday placements, as well as facilitating gap year and year-abroad placements for language students in Scottish schools and universities. Also helps UK applicants find placements in other countries.

The Edinburgh Au Pair Agency

Carrick Cottage, The Walled Garden, Rosewell, EH24 9EQ
0131 440 0800,
aupairs@rosewell.co.uk
Long-established local agency. Three types of placements are available depending on the number of hours you would like your au pair to work. There is a small registration fee and a one-off placement fee.

BABYSITTERS

Some nanny agencies can help you find babysitters, although this is a more expensive option than the traditional options of friends, family or word of mouth. You can, if you wish, employ a neighbouring teenager to babysit. There is no minimum specific age for a babysitter (though 16 is often quoted) – the legal criteria are that the babysitter must be able to look after both himself/herself and the child. As ever, common sense should be employed when deciding who is best to look after your child – and of course it is an offence for anyone over the age of 16, who has responsibility for a child under that age, to wilfully assault, ill-treat, neglect, abandon or expose that child.

Current rates for babysitting range between £6-10/hr, more after midnight, and if you are out late you should ensure that your babysitter gets home safely, either by taking them yourself or giving them the taxi fare.

There are online options, but a few words of caution – "national" often means England and Wales, so check the geographical area the company or organisation covers. Some state that they have screened the babysitters, others do not, so the onus is on you to decide whether you are happy with the arrangement. You might be just as lucky posting an ad and interviewing candidates yourself so you can have a few people on file. Fees for agencies are better kept for nannies, au pairs and maternity nurses.

Babysitting circles

Groups of parents who get together to provide babysitting for each other. To find out about circles in your area ask neighbours, parent and toddler groups, local parents, your health visitor, or your local NCT group. Circles are organised on an purely informal basis and it is up to you to decide if you are happy with the way yours is run. Many arrange for parents and children to meet together at regular intervals so that you can get to know each other better. If the circle is large enough, similar families are matched.

CHILDMINDERS

Childminders care for children in their own homes. They can offer a homely, family environment; most will have had first-hand experience with their own children, and may well be involved with local toddler/ play groups and schools, which may be an advantage for your child later on.

Childminders are self-employed and are legally required to register with the Scottish Commission for the Regulation of Care which involves health, police, fire and home safety checks and is reviewed regularly. Registration is not, however, an evaluation of their skills as a childminder – these are for you to assess.

Childminders are approved to care for a maximum of 6 children up to and including the age of 12 yrs, of whom no more than 3 are under 5 yrs and only one is under 1 yr; these include their own children. You must use a registered childminder: if in doubt ask to see a registration certificate, and check that it is up to date.

Childminders are responsible for their own tax and National Insurance payments and also for Public Liability and Accident Insurance cover. You should check that they are either covered by their domestic insurance or that they have a special childminder's insurance policy.

Scottish Childminding Association (SCMA)

7 Melville Terrace, Stirling, FK8 2ND
01786 445377
information@childminding.org
www.childminding.org
The only Scottish dedicated support organisation for registered childminders. It promotes good quality childcare within a home environment. Provides support, advice and information to all who are interested in childminding. Produces several useful publications for parents and childminders, some of which are free. Also has guides and advice sheets online.

Finding a childminder

There are online lists at:
www.scottishchildcare.gov.uk

or contact the Childcare Information Service, which has a list of all registered childminders, on:
0800 032 0323
childcareinformation@edinburgh.gov.uk

How much will it cost?
Rates vary according to area, but across Edinburgh the average rate is £4/hr/child. The SCMA (see above) produce a guide highlighting pay and conditions within various areas. Rates for part-time places may carry a premium, and some minders offer a reduced rate for siblings.

Payment for holidays and sick pay vary: often a childminder will not charge if unavailable due to holidays or sickness, but if you do not attend you should pay the normal rate or at least a percentage of it.

Choosing a childminder

Decide where you want your childminder to be based: someone close to home is more convenient and may mean your child can make friends locally which will carry on to school. Alternatively, you may prefer someone who lives closer to your place of work. Create a list and phone round – you are unlikely to find many vacancies, however most childminders are very helpful in telling you of any spaces they are aware of, so do ask.

Always visit a prospective childminder in their home with a list of information for them about you and your child, and a list of questions you want to ask. You need to establish the practicalities of hours, rates, holidays, sick pay, overtime (if required) and notice and whether you need to provide food and nappies. You may also want to think about the following:

- Will your child have plenty of play opportunities – indoors and outdoors?
- Will there be outings to the park, playgroup, library etc?
- Will your child be able to rest during the day? If so, where?
- What are the arrangements for meals and snacks?
- Are there other children for your child to play with and are they happy, settled and busy?
- What time will be set aside for you to discuss your child with the childminder?
- Will your wishes for the care of your child be accepted and respected?

Ensure you have a written contract summarising your agreement with your childminder.

NANNIES

You may prefer to employ someone to look after your children in your own home. Nannies may "live in" or "live out". The choice between these options will depend on the nature of your childcare needs, your available accommodation, how you feel about having someone in your home and also on your financial resources.

Nannies are not required to be registered in the same way that childminders are, so you must follow through on references thoroughly.

Remember that whether you choose to search via an agency or through local advertising/ word of mouth, you will still need to spend time interviewing and checking references. Don't rely on the references provided by the agency only – make the calls yourself.

It is worth thinking beforehand about the sort of person you are looking for and to specify your requirements with regard to training, qualifications, experience, age, etc.

Finding a nanny

You can find a nanny through recommendations, by placing advertisements in places like Gumtree, The Scotsman or Friday's Evening News, or through an agency.

If you want a nanny with childcare qualifications, but don't mind if they don't have experience, contact local colleges which offer Early Education and Childcare training courses. The final term (Apr/May) is the best time to do this.

Edinburgh's Telford College

0131 559 4000
www.ed-coll.ac.uk

Jewel & Esk Valley College

0131 344 7100
www.jec.ac.uk

Stevenson College

0131 535 4700
www.stevenson.ac.uk

Nanny agencies

There are a few agencies in Edinburgh who specialise in finding nannies. They will usually charge a registration fee. If you are looking for a part-time nanny, some will try to set up a nanny-share scheme with other clients. If you do appoint someone, you then pay an appointment fee to the agency.

Agencies can sometimes give you information on interviewing, contracts, conditions of employment, tax and National Insurance etc. They should also give some guarantee to find temporary cover if you need it. All nanny agencies are supposed to ensure that everyone on their books has their Disclosure Scotland document. Remember an agency can only be as good as the nannies on its books, and sometimes cannot come up with anyone suitable.

Butterfly Personnel

7 Earlston Place, EH7 5HU
0131 659 5065
enquiries@butterflypersonnel.co.uk
www.butterflypersonnel.co.uk
Specialises in providing permanent nannies and maternity nurses – people who provide support to mothers and their newborn babies. Butterfly Personnel can also register private nannies for the use of childcare vouchers. Other services include experienced babysitters and supply nursery staff.

Butterfly Personnel Childcare
SCSWIS Registered Disclosure
Maternity Care Night Nurses
Nannies Babysitters
We can register your nanny for
Childcare Vouchers
And Tax Credits
Fees can be paid by Childcare Vouchers
leigh@butterflypersonnel.co.uk
www.butterflypersonnel.co.uk
01316595065

Norland Agency

York Place, London Road, Bath, BA1 6AE
01225 904030
agency@norland.co.uk
The Norland College has a strong tradition of well-trained nannies since 1892. Norland has recently started placing nannies in Scotland and they can provide temporary nanny care if you need to travel down south or plan to vacation within the EU.

Conditions of Service
Be clear about your conditions of service in terms of hours, holidays, pay, duties, sick pay, etc. Must your nanny: be able to drive; be a non-smoker; understand a vegetarian diet, know about allergies; observe certain religious practices, and so on?

Apart from looking after the children, nannies' duties can include cooking and being responsible for the cleanliness of the nursery and children's laundry. Nannies with qualifications and experience may not take kindly to being asked to clean a bathroom unless it is the one attached to the nursery, although they may do some light cleaning to help out. Their priority is the children and if there is a downtime during naps – then the nanny deserves a break and to focus on upcoming activities.

Rates vary widely depending on qualifications, age and experience: full-time live-out care can range from £280-£350/wk (remember the additional cost of National Insurance and income tax) or around £7-9+/hr part-time. Live-in pay can be less (£200-£300/week), but don't forget to take account of the hidden domestic costs. When deciding what to pay, take into account training, experience, number of children and level of responsibility required.

Keep in mind that your nanny may wish to go on maternity leave at some point and would not be regarded as self-employed by the HMRC. You need to be clear on what your obligations as an employer are to a pregnant woman.

Interviews
Ask all candidates for CVs – that will give you a good starting point. Prepare your questions in advance and don't feel embarrassed to ask searching ones – you need to find out as much as you can in a very short time! Don't forget to give candidates a chance to ask you questions – they need to assess whether you will be the right family for them. Be sure to obtain references from previous employers or college tutors and follow them up. Have a short list of questions to ask referees, but also give them an opportunity to volunteer their own information.

Contract

A written contract stating the terms and conditions of service and the duties and responsibilities of the job is extremely helpful in preventing problems, or at least making them easier to sort out, for both parties, and the law requires employers to provide certain written particulars.

Employing a nanny

When you do appoint someone, you need to contact your local Inland Revenue office to let them know you are an employer, and they will send you the necessary paperwork. Alternatively you can sign up with a payroll service that sorts out all the paperwork on your behalf ensuring that the nanny receives the correct PAYE pay slips and that you pay the correct quarterly payments to the Inland Revenue. This is highly recommended (unless you or your partner are accountants) because it saves time, it is efficient and you have access to legal and tax advice as part of your membership fee should you have any questions about your obligations as an employer. Here are two payroll services:

Nanny Tax

PO Box 988, Brighton, BN1 3NT
0845 226 2203
mailbox@nannytax.co.uk
www.nannytax.co.uk

PAYE for Nannies

PO Box 38, Hunstanton, PE36 9AD
01485 433322
payroll@payefornannies.co.uk
www.payefornannies.co.uk

Any information you'd like to add? Email us at info@efuf.co.uk

OTHER SOURCES OF HELP WITH CHILDCARE

Doulas

Doulas provide support before and during the birth of your baby, but they can also help mother and child in those vital first weeks.

Doula UK

0871 433 3103
info@doula.org.uk
www.doula.org.uk
The non-profit association for doulas, providing information about the services they offer. It can help you find a local doula.

Edinburgh Doulas

Contact: Kim Bradie
0131 554 6620
info@edinburghdoulas.co.uk
www.edinburghdoulas.co.uk
Provides birth and postnatal support. Postnatal support normally lasts between 10 days and 2 mths depending on your needs. Minimum request is 4 hrs' support a week.

Mother to Mother

Contact: Clare Bartos
0131 445 4445
clare@mothertomother.co.uk
www.mothertomother.co.uk
Provides postnatal doula services for families, as well as one-to-one breastfeeding support.

Scottish Doula Network

info@scottishdoulanetwork.co.uk
www.scottishdoulanetwork.co.uk
A peer support network for doulas working in Scotland. It provides contact details but is not accountable for individual doulas.

A birth doula will work with a pregnant woman to help prepare her for the birth and offer to be one of the attendants during the delivery.

A postnatal doula will work with a mother and her family for a mutually agreed period of time – usually about 6 wks after the birth of a baby, although the extent of the support can vary according to need. She provides physical and emotional support to the mother and her family and will help the mother locate information and support from other sources. She can also free her from some domestic chores so that the mother has time to meet her own and her baby's needs.

Maternity Nurses

Maternity Nurses can be found via the same routes as finding a nanny. They are expensive as they tend to live in for the first 4-8 wks of a baby's life to help the mother adjust to her new situation, establish a routine (if required), and provide support with breastfeeding and sleeping.

Mother's Helps

If you do not need someone to take full responsibility for your child/ren on a regular basis, but feel that you need some help in the home with general housework, as well as childcare, a mother's help may fit the bill. Mother's helps do not need any qualifications or experience and you can specify what you want them to do to help you, but remember the emphasis is on the word "help".

Crèche Services

North Edinburgh Childcare

Crèche Services, 18b Ferry Road Avenue, EH4 4BL
0131 332 8001
info@northedinburghchildcare.co.uk
www.northedinburghchildcare.co.uk
Quality, affordable crèche cover, to enable parents to access either leisure or business opportunities. The crèches are safe, stimulating and, above all, fun. Available for bookings by any group or organisation which is planning an event – anytime, anywhere, on a one-off booking or cover for a regular event. North Edinburgh Childcare can accommodate up to 12 children between the ages of 0-12 yrs (under 1s can be catered for if there are less than 6 other children). Rates vary, depending upon staffing ratios and the venue.

Smilechildcare

17 Calder Grove, EH11 4LZ
0131 476 7800
mailbox@smilechildcare.org
www.smilechildcare.co.uk
Smilechildcare's crèche service is designed to respond to the needs of a broad range of clients. Its offering includes assisting with childcare at weddings, parties and other family occasions, providing a crèche for AGMs, training events, conferences and other corporate events. Each crèche or childcare service is organised to best meet the needs of the individual family or company, including play and care for children with special needs.

Services can be provided in and around Edinburgh, either on a long- or short-term basis or as a one-off event. Smilechildcare will provide qualified childcare staff in the correct ratios; provide or come to a suitable location; complete a risk assessment of your chosen venue; and provide play materials and a healthy snack.

HEALTHCARE

This section includes local NHS, voluntary and complementary health services. It cannot claim to be comprehensive; however, it should provide you with sources of more detailed information.

Emergency Numbers
If your child requires emergency treatment call 999 or 112.

Or go direct to: Royal Hospital for Sick Children, 9 Sciennes Road, EH9 1HF

0131 536 0000.

Or, contact your GP.

Or, if out of hours, call:

NHS 24 Scotland

0845 424 2424
Your call will be answered by a call handler who will take some basic details. Then you will be forwarded to a nurse advisor who will assess the condition of your child and offer advice. You may be asked to attend an appointment at an out-of-hours centre, or to go to the hospital Accident and Emergency (A&E) department. If you need to take your child to A&E, NHS 24 will call ahead and give them your details. NHS 24 works with the Scottish Ambulance Service, GP services, and A&E departments.

NHS Lothian

0131 537 8488
www.nhslothian.scot.nhs.uk
Visit the website or phone to find a General Practitioner (GP), pharmacist or optician. Your local library will have a list of GP practices too. If you are new to the area, you should register with a local GP as soon as possible.

DENTAL CARE

NHS dental care is free for mothers throughout pregnancy and until the baby's first birthday, as well as for children under 18 yrs. Regular attendance is needed to stay registered as an NHS patient. If you wish to change your dentist, you should check whether the new dentist will accept you as an NHS patient. Alternatively there are many dentists offering private treatment in Edinburgh.

It is a good idea to register your child with your family dentist as soon as they are born. The water supply in Lothian does not contain sufficient fluoride to benefit teeth. Your child's teeth should be cleaned as soon as they appear, using a small-headed brush and a smear of fluoride toothpaste containing no less than 1000 parts per million fluoride. For children at high risk of dental decay, dentists may prescribe fluoride tablets or drops.

Dentists

0131 537 8444
Phone to find details of local dentists or contact NHS 24 on 0845 424 2424.

Dental emergencies

If your child is registered with a dentist then contact their dental surgery for emergency treatment.

If your child isn't registered with a dentist, you can take them to the Children's Department at the:

Edinburgh Dental Institute

Level 3, Lauriston Building, Lauriston Place, EH3 9HA
0131 536 4970
Clinics run Mon-Fri 09.00-11.00 and 14.00-15.00. No appointment is necessary. Triage system in operation.

Lothian Dental Advice Line

0131 536 4800
If your chlld is not registered with a dentist, and needs out-of-hours treatment, you can get advice here. This line operates during evenings and at weekends. A dental nurse adviser will take your call and assess the urgency of the symptoms.

GP SERVICES

If you think your child has a medical problem, the normal first contact is your GP. As well as treating most common conditions and referring your child on to a specialist (should this be necessary), most GPs in Edinburgh provide special services for under 5s. These include a Child Health Surveillance Programme, often in conjunction with your health visitor, in which your child will be called for routine medical and developmental checks. In addition, your GP is likely to administer much of your child's basic immunisation programme.

If you want to change your GP practice, you can register with a new one directly, or you can phone NHS Lothian on 0131 537 8488 for advice. If you have been removed from a GP's list, and cannot get another doctor to accept you, then phone 0131 537 8473.

Immunisations

The NHS aims to immunise as many babies and children as possible to promote "herd immunity" and to prevent outbreaks of common, but serious, diseases. Most of the routine vaccines are administered through GP practices, sometimes in conjunction with health visitors. If your child has been registered with a GP, you will be sent an automatic appointment notice when each vaccine is due. If you have any questions or concerns about immunisation your GP should be able to help you.

Check out the latest timetable for immunisation in the timeline in our introduction, p 3. The website for up-to-date information and descriptions of each vaccine, plus details of when they are offered, is: **www.healthscotland. com/topics/health/immunisation/index.aspx.**

Minor Ailments Service

It is worth registering with your local pharmacist's "minor ailments service". This is a new NHS service for groups of patients such as children. It means that if the pharmacist thinks it necessary, they can give you a medicine for no charge, without you having to make an appointment with your GP just to get a prescription. There are a wide range of minor illnesses and ailments which can be treated under the service.

Pharmacies (Chemists)

0131 537 8488
www.nhslothian.scot.nhs.uk
Phone or visit the website to find your nearest pharmacy. To find one that is open out of hours, telephone NHS 24 on 0845 424 2424.

Your local pharmacist can give advice on common health problems and can answer questions about medicines.

HOSPITALS – MATERNITY

There are two hospitals offering maternity services in the Edinburgh area: The Royal Infirmary of Edinburgh (Simpson Centre) and St John's Hospital at Howden:

Simpson Centre for Reproductive Health

Little France, 51 Little France Crescent, Old Dalkeith Road, EH16 4SA
0131 536 1000

St John's Hospital

Howden Road West, Livingston, EH54 6PP
01506 523000

HOSPITAL SERVICES (EXCLUDING MATERNITY)

Royal Hospital for Sick Children

9 Sciennes Road, EH9 1LF
0131 536 0000
This hospital, also known as "Sick Kids", is focussed on the needs of children. It is in Sciennes, south of the Meadows, but it is expected to relocate to the same site as the Edinburgh Royal Infirmary in the near future.

Clinics, waiting areas and the A&E department are all stocked with toys and books for all ages. All parents who wish to stay with their child can do so, and attempts will be made to find beds for as many as possible, either on the ward or in separate areas. Priority is given to parents of very sick children, those who have travelled long distances and breastfeeding mothers. There are no specific visiting times for parents and guardians, and other visitors are welcome until 19.00 at the discretion of the ward charge nurse.

Specialist members of staff ensure that children are encouraged to play during their hospital stay, as well as helping them understand the treatments and investigations they are undergoing. Volunteers work with the play specialists, guiding families around the hospital, taking the mobile library around the wards, befriending a child and reading bedtime stories to the children. Pre-operative play coordinators run pre-admission visits for children who are due to have surgery, to alleviate the anxiety surrounding a hospital admission. Visits can also be organised for small groups of nursery/ primary school children wishing to find out more about hospitals.

With prior arrangement the hospital nursery can accommodate a number of young children of parents visiting the hospital. The nursery is open Mon-Fri 08.00-18.00. For further information contact the play services coordinator, 0131 536 0000.

St John's Hospital at Howden

Howden Road West, Livingston, EH54 6PP
01506 523000
St John's is a modern teaching hospital for adults and children with an A&E department. It provides a full paediatric service including an acute receiving unit, special baby unit, paediatric ward and a range of outpatient services. Parents are welcome to stay and their needs are accommodated where possible on the ward. Siblings are welcome but appropriate adult supervision is appreciated. Visiting times at the discretion of the ward. Playroom and play facilities open when staffing allows.

Western General Hospital

including Minor Injuries Clinic, Crewe Road South, EH4 2XU
0131 537 1330/1331 (minor injuries clinic)
0131 537 1000
The minor injuries clinic is open 09.00-21.00 daily for anyone with a minor injury, for example sprains, cuts, bites, minor burns and small bone breaks (from shoulders to fingers and knees to toes). No appointment is necessary and telephone advice is also available. The specialist staff (nurse, physiotherapy, paramedic) can assess, diagnose and treat your child, and refer them for further treatment if required.

ANTENATAL CARE

www.readysteadybaby.org.uk
As soon as you find out you are pregnant you should call your GP surgery or health centre and ask for an appointment with a midwife. Usually you will be asked to choose where you would like to have your baby, at home or in hospital. A home birth can be arranged with the community midwives in your local area, depending on your medical history.

Maternity services are community based, with most women receiving care in their local area. NHS antenatal care is provided by the local midwifery team, your GP, or, if necessary, a consultant obstetrician. This means that most women only attend hospital for the birth of their baby. The midwives provide information and support on all aspects of pregnancy, birth and postnatal care including breastfeeding. This includes providing information about health in pregnancy, screening tests, parenting skills, and your options for delivery.

You should be offered an opportunity to attend NHS antenatal classes provided by your community midwives along with other health professionals such as health visitors. Courses may vary and, depending on your area, may include: women-only classes; aqua-natal classes; hypnotherapy and physiotherapy.

A 20-wk foetal anomaly scan is now offered by NHS Lothian. Several private companies also offer scans, including 3D and 4D scans.

You may wish to engage the services of an independent midwife or a doula. See the childcare section, above, for more on doulas. During the birth process a doula is a mother's advocate in whatever situation in which she chooses to give birth, be it in a hospital, at home, with or without medical supervision. She will work within the woman's chosen environment as a birth assistant, adapting to her changing needs during labour and birth. Doulas do not offer medical advice.

AIMS

Association for Improvements in the Maternity Services
0300 365 0663
helpline@aims.org.uk
www.aims.org.uk

Provides information and support to parents about their choices in maternity care. A range of booklets on how to make the right decision for you, the second and third stages of labour, the pros and cons of induction, VBAC, breech birth, home birth, water birth, twins etc, plus a quarterly journal, are available. See website for publications list. If you contact the AIMS helpline by email or telephone, you will be connected to volunteers who will respond as soon as possible.

ARC

Antenatal Results and Choices
0207 631 0285
info@arc-uk.org
www.arc-uk.org
A charity which provides support to expectant and bereaved parents through and after the antenatal screening and testing process.

Independent Midwives UK

www.independentmidwives.org.uk
Independent midwives have chosen to work outside the NHS in a self-employed capacity. This website provides information and a search facility to find a local independent midwife. You can also find Scottish independent midwives at: **www.scotbirth.co.uk**.

Independent midwives provide antenatal and postnatal care, and support home births. They are fully qualified midwives, who, like their NHS colleagues, are registered with the Nursing and Midwifery Council. If you plan a home birth and need to go to the hospital an independent midwife can remain with you as an advocate, supporter and friend, but may not have a contract with the hospital to provide midwifery services.

NCT

0300 330 0772 (pregnancy and birth line)
0300 330 0770 (enquiries), 0844 243 6994
(antenatal classes)
www.nct.org.uk
www.nctedinburgh.moonfruit.com
NCT provides support and evidence-based information about pregnancy, birth and the early

days of parenthood. The philosophy of NCT antenatal classes is to empower women and their partners to make informed choices in managing pregnancy and labour. The classes are informal and friendly and many groups stay in touch after their babies are born. Classes run over 8 wks and include relevant anatomy and physiology, preparation for labour including breathing and other relaxation classes, and practising postures for assisting the labour and birthing process. Breastfeeding and early parenting skills are also discussed. There are also intensive weekend courses available.

For more information and to book antenatal classes email: bookings1c@nct.org.uk

Pregnancy and Parents Centre

10 Lower Gilmore Place, EH3 9NY
0131 229 3667
www.pregnancyandparents.org.uk
This centre (previously called the Birth Resource Centre) is a charitable organisation that aims to provide emotional and practical support and information. It provides a variety of classes and workshops for parents during pregnancy and after birth. All sessions provide parents with the information they need to enable them to make decisions about their pregnancies, birth and the care of their babies, as well as an opportunity to meet others in similar circumstances. A full programme of classes is held at the centre throughout the week including music, antenatal and baby yoga, shiatsu and baby massage, as well as one-off antenatal classes. Birth pools, birth balls, a library and a newsletter are available.

NEONATAL CARE

Both Simpsons and St John's have neonatal units to provide specialist care for babies. Parents are encouraged to visit and to participate in their baby's care; siblings are also welcome. Parents may stay if accommodation is available, with priority given to those whose babies are acutely ill or have been transferred to the unit from another hospital. Breastfeeding is encouraged and necessary facilities are provided. Parents and siblings may visit any time but supervision of children is required.

BabyView

www.babylink.info/edinburgh/NeonatalUnit
If your baby is treated within the neonatal unit at the Royal Infirmary of Edinburgh you can use this website to access information about the care and treatment your baby will receive. It has two sections – the first is a public section that covers general information relevant to babies needing neonatal care and what happens within the Simpsons neonatal unit; the second section contains secure pages which can only be accessed by parents and enables them to see medical reports and receive information written by nursing staff about their baby, and, if they choose, to share this with other family members.

Simpsons Special Care Babies (SSCB)

PO Box 12258, North West DO, EH4 1YB
www.sscb.org
A charity that supports the neonatal unit based in the Simpsons unit of the Royal Infirmary of Edinburgh. It is dedicated to fundraising for the care of premature or sick newborn babies, and the support of their parents. The charity is run by volunteers who either work in the unit, or have had a child (or children) go through it.

POSTNATAL & BREASTFEEDING SUPPORT

Postnatal care is provided at home by the local midwifery team. Community midwives will visit you at home after the birth of your baby and will attend the delivery if you have a home birth. They will visit every day until the baby is 10 days old (or for longer if there are any problems), then the health visitor will take over. Both midwives and health visitors will provide breastfeeding support.

Health visitors are registered nurses who have undertaken further extensive training. The focus of much of their work is on families and children. This is achieved through home visits, clinic contact and parenting programmes, and involves helping parents develop an understanding of their child's health and development as well as offering wider support for the family. They have a sound knowledge of the local community and the resources available and can direct families to relevant agencies, e.g. Children and Families Services, and local groups, to obtain the help and support they might require. Health visitors also work closely with other members of Primary Health Care teams such as midwives, doctors, practice nurses, district nurses, community psychiatric nurses and school nurses.

Postnatal doulas can also provide support for between 10 days and 2 mths after the birth – see p 329 for more information.

Bluebell at Parentline Scotland

0800 345 7457
Helpline for postnatal depression. Lines are open from 09.00-17.00, Mon, Wed and Fri and from 09.00-21.00 Tues and Thurs.

Breastfeeding clinic at the Simpson Centre

Little France, 51 Little France Crescent, Old Dalkeith Road, EH16 4SA
The Simpson Centre for Reproductive Health has Baby Friendly status awarded by UNICEF for its support of breastfeeding. There is a weekly drop-in clinic for those with breastfeeding problems – Tues 12.00-16.00. It's recommended you go early! There are 2 play areas on the ground floor of the centre with a selection of toys and children's books. Parents are asked to keep children under supervision at all times.

Breastfeeding Network (BfN)

0300 100 0210
www.breastfeedingnetwork.org.uk
The Supporterline is a helpline staffed by volunteers who have breastfed their own babies and who have received training in breastfeeding.

Breastfeeding Support

www.realbabymilk.org
Midwives and health visitors provide support for breastfeeding and can put you in touch with local support groups. Some are listed in the Edinburgh area of this site.

Edinburgh Postnatal Depression Project

Wallace House, 3 Boswall Road, EH5 3RJ
0131 538 7288
pnd@crossreach.org.uk

8a Palmerston Place, EH12 5AA
0131 220 3547

East Edinburgh PND Centre, near Portobello
The Gate Lodge, 27 Milton Road East, EH15 2NL
0131 454 4315
Also an Outreach Service at **Craigour Community Health Flat in Gracemount, Edinburgh**. This project aims to provide support to women, men and their families with a child under 3 yrs old. You can contact the project direct, or be referred via a health visitor, GP or other health professional. It offers a range of services to families suffering with postnatal depression, including: couple and individual counselling, women's therapy groups and baby massage classes. All services supported with crèche facilities.

La Leche League

0845 120 2918 (UK Helpline)
01620 822260 (East Lothian Leader)
www.laleche.org.uk
www.llledinburgh.wordpress.com
La Leche (pronounced "lalay-chay") is an international organisation that provides breastfeeding support, encouragement and information. The helpline provides telephone counselling from trained volunteers who have personal breastfeeding experience. There are local groups across the UK for pregnant and breastfeeding mothers to meet informally, with

their children as well as friends and relatives.

The Edinburgh group is based at the Pregnancy and Parents Centre (see p 334) and meets monthly, with separate sessions for those breastfeeding toddlers.

National Breastfeeding Helpline

0300 100 0212
Funded by the Department of Health, this helpline is provided by the Breastfeeding Network and the Association of Breastfeeding Mothers. It is staffed by volunteers who have breastfed and received intensive training in order to provide support.

NCT Breastfeeding Line

0300 330 0771
www.nct.org.uk
NCT provides information, support and encouragement for breastfeeding through its network of breastfeeding counsellors who have all breastfed their own children and have been through intensive training. They can also arrange the hire of electronic breast pumps and valley cushions.

NCT Postnatal Support

0300 330 0773 (postnatal support)
0844 243 6123 (Edinburgh North)
0844 243 6124 (Edinburgh South)
www.nct.org.uk
www.nctedinburgh.moonfruit.com
NCT offers extensive postnatal support in the form of local groups of parents who meet on a regular basis. If you go to NCT antenatal classes your name will be given to your local group representative who should contact you around the time your baby is due, if not before. She will give you details of local meetings and may be able to advise you whom to contact if you have any specific problems. You are welcome to join a postnatal support group even if you have not been to NCT antenatal classes. Activities include coffee mornings or afternoons, evening talks, discussion groups, bumps and babies groups, fundraising events, picnics, local newsletter, etc. Members receive a quarterly magazine.

PERINATAL DEPRESSION

Perinatal depression occurs either before (antenatal) or after (postnatal) the birth of a baby. Do not hesitate to ask for help; it is not uncommon and it is a treatable illness. Your GP or health visitor will provide support and advice, including helping you to access other support services.

THERAPY CENTRES FOR CHILDREN WITH ADDITIONAL NEEDS

Bobath Scotland

0141 352 5000
www.bobathscotland.org.uk
These centres – situated throughout the UK – specialise in the treatment of cerebral palsy and acquired neurological conditions in children and adults. The Scottish Bobath Centre is in Glasgow. If you feel your child would benefit, call the Families Coordinator at the children's therapy centre. A letter of referral is required from your child's consultant giving a full medical history.

Craighalbert Centre

01236 456100
sccmi@craighalbert.co.uk
www.craighalbert.co.uk
The Craighalbert Centre is the Scottish Centre for Children with Motor Impairments, providing education and therapy services for children and young people with cerebral palsy and related conditions. Based in Cumbernauld, it is a nursery and school, but children can join one of its regular clubs or attend on periodic placement. The therapy is based on the methods of the Peto Institute – conductive education therapy.

COMPLEMENTARY HEALTHCARE

There are many complementary/alternative therapists offering a range of treatments in the Edinburgh area. Not all would be suitable for children or pregnant women. Individual practitioners offer most services privately and fees for consultation and treatment vary widely. Check that any therapist is registered with the appropriate professional body.

It would not be practical to include all therapists here; your local library may be able to direct you to a national organisation or professional body who can provide details of local therapists. An entry below is not necessarily a recommendation.

You can request an NHS referral to the Homeopathic Hospital if you think this would help you or your child. It is in Glasgow but operates outreach clinics in St John's in Howden.

YOGA & MASSAGE THERAPIES

BabyCalm

25 Inverleith Row, EH3 5QH
0131 552 4830
0871 107 3202
anne@babycalm.co.uk
www.babycalmedinburgh.co.uk
BabyCalm is a unique concept, devised by a mother of 4, which aims to turn crying babies and stressed parents into calmer babies and happier parents. Anne Young, an experienced complementary therapist and baby massage expert, runs BabyCalm Edinburgh and offers BabyCalm Colic and Crying Workshops (newborn to 12 wks) and BabyCalm Parenting Classes (newborn to 20 wks). Classes and workshops can either be at 25 Inverleith Row or at your own home.

From Spring 2012, Anne will also be offering ToddlerCalm.

Have you any information you would like to add? Email us at info@efuf.co.uk

BabyCalm™ is a unique concept presented through classes and workshops helping new parents understand how to calm their baby's crying, avoid colic and aid restful sleep - turning crying babies and stressed parents into calmer babies and happier parents.

Antenatal Workshops
Colic and Crying Workshops
Parenting Classes

Anne Young BSc RN CBMI MIFPA

mob: 07811 073 202
email: anne@babycalm.co.uk

www.scents-of-wellbeing.co.uk

OTHER THERAPIES & SERVICES

Chatterbox Speech Therapy

Contact: Mrs Jane Armstrong
Registered speech and language therapist
0131 445 3965
07952 715609
armstrongjane@sky.com
www.chatterbox-speechtherapy.co.uk
For children of 3½ yrs upwards. Chatterbox offers a range of assessments which can be used to determine any issues with a child's speech and/or language skills. It is a mobile service, coming to your house, where a thorough investigation is made of your child's communication skills.

Discover Chiropractic

240 Queensferry Road, EH4 2BP
0131 332 0063
sayhello@discover-chiropractic.co.uk
Child-friendly family-run business, focused on family care. Consultations available from birth; premises accessible to wheelchairs.

Birthlight

www.birthlight.com
A charity that focuses on the use of yoga and breathing methods to enhance the well-being of you and your baby. The website provides details of local baby massage and baby yoga instructors.

Knotstressed

Contact: Onie Tibbitt and Frances Paulo
07717 783230
relax@knotstressed.com
www.knotstressed.com
Pregnancy and postnatal massage, birth preparation and hypnobirthing, baby massage, baby shiatsu, baby signing, yellow submarine parent, baby and toddler group, great massage for dads too!

The Edinburgh Natural Health Centre

GP Plus, 1 Wemyss Place, EH3 6DH
07950 012501
jncw@enhc.co.uk
www.enhc.co.uk
Appointments at Wemyss Pl on Mons only. Acupuncture, homeopathy, acupressure massage, Chinese herbal medicine and nutrition are available with advice on and treatment for vaccinations. Consultation by appointment.

Elemental Birth

07891 059677
admin@elementalbirth.co.uk
www.elementalbirth.co.uk
Services include waterbirth pool hire, birth preparation workshops and YogaBirth classes.

Glovers Integrated Healthcare

10 William Street, EH3 7NH
0131 225 3161
info@glovers-health.co.uk
www.glovers-health.co.uk
Health consultations with homeopathy for adults and children. Offers homeopathic support package for pregnancy and childbirth.

Health All Round

Springwell House, Ardmillan Terrace, EH11 2JL
0131 537 7530
info@healthallround.org.uk
www.healthallround.org.uk
A local charity identifying and responding to a range of health needs and issues within the community of Gorgie, Dalry and surrounding areas. Offers counselling, complementary therapies, exercise groups and yoga. Weekly multicultural women's group.

Hypnotherapy Directory

www.hypnotherapy-directory.org.uk
Searchable website that helps you find a hypnotherapist near you. Only lists hypnotherapists who are registered or who have sent in proof of qualifications/insurance cover.

Medicalternative

Waterside House, 19 Hawthornbank Lane, EH4 3BH
0131 225 5656
reception@medicalternative.com
www.medicalternative.com
A private healthcare centre, which encompasses both conventional and alternative care. You can walk in off the street and see a qualified GP (no referral or appointment needed). There are numerous alternative therapists, all highly qualified and specialists in their own field. Nappy-changing facilities.

Mulberry House

21 Manor Place, EH3 7DX
0131 225 2012
0131 220 6885
enquiries@mulberryhouse.co.uk
www.mulberryhouse.co.uk
A complementary health centre offering an extensive range of therapies, classes and workshops – many geared towards mother and baby. There is also a low income clinic.

Napiers Dispensary

18 Bristo Place, EH1 1EZ
0131 225 5542
and
35 Hamilton Place, Stockbridge, EH3 5BA
0131 315 2130
www.napiers.net
Parent/child herbal clinic by appointment. Baby/child homeopathic clinic (monthly) by appointment. Consultations in herbal medicine, aromatherapy, osteopathy, homeopathy, acupuncture and counselling. The parent and child herbal clinics provide dedicated support for pregnant women, babies and children. Specialists in women's health problems also available. The shops stock a range of traditional herbal remedies, nutritional supplements, aromatherapy products and organic skin care as well as their own mother and baby range. Mail order available.

Neal's Yard Remedies

102 Hanover Street, EH2 1DR
0131 226 3223
edinburgh@nealsyardremedies.com
www.nealsyardremedies.com/edinburgh-store
Stocks organic skin care, aromatherapy, homeopathic, herbal and flower remedies. A wider variety of complementary therapies are offered through its treatment rooms. Mail order available.

SOMA Osteopathy

21 Queen Charlotte Street, EH6 6BA
0131 553 3388
info@somauk.com
www.somauk.com
Healthcare clinic specialising in the physical well-being of the whole person. Offers maternity support for mothers, babies and children – osteopathy, massage, reflexology, acupuncture, postnatal pelvic checks, and cranial osteopathy.

The Whole Works Complementary Therapy and Counselling Centre

Jackson's Close, 209 Royal Mile, EH1 1PZ
0131 225 8092
enquiries@thewholeworks.co.uk
www.thewholeworks.co.uk
Offers a range of complementary health therapies, counselling and psychotherapy services, including craniosacral therapy, massage, homeopathy, chiropractic, acupuncture and herbal medicine.

USEFUL ADDRESSES

This list is not intended to be exhaustive but it may help point you in the right direction if you are seeking local information. Your local GP, health visitor, NCT group, library and community centre are also useful sources for contacts.

Action for Sick Children (Scotland)

22 Laurie Street, EH6 5AB
0131 553 6553
www.ascscotland.org.uk
A charity for all children in hospital and for adults caring for them. It provides information for parents with babies in special care units and parent packs to help children prepare for a hospital visit.

Chalmers Sexual Health Centre

2A Chalmers Street, EH3 9ES
0131 536 1070
www.nhslothian.scot.nhs.uk
Offers a range of contraception, pregnancy testing, gynaecological services and testing and treatment for STIs. The website also provides information about local sexual health clinics but the Chalmers is the main HQ. You do not need to be referred by a GP. Walk-in clinic open Mon-Fri 08.30-10.00, otherwise call to make an appointment. Phone lines open Mon-Thurs 08.30-20.00, Fri 08.30-16.00.

Child Accident Prevention Trust

0207 608 3828
safe@capt.org.uk
www.capt.org.uk
A national charity committed to reducing the number of children and young people killed, disabled and seriously injured as a result of accidents. Their website provides safety advice for babies, toddlers, and children aged 3-5 yrs.

NHS 24

0845 424 2424
www.nhs24.com
Provides up-to-date health information and advice for people in Scotland. The telephone service operates 24/7 and can help you if your GP surgery is closed. The website's email enquiry service provides information about named health conditions, treatments and NHS services within 5 days.

St Andrew's First Aid

Edinburgh, Lothian and Borders
Strachan House, 16 Torpichen Street, EH3 8JB
0131 229 5419
www.firstaid.org.uk
Offers courses to the public including baby and child first aid.

HELP & ADVICE

While this section is not able to cover all of the support and services available to families, we hope it's useful. A number of services are listed that families can contact for further information. Kindred, for example, is a very valuable resource for parents of children with special needs in the Edinburgh area looking for information or support.

ADVICE CENTRES

Adviceguide

www.adviceguide.org.uk
The online advice service of the National Association of Citizens Advice Bureaux.

Citizen Advice Bureaux Edinburgh

www.citizensadviceedinburgh.co.uk
Free, confidential service providing general advice and information on topics such as housing, family, employment, benefits and consumer issues. Offers money advice and debt negotiation, representation at employment and social security tribunals, and some court representation. Most offices have legal clinics on a weekly basis. Check website for opening hours.

Local offices throughout Edinburgh can be found at:

CAE Dundas Street
58 Dundas Street, EH3 6QZ
0131 557 1500 (advice), 0131 558 3681 (appts only)

CAE Gorgie/Dalry
Fountainbridge Library, 137 Dundee Street, EH11 1BG

0131 474 8080 (advice), 0131 474 8081 (appts only).

CAE Portobello
8a-8b Bath Street, Portobello, EH15 1EY

0131 669 7138 (advice), 0131 669 9503 (appts only)

The Leith and Pilton offices offer a "drop-in" service (no appointment needed):

CAE Leith
166 Great Junction Street, Leith, EH6 5LJ

CAE Pilton
661 Ferry Road, Pilton, EH4 2TX
0131 332 9434 (advice)

Citizen Advice Bureaux Scotland

www.cas.org.uk

The City of Edinburgh Council Advice Shop

85-87 South Bridge, EH1 1HN
0131 225 1255
Consumer advice, debt advice and advice on welfare benefits.

Gingerbread Edinburgh and Lothian Project

c/o Tollcross Primary School,
117-119 Fountainbridge, EH3 9QG
0131 478 1391
gingerbread@wwmail.co.uk
www.gingerbreadchildcare.org.uk
Information and advice centre for lone parent families. Also provides legal and informal counselling by appointment, childcare services and after-school care clubs. Two-partner families welcome to use childcare facilities. Holiday information packs and leaflets on all of the above available on request.

Granton Information Centre

134-148 West Granton Road, EH5 1PE
0131 552 0458
info@gic.org.uk
www.gic.org.uk
Information and advice on benefits, debts, housing, employment etc. Also available for development of local self-help/support groups. Youth and disability rights.

The Rights Office

Southside Community Centre, 117 Nicolson Street, EH8 9YG
0131 667 6339
Advice sessions, independent advice and representation on welfare benefits, disability rights, employment rights, debt and housing.

BENEFITS & SOCIAL SECURITY INFORMATION

There's a good deal of information online. A few useful resources are:

Benefit Enquiry Line

0800 882 200
A confidential telephone service for people with disabilities, their representatives and their carers.

Benefits Now

www.benefitsnow.co.uk
The website has detailed information about claiming Disability Living Allowance, along with discussion lists where parents can exchange advice and information, as well as links to equipment suppliers and information about the Motability scheme. The site also contains the full text of the Disability Handbook, used by the Benefits Agency when assessing claims and which has useful information about the appeals process.

Child Benefit

0845 302 1444
www.hmrc.gov.uk/childbenefit

Child Tax Credit

0845 300 3900, 0845 300 3909 (textphone)
www.hmrc.gov.uk/taxcredits
(general queries)
For help or information regarding child tax credit

see the relevant section of www.direct.gov.uk, which includes a tax credits online questionnaire to check eligibility. You can contact the helpline or write to the social security office. You will need your NI number (and your partner's if the claim is joint). The helpline can be extremely busy, but it's still quicker than writing.

Department for Work and Pensions

www.direct.gov.uk
Provides details of all public services including the different types of benefits available and how to make a claim.

Parents at Work

www.workingfamilies.org.uk
Has a wide range of information including a Tax Credit online calculator and fact sheets about rights during maternity leave and flexible working. Aims to help children, working parents and their employers find a better balance between responsibilities at home and work.

Their Children with Disabilities Project produces a newsletter – "Waving not drowning", for parents of disabled children who work or want to work.

Social Security Office

38 Castle Terrace, EH3 9SJ
0131 229 9191
www.edinburgh.gov.uk
General information and advice about social security and child benefits. More information concerning benefits can be found on Edinburgh City Council's website under Council and Government. You can also find local social security and job centre plus offices on this website.

HOUSING

The following listings should be particularly useful for people with disabilities or those caring for people or children with disabilities.

City of Edinburgh Housing Department

www.edinburgh.gov.uk
Part of the official council website is devoted to housing issues. Links to sections on adaptations, information for tenants and details of houses available for exchange.

Council Tax Reduction

To qualify for the council tax reduction (which would move your council tax bill down by one band), households must include a child or adult who is permanently disabled. They must also either: use a wheelchair indoors; need a second bathroom or kitchen; or need one room as a living space.
The reduction is granted regardless of income or savings, and claims can't be backdated indefinitely if applicants can prove that they met the criteria in the past. Contact your local council tax office for further information by phoning your local council switchboard (for City of Edinburgh Council call 0131 200 2000).

Ownership Options in Scotland

0131 661 3400
moira@oois.org.uk
www.ownershipoptions.org.uk
A charity providing information, advice and other support (although not financial) to disabled people and their families, carers and professionals to improve access to housing in owner-owned, social and rented accommodation.

MEDIA LISTINGS

Edinburgh Life

PO Box 28948, Gorebridge, EH22 9BD
info@edinburgh-life.co.uk
www.edinburghlifemagazine.com
Heritage, history, people, places, where to go, what to eat, what to do, where to meet. Edinburgh Life explores the myriad aspects of our capital city and its surrounding areas.

EdinburghLife
January/February 2012 £2   and the Lothians
www.edinburghlifemagazine.com

The Scottish National Portrait Gallery Opens

Famous Oyster Club

Beautiful Snowdrop Walks

Chinese New Year

The Pandas ar~

The magazine for people who love their city.
On sale everywhere across the city or visit www.edinburghlifemagazine to subscribe.
Tel: 07850 938407

WIN!
A family pass to Edinburgh Zoo

Families Edinburgh

0131 622 0405
www.familiesedinburgh.co.uk
Free bi-monthly magazine – printed and online – for families with young children. Printed version distributed at playgroups, nurseries, leisure centres, etc. Local listings, advertisements, features.

The List

14 High Street, EH1 1TE
0131 550 3070
newwriters@list.co.uk
www.list.co.uk
Published fortnightly and online, includes a small section "Kids' List" which provides information about events in and around Edinburgh and Glasgow. Printed version available at newsagents.

MADE (Mums and Dads Edinburgh)

PO Box 28825, Edinburgh, EH14 9BA
07738 068022
mademag@live.co.uk
www.mademagazine.co.uk
The free, glossy, handbag-friendly, lifestyle magazine for parents across Edinburgh. Published bi-monthly and distributed via libraries, nurseries, shops, cafés, leisure centres etc. MADE has all the latest in Edinburgh news, reviews and interviews.

The Scotsman Group

108 Holyrood Road
0131 620 8680 (reception)
0131 620 8874 (online advertising)
0131 620 8342 (display advertising)
www.scotsman.com

The Scotsman

Carries birth announcements. Has daily section with details of exhibitions, theatres, art galleries, etc. Weekend section on Sat with "What's on" information.

Evening News

Daily afternoon and evening paper full of local news. "Daily Plan-It" has details of events.

Scotland on Sunday

Scottish Sunday Paper with events page.

SOCIAL WORK SERVICES

For all first-time contact with children and families social care services contact Social Care Direct.

Social Care Direct

0131 200 2324
socialcaredirect@edinburgh.gov.uk

Opening hours: Mon-Thurs 08.30-17.00, Fri 08.30-15.55. Outside of these hrs and on public holidays contact the Emergency Social Work Service – 0800 731 6969.

Social work services provide a range of services to support children with disabilities and illness. For more information about any of these services contact your nearest Social Work Centre (below).

SOCIAL WORK CENTRES

Captains Road Social Work Centre

40 Captains Road, EH17 8QF
0131 529 5300

Visit our website for updates:
www.efuf.co.uk

Craigentinny Social Work Centre

Loaning Road, EH7 6JE
0131 661 8291

Craigmillar Social Work Centre

171 Duddingston Park South, EH15 3EG
0131 657 8500

Leith Social Work Centre

St John's House, 71 Constitution Street,
EH6 7AF
0131 553 2121

Muirhouse Crescent Social Work Centre

34 Muirhouse Crescent, EH4 4QL
0131 343 1991

Murrayburn Gate Social Work Centre

5 Murrayburn Gate, EH14 2SS
0131 442 4131

Oxgangs Path Social Work Centre

4 Oxgangs Path, EH13 9LX
0131 445 4451

Springwell House Social Work Centre

1 Gorgie Road, EH11 2LA
0131 313 3366

Victoria Street Social Work Centre

11 Victoria Street, EH1 2HE
0131 226 6731

West Pilton Gardens Social Work Centre

8 West Pilton Gardens, EH4 4DP
0131 529 5400

Westfield House Social Work Centre

5 Kirk Loan, EH12 7HD
0131 334 9933

SUPPORT & ASSISTANCE

This section contains alphabetical listings of organisations and voluntary groups who offer support and assistance on a wide range of issues.

The Action Group

advice@actiongroup.org.uk
www.actiongroup.org.uk
A voluntary organisation that has developed a range of services for people with support needs and learning disabilities and their carers throughout Edinburgh and the Lothians. They offer a family info and support service, playschemes, welfare rights advice, holidays, leisure schemes, sitter service, information and newsletters.

AFASIC Scotland

01382 250060
www.afasic.org.uk
www.afasicscotland.org.uk
www.talkingpoint.org.uk
www.actiongroup.org.uk
Charity supporting children and young adults with speech, language or communication impairments and their parents/carers.

Opening hours: Mon-Fri 10.30-14.30 (helpline).

AFASIC Edinburgh

0131 557 9755,
afasicedinburgh@btinternet.com
Local AFASIC support group.

Allergy UK

01322 619864
www.allergyuk.com
UK charity providing information on all aspects
of allergy.

Ask Nanny

Contact: Trudi on 0131 476 0004
www.asknanny.com
Offers parent coaching to advise parents on all
stages of baby and childhood including sleep,
feeding and behaviour.

Asthma UK Scotland

4 Queen Street, EH2 1JE
0131 226 2544, 0845 701 0203 (helpline)
info@asthma.org.uk
www.asthma.org.uk/scotland
Helpline available Mon-Fri 09.00-17.00. An
independent UK charity, based in London,
Edinburgh, Belfast and Cardiff, which works to
conquer asthma.

BEMAS

Black and Ethnic Minorities Advice Service
The Action Group, Norton Park
57 Albion Road, EH7 5QY
0131 475 2315
advice@actiongroup.org
Provides practical advice and assistance
regarding social work services, education,
health and housing to black or ethnic minority
families who care for children and adults with
additional support needs. The service is free
and confidential. Interpreters can be arranged
upon request.

Birthlink Adoption Counselling Service

21 Castle Street, EH2 3DN
0131 225 6441
mail@birthlink.org.uk
www.birthlink.org.uk
The adoption contact register for Scotland.
Counselling, support and advice for adopted
people, birth parents and adoptive parents.
24hr answering service, call to make an
appointment.

Capability Scotland Advice Service

11 Ellersly Road, EH12 6HY
0131 337 9876
0131 346 2529 (text phone)
www.capability-scotland.org.uk
Provides information and advice on any
disability matter.

Child Brain Injury Trust

0845 601 4939
www.childbraininjurytrust.org.uk
Works with children who have an acquired brain
injury, and their families. They have a number
of new parents' groups which meet to talk
about brain injury, to share ideas and to have a
night out. There are groups in Edinburgh, West
Lothian and Glasgow.

Children in Scotland

Princes House, 5 Shandwick Place, EH2 4RG
0131 228 8484
www.childreninscotland.org.uk
National agency for voluntary, statutory and
professional organisations and individuals
working with children and their families in
Scotland. It exists to identify and promote the
interests of children and their families and to
ensure that the relevant policies, services and
other provisions are of the highest possible
quality.

The Compassionate Friends

0845 123 2304 (helpline)
0845 120 3785 (office)
info@tcf.org.uk
www.tcf.org.uk
A self-help group for parents and their families who have suffered the loss of a child of any age through any cause.

Contact a Family Scotland

Craigmillar Social Enterprise & Arts Centre, 11/9 Harewood Road, EH16 4NT
0131 659 2930, 0808 808 3555 (helpline)
www.cafamily.org.uk
Introduces and links families whose children have special needs. Provides support and advice to parents whatever their child's medical condition. Website covers a huge number of conditions and syndromes, with details of support groups. Very useful helpline – a one-stop advice service for parents of children with additional needs – which gives advice on a wide range of topics: medical conditions, benefits, holiday funding, and how to make contact with other parents for mutual support.

Couple Counselling Lothian

9a Dundas Street, EH3 6QG
0131 556 1527
info@cclothian.org.uk
www.cclothian.org.uk
A range of counselling and other services for couples, individuals, young people and extended families who are experiencing relationship difficulties.

Cruse Bereavement Care Scotland

3 Rutland Square, EH1 2AS
0845 600 2227 (use this central number to get a referral to Edinburgh office)
edinburgh@crusescotland.org.uk
www.crusescotland.org.uk
Bereavement counselling, advisory services and friendship groups for adults. Also offers bereavement counselling to children.

Depression Alliance

information@depressionalliance.org
www.depressionalliance.org
Resources for those suffering from postnatal or antenatal depression. There isn't currently a helpline but you can contact DA to request an information pack.

DisabledGo Edinburgh

www.disabledgo.info
An internet guide to accessibility of venues throughout the UK, including Edinburgh.

Down's Syndrome Scotland

158-160 Balgreen Road, EH11 3AU
0131 313 4225
info@dsscotland.org.uk
www.dsscotland.org.uk
Support and information for families of people with Down's Syndrome.

Edinburgh & Lothians Regional Equality Council

14 Forth Street, EH1 3LH
0131 556 0441
admin@elrec.org.uk
www.elrec.org.uk
Aims to work towards the elimination of racial discrimination.

The Edinburgh Parent Centre

28 Kirk Brae EH16 6HH
0131 664 5388
info@theparentcentre.co.uk
Offers courses to support parents in the tasks of parenting. Fees apply.

Edinburgh Twins Club

www.edinburghtwins.co.uk
Support group for families with twins, triplets etc, providing help, advice and friendship. See also TAMBA.

Edinburgh Women's Aid

4 Cheyne Street, EH4 1JB
0131 315 8110 (helpline)
info@edinwomensaid.co.uk
An all-women, confidential organisation which provides information, support and, where appropriate, refuge accommodation for women and any accompanying children who have experience of or are at risk of domestic abuse.

Opening hours: Helpline Mon-Wed, Fri 10.00-15.00, Thurs 10.00-19.00, Sat 09.30-12.45.

Edinburgh Women's Rape and Sexual Abuse Centre

1 Leopold Place, EH7 5JW
0131 556 9437 (helpline)
info@ewrasac.org.uk
www.ewrasac.org.uk
Information, practical and emotional support for women who have been raped or sexually assaulted at any time in their lives. Run by women for women.

Enquire

Children in Scotland, 5 Shandwick Place EH2 4RG
0845 123 2303 (helpline)
info@enquire.org.uk
www.enquire.org.uk
Scottish advice service for additional support for learning. Offer independent and impartial advice and information to parents, carers, practitioners, children and young people. Provide a range of clear and easy to read guides and fact sheets explaining everything from how to find out if your child needs extra help at school to what should happen when they leave school.

Opening hours: Helpline Mon-Fri 09.00-16.30.

Epilepsy Scotland Edinburgh Office

Orchard Brae House, Queensferry Road, EH4 2HG
0131 226 5458, 0808 800 2200 (helpline)

enquiries@epilepsyscotland.org.uk
www.epilepsyscotland.org.uk
Provides information on the causes and treatment of epilepsy and campaigns for more epilepsy services in Scotland. The Edinburgh office runs a support group for adults, as well as a parents' support group and youth groups. For more information contact Michael Adair by phone or email **madair@epilepsyscotland.org.uk**

Equality and Human Rights Commission

0845 604 5510 (Scottish helpline)
www.equalityhumanrights.com
Helpline can give information on disability.

ERIC – Enuresis Resource and Information Centre

0845 370 8008 (helpline)
info@eric.org.uk
www.eric.org.uk
Provides advice and information to children, young people, parents and professionals on bedwetting, day-time wetting and soiling.

Opening hours: Helpline Mon-Fri 10.00-16.00.

FAIR

Family Advice and Information Resource
95 Causeway, EH9 1QG
0131 662 1962
fair@fairadvice.org.uk
www.fairadvice.org.uk
Information and advice service for people with learning disabilities, parents, carers and people who work with them in Edinburgh. Call them or pop into their office – open Tues-Fri.

The Family Fund

0845 130 4542
info@familyfund.org.uk
www.familyfund.org.uk
Helps families of disabled children under 17 with the cost of holidays, leisure, laundry equipment, driving lessons and more. Provides a range of

information on benefits, holidays, transport etc. Apply by phone, online or in writing. You'll need to supply your child's name, date of birth, disability and the help you need. Only those entitled to certain benefits/tax credits may apply.

http://ellp.net/firststep/
Community project working in partnership with parents and the local community to support families with children aged up to 8 yrs. Open Mon-Fri.

Family Mediation Lothian

37 George Street, EH2 2HN
0131 226 4507
info@familymediationlothian.org
www.relationships-scotland.org.uk/fmlothian
Offer relationship counselling, family mediation and family support.

Opening hours: Mon-Thurs 09.30-16.30, Fri 09.30-13.00.

Family Support Group

Queensferry, Dalmeny and Kirkliston area
0131 319 3200 (Queensferry High School)
Contact: Sean McCarthy, Principal Teacher for Support for Learning and Behaviour at Queensferry High School. Group provides support for parents of children with additional learning needs – the Family Support Group has been integrated into the Parent and Community Council.

Firsthand

39 Broughton Place, EH1 3RR
0131 557 3121
info.firsthand@gmail.com
www.firsthand-edinburgh.org.uk
A charity, established in 1992, that aims to increase resiliency and improve well-being of vulnerable families, children and young people who are isolated as a result of their caring duties, disability or mental health. They provide a sitter service to lone parents and families affected by disability, and a befriending service to isolated young people with disabilities and/or mental health issues.

First Step Community Project

37 Galt Avenue, Musselburgh, EH21 8HU
0131 665 0848
firststep1@btconnect.com

Grapevine

Norton Park, 57 Albion Road, EH7 5QY
0131 475 2370
grapevine@lothiancil.demon.co.uk
www.lothiancil.org.uk
Provides free, confidential information to disabled people, their supporters and any organisation or individual looking for disability-related information in Edinburgh and Lothian. You can contact Grapevine about a wide variety of issues, including: disability benefits, transport, aids and equipment, access issues, community care and direct payments, housing and adaptations, holidays and leisure, education and employment, and the Disability Discrimination Act.

Home Link Family Support

Unit 5, Abbeymount Techbase, 2 Easter Road, EH7 5AN
0131 661 0890
administrator@homelinkbefriending.org
www.homelinkbefriending.org
Provides emotional and practical support to families with young children, using trained befrienders.

Homestart

0800 068 6368
www.home-start.org.uk

Leith and North East Edinburgh Branch
247 Leith Walk, EH6 8NY
0131 553 7819
admin@homestartleith.co.uk
www.homestartleith.co.uk.

Edinburgh West and South West Branch
108a-110a Gorgie Road, EH11 2NP
0131 347 2881
homestart.edinwsw@btconnect.com.

UK-wide organisation offering help, friendship, advice and support to families with a child under 5. Trained volunteers visit families once a week for 2-3 hrs offering emotional support and practical help.

Humanist Society of Scotland

272 Bath Street, Glasgow, G2 4JR
0870 874 9002
www.humanism-scotland.org.uk
Information about non-religious ceremonies, including baby naming ceremonies.

Hyperactive Children's Support Group

01243 539966
hacsg@hascg.org.uk
www.hacsg.org.uk
Considers non-drug therapies (dietary ones in particular) important for under 6s.

Independent Special Education Advice (ISEA) Scotland

164 High Street, Dalkeith, EH22 1AY
0131 454 0096
isea@isea.org.uk
www.isea.org.uk
Provides advice, information, advocacy and representation to parents throughout Scotland who have a child or young person with additional support needs.

Kindred

14 Rillbank Terrace, EH9 1LN
0131 536 0583 (helpline), 0131 536 0360
kindred.enquiries@gmail.com
www.kindred-scotland.org
Provide advocacy and information on services available to children with additional support needs and their carers. You don't need a specific question, they also provide a listening ear. Kindred also runs support groups and has a "funder finder" for grants for holidays, equipment etc.

Lothian Autistic Society

Unit 22, Castlebrae Business Centre
40 Peffer Place, EH16 4BB
0131 661 3834
office@lothianautistic.org.
www.lothianautistic.org
Provides monthly support meetings for all parents of children with ASC.

Mindroom

PO Box 13684, Musselburgh, EH21 1YL
0131 317 1016
moreinfo@mindroom.org
www.mindroom.org
A charity dedicated to raising awareness of learning difficulties as well as providing direct help and support for children and adults with learning difficulties, and their families.

The Miscarriage Association

01924 200799 (helpline)
www.miscarriageassociation.org.uk

Opening hours: Helpline Mon-Fri 09.00-16.00.

Mosaic Down's Syndrome UK

www.mosaicdownsyndrome.org
Support and information for families of those with Mosaic Down's Syndrome.

Muscular Dystrophy Campaign

0800 652 6352 (information and support)
www.muscular-dystrophy.org

NCT

0844 243 6994 (UK Switchboard)
0300 330 0771 (NCT Breastfeeding Line – 08.00-22.00)
www.nct.org.uk
www.nctedinburgh.moonfruit.com
Provides classes, groups and counselling services, offering parents information and support during pregnancy and the early years of parenthood.

Local bumps and babies groups, postnatal support groups, social events and Nearly New Sales.

National Deaf Children's Society Scotland

Second Floor, Empire House
131 West Nile Street, Glasgow, G1 2RX
0141 354 7850
0808 800 8880 (freephone helpline)
ndcs.scotland@ndcs.org.uk
www.ndcs.org.uk
An independent UK charity supporting children and young adults with deafness, and their parents/carers.

National Domestic Violence Helpline

0808 200 0247 (24 hrs)
www.nationaldomesticviolencehelpline.org.uk

National Eczema Society

0800 089 1122
helpline@eczema.org
www.eczema.org
An independent UK charity dealing with the management and treatment of eczema.

Opening hours: Helpline Mon-Fri 08.00-20.00.

North West Carers Centre

34a Muirhouse Crescent, EH4 4QL
0131 315 3130
Offers a free, flexible sitter service for people living in, or caring for someone in, North West Edinburgh. Trained paid support workers give people a short break from their caring responsibilities by providing support either to the carer or to the person being cared for.

One Parent Families Scotland

13 Gayfield Square, EH1 3NX
0131 556 3899
info@opfs.org.uk
www.ofps.org.uk

Information and help for lone parents. National Lone Parent Helpline also available: 0808 801 0323.

Parent Network Scotland

0141 948 0022
mail@parentnetworkscotland.org.uk
www.parentnetworkscotland.org.uk
Provide information, courses and workshops for parents to learn and develop parenting skills.

Parenting Across Scotland

1 Boroughloch Square, EH8 9NJ
0131 319 8071
pas@children1st.org.uk
www.parentingacrossscotland.org
A partnership of seven charities across Scotland working together to focus on issues affecting families. Visit the website to find out more about the information and support available.

Parentline Scotland

0808 800 2222
parentsupport@parentlineplus.org.uk
www.parentlinescotland.org.uk
Information, advice, or someone to listen to you on the telephone. Telephone support and advice for parents provided by trained volunteers.

Opening hours: Helpline Mon, Wed, Fri 09.00-17.00, Tues, Thurs 09.00-22.00, Sat, Sun 12.00-20.00.

The PF Counselling Service

8 Ballcarres Street, EH10 5JB
0131 447 0876
info@pfcounselling.org.uk
www.pfcounselling.org.uk
Counselling available for individuals and couples (over 18 yrs) on a wide range of problems and difficulties.

Opening hours: Service open Mon-Thurs 09.00-21.00, Fri 09.00-14.00.

351

PINS – Pelvic Instability Network Scotland

01463 782801
info@pelvicinstability.org.uk
www.pelvicinstability.org.uk
A Scottish charity supporting women with Symphysis Pubis Dysfunction, also known as Pelvic Girdle Pain. Their aim is to provide support and information to women with this condition and to raise awareness of the condition amongst health professionals and the general public.

Positive Help

13a Great King Street, EH3 6QW
0131 558 1122
office@positivehelpedinburgh.co.uk
www.positivehelpedinburgh.co.uk
Voluntary organisation for people living with HIV.

Prison Advice and Care Trust Family Support Service

0808 808 2003 (Offenders' Families Helpline)
info@prisonadvice.org.uk
www.prisonadvice.org.uk
Advice, information and support for the families of those in prison.

RNIB Scotland

12-14 Hillside Crescent, EH7 5EA
0131 652 3140
0303 123 9999 (helpline)
rnibscotland@rnib.org.uk
www.rnib.org.uk
Offers practical support and advice to anyone with a sight problem.

Opening hours: Helpline Mon-Fri 08.45-19.30.

The Rock Trust

55 Albany Street, EH1 3QY
0131 557 4049
admin@rocktrust.org
www.rocktrust.org

This charity helps homeless and socially excluded young people in many ways, including providing supported accommodation for young mothers and babies.

Saheliya

125 Mcdonald Road, EH7 4NW
0131 556 9302
info@saheliya.co.uk
www.saheliya.org.uk
Supports and promotes the positive mental health and well-being of black and minority ethnic women and girls in the Edinburgh area.

SANDS

0207 436 5881 (helpline)
helpline@uksands.org
www.uk-sands.org
Offers support for those affected by stillbirth or the death of a baby in the early weeks of life.

SANDS Lothian
Craiglockhart Centre Tournament Building, 177 Colinton Road, EH14 1BZ
0131 622 6263
www.sands-lothians.org.uk
Offers a range of befriending and counselling services and can also offer helpful advice with a baby's funeral.

Scottish Autism

01259 720044
autism@scottishautism.org
www.scottishautism.org
Exists to help those diagnosed with autism to lead full and enriched lives and become valuable members of the community they live in.

Scottish Cot Death Trust

0141 357 3946
www.scottishcotdeathtrust.org
Gives personal support to bereaved families by letter, telephone and leaflets and may put parents in touch with other bereaved parents.

Scottish National Federation for the Welfare of the Blind

01738 551351
www.snfwb.org.uk
Coordinates organisations working for blind people in Scotland.

Scottish Spina Bifida Association

0131 332 0743 (office)
0845 911 1112 (family support lo-call)
mail@ssba.org.uk
www.ssba.org.uk
Phone the family support service for local contacts.

Sexual Health Line

0800 567 123
Free and confidential service – can give information about local services.

Shakti Women's Aid

Norton Park, 57 Albion Road, EH7 5QY
0131 475 2399 (helpline)
info@shaktiedinburgh.co.uk
www.shaktiedinburgh.co.uk
Offers information, practical and emotional support and safe, temporary accommodation to all black/ethnic minority women and their children who are being abused either physically or mentally by their partners, husbands or families.

Siblings of Children with Autism

Scotland Yard Adventure Centre, 22 Eyre Place Lane, EH3 5EH
0131 557 8199
A parent and toddler group for children 3 yrs and under who have a brother or sister with autism.

Simpson House Drugs Counselling and Related Services

52 Queen Street, EH2 3NS
0131 225 1054
0131 225 6028
counselling@simpson-house.org

353

www.simpson-house.org/counselling
Free and confidential counselling service to drug users, friends and families.

Opening hours: Mon-Fri 09.00-17.00.

The Sleep Lady

Contact: Linda Russell
07827 930830
linda@thesleeplady.co.uk
www.thesleeplady.co.uk
One-to-one support in your own home either by telephone or home visits. Fees apply.

Childrens Sleep Clinic

Are you struggling with your child's sleep ?

Then pop down to the children's sleep clinic for a one to one session with Linda Russell, The Sleeplady, at The Ceramic Experience Ocean Terminal.

Linda also offers a home visiting service as well as working with families by telephone and internet.

For more details visit:
www.thesleeplady.co.uk
or call: **07827930830**

Sleep Scotland

8 Hope Park Terrace, EH8 9NW
0131 651 1392 (support line)
sleepscotland@btinternet.com
www.sleepscotland.org
Support for families of children with additional support needs and severe sleep problems.

Opening hours: Mon-Fri 09.30-17.00.

Smokeline

0800 848 484
www.canstopsmoking.com
Call or chat online.

Opening hours: 09.00-21.00.

Stepfamily Scotland

Gillis Centre, 113 Whitehouse Loan, EH10 1BB
0845 122 8655 (helpline)
0131 623 8951 (office)
info@stepfamilyscotland.org.uk
www.stepfamilyscotland.org.uk
Offers support and information to all members of stepfamilies and those working with them.

Opening hours: Helpline Mon-Thurs 12.00-16.00.

Stepping Stones (North Edinburgh)

10 Wardieburn Road, EH5 1LY
0131 551 1632
A chance for young parents who live in the Greater Pilton area to meet and participate in various activities. Also provides support for young parent families and pregnant teenagers.

TAMBA Twinline

0800 138 0509
www.tamba.org.uk
A confidential listening support and information service run by trained volunteers, all of whom are parents of twins or triplets.

Opening hours: 10.00-13.00 and 19.00-22.00.

VOCAL – Voices of Carers Across Lothian

0131 622 6666 (helpline)
centre@vocal.org.uk
www.vocal.org.uk
A carer-led organisation which campaigns for carers and their needs, giving them a real voice. It provides information and advice to carers and professionals and an advocacy and counselling

service is available to carers free of charge. VOCAL also run free courses for parents on lifting and handling – these can be very useful.

Wellspring

13 Smith's Place, EH6 8NT
0131 553 6660
mail@wellspring-scotland.co.uk
www.wellspring-scotland.co.uk
Offers psychotherapy and counselling to individuals, couples and groups, including families and young people. Fees may apply.

West Lothian parent groups for children with communication difficulties or autism

01506 777598
louise.jarman@wlt.scot.nhs.uk
At this group parents of children with communication difficulties or autism have the opportunity to discuss various topics, including using a variety of visual strategies to improve communication. There is also a library with books on autism and a crèche.

Women's Groups

City of Edinburgh Council, Equality Unit, 12 St Giles Street, EH1 1PT
0131 469 3726
0131 469 3828
For comprehensive information on Women's Groups.

YWCA Scotland

4B Gayfield Place, EH7 4AB
0131 558 8000
reception@ywcascotland.org
Work primarily for and with girls and young women aged 9 to 30 in Scotland, particularly where they face social, economic or educational exclusion. Also engage in activities that have a positive impact on young women and girls. Work in partnership with Aberlour Childcare Trust to provide advice and support to young mothers who have substance misuse issues.

OTHER GUIDES TO EDINBURGH

A-Z guide

Produced by City of Edinburgh Council, listing contacts, community updates, council lists, and general information regarding the city.

City of Edinburgh Council

www.edinburgh.gov.uk
Council-run information website, which provides information about your local community and council departments.

Mumsnet local

www.mumsnet.com/local/edinburgh
Local events, nearly new swaps and sales, a directory of local services, the opportunity to meet local mothers or just chat online on a variety of topics.

Netmums – Edinburgh

www.netmums.com/edinburgh
Includes information on events, activities and meeting local mothers.

Skootkidz

0131 317 1270, 07827 930830
linda@skootkidz.com
Local events guide available through an e-newsletter. Weekly updates on events, clubs, classes, workshops, special offers, family friendly eating out and shopping. To receive Skootkidz send your email address to linda@skootkidz.com.

Visit our website for updates:
www.efuf.co.uk

Index

INDEX

Acknowledgements

Our Researchers and Contributors
Our Advertisers
Our Donors and Helpers

Our researchers and contributors

A great big thank you to this edition's researchers and contributors, and their under 5s!

Emma Anderson	Rhian Hastie	Nicola McLaughlan
Vicky Allan	Susan Heaton	Pamela McMeeken
Jennifer Angus	Joe Hind	Steve Murray
Fay Ballantine	Orla Hobson	Meg Nelson
Val Baillie	Elisabeth Houghton	Felicity Neyme
Cat Bergman	Carolyn Hutchinson	Stephie Phipps
Jane Boardman	Joy Hutchinson	Gillian Platt
Fiona Burden	Andrew Jamieson	Samantha Pringle
Anne Cameron	Catriona Johnson	Judith Rintoul
Christine Carlton	Sheelagh Jones	Nadine Roberts-Leivesley
Pauline Colles	Sarah Joss	Mary Ross
Lindsay Coulton	Aileen Kelly	Imogen Russon-Taylor
Allison Davis	Sophie Kelsall	Hannah Sanguinetti
Ruth Dawkins	Olga Kennedy	Tasca Shadix
Paula Dawson	Amanda Kerr	Jennifer Shooter
Fiona Dill	Rachel Kerr	Paula Skerry
Dani Dinwoodie	Kirsty Lamb	Deborah Smith
Jo Drew	Tara Macdonald	Laura Smith
Louise Duff	Alison Mackenzie	Lizzie Smith
Kate Farrell	Angela Macnamara	Nina Smith
Sean Farrell	Olivia MacPherson	Morag Snaddon
Jenny Fausset	Jane MacSorley	Claire Stevenson
Joanne Finnie Jones	Liz McCabe	Rheona Warrender
Karen Fleming	Gillian McDonald	Jane Watt
Andrea Foster	Louise McGeough	Diahann Whitefield
Rachel F Freeman	Kathy McGlew	Sue Widdicombe
Ruth Harrison	Katie McGlew	

If you'd like to volunteer to become a researcher or contributor for Edinburgh for Under Fives, drop us an email at ed@efuf.co.uk. Work for the 14th edition, out in 2014, will begin in April 2013.

You don't need to be the world's greatest writer. All you need is a bit of time, some commitment – and an under 5!

Our advertisers

All the revenue we make at Edinburgh for Under Fives goes to help us produce the next edition and support Edinburgh NCT. In the past we have supported the former Edinburgh Office at the Stockbridge Health Centre and trained NCT antenatal teachers and breastfeeding counsellors. A big chunk of this revenue comes from advertising – we couldn't produce Edinburgh for Under Fives without it!

So a big thanks to:

Almond Valley Heritage Centre
Baby Calm
Baby Singing
Butterfly Personnel Childcare
Clear Photography
Doodles
Edinburgh Academy Nursery
Edinburgh Libraries
Edinburgh Life
Edinburgh Nursery and School Guide
Head Start Nursery
Maddie and Mark's
MADE Magazine
Monkey Music
NCT bra sales and fitting

Picture House Studios
Plu
Rugby Tots
Safestore UK
Scents of Wellbeing
Scottish Autism
Sleep Lady
The Spartans Community Football Academy
St George's School for Girls
Stina Sparkles
SwimEasy
Totseat
Tumble Tots
Waterbabies

If you'd like to support us by advertising in the next edition, contact business@efuf.co.uk **or look at the business pages on our website** www.efuf.co.uk

Our donors and helpers

Our donors

At Edinburgh for Under Fives we've got so many ideas. We want to do much more for Edinburgh parents and carers to make their lives with their little ones easier, more interesting and more supported. However, as a volunteer committee our time is tight, and we can only work with the funds produced by the sales of the previous edition and the advertising that appears in it.

The following generous organisations have donated money for projects to ensure that we can start realising our vision for the future of Edinburgh for Under Fives.

A huge thanks to the following donors:
Burness LLP
Deloitte
Ernst & Young
KPMG
The Spartans Community Football Academy

Our helpers

Thank you also to PwC parents' group for their support, Marketing Edinburgh for marketing help and advice, Susan Heaton of Clear Photography for her time and skill in capturing such fantastic images for the cover and some of the book's inside pages, and to Safestore UK for generous donation of storage space.

Special thanks to Steve Murray for his fundraising.

If you'd like to know more about becoming a donor for Edinburgh for Under Fives, or if you have any ideas about how else you could help us, email info@efuf.co.uk

No space to swing one?

Convenient, dry and secure self storage

SAFESTORE PRICE GUARANTEE

UP TO 4 WEEKS FREE STORAGE*

*Terms and conditions apply.

- ☑ Short or long term - store from just a week.
- ☑ Wide range of room and locker sizes to suit your needs.
- ☑ You are the only key holder with FREE unlimited access.
- ☑ Wide range of boxes and packaging materials available.
- ☑ 24 hour CCTV security.
- ☑ Business rates available.

SAFESTORE EDINBURGH LEITH:
1 Carron Place, Salamander Street, Edinburgh EH6 7RE.
Tel: 0131 554 4888

Scotland's No.1 for Self Storage

safestore™ self storage

www.safestore.co.uk   We know the value of space!

Notes

Key to our icons

Throughout, we've used a series of icons so you can check facilities at a glance.

Parking – Lots of free on-street parking nearby, or a car park.

Accessibility – Venue is pretty easily accessible to people with mobility issues, or a service is of special use to people with disabilities.

Pushchair friendly – Easy pushchair access.

Toilets – Toilet(s) the public can use.

Nappy changing – Pull-down or freestanding changing table(s).

Eating and drinking – Venues aren't cafes and restaurants but you can buy food/drinks.

Play area – Venues aren't dedicated play areas in themselves but have play areas – anything from a dedicated space with toys and books to an outside multiplay.

Birthdays/celebrations – Happy to host or help with parties, given prior notice.

Highchairs – At least one highchair.

Children's menu – A specific children's menu.

Vegetarian options – A number of vegetarian options offered.

Gluten free – Gluten-free options offered.

Licensed – Licensed to serve alcohol.

Food heating/bottle warming – Equipment provided for you to heat food/bottles yourself (e.g. a microwave).

Breastfeeding – Dedicated area for nursing mothers.

The notes in italics under the main review provide extra information where necessary.

Finally, bear in mind ...

We rely on a team of volunteers who are busy parents and carers. Where they haven't managed to get to a venue we've verified that last edition's review still stands. If you think we've included out-of-date or incorrect information please get in touch.

Occasionally there are gaps where people haven't told us about the presence of facilities such as toilets, highchairs or a children's menu. We'd recommend contacting the venue directly if you have any questions that we haven't covered – and then let us know about those facilities!

Addresses are in Edinburgh, unless stated otherwise.

Edinburgh's areas

Postcodes were used to decide the areas within Edinburgh City boundaries within this book. The map, in conjunction with this table, should help you see exactly which area falls where.

Wherever possible we've included postcodes in listings so that you can easily find venues using a more detailed map on the internet, your mobile phone or a sat nav.

Area	Places and postcodes	Example attractions
Central Edinburgh	Broughton, Canonmills, New Town, Old Town, Stockbridge, Tollcross, West End EH1, EH2, EH3	Edinburgh Castle National Gallery National Museum of Scotland Royal Botanic Garden Scottish National Portrait Gallery Scottish Storytelling Centre
North Edinburgh	Barnton, Blackhall, Clermiston, Comely Bank, Craigentinny, Craigleith, Cramond, Crewe Toll, Dean Village, Drylaw, Granton, Leith, Meadowbank, Muirhouse, Newhaven, Pilton, Ravelston, Restalrig, South Queensferry, Trinity EH4, EH5, EH6, EH7, EH30	Cammo Estate Cramond Beach Dalmeny Estate Inverleith Park and Playing Fields Ocean Terminal Scottish National Gallery of Modern Art (One and Two)
East Edinburgh	Cameron Toll, Canongate, Craigmillar, Duddingston, Ferniehill, Gilmerton, Holyrood, Joppa, Liberton, Moredun, Mortonhall, Mountcastle, Newington, Niddrie, Northfield, Piershill, Portobello, Prestonfield EH8, EH15, EH16, EH17	Craigmillar Castle Holyrood Park Inch Park Our Dynamic Earth Portobello Beach and Promenade Royal Commonwealth Pool
South Edinburgh	Blackford, Bruntsfield, Fairmilehead, Grange, Marchmont, Merchiston, Morningside EH9, EH10	Braidburn Valley Park Bruntsfield Links Hermitage of Braid The Meadows Pentland Hills Regional Park (also West Edinburgh)
West Edinburgh	Balerno, Chesser, Colinton, Corstorphine, Craiglockhart, Currie, Gorgie, Gyle, Haymarket, Juniper Green, Kirkliston, Longstone, Murrayfield, Newbridge, Oxgangs, Ratho, Saughton, Sighthill, Slateford, Stenhouse, Wester Hailes EH11, EH12, EH13, EH14, EH27, EH28, EH29	Corstorphine Hill Local Nature Reserve Edinburgh Zoo Gorgie City Farm Gyle Shopping Centre Pentland Hills Regional Park (also South Edinburgh) Water of Leith Visitor Centre

Please note the map is intended to be a guide only.